Development and Stabilization in Small Open Economies

Theories and Evidence from Caribbean Experience

DeLisle Worrell

Routledge
Taylor & Francis Group
LONDON AND NEW YORK

Designed cover image: © Shutterstock

First published 2023
by Routledge
4 Park Square, Milton Park, Abingdon, Oxon OX14 4RN

and by Routledge
605 Third Avenue, New York, NY 10158

Routledge is an imprint of the Taylor & Francis Group, an informa business

British Library Cataloguing-in-Publication Data
A catalogue record for this book is available from the British Library

Library of Congress Cataloging-in-Publication Data
A catalog record has been requested for this book

ISBN: 978-1-032-16218-8 (hbk)
ISBN: 978-1-032-16229-4 (pbk)
ISBN: 978-1-003-24760-9 (ebk)

DOI: 10.4324/9781003247609

Typeset in Times New Roman
by Taylor & Francis Books

For Monica, whose love makes me whole.

Contents

Illustrations

Figures

Tables

Box

Preface

At an age when many of my colleagues and contemporaries are writing or have written autobiographies, I have been offered the opportunity to do something much more satisfying, to reflect on what a lifetime of economic policy making and advisory work in small economies across the world has taught me about how these economies work, and how best they may be managed. For this offer I must thank Robert Looney, who extended the invitation to make a contribution to a Routledge series of which he is general editor, and Cathy Hartley, my editor at Routledge. I am also in debt to my copy editor, Tessa Ottley, who combines an unassuming manner with an exceptional talent.

Writing this book has been a rewarding exercise of self-discovery, as I retraced my intellectual and leadership journey, from its beginnings at the University of the West Indies in the 1960s, through the accident that made me a central banker, the challenges of leading the establishment of the economic, banking supervision and information technology systems of the Central Bank of Barbados from its foundation, decades of research collaboration with colleagues at the Smithsonian Institution, Princeton and Yale Universities, the Peterson Institution, the Wharton School and the International Economic Association and elsewhere, a decade of experience at the International Monetary Fund, and seven years as Governor of the Central Bank of Barbados. My debt to the many who inspired, encouraged and supported me, and to those who have opened doors for me, right up to the present day, is enormous, and I am grateful beyond words to them all. The insights that this experience has provided me are what I have set out to share in this book. I have enjoyed the writing, and I hope my readers will find it appealing and thought-provoking.

DeLisle Worrell
July 2022

1 Introduction

A Novel Approach to Policy Making in Small Open Economies

The banner headline in the Barbados *Sunday Sun* newspaper of October 28, 2012 read "IMF Clash", under juxtaposed photos of Christine Lagarde, then Managing Director of the International Monetary Fund, and myself, Governor of the Central Bank of Barbados. The article reported on a leaked transcript of a meeting in Tokyo, Japan, two Sundays earlier, between the Managing Director and Caribbean delegates to the annual meetings of the IMF and World Bank, which had concluded in the Japanese capital that week. The transcript "showed a vigorous debate between Worrell and Lagarde, a former French minister of finance, over the merits of devaluation, and how economic growth could be achieved", according to the article. Lagarde's experience would have been that when the value of the euro falls relative to the dollar, travel to France becomes more affordable, resulting in a surge of visitors to that country. In contrast, everyone in the Caribbean knows that airfares to the region, hotel rates, restaurant menus, taxi fares, access fees to tourist attractions, souvenirs, spa treatments, hair braiding and all services targeted at the tourist business, are priced in US dollars. When the value of the Trinidad and Tobago currency fell from 4.25 to the dollar to 6.00 in 1993, the taxi fare from Piarco International Airport to downtown Port-of-Spain increased from 95 in local currency to 132, but it remained unchanged in US dollars at US$22. The prices at which small economies sell to the international market are set, usually in US dollars, and are unaffected by changes in the value of the local currency.

The fact that devaluation has no effect on the prices at which tourist services and all other exports from small open economies are sold is baked into all economic models developed in the Caribbean, but this essential feature is absent from the models used by IMF staff and others to assess Caribbean economies, to comment on policies and to conduct negotiations for programmes of financial assistance. That is no doubt because the builders of conventional models base their specifications on their experiences, which are of European and North American countries. Very recently mainstream economists have come to recognise what has been termed "the dominant currency paradigm";[1] dominant currency pricing is a feature that defines economies of the size with which this book is concerned.

DOI: 10.4324/9781003247609-1

Another distinctive feature of small economies is that their international commerce operates, in terminology which has become familiar in the context of small scale renewable energy production, on a "buy all/sell all" basis.[2] Because of a small population and a limited range of skills, resources and productive capacity, there are only a handful of goods and services which small economies can produce in quantity at internationally competitive prices. Their most efficient strategy is to export everything they produce and buy everything they need, all of which they can buy abroad more cheaply than they can produce at home, if they are able to produce the item at all. The only things produced and consumed in an efficient small economy are government services, public utilities, distribution and other nontradables. The stability of the small economy is secured by a balance between what they earn from foreign sales and prudent foreign borrowing, and what they spend on purchases from abroad. The growth of the economy depends on selling more abroad, through increased productivity and increased capacity to produce competitive products and services.

There is a continuum of country sizes, from large, continental nations with large populations and the resources to sustain a diversified, modern economy with relatively little foreign input, and the small economies with which this book is concerned. A country like Canada, for example, will have considerable potential for domestic production for domestic consumption, though that may not be the most efficient disposition of resources. A country like Saudi Arabia may affect world oil prices through its production and exports, even though oil price contracts are usually written in US dollars. Such qualifications do not arise with respect to the 41 countries on which our discussion is based, which are all towards the extreme end of the ranking of size in descending order. Cuba has the largest economy among them, somewhat less than US$100 billion; Ghana, the most populous country, has a population that is slightly less than 30 million. These countries are all price takers on the international market, and they are all limited in what they can produce at scale and sell profitably at ruling international prices of any tradable good or service. The aim of this book is to outline an economic model and framework which equips policy makers in economies with these characteristics with the tools to attain goals and targets for stable, sustainable economic development.

Our development target is improvement in the material well-being of the average household; the best measure of well-being that is available for all countries is the Human Development Index, developed by the United Nations Development Programme in 1990, when the first report already included a majority of the world's nations. The remainder were added by 2000. We therefore have two or three decades of data to permit comparative analysis of the performance of all countries. The HDI incorporates the GDP, the most commonly used economic yardstick, and corrects the GDP data to account for differences between the purchasing power of one US dollar in different countries. In addition to GDP per person at purchasing power parities, the HDI incorporates indicators of health and education status, both of which are known to be important qualities contributing to the well-being of individuals and households. The index is flexible, and can be extended to incorporate other aspects of well-being such as housing, water and sanitation, though these indices are not available on a comparable basis for all countries. Chapter 17 is a primer on the HDI, its merits and extensions.

This book is about the implications of small size for the design, targets and implementation of macroeconomic policy, a topic which has not received the attention it deserves during the last four decades. By 1980 macroeconomic development, which had been a major preoccupation of the economic profession since the end of the Second World War, had gone off the agenda, and development was relegated to the realm of microeconomics, a field which receives little attention outside the economics discipline itself. Important microeconomic insights which have come to light in the period since 1980 have gone largely unnoticed by economic policy makers at the macro level. Those of us who continued to argue for specific attention to macroeconomic issues affecting the design of policy for small economies had to overcome the scepticism of critics who pointed to the outstanding growth performances of small economies like Iceland and Singapore. Thanks largely to the outstanding research of the Islands and Small States Institute of the University of Malta, and the leadership of its founder, Lino Briguglio, that scepticism has been overcome, and issues related to small economies have now been placed on the agenda of the IMF, the World Bank and the United Nations. However, the concerns that command interest do not yet extend to the formulation of macroeconomic policy, though research has thrown light on some puzzles, including the policies to strengthen resilience which have contributed to the success of countries like Iceland and Singapore that share the vulnerabilities to which all small economies are subject. The lacuna with respect to the design and implementation of macroeconomic policy take account of the implications of small size is the vacuum this book aims to fill.

Comments on the practice of economic policy making

Economists use what we call "models" as a framework for thinking about the subject matter of our discipline. It is the best image we have found for what we do, which is to separate out everything the farmer, the teacher, the politician, the philosopher does every day in the way of producing, exchanging, consuming or accumulating products or services for values that are measured by society by some agreed standard, which is called money. Economists collect various aspects of these activities in groups that we label output or product, consumption, investment, imports, exports, prices, employment and so on, and we then try to identify and describe the relationships between the entities we have conceptualised.

We will provide a drone's camera view of this landscape in Chapter 14; the point to be made up front is that there are many different approaches to model-building, operating at different levels of abstraction; I have experimented with several over the course of my career. Based on that experience I advocate the use of behavioural models for policy use. The equations of the policy model described in Chapter 6 all represent identifiable behaviour of economic agents whose actions will produce the results expected from the activity described by the equation, if it is well specified. For example, I am able to describe the factors affecting investment decisions (Equation 6.1) in terms that an investor would recognise as reflecting the things she worries about. The strength of this approach for the policy maker is that it soon becomes apparent if you've got something wrong, and you can investigate to find ways to get back on track. As we shall see, the management of an economy is a continuous process of trial, error, correction and adjustment, repeated endlessly. The policy making process should be fertilised by continuous research, to tease new insight from this trial and error process.

The behavioural approach to modelling contrasts with the highly abstract general equilibrium models used by the IMF and many central banks, and the autoregressive models that appear in much empirical economic analysis nowadays. The general equilibrium models are technically so complex that simplifications are needed to derive useful ideas for policy. These simplifications may unwittingly invalidate the results derived from the model by misrepresenting some crucial aspect of the structure of the economy. An example would be to apply to a small economy a model which allows for any imported item to be produced locally. Anomalies like this are easy to miss because of the level of abstraction at which these models operate. They are seldom sufficiently realistic to allow policy makers to trace the impact of a particular policy change, such as an interest rate increase. The same is true of autoregressive models, which are exercises in detecting regularities in a series of values of a variable such as the national income. These and other model approaches may be a useful supplement to the behavioural model, but none is as useful to the policy maker.

The reason is that it is the behaviour of all those economic agents, and how they are motivated to alter that behaviour in response to changes in interest rates, changes in the exchange rate, import tariffs and barriers, that will determine the outcomes of policy. Whether the government's intentions are achieved, and whether, in the end, there is any improvement in the average well-being of the society, will depend on the extent to which economic agents are motivated to use and consume resources, and to buy and sell, in ways that produce the desired outcomes. The most successful policies – arguably the only policies that will succeed in bettering average well-being – are those which are devised to incentivise behaviour of all economic agents in ways consistent with the objectives of the policies. What those ways are can never be known with certainty in advance; they can only be uncovered by the process of trial, error, learning and adjustment described earlier. Absent a model where behaviours can be checked against expectations, policy makers may find that the policies they choose to guide or compel economic agents push them in directions the latter perceive as against their interests. In such cases, rather than react in the way policy makers hoped, economic agents devote energies to getting around or supplanting the proscribed activities, including hoarding, resorting to informal markets and switching to channels which lie beyond the regulated guidelines.

Even with a good behavioural model, designing effective economic policy is a very complex and challenging business, and it must be assigned to a trained and experienced team of economists and finance specialists. Their work must be informed by economic and financial statistics as well as by relevant research and information networks. It helps to review policies and strategies with the help of think tanks, nongovernmental organisations and other interest groups, in advance of discussion and endorsement by the Parliament. It will never be possible to fully satisfy all interests, but such discussions help in developing persuasive arguments to address the concerns of dissenting elements. The most convincing argument is by demonstrating how the policy improves average well-being, by a government which has built a reputation for delivering such improvements in the past. The achievements of Iceland and Singapore are so difficult for other governments to imitate precisely because few governments have built a record of achieving consistent improvement in the level of living and quality of life comparable to the governments of these two countries.

The small open economy is fuelled by foreign currency

Figure 1.1 illustrates the mechanism of a small open economy. Its internationally competitive tourism and exports earn foreign currency, and thanks to the productivity of local labour and the attractiveness of the local investment climate it attracts foreign investment. Together these sources provide US

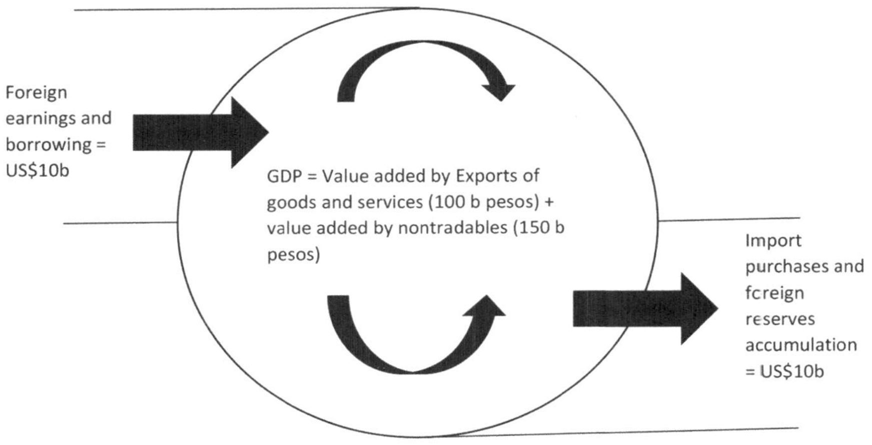

Figure 1.1 The small open economy
Source: Author's construction.

$10 billion of foreign exchange, which is converted to local currency at the exchange rate of 10 pesos to the dollar, generating an additional 150 billion in pesos of added value by public utilities, transport, communications, banking and insurance services, wholesale and retail activity, for a total GDP of about 250 billion pesos. This spending in turn generates imports of fuels, vehicles, equipment, building materials and consumer items. Any surplus which is left of the US$10 billion inflow is added to the country's store of foreign reserves, invested by the central bank with the US Federal Reserve Bank in New York.

Figure 1.2 illustrates the conditions for economic stability and economic growth in the small open economy. Stability is defined by the balance of external inflows and outflows. With any given ratio of imports to GDP (the propensity to import, in economic terms), the most imports that can be sustained over successive years is the amount of each year's inflow of foreign currency. Any year there is an excess of imports, the central bank draws on the reserve balances held with the New York Fed; to maintain stability,

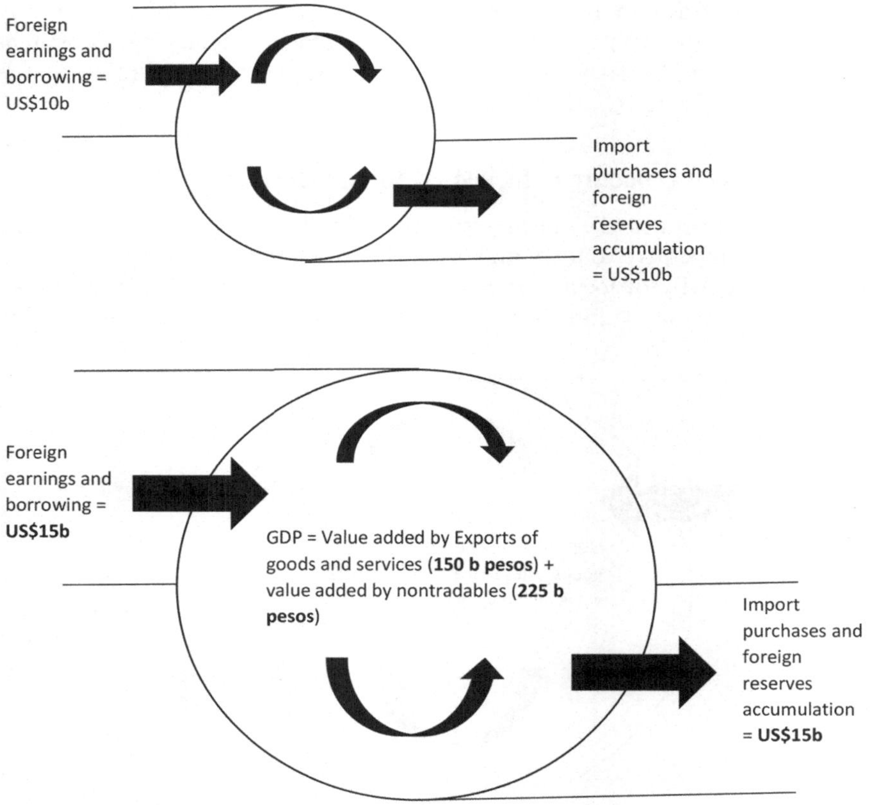

Figure 1.2 Economic growth
Source: Author's construction.

government must take action to reduce the next year's imports below expected inflows, so as to build reserves back to the previous level, as a precaution in case of another case of excess imports.

The economy will grow only when the earnings of foreign currency increase, or when there is major foreign investment, as shown in Figure 1.2. Government spending on public utilities, health infrastructure or housing may be a national priority, but unless such spending is funded by borrowing abroad it will be counter-productive, because the imports that would result from the additional activity will deplete the foreign reserves. From the point of view of both growth and stability, the conclusion that foreign currency is what animates the small open economy is inescapable.

The plan of this book

The chapters of the book are collected into four sections: the chapters in Section A describe the evidence on which the theory and model of Section B are based. That evidence is drawn from a selection of 41 small open economies drawn from all around the world. Section C expands on the practice of economic policy making, including the skills and knowledge required as well as the proper use of the tools of the discipline. Section D contains chapters on institutions, the global context and changes, and a technical overview of the Human Development Index.

There are four chapters in Section A. Chapter 2 is devoted to comparative analysis of all 41 countries in our sample, with respect to the indicators of the quality of human well-being and the changes over three decades. Individual stories of the performance of a smaller selection of countries are recounted in Chapter 3; we compensate for the smaller selection by extending the analysis as far back as the data that we have will allow in each case. Chapter 4 is a survey of the main sources of foreign earnings for countries of Central America and the Caribbean. Chapter 5 recounts the Caribbean experience with attempts to achieve a single economy through integration of individual states.

Chapter 2 surveys the small economies chosen for discussion in this book in terms of their economic performance, as measured by the Human Development Index. Two-thirds of the sample have Human Development Indices which put them in the categories of *High* and *Very High* Human Development. The remainder are in the *Medium* category, with only one, the Gambia, with a score below 0.500, the cut-off below which countries are classified as having *Low* Human Development. Iceland is the country that tops the list, with the fourth highest score of all countries in the 2020 Index. Mauritius is rated the best-performing in our sample: not only does it sit in the highest category; the country has also made the largest gain in human development in the past 30 years. Comparative analysis among the 41 countries indicates that improvements in health and education have a much more powerful impact on the HDI score than does an increase in purchasing power of the same percentage. We infer that although growth is needed to provide additional resources, the effectiveness with which resources are deployed to improve health and educational achievement is more important than the rate of growth. Capsules of the growth performances of all 41 countries revealed the expected variety, but in general we find that the impact of downturns in global economic cycles appears to be less pervasive than is usually assumed. Also, only prolonged slow growth and deep contraction retard improvement in the HDI score. Extreme economic volatility may also depress the HDI score, but such volatility is rare. Wars and civil strife cause lasting damage, but hurricanes and natural disasters have no lasting impact on the growth rate.

The chapter concludes with a survey of my research on comparative studies of economic policy and growth over the past four decades. It presages many of the themes that will be developed in the course of this book, including: the central importance of prudent management of public sector finance; the impact of currency devaluation on domestic inflation; the fact that devaluation of the local currency does not attract additional foreign earnings because prices for foreign buyers are quoted in US dollars; and the limited discretion available for interest rate policy. The studies also speak to the need to ensure consistency between fiscal policy and private expenditure intentions; ways in which small open economies can build confidence by borrowing credibility from large countries through interest and exchange rate policies; and the use of competitive strategies based on increased productivity and higher added value.

Whereas Chapter 2 deals with comparative analysis, Chapter 3 surveys individual country experiences in greater depth. The Caribbean is over-represented, but there are capsules of development experiences of countries from all regions of the globe. *Barbados* was transformed from an economy based on export agriculture with poor human development in 1945, to one based on tourism, with an HDI score that puts the country in the top category of human development. Although gains have continued to be made in the years since Independence in 1966, the essential transformation was achieved in the 1950s and 1960s. Government budgeting was characterised as prudent in the early years of Independence, and the public services demonstrated relatively high productivity. Government savings contributed one-third of capital spending over the period from 1945 to 1980. In stark contrast, the public sector was described in 2016 as overstaffed, poorly skilled and with low productivity. The relaxation of fiscal discipline from the mid-1980s resulted in a balance of payments crisis which required deep economic contraction in 1991, and that pattern was repeated from 2013 to 2018, with another balance of payments crisis in that year. The economies of the *Eastern Caribbean Currency Union* (ECCU) have maintained an advantage over the Caribbean average HDI score in the past two decades, a period during which they completed the switch from export agriculture to tourism. The ECCU experience shows that large current account deficits are sustainable over many years, and healthy levels of foreign reserves bear testimony to the region's resilience in the face of hurricanes and other natural disasters. The economic transformation of the *Dominican Republic* came with political stability and the development of the tourism industry. *Trinidad & Tobago*, the insular Caribbean's major oil exporter, recorded modest success in managing volatile foreign earnings, particularly in the 1970s, when a major new industrial zone was established with the proceeds of an oil bonanza. *Belize* bettered the average Caribbean HDI score on the basis of tourism revenues, plus exports of sugar, fruits, clothing and other manufactured goods. *Cuba* suffers from a combination of geo-political victimisation and bad economic management. Health and education indicators are outstanding, but income levels are low, productivity is falling and the outlook is discouraging. The strength of an economy which had benefited from long periods of sustained growth and sound finances enabled *Iceland* to emerge unscathed from what was, in relation to its GDP, the worst single country financial crisis triggered by the Global Recession of 2008.

Chapter 4 tells the stories of changing production structures in the foreign earnings sectors of countries, and in foreign finance in the Caribbean and Central America; we chart the manner in which the changes came about and the main factors influencing these developments. In doing so, we explore the associated themes of wages and labour productivity, inflation, migration into and out of the region and the exploitation of natural resources. The sectors and activities discussed in this chapter are tourism, other services such as data processing, call centres and international business services, exports of clothing, processed food and other manufacturing, mineral and other primary extractive industry exports and remittances. The Bahamas, Barbados and the countries of the Eastern Caribbean Currency Union derive most of their foreign earnings from tourism and related activities. Tourism was also the largest contributor to inflows in Cuba and Jamaica. The Dominican Republic, along with three Central American countries (Costa Rica, Nicaragua and Panama) are mainly exporters of manufactured goods such as pharmaceuticals and medical equipment. Exports of bananas, sugar, coffee, fruits and other agricultural products are the largest sources of foreign earnings for Guatemala and Honduras, followed by workers' remittances. Trinidad and Tobago is the only country in this region which exports petroleum and related products, accounting for approaching 90 per cent of inflows, although in the early 2020s Guyana is poised to become the second oil exporter from the Caribbean. There are two countries for which remittances have become the main source of foreign currency, El Salvador and Haiti, tragically in both cases as a result of social and political instability. International business services, including legal, accounting, insurance, finance and marketing, are now of importance mainly in the Cayman Islands, Bermuda and the smaller UK dependencies in the Caribbean.

One possible way to ameliorate the limitations of small size is by way of economic integration with other countries. However, economic integration brings its own challenges, as Caribbean experience demonstrates. That experience is summarised in Chapter 5. The international competitive success of the Caribbean, which rests mainly with tourism, owes little to official policy, and nothing to regional cooperative efforts. Ironically, the Caribbean has become more integrated socially, culturally and, on a sub-regional basis, economically, at the same time that the official institutions of integration have lost their credibility. The region has developed a small but remunerative cultural industry that fuels the economic activity of Caribbean people in ways which economic statistics do not record. Opportunities for migration within the region, to the mutual benefit of sending and receiving countries, have grown in response to employment opportunities, even though the limited and impossibly bureaucratic formal arrangements for intra-regional migration have proven completely ineffective. There has been an intensification of financial integration within the Caribbean. The facts of geography dictate that the Caribbean has an American destiny, and the economic weight of the US makes it inevitable that the region's economic fortunes depend on the nature of its relationships with that country. It may however be argued that the Caribbean has not used the unequal relationship to its best advantage because of the pursuit of futile attempts to resist American influence, rather than finding ways to take advantage of the relationship to further the goals of the Caribbean people. What emerges from an overview of Caribbean economies today is a picture of exceptional achievement by the people of the region, in virtually every field of human endeavour, and the achievement of levels of living in the region that, with few exceptions, are not far short of those typical of countries in Europe and North America. In contrast, the landscape of policy and governance is one of unrelieved failure to attain the often lofty intentions of the region's independent nation-states. In order to fully appreciate the sources of improvements in Caribbean well-being, it is helpful to think of the Caribbean as including the diaspora, up to now mainly in North America and Europe, but increasingly spreading to the Middle East, Asia and elsewhere. The diaspora is also perhaps the most powerful instrument of integration of the Caribbean nation.

Section B on monetary, fiscal, financial and exchange rate policy in the small open economy comprises Chapters 6 to 11. Chapter 6 presents a behavioural model which incorporates the distinguishing features of small open economies (SOEs): their growth depends on investment in the capacity to produce internationally competitive tradable goods and services, sold abroad at ruling world prices; there is no substitutability between the tradables they sell to earn foreign exchange, the imports they need to sustain production and lifestyles, and government services and other nontradables; and their financial markets cannot be insulated from the international financial markets which enable their external commerce, the lifeblood of their economies. The key to successful policies for stable growth and long term prosperity in SOEs is fiscal policy designed to manage aggregate demand with a view to external balance and a stable exchange rate, while at the same time deploying tax, expenditure and government borrowing policies to sustain and improve international competitiveness. In this chapter the effectiveness of this strategy is brought to light with the use of the SOE-specific model, and its conclusions are compared with conventional wisdom.

Growth in the SOE comes by way of nurturing and developing the products and services in which the country has an established international competitive advantage and following up selectively on clues as to future activities which show promise for sales to foreigners, given the society's endowments. The SOE is an atomistic producer of any product or service offered to the rest of the world. It may sell an unlimited amount at the ruling international price, and it will do so, up to the point where marginal sellers fail to make a profit sufficient to keep them in business. The way to increase sales and foreign currency earnings is by increasing the productivity of labour and other domestic factors, and by adding value to established products that are being sold competitively at ruling world prices.

Economic stabilisation in the SOE is attained by ensuring that the external accounts are always in balance with the expected levels of investment and output. In the event that inflows of foreign currency fall short of payments for imports, foreign debt service and other outflows by a substantial amount or over several successive years, economic policy makers in SOEs need to take decisive action. In such cases there is a danger that the country's foreign reserves held with the US Federal Reserve Bank will eventually be exhausted, no matter how large they might be. The way to avert this is by way of fiscal contraction, through tax increases, cuts in expenditure – less additional foreign borrowing, if the country's external credit rating is strong – in a package that is sufficient to fully restore the level of foreign reserves, through a large enough cut in imports. The chapter presents a detailed explanation of the workings of the SOE-specific model, and how it differs from models in use by the IMF and elsewhere.

Chapter 7 proposes that small open economies treat the foreign currency market as one where the exchange rate is fixed in advance, much like prices in a supermarket, and recommends that government manages tax policy, its own expenditure and its finances, to moderate total imports in line with the amount of foreign currency that is available. Arguably, this is the only approach that enables the government of a small open economy to avoid a steep devaluation of the local currency under all circumstances. We offer guidelines for fiscal policies to improve productivity in the public service, to respond to international shocks such as the Covd-19 pandemic, to correct for the impact of election cycles on fiscal balances and to arrest runaway inflation in property prices. The advantage of using fiscal tools is that they are varied and flexible, and strategies may be tailored to the circumstances by calibrating each tool to fit into the overall picture. The tools also have the advantage that they comprise actions which are directly within the government's purview – that is, direct spending – and actions which are designed to affect the behaviour of actors in the private sector, which offers a wealth of options for custom design to fit each circumstance. Using the balance of payments to define the overall stance of fiscal policy gives us an objective measure of fiscal space, depending on the surplus of foreign currency over the demand for imports which is available to support additional stimulus. The chapter offers case studies of adjustment based on Caribbean experience, contrasting the approach using fiscal policy to manage the external balance with conventional strategies.

Chapter 8 shows how the small open economy maintains international competitiveness and sustained economic growth while anchoring policy on a managed exchange rate. Suggestions for the design of fiscal strategies to stimulate competitiveness are drawn from Caribbean experience, beginning with the design of the tax system. Because foreign currency is essential for growth in small open economies the corporate tax system should be biased towards tradable activities; because there is no case for protecting domestic production of importables, a low border tax is preferable; the main indirect tax should be a simple tax on goods and services. Because the use of value added taxes is now so prevalent, it should be noted that they are markedly less efficient than simple sales taxes, especially in economies where tourism and other services predominate. State entrepreneurship plays a crucial role in improving international competitiveness. The starting point should be by way of leveraging existing skills, knowledge, experience and networks, retooling, repositioning and modifying products, services, processes and organisation to take advantage of emerging opportunities. Government needs to devise a comprehensive, internally cohesive and consistent strategy for maintaining and enhancing competitiveness, in close collaboration with the private sector. Investment in roads, ports, airports and other transport and communications infrastructure are a vital catalyst for investment. The same is true for the supply of electricity, water, sanitation and other essential services. The speed, predictability, pertinence and courtesy which characterise public services are factors which rank highly in surveys of businesses investment. Affecting all aspects of policy is the availability – or lack thereof – of analytical tools and perspectives fashioned to the circumstances and needs of SOEs.

Chapter 9 describes how monetary policy may be employed, in an essential but supporting role alongside fiscal policy, in the framework of macroeconomic policy. Monetary policy tools are important because they are quick-acting, in contrast to fiscal tools, which are powerful but slow to take effect. A coordinated approach to economic shocks, simultaneously deploying fiscal tools sufficient to restore external balance and monetary tools to calm financial markets, offers the best chance of successful adjustment. The monetary authority should also offer guidance to financial markets through interest rate policy, moral suasion and information sharing. The path for domestic interest rates in small open economies is defined by the trend in the US Treasury bill rate – or other international benchmark rate – plus the costs of currency exchange and a country risk premium, which rises when there is a perceived risk of currency devaluation. Even in the absence of an active market in short-term finance – something of which only a handful of countries can boast – the monetary authority can influence the domestic treasury bill rate in any desired direction through repeated intervention in a weekly auction. In this way the local rate can be kept in line with the underlying trend in the international benchmark rate. The monetary authority may then provide guidance to the market with respect to longer term rates, using the offer rates on longer term government bonds.

Chapter 10 explores the relationship between the financial sector and development that improves the quality of human lives. The first part of the chapter deals with the financing of investment, the efficiency of banking services and other credit mechanisms and the functions of capital markets, issues that directly affect employment, income spending and well-being. The second part of the chapter, on issues of financial stability, evaluates risks and mitigation strategies in terms of their potential to impair the material well-being of the population.

Perhaps the clearest and most widespread benefit of the broadening and deepening of the reach of banks and other deposit and pooled liquidity institutions has been in improving the access of households to durable consumption goods. The availability of mortgages and credit for the purchase of items of lasting value has lifted the average quality of life everywhere these facilities have been made available. The banking system broadly defined has provided a vital lubricant to trade, domestic and international, at wholesale and retail levels, through the provision of trade credit and working capital to producers, traders, distributors and the providers of transport, freight and a myriad of other supporting services. Household needs are still mainly satisfied by commercial banks in most countries, but there are signs in the US, the Caribbean and elsewhere, that co-operative financial institutions are outcompeting international commercial banks in providing financial services to individuals. Financial failures do not appear to have inflicted any lasting damage on the well-being of countries, even in those cases where there have been well-publicised systemic failures. The public sector should aim to address the provision of equity for small and medium enterprises and for new ventures. Possible mechanisms for consideration are guarantees intended to share the risk inherent in this market, performance-based subsidies, tax incentives and other initiatives, all guided by the principle that there is a sound business case, as assessed by knowledgeable and experienced practitioners.

Weaknesses in the current analysis of the stability of financial systems are identified. They include the underdeveloped nature of stress testing methodologies. The divided international institutional framework for the assessment and surveillance of financial soundness, and for the development and implementation of regulations, is a major defect of the international system. The international surveillance of financial institutions suffers from over-reliance on elaborate lists of judgmental "standards and codes" for banking supervision, anti-money laundering, tax compliance and financial conduct, evaluated by complicated and largely defective methodologies.

In Chapter 11 we put the case that the domestic currencies of small open economies are an anachronism in a digital world. Currency was essential for payments when all purchases were made using notes and coins. Those days are long gone; nowadays all payments and transfers of significance are made by way of a secure instruction to transfer value from the payer's bank account to the account of the seller. Increasingly, such instructions are communicated digitally, via credit and debit cards, online bank portals, digital wallets and similar devices. The prices of imports, denominated in US dollars, determine domestic inflation in small open economies; the existence of a local currency increases the risk of excessive inflation, beyond imported price increases as a result of exchange rate depreciation. The use of the US dollar as local currency facilitates seamless payments, domestic and international.

Section C comprises three chapters that elaborate on practical aspects of economic policy making. Chapter 12 describes in some detail one possible framework of institutions and coordination which may be used to manage the small open economy, using the concepts and tools of Section B. Because the approach offered in this book conflicts with orthodox strategies in critical ways, it is very important that those who adopt this approach be cognizant of the orthodox approaches, their weaknesses and how and why the strategies of Section B differ. That is the burden of Chapter 13.

Chapter 14 offers wide-ranging observations on the unsatisfactory state of contemporary economic practice, something which all economists should be much more conscious of than seems to be the case. The tools economists use are all crude, in terms of their ability to answer the questions that the policy maker confronts, and the answers they produce are far more uncertain than most economists and policy makers are willing to admit.

Chapter 12 outlines a forecasting model and framework for policy making in small open economies which follows the logic of Chapter 6, to ensure that the inferences drawn and the forecasts made are what one should expect of a small open economy. The chapter may be considered something of a practical manual for economic policy makers in these economies. The essential modules within the economic policy framework are:

- a model of long term investment, competitiveness and growth, which serves to provide a benchmark for the growth of competitive production capacity in the economy;
- structural forecasting models of sectoral growth, the balance of payments, public sector revenue/current expenditure/capital expenditure/financing, and the monetary accounts. Two models with similar structure are needed, a quarterly model with a rolling 18-month horizon, and an annual model with a rolling five-year horizon;
- quarterly and annual financial control frameworks for the public sector accounts, structured to provide data that is incorporated into the forecasting framework;

- a weekly forecast for domestic and foreign currency liquidity, which is used to manage the public sector's cash requirements, consistent with the foreign reserve targets.

The system works well only when all the elements are in place: careful preparation of realistic public sector budgets, with a match for each spending unit between funds allocated and services to be provided, timely public accountability by way of published annual reports and accounts, a top-flight coordinating committee for monetary and fiscal policy with the requisite authority, and a fully functional system of financial control.

Chapter 13 provides a survey of recent literature showing how conventional views have come around to accept that small open economies need to actively manage their exchange rates. However, the orthodoxy still believes that managing the exchange rate can be achieved by accumulating very large reserves of foreign currency. We show why small open economies do better by managing aggregate demand so as to keep the external accounts in balance. In this chapter we discuss the realistic options open to small economies to manage economic and financial risks, and demonstrate some of the risk mitigation strategies and tools that are most useful for these countries. The importance of devoting resources to the preparation of thoroughly researched, statistically rich presentations by small economies in the international context is highlighted.

Chapter 14 deals with a wide variety of issues in the practice of economics which have a bearing on the inferences we may draw from economic analysis and the advice and guidance that may be offered for economic policy. The variables used in economics are all abstractions, conceptually and in time and space. The universally used measure of economic activity, the gross domestic product, is "a made up entity" (Coyle, 2014) whose measurement is controversial and riddled with logical compromises. It is never self-evident what data is to be collected and aggregated to address any issue. Careful consideration has to be given to the options in every case. Considerations of practicality and cost determine who collects what data, and how often they do so. Careful consideration is also needed to ensure that raw data are aggregated using techniques which are most suitable for the analysis at hand. Economists have no way of establishing beyond question the impact of economic policies such as interest rate changes on intended targets such as inflation, because the impact of the policy cannot be isolated from the many other events that may be impacting the target.

Economic forecasts are an essential tool for decision makers in business and government because they establish a benchmark against which to evaluate success or failure in implementing policy; it is not helpful to share forecasts with the general public because of the myriad circumstances which always impact on the actual outturn. The forecast is to guide the decision maker as to what actions are necessary to stay on course. The nation state is not always the most useful way to define an economy because national borders define patterns of production and exchange only when there are geographical, language, wars or other barriers in the way of commerce.

Economics concerns itself with value in production, consumption and exchange, but the discipline has no objective measure of value. We are able to assign value only when there is a purchase, and the value assigned is whatever the buyer and seller agreed to, once the transaction is legal. Economics struggles with issues relating to measuring variables at monthly, quarterly, annual or other intervals, ensuring that what is measured on each occasion is identical with that item as recorded on all other occasions. The choice of methods used to draw inferences about economic relationships is not a straightforward matter.

Economics continues to be in a state of internal intellectual turmoil. Chapter 14 includes summaries of some of the unconventional currents within the discipline. There is a section on evolutionary economics, the approach within our discipline which I find most appealing. We also comment on the use of terms and concepts in economics which are misleading or outmoded. Finally, we renew Diedre McCloskey's 40-year-old plea for polite, sensible, reasoned discussion among economists (McCloskey, 1983).

The chapters in Section D deal with a selection of issues that have been in the background of everything that has been discussed up to this point. The chosen topics are matters on which I offer a perspective which differs from economic orthodoxy and popular perceptions in ways that are crucial for the success of macroeconomic policy. The chapters in this section cover the role of central banks in small open economies; factors that affect the degrees of freedom of policy makers, including history, geography and technology; the rationale for the use of the Human Development Index as the measure of well-being in this book, with an explanation of how the Index is computed; and some observations on anti-globalisation sentiments.

Chapter 15 is about the role of the central bank in the framework of economic policy. Conventional views restrict the role of the central bank to the conduct of monetary policy and, in some cases, the oversight of the financial system. Chapter 15 presents the case for a much broader mandate for the central bank in small and developing countries, to include a leading role in a joined-up management of the economy as well as in the financing of investment that increases the competitiveness of the economy.

Chapter 16 offers brief commentaries on the boundaries to the space for policy discretion that leaders of small nations should always be conscious of. Small countries are mistaken if they suppose that sovereignty equips them with greater economic resources than they had before they were independent nations; we explain why. The possibilities and potential for the future of the economy will have as their point of departure the patterns of wealth distribution, infrastructure, language and other endowments and legacies which history has bequeathed to the society. These will be unique, and lessons drawn from others will be filtered through this unique historical lens. Geography defines the nature and possibilities of the small nation's engagement with the rest of the world. The chapter also offers some comments on how small open economies might seek to reap most benefit from technological change.

Chapter 17 explains why the Human Development Index (HDI) is the best indicator of well-being for the purposes of evaluating the success of economic policy. The Index most closely reflects observed conditions of living in a wide variety of countries, and data is available for all countries, for 20 to 30 years. The chapter explains the construction of the index in some detail, explaining the rationale for the selection of the indicators for purchasing power, health and education, and the technique by which they are combined into a single index. The HDI meets minimum standards of objectivity and it is flexible enough to incorporate additional dimensions of well-being, such as equitable income distribution, gender equality and the quality of health and educational services, in countries where data are available.

The basic HDI may be enriched to capture inequities over various kinds, to provide a framework for judging the quality of services under each dimension of the index, and to highlight inconsistencies and resource limitations. There is no other measure of economic success that comes close to matching these attributes. It follows that macroeconomic policies and strategies that use the HDI and extensions as the target they seek to attain, employing the HDI to monitor progress along the way and adjusting policies and targets where necessary, will have a greater chance of success than any other metric. What is more, because success would have been achieved by securing increases in life expectancy at birth, in the mean and expected years of schooling and in the purchasing power of average incomes, along with other desirable changes, the credibility and authority of economists and policy makers would be restored, over time, by the match between claims of success and the lived experience of the population.

Chapter 18 is a commentary on the topic of globalisation, from the perspective of the policy maker in a small open economy. In contrast to populations in large countries, where the world outside the home country may be peripheral to their daily business activity for a large majority, the world at large and economic exchanges with their main trading and financial partners impact daily on the economic activities of the populations of small nations. Interactions with the rest of the world may only recently have been given the title of globalisation, but those interactions have always been paramount in small open economies. Chapter 18 offers suggestions on the new opportunities that technologies have opened up, and comments on emerging challenges.

The chapter concludes with suggestions for first steps in the reform of global governance. The World Bank, the International Monetary Fund and the United Nations must be the foundation for the reform of global governance because these institutions have membership of all countries. The International Monetary Fund and World Bank both have a governance structure that reflects global power relationships. A number of reforms are essential to restore the influence and effectiveness that the Fund and the Bank once enjoyed. The first and most important must be to end the farce which perpetuates the European monopoly of the posts of Managing Director of the Fund and the US monopoly of the Presidency of the Bank. The second crucial reform is the revision of the capital contributions of the Bank and Fund to bring them in line with current realities of international economic relationships, and realignment of constituencies on the Executive Boards accordingly. The governance structures of the United Nations and its agencies must be reformed along the lines of the Executive Boards of the Fund and the Bank. All international laws, frameworks, guidance, standards and regulations would ultimately need to be captured under the inclusive umbrella of the Fund, Bank and the United Nations.

These first steps are now urgent, in a journey to the destination of a global system of governance that gives humanity a fighting chance of reversing trends that, on our present course, threaten to wipe civilisation from this planet prematurely. Humanity can no longer resist these initiatives for reform unless we are utterly fatalistic about our future. To continue as we are, on the basis of national commitments, means that the world moves further and further away from the goals for sustainability of the civilisation we now enjoy.

The final chapter offers some practical policy suggestions for economic authorities in small open economies. Policy makers everywhere will gain credibility from the use of the Human Development Index as the measure of economic success. It assures that there will be congruence between claims of economic success and improvements in health, education, purchasing power and other public services. It also tempers expectations: everyone will know that improvements in the quality and availability of public services, public utilities and infrastructure are not achieved overnight. Policy makers in small economies should use a model which targets their international competitiveness in a limited range of products and services, ensuring that the most affordable products and services are secured in exchange to meet their consumption and investment needs. The strategy they devise with the help of this model must be sold to the population and the investor community. There should be final and intermediate targets and a benchmark of the paths to the final targets. This benchmark should be used for ongoing monitoring and making course corrections as needed to stay on track. It is not necessary to begin with a perfect plan, nor can the outcome be predicted at the outset. However, the targets of any strategy may be attained by this process of continuous monitoring and adjustment, as policy makers and economic agents incorporate the lessons of experience.

Notes

1 See Gopinath, Gita, Emine Boz, Camila Casas, Federico Diez, Pierre-Olivier Gourinchas and Mikkel Plagborg-Moller (2019), Gevorkyan and Khemraj (2022), and IMF (2020).

2 The term describes small solar photovoltaic systems on the roofs of buildings which sell all the electricity they produce to the grid, from which they continue to purchase all the building's own requirements.

3 Donald N. McCloskey, the author whose name will be found on the 1983 paper, is the person who is now Diedre McCloskey.

References

Coyle, Diane. 2014. *GDP: A Brief but Affectionate History.* Princeton, NJ: Princeton University Press.

Gevorkyan, A and T. Khemraj. 2022. "*Dominant currency shocks and foreign exchange pressure in the periphery.*" Schwartz Center for Economic Policy Analysis and Department of Economics, The New School for Social Research, Working Paper Series 2022–1, January.

Gopinath, Gita, Emine Boz, Camila Casas, Federico Diez, Pierre-Olivier Gourinchas and Mikkel Plagborg-Moller. 2019. "Dominant currency paradigm". Working Paper, National Bureau of Economic Research Revised March.

International Monetary Fund. 2020. "Dominant Currencies and External Adjustment." Staff Discussion Note, July.

McCloskey, Diedre (Donald N.)[3]. 1983. "The rhetoric of economics." *Journal of Economic Literature*, Volume 21, Number 2, June, pp. 481–517.

Section A

Country, Regional and Comparative Studies: The Varieties of Economic Performance in SOEs

Section A provides evidence of the development performance of 41 small economies whose experiences provide the evidence which supports the theory and model which we expand on in Section B. The countries on which the analysis of this book is based have economies whose GDP is US$100 billion or less, and whose population is less than 30 million. The cut-off point between large and small countries cannot be sharply defined, but, based on defining structural characteristics, the sizes of the economy and the population are the strongest indicators of the differences in the way policy should be approached in the small open economy. The classification of economies by size is discussed in Moore, Beckles and Worrell (2015), which compares lists published by the Commonwealth Secretariat and the World Bank, as well as others appearing in other economic research (see Moore, Beckles and Worrell, 2015, Table 1, p. 7). The study compares a comprehensive list of small economies from these sources with selected large economies with respect to two characteristics which determine how they should be managed for best results, namely their openness to trade in goods and services, and the (limited) extent of diversification of their sources of foreign earnings. The countries chosen for analysis in their paper were those that are most open and that are most specialised in terms of foreign earnings.

The 41 SOEs included in the analysis of Section A of this book all exhibit a high degree of openness and a high concentration of foreign earning activities. The country with the highest degree of openness among them is Malta, with trade in goods and services that are almost three times its GDP. The lowest figure, for the Comoros, is 43 percent of GDP. The majority of ratios are clustered between 50 percent and 150 percent of GDP. By way of contrast, the ratio for China, the world's largest trading nation, is 41 percent, and for the US it is 29 percent (see Figure A.1.)

There is a similar pattern with respect to export concentration. At the top extreme the Maldives earns 96 percent of foreign exchange from the top five earners, principally tourism, while for Mauritius, the most diversified in our

DOI: 10.4324/9781003247609-2

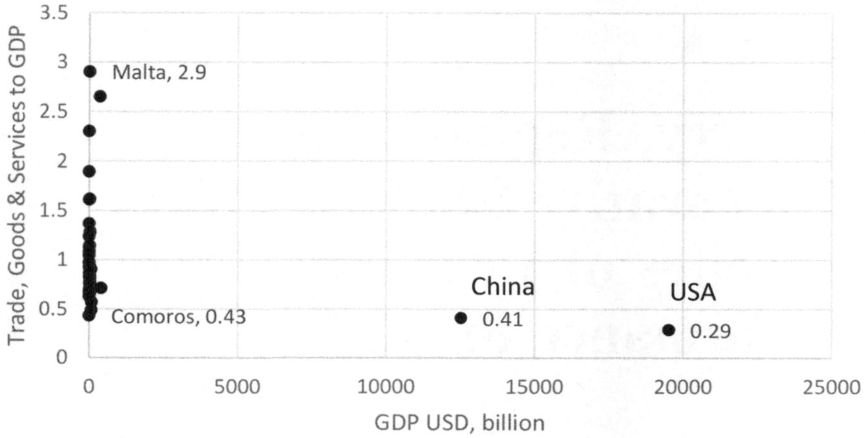

Figure A.1 Economic size and openness
Source: Moore, Beckles and Worrell, 2015.

sample, the figure is 49 percent. The US, in contrast, earns about one-third of exports from the top five earners. In the UNCTAD report on export diversification (2017) Mauritius has a score of 7.3, compared with 11.6 for the US and 11.9 for China (see Figure A.2). However, this index excludes services, so that countries in the Caribbean, Seychelles, Maldives and others whose main source of foreign earnings is tourism appear more diversified (with higher index) than is in fact the case.

The selection of countries in our sample is heavily influenced by my own experience. Included are all the independent nations of Central America and

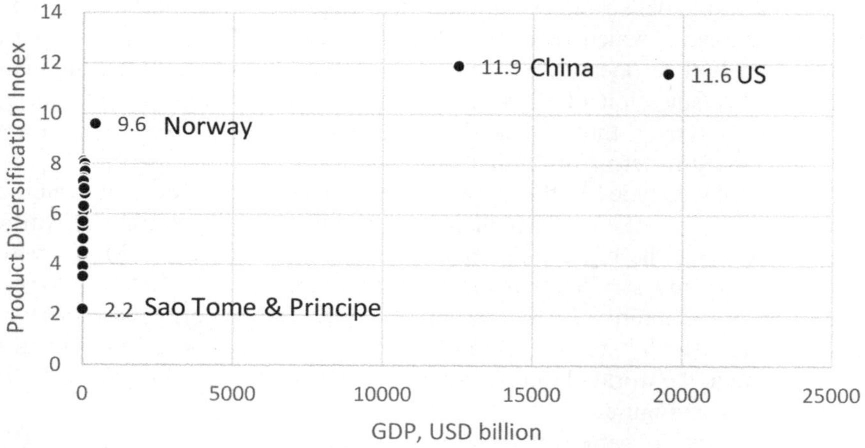

Figure A.2 GDP, Product Diversification Index
Source: United Nations Conference on Trade and Development (UNCTAD), 2017.

Table A.1 Size, structure and human development

Country	*GDP, USD b*	*Popula-tion, m*	*Trade (G&S)/ GDP*	*5 FX Sector Ratio*	*WTO Index*	*HDI score*	*Quartile*
Small Open Economies							
Bahamas	12.2	0.4	0.83	84	5.4	0.814	VH
Barbados	5.0	0.3	0.93	85	5.1	0.814	VH
Belize	1.9	0.4	1.24	75	5.5	0.716	H
Bosnia-Herzegovina	16.9	3.5	1.15	n.a.	8.1	0.768	H
Botswana	18.3	2.3	0.76	87	4.5	0.735	H
Comoros	1.1	0.8	0.43	95	3.5	0.554	M
Costa Rica	58.0	5.0	0.74	82	8.0	0.810	VH
Cuba	96.9	11.5	0.38	89	6.1	0.783	H
Cyprus	24.0	1.2	1.62	60	n.a.	0.887	VH
DR	78.7	10.9	0.57	85	7.8	0.756	H
El Salvador	25.0	6.4	0.82	77	7.2	0.673	M
Fiji	5.4	0.9	1.09	68	6.2	0.743	H
Gambia	1.5	2.2	0.68	78	n.a.	0.496	L
Ghana	58.1	29.5	0.90	n.a.	7.0	0.611	M
Guatemala	71.6	17.2	0.49	n.a.	7.7	0.663	M
Guyana	3.6	0.8	1.89	64	5.4	0.682	M
Honduras	23.0	9.4	0.83	89	7.4	0.600	M
Iceland	25.1	0.3	0.83	n.a.	7.3	0.949	VH
Jamaica	15.3	2.9	0.94	79	6.2	0.734	H
Kiribati	0.2	0.1	1.04	70	n.a.	0.630	M
Latvia	32.1	1.9	1.28	n.a.	n.a.	0.866	VH
Maldives	4.9	0.4	1.61	96	4.5	0.740	H
Malta	13.6	0.4	2.90	74	n.a.	0.895	VH
Mauritius	13.7	1.3	0.92	49	7.3	0.804	VH
Montenegro	5.2	2.1	1.13	74	5.5	0.829	VH
Namibia	14.6	2.6	0.71	64	5.9	0.646	M
Nicaragua	13.5	6.3	0.87	87	6.8	0.660	M
Panama	62.3	4.2	0.90	73	6.8	0.815	VH
PNG	19.8	8.4	0.78	n.a.	6.1	0.555	M
Paraguay	39.2	6.9	0.67	n.a.	7.0	0.728	H
Sao Tome	0.4	0.2	0.63	94	2.2	0.625	M
Seychelles	1.5	0.1	2.30	76	5.0	0.796	H
Suriname	3.4	0.6	1.37	88	5.7	0.738	H
Trinidad-Tobago	22.8	1.4	0.77	83	6.3	0.796	H
Vanuatu	0.9	0.3	0.97	86	4.4	0.609	M
Eastern Caribbean Currency Union			*0.76*				
ANB	1.4			90	3.5	0.778	H
Dominica	0.5			78	4.4	0.742	H

Country	*GDP, USD b*	*Population, m*	*Trade (G&S)/ GDP*	*5 FX Sector Ratio*	*WTO Index*	*HDI score*	*Quartile*
Grenada	1.0			n.a.	3.6	0.779	H
SKN	0.9			80	4.5	0.779	H
SLU	1.5			73	3.9	0.759	H
SVG	0.7			67	3.5	0.738	H
Large economies, highest HDI							
Norway	401.4	5.4	0.71	74	9.6	0.957	VH
Ireland	360.3	4.8	2.65	53	n.a.	0.955	VH
US	19,519.4	326.8	0.29	37	11.6	0.926	VH
China	12,520.1	1415	0.41	n.a.	11.9	0.761	H

Notes:
GDP, USD b: GDP, US dollars, billion (IMF, 2022).
Population: Latest estimates millions
Trade (G&S)/GDP: Ratio of trade in goods and services to GDP (IMF, 2022).
5FX Sector Ratio: Percentage of foreign currency receipts due to the 5 largest exports & services (Moore, Beckles and Worrell, 2015)
WTO Index: Product diversification index (higher values indicate more diversified) (United Nations Conference on Trade and Development (UNCTAD), 2017).
HDI Index (United Nations Development Programme, 2020).
Quartile: Countries in the HDR are assigned to one of 4 categories: Very High (VH), High (H), Medium (M) and Low (L)
Norway is ranked first in the HDI and Ireland is ranked fourth
Country abbreviations: ANB Antigua & Barbuda; DR Dominican Republic; PNG Papua New Guinea; SKN St Kitts-Nevis; SLU St Lucia; SVG St Vincent and the Grenadines

the Caribbean, about which I have written and researched over many years. I have also worked on all other countries in the sample, except for Botswana, Cyprus, Iceland, Maldives, Malta, Montenegro, Namibia and Paraguay. The exceptions were included in the sample to ensure there was adequate representation from all regions and all levels of human development. The emphasis on personal experience reflects the fact that much of the insight I have gained over the years has come from being on the ground and from in depth understanding of the culture, history and circumstances of individual countries. Local knowledge is the most effective way to uncover unconscious bias and unwarranted assumptions.

The structural features that define the 41 countries in our sample are summarised in Table A.1, together with their scores on the Human Development Index. The one thing that is immediately evident from the table is that size does not limit the capacity of an economy to attain a superior material quality of life for the population. Two-thirds of these SOEs are above the median HDI score for all countries, and of these ten are in the highest category, indicating that material living conditions in those countries are on par with the world's most advanced societies. Perhaps the thing that recommends the HDI more strongly than any other indicator that is available for the countries of our sample is the fact that anyone who has visited these ten countries – The Bahamas, Barbados, Costa Rica, Cyprus, Iceland, Latvia, Malta, Mauritius, Montenegro and Panama – can bear witness to the high standard of living. More than half of the remaining countries of the sample, 18 SOEs, have a material quality of life which is indicated as High, a category which includes China, the world's second largest economy. There are 13 SOEs that remain below the global median, and of them only the Comoros, Gambia and Papua New Guinea are among countries with the lowest HDI scores in our sample. Even though our country selection is somewhat idiosyncratic, the conclusion that other factors trump size in explaining the performance of SOEs seems reasonable. Our task is to arrive at some informed notion of what are the most important economic factors that account for the observed performances.

2 Human Development and Economic Stabilization

Comparative SOE Experiences

We have seen that a majority of small economies have attained a material quality of life for their populations which appears to be above average, and in a significant number of cases well above average. In this chapter we will find out how countries have performed in the recent past, reaching as far back as data will allow. We will discuss improvements in human development, and how much income, education and health have each contributed to that development. Then we focus on further elaboration of the income contribution, since that is our area of expertise and the area where we hope to derive insight for future policy, analysing patterns of growth and economic stabilisation. The third section of this chapter colours our analysis with a literature review of comparative studies of economic performance in SOEs.

Human development since 1990

Iceland, with a population of just about 300,000, is the highest-ranking economy in our sample, on the Human Development Index scale. Not only is it the highest scoring, ranking fourth in the world in 2019, it also boasts a combination of income, health and education that provides residents with a quality of life superior to what is available in the US, most of Europe and the average of countries that appear in the category of Very High Human Development. What is more, the country has improved its standing relative to the category average since 1990. Malta has also done very well, with an HDI score which is on par with the category average, having also improved relative to the group since 1990. Two European countries, Cyprus and Latvia, lie somewhat below the category average, but they, like the high flyers, have gained on the group since 1990. Although Panama, Costa Rica and Mauritius ended with HDI scores below the average for the Very High group, these countries recorded strong development gains, narrowing the gap with the group average in each case. Two Caribbean countries, The Bahamas and Barbados, round out the countries in our sample in the top group; both registered improvements in human development, but they lagged the category in terms of the gain, and they fell further below the category average.

DOI: 10.4324/9781003247609-3

The strongest performers in the High Human Development category are Bosnia-Herzegovina, Cuba, the Dominican Republic and Trinidad and Tobago. They all kept pace or outperformed the category average, and they all ended with scores higher than the average. The countries in this group, the largest in our sample, were clustered around the group average, with the weakest performer in this group, Paraguay, only 3.3 percent below the average.

Of the 12 countries whose HDI scores put them in the medium category, five were higher than the category average. They include three Central American countries, El Salvador, Guatemala and Nicaragua, plus Guyana and Namibia. However, the gains since 1990 were less robust than for the group as a whole. For example, Guyana, with the highest score in this group, was 27 per cent higher than the medium group average in 1990; by 2019 the gap had narrowed to an eight per cent advantage. Ghana was the weakest performer in this group: its HDI score rose by almost a third in the three decades to 2019, but the group performance was even better, and whereas Ghana bettered the group average by seven per cent in 1990, by 2019 it had fallen below by three per cent.

The three countries with scores at the bottom of the rankings, the Comoros, The Gambia and Papua New Guinea, all showed considerable improvement between 1990 and 2019, even though in all cases the gains were somewhat less than their group average. The average score for the Low Human Development category improved by almost 50 per cent, indicating a significant improvement in the living standards of the citizens of some of the world's poorest nations.

In general, there appears to be some convergence in HDI scores worldwide over the past three decades. The percentage increases are larger, the further down the scale you go: 15 per cent for countries with Very High Human Development, almost two-thirds for those with High Human Development, and 46 per cent for the Medium category. This convergence tendency may be observed in the 41 SOEs in our sample. The countries in the Low and Medium categories show the larger improvements, with few exceptions, with scores that rise by a third or more in some cases (see Table 2.1).

We may derive very important guidelines for economic policy from an analysis of the contributions of GDP, life expectancy at birth and schooling to the improvement in the HDI. Figure 2.1 shows calculations based on data for 2019 of the impact of a ten per cent increase in GDP, compared with a similar increase in life expectancy and expected years of schooling.[1] The clear inference is that the most effective policies for advancing material well-being are those which improve the quality and availability of health services, resulting in an increase in life expectancy. A ten per cent improvement in life expectancy has over twice the impact on the HDI score, compared with a similar increase in expected years of schooling. Compared with a ten per cent increase in GDP per capita at purchasing power parity, that increase in life expectancy is almost 26 times more powerful. An increase in years of schooling is ten times as influential as a similar percentage increase in GDP.

Table 2.1 HDR trends 1990–2019

1990–2019	*1990*	*2000*	*2010*	*2014*	*2015*	*2017*	*2018*	*2019*	*Annual % change 1990–2019*
Bahamas		0.797	0.805	0.805	0.808	0.812	0.812	0.814	0.12
Barbados	0.732	0.771	0.797	0.808	0.809	0.81	0.81	0.814	0.37
Belize	0.610	0.640	0.695	0.705	0.710	0.714	0.714	0.716	0.55
Bosnia-Herzegovina		0.679	0.721	0.758	0.761	0.774	0.777	0.780	0.88
Botswana	0.573	0.581	0.663	0.711	0.717	0.726	0.730	0.735	0.86
Comoros		0.465	0.521	0.543	0.545	0.550	0.552	0.554	0.68
Costa Rica	0.665	0.721	0.765	0.796	0.797	0.804	0.808	0.810	0.68
Cuba	0.680	0.691	0.781	0.767	0.772	0.777	0.781	0.783	0.49
Cyprus	0.735	0.804	0.856	0.863	0.865	0.878	0.885	0.887	0.65
DR	0.599	0.659	0.706	0.730	0.738	0.746	0.751	0.756	0.81
El Salvador	0.536	0.615	0.668	0.668	0.668	0.671	0.67	0.673	0.79
Fiji	0.662	0.695	0.715	0.733	0.737	0.740	0.742	0.743	0.4
Gambia	0.349	0.403	0.459	0.468	0.471	0.480	0.487	0.496	1.83
Ghana	0.465	0.494	0.565	0.590	0.590	0.602	0.606	0.611	0.95
Guatemala	0.481	0.549	0.606	0.648	0.652	0.655	0.657	0.663	1.11
Guyana	0.548	0.616	0.649	0.671	0.674	0.677	0.680	0.682	0.76
Honduras	0.519	0.566	0.610	0.616	0.618	0.630	0.633	0.634	1.64
Iceland	0.807	0.867	0.898	0.931	0.934	0.943	0.946	0.949	0.56
Jamaica	0.645	0.678	0.732	0.729	0.731	0.734	0.734	0.734	0.45
Kiribati		0.553	0.593	0.617	0.625	0.627	0.628	0.630	0.67
Latvia	0.711	0.735	0.824	0.845	0.849	0.859	0.863	0.866	0.68
Maldives		0.622	0.685	0.718	0.724	0.731	0.734	0.740	0.86
Malta	0.738	0.804	0.870	0.888	0.891	0.896	0.898	0.900	0.6
Mauritius	0.624	0.678	0.751	0.789	0.789	0.797	0.801	0.804	0.88
Montenegro			0.802	0.813	0.816	0.822	0.826	0.829	0.37
Namibia	0.581	0.544	0.589	0.631	0.638	0.644	0.645	0.646	0.37
Nicaragua	0.497	0.577	0.622	0.649	0.652	0.661	0.659	0.660	0.98
Panama	0.675	0.735	0.774	0.795	0.799	0.811	0.812	0.815	0.65
PNG	0.38	0.45	0.522	0.542	0.548	0.549	0.549	0.555	1.31
Paraguay	0.598	0.643	0.696	0.715	0.721	0.726	0.727	0.728	0.68
Sao Tome	0.452	0.498	0.561	0.591	0.604	0.619	0.624	0.625	1.12
Seychelles		0.714	0.764	0.775	0.786	0.789	0.790	0.796	0.46
Suriname			0.710	0.735	0.740	0.732	0.734	0.738	0.43

1990–2019									*Annual % change*
	1990	*2000*	*2010*	*2014*	*2015*	*2017*	*2018*	*2019*	*1990–2019*
Trinidad-Tobago	0.668	0.717	0.784	0.785	0.792	0.795	0.795	0.796	0.61
Vanuatu			0.590	0.594	0.598	0.601	0.603	0.609	0.35
Very high HDI	0.782	0.826	0.87	0.885	0.889	0.894	0.896	0.898	
High HDI	0.567	0.629	0.705	0.730	0.735	0.744	0.748	0.753	
Medium HDI	0.433	0.492	0.571	0.601	0.609	0.624	0.627	0.631	
Low HDI	0.345	0.381	0.468	0.497	0.500	0.507	0.509	0.513	
World	0.601	0.644	0.699	0.720	0.724	0.732	0.734	0.737	
ECCU									
ANB			0.763	0.76	0.762	0.768	0.772	0.778	0.22
Dominica		0.703	0.740	0.741	0.739	0.736	0.738	0.742	0.03
Grenada			0.754	0.766	0.770	0.770	0.773	0.779	0.36
SKN			0.746	0.768	0.768	0.770	0.773	0.779	0.48
SLU		0.695	0.730	0.735	0.747	0.759	0.758	0.759	0.43
SVG		0.681	0.718	0.733	0.733	0.734	0.736		0.31

Source: United Nations Development Programme, 2020.

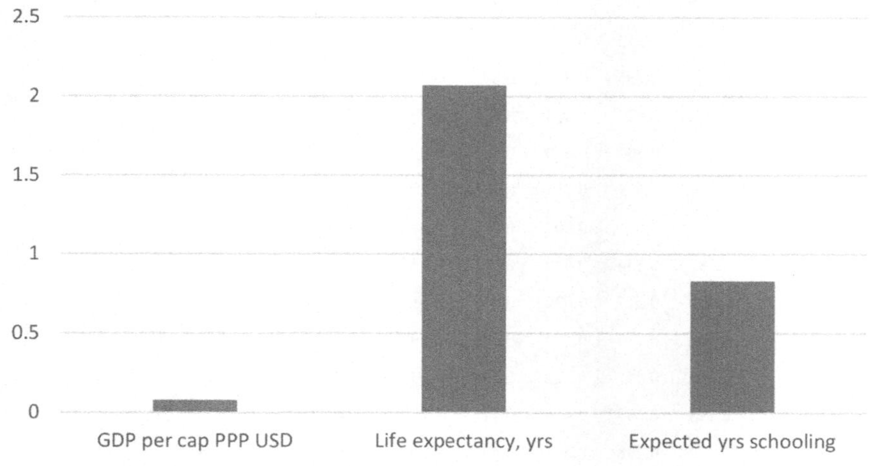

Figure 2.1 Relative contributions to HDI, 2019
Source: United Nations Development Programme, 2020.

Very clearly, improving the quality and reach of health and educational services are the most effective policies governments should prioritise if they wish to accelerate human development.

A look at the top performers reinforces the importance of health and education in human development

Mauritius is the highest ranking country in our sample of 41 SOEs when the HDI ranking is combined with the magnitude of the improvement since 1990; even though Mauritius lies only in tenth place in the HDI 2019 ranking, it has improved its HDI score since 1990 at an annual rate of 0.68 per cent per year, to gain eighth place in the growth ranking. Iceland, Number 1 in the 2019 HDI ranking, improved at an annual rate of 0.56 per cent, sufficient to secure only 24th place for its growth performance, leaving the country tied with Malta for fifth place in the combined rankings.

Table 2.2 shows the contributions of health, educational and income indicators to the country's overall performance, for the ten best performing countries in our sample, when we combine rank in the HDI scores and the improvement since 1990. For each country the table shows the difference between the value for that country and the world average. One thing that is very striking is that Cuba is the tenth best performer, even though income per capita in that country is only about half the world average. The main reason

Table 2.2 Top ten performers

Combined rank	*Country*	*LEB/World*	*EYS/World*	*GNIpc PPP/World*
1	Mauritius	3.0	18.9	51.0
2	Latvia	3.4	27.5	81.0
3	Bosnia-Herzegovina	6.3	13.1	-11.2
4	Cyprus	11.3	19.7	128.3
5	Iceland	14.0	50.4	226.8
5	Malta	13.3	26.8	136.4
7	Costa Rica	10.3	23.6	10.5
7	Panama	7.8	1.6	76.6
9	T&T	1.0	2.4	56.8
10	Cuba	8.2	12.6	-48.5
	Mean	*7.9*	*19.7*	*70.8*
	Standard deviation	*4.4*	*14.1*	*79.8*

Source: United Nations Development Programme, 2020.

Notes:
LEB/World: Life expectancy birth, compared with world average.
EYS/World: Expected years of schooling, compared with world average.
GNIpc PPP/World: Purchasing power, compared with world average.

is that the Cuban life expectancy is almost 79 years, eight per cent higher than the world average, which is just below 73 years.

In general, the health indicator is the most powerful indicator of human development, which is as should be expected. Life expectancy, which exceeds the world average by 14 per cent, secures Iceland fourth place in the world rankings overall; that represents an average life expectancy at birth of 83 years, a figure which is extraordinarily difficult to achieve. All the top performing countries in our sample have life expectancies that exceed the world average, and except for Trinidad and Tobago, the margin of advantage is significant.

Educational achievement is less influential in improving the level of human development than is health, but it may be seen to matter far more than does the level of income. On average, an advantage of 20 per cent over the world average expected years of schooling secures a country a spot in the top ten performers in our sample. For the more powerful health indicator, a country in the top ten records an eight per cent advantage over the world average life expectancy at birth. For the income indicator, the least powerful, it takes a 71 per cent advantage over the world average to put a country into the top ten. However, the range of income performance in the top ten is very wide: two countries – Cuba and Bosnia-Herzegovina – have per capita incomes below the world average. The standard deviation of per capita incomes in the group is greater than the group mean, in contrast with the other two indicators. Years of schooling and life expectancy are more reliable indicators of human development than income, even though the best guide is one which incorporates all three.

The way resources are employed is more important than the rate of growth

In designing development policies governments will get the greatest bang for their buck if they direct efforts to increase competitiveness while at the same time ensuring that, for every dollar of extra income, the lion's share goes to health services and then to foundational educational services. Furthermore, in times of austerity, the priority ought to be to ensure that the quality and general availability of health services are not impaired, and that educational standards are maintained. This explains why countries like Iceland, a country which suffered a major loss of real income during the financial crisis of 2008, and Cyprus, where there was a debt crisis which captured world attention in 2013, have both remained in the highest category of human development throughout. Even though real output declined, the delivery of health and educational services did not deteriorate. The population as a whole continued to enjoy a superior standard of living, when compared internationally.

We may conclude from the HDI that a country with a low growth rate will enjoy a greater improvement in human development than a country with a much higher growth rate, if the first country devotes most of the additional resources from its meagre growth to health and education. Equally, in cases of downturn, the country which better protects health and educational services will cushion the impact of the economic losses on the livelihoods of the population.

There are other public services such as housing, water and sanitation, electricity, roads and communication, which also greatly magnify the material benefits of foreign earnings. We are unable to make definitive statements about their impact only because comparative data for the countries in our sample are not readily available and are not included in the annual HDI scores for all countries, but it is reasonable to expect that priority given to these public services will contribute to lasting gains in human development. This discussion also puts the spotlight on the efficiency of public service delivery. All too often, the extent of government expenditures on health, education and other public services is not reflected in the quality and coverage of services. In order to achieve and maintain a Very High level of human development governments should allocate resources well and put systems in place to ensure high productivity in the delivery of public services.

In addition to these direct improvements in well-being, enhancements of health, educational and other public services have second round effects in promoting faster GDP growth in a virtuous cycle. As we shall see in Section B of this volume, these are among a range of facilities which contribute to a country's competitiveness and ability to attract investment. That in turn increases productive capacity and the country's ability to earn foreign exchange to accelerate sustainable growth in the economy.

Questions of the allocation of public financial resources and efficiency in the delivery of public services – whether or not they are provided by the government or state companies or agencies – have not received the attention they deserve in research that informs macroeconomic policy. That is unfortunately reflected in the paucity of studies cited in this volume, and the inadequacy of guidance which is available to policy makers on these two issues, which, it is evident, are far more critical than is the GDP, in evaluating the level of human development in any nation.

Context – the world economy since 1970

Always bearing in mind the importance of the allocation of available economic and financial resources, we now turn our attention to the amount of resources at the society's disposal, and to ways of augmenting that amount, that is to say, to the GDP and to economic growth. While we have made the point that the misallocation of resources may squander the potential of high income, it remains the case that higher income, efficiently employed, is the ultimate goal.

Our concern is with small economies which are outward-oriented, so we need to evaluate their performance in the context of the international economy with which they do business. Our first task is to paint in the background,

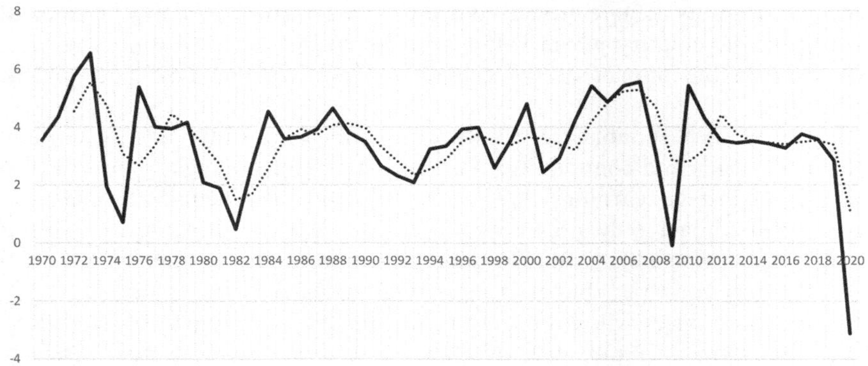

Figure 2.2 World real GDP growth, %
Source: IMF, 2022.

by providing ourselves an overview of the recent history of the world economy. We begin our review in 1970, at a time when the Nixon administration is soon to make the momentous decision that eventually results in the abandonment of the anchor for the US dollar to gold at US$35 per ounce. The events leading to that decision, and its far-reaching consequences, vividly recalled in Jeffrey Garten's marvellous book (Garten, 2021), proved to be a watershed in post-war international financial and exchange rate arrangements.

The performance of the world economy since 1970 may be divided into four periods, according to the general tendency of change in overall growth (Figure 2.2). The period from the early 1970s to 1982 witnessed a declining trend of growth from a peak early on to a low in the early 1980s. The 1980s were a period of modest growth, in comparison with the early 1970s, once the world economy had recovered from the 1982 low point. Growth fell away somewhat to a low in 1993, which marks the beginning of a third period, lasting to the onset of the Global Recession in 2008/09. During this third period global growth strengthened, interrupted twice, by the Russian Financial crisis and the September 11 attacks on the World Trade Center in New York in 2001. The fourth period, from 2009 to 2019, was one of modest growth in the world economy, following a sharp recovery in 2010.

From Camp David (August 1971) to the bottom of the early 1980s recession (1982)

The US decision to close the gold window, where the Federal Reserve had previously committed to sell gold to other central banks at US$35 per ounce, was initially welcomed by everyone. The Fed was known to have gold reserves that were only a quarter of the value of outstanding liabilities at the 35 dollar price. Speculators saw a one-way winning bet, if they put enough collective pressure on the gold reserves at that price, and some central banks were under pressure to buy gold when they might not otherwise have done so, in case panic buying caused the price to rise. Suspending all sales until a new equilibrium price for gold could be found appeared sensible in these circumstances. The international economy reacted favourably, with growth accelerating from 3.5 per cent in 1970 to 6.6 per cent in 1973.

World economic growth tanked in 1974, in the wake of the action by the Organization of Petroleum Exporting Countries in October 1973 to boycott countries that had supported Israel during the Yom Kippur War. The price of oil rose four-fold, and the global rate of growth fell to less than one per cent in 1975. There was an impressive recovery in 1976, thanks to a boom in commodity prices, but it did not last, and the global rate of growth fell continuously until 1982, to just half of one per cent. An incipient recovery in 1979 was cut short by a new energy crisis triggered by the Iranian Revolution in 1979, followed by the Iran–Iraq War in 1980. At the end of the 1970s decade US inflation was driven to levels unprecedented in recent history; strong interest rate medicine by the Federal Reserve is credited with taming inflation, but at the cost of economic growth.

From 1982 to the bottom of the early 1990s recession in 1993

The Reagan administration's expansionist fiscal policies were the major factor in the strong acceleration of world economic growth to 4.5 per cent in 1984. Meanwhile the Latin American debt crisis emerged, weakening confidence and arresting world economic growth. Commercial bank lending to Latin American countries had ballooned in the late 1970s and early 1980s; in August 1982 Mexico, among the largest of the Latin American borrowers, defaulted, leading to a "sudden stop" in financial inflows and refinancing of maturing debt. This triggered a debt default crisis that affected most of Latin America, depressing direct investment inflows and productive capacity, leading to the "Lost Decade" for the region (Williamson, 1990). The lingering effects of the Latin American debt crisis were a drag on the regional economy for most of the 1980s decade and, in some cases, into the 1990s.

Other crises took the steam out of the global economy in the 1980s and early 1990s. They included another oil price shock at the time of the Iraqi invasion of Kuwait (1990), followed by the Gulf War in the following year. A decrease in defence spending in Western nations after the collapse of the Soviet Union was a drag on expenditure. Another depressing factor was a slow-burning crisis among small savings and loan banks in the US, from the mid-1980s to the mid-1990s.

From 1993 to the great recession of 2009

The taming of US inflation after 1982, a retreat in oil prices from their 1990 peak, and expansionary US fiscal policy brought on a global recovery from

1994 onwards. Growth was tempered, however, by the Mexican debt crisis and the onset of financial crises in East Asia in 1997 and in Russia in 1998. The strengthening trend in global growth was interrupted in 1998 as a result. However, an IMF-supported adjustment programme (promoted by the US Treasury) in 1995 brought an end to the Mexican crisis, to be followed in the second half of the decade by admittedly painful resolution of the Asian and Russian financial crises, and world growth recovered to almost five per cent in 2000. The shock of the terrorist attack on the world's financial capital in 2001 caused a deceleration to only two per cent growth in that year, but two years later global growth had recovered to exceed five per cent. The most important driver, from the turn of the millennium, has been the extraordinary rate of expansion in Chinese production. In 2007 the world economy grew by almost six per cent, the fastest pace since 1973.

From the global recession (2008) to the onset of the COVID pandemic

We end our story in 2019, just before the onset of the COVID-19 pandemic, an unprecedented event whose consequences, deep and long-lasting, cannot yet be discerned. The crisis in the financial market in New York City, which stands at the centre of global commerce, was a shock felt principally in North America and Europe. The US and the larger European countries reacted swiftly, with central banks and governments intervening to prevent any serious loss of wealth. However, debt problems emerged in smaller and weaker economies. The extent and magnitude of the problem created an international period of financial uncertainty that put a damper on direct investment flows, taking the steam out of global growth. Debt crises broke out in Russia, Ireland, Spain, Latvia and Iceland in 2008, followed by Greece in 2009 and Portugal in 2010. The problems in Russia, Ireland and Latvia were quickly resolved, but the economic malaise lingered on for several years elsewhere. Asian countries were largely unaffected by the fallout from the financial crisis and countries like China and South Korea were the main engines of global growth of a little better than three per cent during the decade to 2019.

Economic growth performances – top ten countries

The top performances in the HDI rankings in Table 2.2 all saw consistently strong economic growth performances in all phases of the world economy's evolution, with the exceptions of Cuba and Trinidad and Tobago. Their growth rates were substantially above the strong global average recorded in the first half of the 1970s, and they recovered from the 1982 slump to achieve rates of growth better than the moderate world average. They all kept pace with or bettered accelerating world growth through the 1990s and early 2000s, and they all recovered strongly from the impact of the global recession in 2008–09. The fortunes of Trinidad and Tobago, the only oil exporting country in the group, strongly reflected trends in the world price of oil. In the case of

Cuba, the collapse of the Soviet Union deprived that country of its main market for exports and source of investment. Without a means to compensate for the tight US embargo, the Cuban economy contracted and entered an extended period of economic stagnation.

Mauritius, which stands at Number 1 among the countries in our sample in the combined HDI score and improvement since 1990, recorded growth well above the world average in the period of the commodity price boom, with peaks of over ten per cent in some years. In only two years, 1979 and 1980, did the country underperform relative to the world average. The economy recorded growth rates consistently above the world average up until 1998, after which the rate became more volatile from year to year, while still keeping pace with world growth, as the rate of growth accelerated through the early 2000s. The Mauritius economy matched the modest world growth rates in the decade to 2019, with only a slight deceleration of growth (to three per cent) in 2009.

Cyprus' economic performance was especially strong in the early years of our review period. Growth rates in the 1970s were substantially above the world average, with a peak of 20 per cent in 1975. Growth rates were better than the world average in most years of the 1980s and up to 1998, ranging between five and ten per cent. The growth rate fell behind in 2004, and slumped in 2008, bottoming out in 2012, with a contraction of almost seven per cent. The following year GDP recovered by the same percentage, and the growth rate remained above five per cent until the onset of the COVID-19 pandemic.

The Icelandic economy outperformed the world average consistently through the ups and downs of the 1970s, decelerating, but less quickly than the world average, to fall into brief recession in 1983, a year after the bottom of the global cycle. Recovery was swift to 1987, when the growth rate was eight per cent. However, the economy then stagnated for the remainder of the 1980s and into the early 1990s, with a low in 1992, when the economy contracted by three per cent. Strong and persistent growth, starting in 1993, heralded a period that lasted until a peak of eight per cent in 2007, during which growth strengthened every year, except for brief lapses in 1995 and 2002–03. The large overseas overexposure of Icelandic banks resulted in a crisis which attracted world-wide attention and resulted in an eight per cent contraction in 2009, followed by a further three per cent loss in 2010. The long climb back to economic health started in 2011, with another persistent climb to eight per cent growth in 2016, and over-performance, compared to the world average, lasting to the end of the period.

Malta recorded exceptional growth from 1974 to 1982, with a peak of 20 per cent in 1975. Strong growth continued in the period 1988 through to 2000, after a brief slowdown from 1983 to 1985. There followed a period of underperformance, with growth well below the world average, after a slump in 2001. The economy hit a nadir with a one per cent contraction in 2009. Recovery was slow, and the economy did not hit its stride until 2012, after which very strong growth was recorded, with a peak of ten per cent in 2015.

Costa Rica bettered the average world economic growth even in the peak year of 1975, when the country recorded a growth rate of eight per cent compared with the world average of six per cent. Strong performance was interrupted by a slump in 1981 and 1982, which saw a contraction of seven per cent in the latter year. However, the economy recovered strongly, with a growth rate of eight per cent in 1984, and above average growth persisted, with some volatility, to 2008. The peak was in 1992 (nine per cent), with a low of one per cent in 1996. There was a one per cent contraction in 2009, but a sharp recovery in 2010 brought the growth rate back to the global average for that year (five per cent), where it remained.

Panama recorded very strong growth at the beginning and end of the seventies decade, and extending to 1982. Growth peaks were recorded in 1973, 1978 (both ten per cent) and 1981 (nine per cent). The 1980s were a problematic decade for political reasons, and the economy underperformed, reaching a nadir in 1988, with a 13 per cent contraction. Rapid growth resumed after the transfer of control of the Panama Canal in 1990; since then growth rates have generally been in excess of five per cent every year, with a high of 12 per cent in 2007, and peaks approaching that figure in 1992 and 2011. The growth rate never fell below two per cent, except in 2001 (one per cent growth) and 2009, when there was no growth.

Other countries with high or very high human development

This segment includes countries in the top two categories of the HDI which did not achieve the combination of improvements over the past 50 years and final quality of life, to qualify them for the top ten. At one end of the spectrum, we have countries in this group which recorded consistently high growth over all four periods of the evolution of the world economy. They are Botswana (with an average growth rate of 8.1 per cent over the period), Maldives (6.5 per cent), the Dominican Republic (4.9 per cent) and Seychelles (4.2 per cent), compared with the world average of 3.6 per cent over the period. At the other end of the spectrum were economies which recorded low rates of growth pretty much in all phases of the evolution of the world economy: Jamaica (with an average growth rate of 1.4 per cent), The Bahamas and Barbados (both 2.1 per cent) and Fiji (2.9 per cent). Between these extremes we find a variety of country experiences. We offer short capsules for each country, proceeding in descending order of the scores in the 2019 HDI.

There are three countries with Very High Human Development which did not register improvements sufficient to place them in the list of top ten performers. Montenegro, a new nation, suffered a large economic contraction in 1999, when our series for this country begins, and the rate of growth has lagged the world average ever since. However, because it has enjoyed the high quality of life of its European neighbours it remains ahead in the HDI rankings.

The Bahamas, the second country in this group, experienced large swings in GDP performance in the first half of the 1970s, but recovered in the second half of that decade, with growth rate reaching 11 per cent in 1979. The economy recorded strong growth in the early 1980s, but performance trailed off to four per cent contractions in 1991 and 1992. The economy recovered to record growth rates slightly better than the average for an accelerating world economy over the 1990s decade to reach a peak of seven per cent in 1999. However the economy has stagnated for the most part since then.

The Barbados economy performed well in the 1970s, with growth rates in excess of the world average, reaching a peak of 16 per cent in 1975. However, the country began the 1980s with two years of economic contraction, and a weak recovery over that decade ended with three years of contraction, from 1990 to 1992. The pattern of weak recovery followed by deceleration was repeated in the 1990s, ending with a 2.4 per cent loss in GDP in 2001, and again in the 2000s, ending with a five per cent contraction in 2009.

Next we consider the four countries that recorded growth rates that were better than the world average consistently over the period of our review, and they all sit in the category of High Human Development. We review their performance in the order of their rank in the Human Development Index.

Seychelles sits at the top of the High Human Development rankings, just below Mauritius, which has the lowest score in the Very High category. Since the break points are of necessity arbitrary, this means that in practice there is nothing to choose between the quality of life in these two countries. Seychelles recorded growth rates ranging between five and 16 per cent in the 1970s, except for 1979, when the growth rate fell to two per cent. Following a contraction in the first four years of the 1980s, growth jumped to ten per cent in 1985, and GDP expansion continued at rates between four and 12 per cent to 2000, except for a brief slump in 1994 and 1995. There was a short period of poor performance in the first half of the 2000s, but a strong recovery in 2005 (nine per cent growth) was followed by performance that bettered the world average to 2019, except for contraction of about two per cent each year in 2009 and 2010.

The Dominican Republic recorded growth rates between two and 13 per cent per annum during the 1970s. Growth was very erratic in the 1980s, with contractions of two per cent in 1984 and six per cent in 1989, and a peak of ten per cent in 1986. The 1990s opened with 11 per cent growth in 1991, followed by a period lasting to 2002 when growth rates ranged between three and nine per cent. After a one per cent contraction in 2002, growth resumed and continued at rates exceeding five per cent most years, up to the end of our period.

After underperforming in the 1970s, the Maldives' GDP growth rate was better than the world average every year to 2019 except for 1990 (five per cent contraction), 2005 (down 13 per cent) and 2009, when GDP fell seven per cent. In the 1980s growth ranged between five and 19 per cent, in the 1990s between five and ten per cent and in the 2000s between two and 26 per cent. The range in the past decade was two to eight per cent.

Botswana outperformed the world economy average by wide margins, up to ten percentage points from the 1970s to the early 1990s. Thereafter the pattern of out-performing the world average continued almost to the end of our period, although the margins were much lower, in the region of two or three percentage points better than the world average most years. There was only one year of contraction in this period, by eight per cent in 2009.

The remaining countries in the High Human Development group are Fiji, Paraguay and countries in the Caribbean – the member countries of the Eastern Caribbean Currency Union (ECCU), Suriname, Jamaica and Belize.

The countries of the ECCU all turned in creditable performances in the 1970s, exceeding the global average, with rates of growth in excess of ten per cent for some years. Dominica was hit by a major hurricane (David), leading to an 18 per cent GDP loss in 1979, but with increases of 13 per cent and 11 per cent in the following years, the GDP was soon well ahead of its previous trend. Antigua and Barbuda and St Kitts-Nevis experienced set-backs in GDP in the early 1980s, but quickly recovered to join other ECCU countries with growth rates that exceeded the world average by margins of over five percentage points most years. Performances diverged from the 1990s onwards. Grenada's economy recovered from recession in 1991–92 to achieve 12 per cent growth by 1998. Hurricane Ivan depressed GDP in 2004, but hurricane relief inflows and investment in rehabilitation meant that losses had been repaired by 2008, only for the economy to suffer its deepest contraction, worse than the hurricane impact, with a loss of seven per cent in 2009. Grenada's tourism, remittance flows and inward investment were all hard hit by the global recession of 2008. Recovery was gradual, but strengthened each year to a peak of seven per cent growth in 2014.

St Kitts-Nevis registered growth rates ranging between three and ten per cent through to 2001. Since the turn of the millennium performance has been erratic, below the world average, with contractions of about four per cent in 2003, 2009 and 2012, all hurricane-related. As is typical, each episode was matched with swift recovery in subsequent years, as relief and rehabilitation efforts kicked in.

Antigua and Barbuda made a swift recovery from a five per cent contraction in 2001 to achieve a growth rate that topped out at 13 per cent in 2006. The economy suffered a 12 per cent contraction in 2009, recovering steadily to reach a high of seven per cent in 2018.

In St Lucia a slump in 1991, when there was no growth, began an extended period of weak performances lasting to 2019. The last three decades saw a disappointing performance in Dominica also, where growth rates did not rise above three per cent in the 1990s. Growth was stronger in the 2000s, around five per cent, but the economy then stagnated during the last decade. In St Vincent and the Grenadines the economy kept pace with the world average, albeit with wide swings, up to 2008. After a two per cent contraction in 2009, the economy stagnated for the next decade.

Fiji recorded three years of growth in the early 1970s, followed by a period of stagnation that lasted to 1978. After that came a period of wide economic fluctuations, alternating between contractions of up to seven per cent and growth rates that sometimes exceeded ten per cent. Up to 2001 the average growth over the years compared favourably with world trends, but a slump in that year was the beginning of a period of modest growth for the rest of the decade. Growth rose above the world average from 2013.

Starting with five per cent growth in the early 1970s the Surinamese economy recovered from a seven per cent loss in 1974 to achieve growth rates of ten to 17 per cent in the last years of the decade. The 1980s were an extended period of contraction, through to the mid-1990s. There was a period of better than ten per cent growth lasting from 1996 to 1998, followed by two years of no growth, after which the growth rate climbed back to peak at seven per cent in 2004, remaining in the region of five per cent per year until 2013. Performance deteriorated afterwards, with a nadir of five per cent contraction in 2016.

Jamaica has had a record of poor economic performance for the past 50 years. The 1970s began with growth rates ranging between a low of four per cent and a high of 12 per cent, but the economy then contracted in the second half of the decade. In the 1980s the economy struggled to maintain a growth rate of two to four per cent most years. The years 1996–1998 saw a recession, with a slow climb back to a growth rate of four per cent in 2003. Afterward the growth rate fell away, with a low point of three per cent contraction in 2009. Since 2010 growth has remained less than two per cent per year.

Paraguay outperformed the world economy by wide margins (between two and eight percentage points) in the 1970s and 1980s, up to 1994, with just one slump, an average two per cent contraction in 1982–83. The years 1998 to 2002 were a period of weak performance, falling to minus two per cent in 2000. A steady recovery brought the economy to a growth peak of six per cent in 2008. The effect of the global recession was reflected in zero growth in 2009, but recovery was exceptionally strong and was followed by above average growth rates.

Although the growth rate was quite volatile, Belize's GDP bettered the world average in the 1970s and up to 1982, when the economy contracted by eight per cent. Strong recovery with growth exceeding the global average by ten percentage points or more followed until 1994, when there was no growth. The economy then recovered to peak at 13 per cent growth in 2000. Growth slowed to 2009, when again there was no growth. Growth has been slow ever since, ranging from zero to four per cent.

The remaining countries in our sample all sat in the Medium Human Development category, with the sole exception of The Gambia

Of the remaining 13 countries in our sample, only The Gambia has an HDI score which is below the cut-off for the Medium HDI group. We summarise their performance, as before, in descending order of their rank in the HDI.

The 1970s and 1980s were disastrous for the Guyanese economy, which contracted every year, except for a brief interval in 1973 to 1976. The 1990s saw a revival, with growth rates between five and nine per cent each year. This period ended in 1999, and the economy stagnated between 2000 and 2005. GDP recovered to five per cent growth in 2006, a rate which was maintained to 2018.

El Salvador's growth rate of about five per cent per year in the 1970s was somewhat better than the world average, but the decade ended with a 16 per cent contraction in 1979. The economy recovered gradually in the 1980s to reach a growth rate just above seven per cent in 1991. Growth slowed in 1995 and remained below the world average until 2018.

Guatemala's GDP growth rates in the 1970s, ranging between five and seven per cent most years, bettered the world average. The economy contracted by four per cent in 1982, followed by a gradual recovery to three per cent in 1990. In the 1990s growth ranged between three and five per cent, continuing at that pace until 2006. A one per cent contraction in 2009 was followed by a period of slow growth of around three per cent per year that lasted through the 2010s.

In Nicaragua growth rates of five per cent or more in the 1970s ended with a huge contraction (over 25 per cent) in 1978–79. The economy did not grow at all in the 1980s, and in 1988 there was a 12 per cent contraction. Growth rates of about five per cent were once more achieved from 1994 to 2008. The economy contracted by three per cent in 2009, recovering to the five per cent pace between 2010 and 2017.

The Namibian economy accelerated steadily from economic stagnation in the early 1980s to reach a plateau of between four and six per cent growth per annum from 2002 to 2016. There were just two setbacks, a two per cent contraction in 1993 and a year of no growth in 2009.

The Kiribati economy expanded rapidly in the early 1970s, but most of the gains were lost through economic contraction in the second half of the decade. The economy recovered to reach seven per cent growth in 1982, but then slowed, bottoming with a contraction of nine per cent in 1987. Recovery, with steadily accelerating growth which reached a peak of seven per cent in 1998, was followed by a period of high volatility lasting to 2017, with swings of five to ten percentage points and GDP changes from minus two to plus five per cent.

In São Tomé exceptional growth rates in the late 1970s were undone by a prolonged period of economic contraction which lasted throughout the 1980s. Growth rates in the 1990s were in the range of one to two per cent, accelerating in the 2000s to a peak of nine per cent in 2006. After a year of no growth in 2009 the GDP expanded by about five per cent per year in the last decade.

The period 1970 to 1983 was one of poor performance by the Ghanaian economy, with GDP changes ranging between two per cent growth and a 12 per cent contraction. GDP recovered to nine per cent in 1984, followed by a long period of growth rates in the region of five per cent which lasted to 2007. There was a sharp acceleration of growth to a peak of 17 per cent in 2011, slowing afterwards to end at six per cent growth in 2018.

The 1970s were a period of volatile growth in Vanuatu, on a rising trend which peaked at nine per cent in 1978. Growth then slowed but remained above the world average to 1984. The 1980s were a period of poor performance, with a nadir of minus three per cent in 1987. The 1990s were much better, with growth on a rising trend that lasted to 2006, when growth of eight per cent was recorded. There were only two years when the economy faltered, 2001 and 2002, with contractions of three and five per cent respectively.

The Honduran economy recorded high volatility from 1970 to 2000, with annual changes ranging from minus three to plus ten per cent. There were swings of six to eight percentage points in 1982–84, 1986–87, 1990–92, 1993–94 and 1999–2000, with a giant reversal (down nine percentage points, followed by a 14 point gain) in 1974–76. A slowdown in 2001, when two per cent growth was recorded, was followed by acceleration to six per cent in 2007. A two per cent contraction in 2009 was followed by recovery to a rate of around four per cent for the remainder of the period.

The Papua New Guinea economy has underperformed over the last 50 years, with growth rates seldom reaching three per cent, and interspersed with frequent deep contractions. Real GDP declined at an annual rate of 3.5 per cent over the period, by far the worst performance in our sample.

Patterns of economic growth in the Comoros have been very erratic, except for the eighties and the 2010s. In the 1970s GDP growth fluctuated between zero and seven per cent, with swings of three to seven percentage points. Growth rose to a peak of almost ten per cent in 1979, falling off to zero in 1989. The year 1990 began a period of fluctuation with swings of four to 14 percentage points, which lasted to 2008. Modest growth of between one and four per cent per year was recorded between 2008 and 2018.

The Gambia recorded growth rates of five to 13 per cent between 1972 and 1977. There followed a period of violent swings, between 17 and 30 percentage points from 1978 to 1984, after which a period of slow growth extended to 1992, with rates between two and four per cent per year. A contraction of four per cent in 1994 was followed by a gradual climb back to almost seven per cent growth in 1998. Growth continued at that pace until 2004, except for a three per cent contraction in 2002. There was a period of high volatility from 2002 to 2015, with swings ranging between five and ten percentage points.

Observations on SOE economic performances

The great variety of experiences among the 41 SOEs in our sample raises questions about some of the generally accepted notions about their economic performances and possibilities. The impact of world economic cycles and lesser downturns may be less pervasive than is usually assumed. Only two major global economic events are reflected in the performances of most, but not all, SOEs: the commodity price boom of the mid-1970s and the global recession of 2008–09. Secondly, it seems that only prolonged slow growth and deep contraction will serve to arrest improvements in the HDI score. Prolonged volatility is also costly, in terms of a country's HDI score. However, such extreme volatility is rare, characterising just five countries in our sample: Fiji, Honduras, Comoros, The Gambia and Kiribati (in the 2000s). Wars and civil strife cause lasting damage and depress the HDI score, but hurricanes and natural disasters generally have no lasting impact on the GDP growth rate, because inflows for relief and rehabilitation quickly restore the growth trajectory.

Assessments of economic policy and performance, comparative studies, 1960s to the present

This section summarises insights of my research on comparative studies of SOEs, as seen now with the benefit of hindsight.

In 1980 I compared the policies of Barbados and Jamaica in response to the terms of trade shocks of the 1970s (Worrell, 1980). The real costs of adjusting to the changes in the 1971–73 period were very large in both countries, and proportionately larger in Jamaica. In both cases there was a sharp decline in output. Both countries attempted to lessen the impact by expansionary fiscal policy, Jamaica more aggressively so, including the "socialisation" of large private enterprises.[2] In Barbados the expansion was biased toward investment activities, with ten per cent of the investment being financed from Government savings. The extent of Government borrowing from the central banks boosted official and total credit, breaching quantitative credit limits which had been set in both countries. In Barbados the public sector crowded out the private sector to some extent, slowing the overall growth of credit. As a result of its less aggressive fiscal expansion, the fact that it focussed on investment and was partly financed by public sector savings, there was no excess pressure on the foreign exchange market in Barbados, and the peg to the US dollar remained intact. Responding to excess market pressure, the Jamaican authorities devalued the exchange rate by 27 per cent in hopes of increasing relative domestic prices by 19 per cent, but the actual change turned out to be only one per cent. I concluded that countercyclical fiscal policy may be effective if it focussed on capital formation in the public sector. I observed that "It is difficult to obtain effective results from any other policy instrument if the fiscal deficit grows large enough to require substantial money creation" (Worrell, 1980, p. 147).

Worrell (1984) was a comparative analysis of the experiences of Barbados, Costa Rica, Jamaica and Nicaragua in the 1970s and early 1980s. The common sources of terms of trade shocks were price increases for oil and other commodities, leading to foreign currency shortages in all four economies. It proved impossible to increase the supply of foreign currency in the short run. To make matters worse, investment slowed due to "uncertainty about markets and costs" (Worrell, 1984, p. 168). No country was able to attract adequate balance of payments support, and capital flight aggravated foreign currency shortages. In the second half of the seventies and early eighties all four governments took measures to cut budget deficits, though the gap was so wide in Jamaica that the improvement in the balance of payments outcome was not significant. Barbados was the only country to escape very high inflation, which was associated with sharp currency devaluation in Jamaica and Costa Rica. Jamaica and Nicaragua maintained extensive quantitative controls on foreign exchange markets, leading to distortions in relative prices and misallocation of resources. Interest rate policy changes in Jamaica and Costa Rica failed to secure the intended increase in the real rate of return on investment.

Worrell (1987) is an exhaustive analysis and evaluation of the policies and performance of The Bahamas, Barbados, Guyana, Jamaica, Trinidad and Tobago and the ECCU states between 1970 and the mid-1980s. My main conclusions were as follows. Fiscal policies were the cornerstone of adjustment programmes that maintained economic stability in all external circumstances. It proved difficult to isolate local money and credit markets from external transfers. In Jamaica, currency devaluation did not produce any measurable expenditure switching in favour of the consumption of local production; instead, devaluation reduced real income through inflationary effects. The main impact of credit restrictions was to stimulate inventive ways to evade them, with no discernible impact on the total credit. Financial flows responded to perceived country risk premiums, irrespective of the tightness or otherwise of exchange controls. The "budgeting" of available foreign currency according to supposed national priorities was universally unsuccessful in every country where it was attempted. Discretionary interest rate policy only produced desired effects when it was exercised within a corridor set by the cost of exchange. General controls on prices had no measurable effect. Direct government investment in commercial ventures had no positive effect on total output, except in the case of Trinidad and Tobago, where I reserved judgement. My overall assessment was that the successful economic policies were those of The Bahamas and Barbados in response to the terms of trade shock of 1981–83. Trinidad and Tobago's strategy at the time of the first oil crisis (1973–74) was deemed to be a qualified success. The Guyanese strategy in 1966–67 and Jamaica's in 1974–76 were judged to have had harmful effects, which damaged the long term growth prospects of their economies. The Jamaican policies in the 1977–84 period, and those of Guyana between 1980 and 1984 were also deemed to have failed, though they were thought to be in the right direction.

Worrell (1989) concluded, in a review of countries of the Caribbean Community (CARICOM), that state enterprises in the region had a record of unrelieved failure, except perhaps for hotel investments in Belize, due largely to managerial and other administrative inefficiencies:

> State acquisitions were too precipitate, with no time allowed for organic changes to new administrative structures. Information systems were

> inadequate and neglected, as governments failed to realize that knowledge was the principal factor determining the share of rewards between locals and foreigners. This failure is reflected in the frequent use of management, technology and marketing contracts by nationalised companies. Public administration in the Caribbean was not structured to deal effectively with enterprise. In particular, the lines between policy and its execution, and the responsibilities for each, were often blurred, opening the way for political interference in the firm's operations. State enterprises often failed to provide themselves with the capability for forward thinking and strategic planning.
>
> (Worrell, 1989, p. 71)

The study also concluded that government spending and taxation proved more effective in adjusting national aggregate expenditures than in increasing output.

Worrell and Bourne (1989) was a collection of studies, each reviewing research on an aspect of Caribbean policy over the 1969–1986 period, that were undertaken under the auspices of the Caribbean Regional Monetary Studies Programme (RPMS), a collaborative network between the regional central banks and The University of the West Indies. The English-speaking Caribbean was seen to have a rather dismal record in the 1970s and 1980s, compared with the creditable growth rates and low inflation recorded in the 1960s. The problems identified in the studies were that investments in mineral production and tourism were thought to have exhausted their potential, that there remained an unacceptably high level of hard core unemployment throughout the region, that the degree of export concentration was very high, and that the region was burdened with an aging manufacturing sector. Buoyant foreign earning in the early 1970s had aroused high hopes of accelerated growth with improved equity, but these hopes were all dashed. The findings included the following points: money supply was endogenous; the importance of import prices in domestic inflation was established; export-led growth was evident; imports increased with income but there were no relative price effects; and devaluation was inflationary. With respect to individual country studies the survey found the uncovered interest parity held for The Bahamas and for Belize; that procyclical fiscal policy kept the exchange rate peg secure in Barbados; that in Guyana delayed fiscal contraction in the late 1970s was unsuccessful in stabilising the external accounts and averting a severe depression; that in Jamaica repeated failure to reach fiscal targets was accompanied by contraction in real income and high inflation; and that in Trinidad and Tobago an oil price boom had generated high inflation because of limited absorptive capacity.

Worrell (1990) is a review and analysis of the performance in the 1980s of five Caribbean countries: Barbados, the Dominican Republic, Guyana, Jamaica and Trinidad and Tobago. Barbados maintained tight fiscal policy in the face of terms of trade and other shocks. Even though there were lapses, fiscal prudence meant that the country avoided the build-up of debt and the depreciation of the value of the local currency which made the countries of Latin America and the Caribbean notorious during the 1980s. Private investment in tourism propelled the modest growth rate which the country achieved. In the Dominican Republic fiscal tightening was insufficient to protect the exchange rate of the domestic currency. Depreciation fuelled a surge in inflation. However, major investment in tourism and the development of free trade zones led the revival in growth. A series of policy packages, featuring fiscal contraction and currency devaluation failed to restore external balance in Guyana, and the economy contracted during the 1980s. It was a similar story for Jamaica, where a succession of adjustment programmes, all with the support of the International Monetary Fund and other international financial institutions, failed to restore balance to external payments, while the economy stagnated. The decade was not a good one for the economy of Trinidad and Tobago either. A currency devaluation in December 1985 reduced aggregate demand, but not by enough to achieve external balance, and real output fell. The volume in which this article appeared (Williamson, 1990) popularised the term "Washington Consensus" to describe a package of economic adjustment which had emerged as conventional wisdom at the International Monetary Fund, the US Federal Reserve and other leading policy institutions and think tanks in North America and Europe. I ended my essay with two comments on elements of the Washington Consensus: first, a persistent balance of payments deficit in the open economy is best understood, from the policy maker's perspective, as an indication that public sector saving is too low, given the level of private spending. Secondly, the appropriate interest rate policy was to anchor the nominal rate on the most relevant rate in international financial markets. Both were at variance with consensus perceptions, though not necessarily inconsistent with them.

Worrell (1992) is a taxonomy of policy options and effects in SOEs, based on Caribbean experience, with economic forecasts for the same five countries as in the previous paragraph. The chapters of the monograph cover the economic characteristics shared by Caribbean economies, fiscal and monetary policies, exchange rate issues, investment policy, market structure and regulation, and the international economic environment as it impacts the region. Observations on Caribbean experiences include: "Getting the official exchange rate 'right' is a delicate confidence act, depending mainly on the use of fiscal policy to establish the credibility of the rate" (Worrell, 1992, p. 5); adjustment policies can be improved by fuller articulation of the elements that make up "fiscal policy"; artificially high values of local currency will not hold, but attempts to alter relative prices through exchange rate changes have no better chance of success; informal markets are grossly inefficient and all financial and economic markets need official guidance to function efficiently. In addition, adjustment programmes should be designed with a view to avoid deterioration of human resources:

> It is now accepted that programmes which fail to incorporate the effects on income distribution may stand little chance of stabilising the balance of payments even in the short run, because of the decline in productive effort. Moreover, such programmes have virtually no chance of reviving output because of the deterioration of human resources.
>
> (Worrell, 1992, p. 6)

Forecasts derived from econometric models were as follows. The projection for the Barbados economy showed no growth over the first half of the 1990s, with the possibility of a balance of payments crisis. Fiscal cutbacks were recommended, along with incentives to improve product quality to attract new investment. The Dominican Republic was projected to enjoy healthy economic growth, but with an unsustainable external balance. Fiscal contraction and exchange rate adjustment were indicated. A decline in Guyanese output was projected, but the external accounts were projected to be in balance, albeit with the persistence of a large informal market for foreign exchange. Structural reforms would be needed to revive the economy and stimulate growth. No increase in Jamaican output was projected, with a deficit in overall external payments. Further fiscal contraction with incentives for investment in exports were indicated. Output decline was projected for Trinidad and Tobago, with fiscal prospects that would depend on oil revenues. More investment in manufacturing was needed.

Worrell (1993) finds the performance of English-speaking Caribbean countries between 1960 and 1991 to have been disappointing. The reasons were assessed to have been a mixture of adverse external circumstances, policy errors and policy weaknesses and omissions. The external circumstances included unstable oil and commodity prices, adverse terms of trade movements, recessions in the main markets for Caribbean exports, and rising international interest rates. The policy errors included restrictive credit, price and exchange controls, nationalisation of commercial enterprises, excessive fiscal expansion and reckless liberalisation of financial, exchange and economic markets. The policy weaknesses mentioned were poor design of fiscal policy, with a lack of prioritization of objectives, and inefficient export promotion agencies and policies.

Fairbairn and Worrell (1996) is a comparative study of island economies in the Caribbean (Barbados, Dominica, St Lucia and St Vincent and the Grenadines) and the South Pacific (Fiji, Kiribati, Vanuatu and Western Samoa), covering the period from the early 1980s to the mid-1990s. Income per head in the Caribbean is much higher than for South Pacific countries, and from the mid-1980s the Caribbean growth rates were also higher; the situation was reversed in the 1990s. Social indicators in the Caribbean were also much better. A big advantage for the Caribbean over the South Pacific, all small islands that are export-driven, was proximity to the enormous US market, in contrast to the South Pacific countries, which are remote from all large markets. That makes it much easier for the Caribbean to take advantage of the tourism potential common to both regions. The key issues for governments in both regions were identified as maintaining "an environment of economic stability, with guaranteed rights of property and a climate of fair play" (Fairbairn and Worrell, 1996, p. 36); ensuring that policies were developed and designed in such a way as to ensure national ownership and widespread commitment to their success; improving the efficiency of public administration; establishing and maintaining active frameworks of collaboration between government and the private sector, and establishing "an effectively functioning coordinating mechanism, involving key macroeconomic, planning and sectoral ministries, as a basis for achieving sound and effective execution of government development goals" (Fairbairn and Worrell, 1996, p. 41). In order to accelerate growth and stimulate development it would be necessary to improve productivity in traditional exports, improve their quality and diversify export offerings where possible.

Worrell (2013) assesses the economic prospects for the English-speaking Caribbean based on an analysis of the region's competitiveness. While supporting export diversification in activities which show promise, the paper advises that diversification should not be at the expense of untapped potential of existing markets in North America and Europe for products and services in which the Caribbean has an established competitive advantage. In these established markets the Caribbean should target countries, states, provinces and municipalities that are the most prosperous and that would be attracted to the region's up-market and specialised tourism offerings and the high quality rums, coffee, and other unique foods, beverages and other products. Strategies should include building loyalty to Caribbean brands, and improvement in service quality very generally. The paper reiterated the importance of maintaining economic stability through the use of fiscal policy for aggregate demand management. It emphasised the need for an effective framework for the design and management of economic policy, incorporating macroeconomic forecasting, monitoring and feedback to ensure timely policy tweaks when necessary, in order to stay on course for the economic growth targets. The benefits of active management of the exchange rate were seen to be to minimise the inflation rate, protect the real value of household savings, lend credibility to government policy and reduce uncertainty, all of which contribute to a favourable climate for investment.

Worrell, Lowe and Naitram (2013) was an exploration of the limits to growth potential that might be imposed by scarcity of foreign exchange. The foreign exchange available to boost investment is measured as the surplus of foreign currency receipts over foreign payments of all kinds, minus any amount needed to top up reserves, if they are below a level with which the market is comfortable. Tests were run to estimate whether growth in Barbados, Jamaica and Trinidad and Tobago had been inhibited by the limited availability of foreign exchange; no evidence of the foreign exchange constraint was detected in any of the three countries during the period from 1980 to 2010.

Worrell (2020) is an evaluation of human development in Central American countries and the larger economies of the Caribbean. The majority of the countries in this region are classified as having High or Very High Human Development and in every case there has been steady improvement over the past 30 years. In terms of the growth performance, the gains in per capita income were greatest in countries whose main source of foreign earnings was manufactured goods, along with a significant tourism sector and at least one other export that contributes ten per cent or more to foreign earnings. External shocks had no lasting effects, except in the case of some tourism countries at the time of the Great Recession in 2008–09. Costa Rica was judged to be the region's most consistently competitive country. It was able to improve its overall market share in major exports and tourism through all phases of three international economic cycles since 1980, in spite of the fact that its relative prices rose compared to the regional average. This is seen as evidence that the country's exports and services have added value and improved product quality and variety over time, sufficient to increase clientele, who are satisfied with the value they get for the premium prices they pay. A footnote to the study was the observation that exchange rate changes had no discernible effects on relative prices.

Notes

1 The calculation is based on the coefficients of HDI scores with respect to each of the elements of the index, using 2019 data.
2 The term "socialisation" was used to describe official policy that combined the nationalisation of some financial and commercial enterprises with government-sponsored cooperatives in other areas.

References

Fairbairn, Te'o and DeLisle Worrell. 1996. *South Pacific and Caribbean Economies: A Comparative Study*. Brisbane: The Foundation for Development Cooperation.

Garten, Jeffrey. 2021. *Three Days at Camp David: How a Secret Meeting in 1971 Transformed the Global Economy*. New York: HarperCollins.

International Monetary Fund. 2022. "International financial Statistics." International Financial Statistics – At a Glance.

United Nations Development Programme. 2020. "Human Development Report." New York: United Nations.

Williamson, John (ed). 1990. *Latin American Adjustment: How Much has Happened?* Washington, DC: Institute for International Economics.

Worrell, DeLisle. 2020. "Economic progress in Central America and the Caribbean in the past 30 years," Working Paper. www.DeLisleWorrell.com.

Worrell, DeLisle, 2013. "The economic prospects for the English-speaking Caribbean," Working Paper Central Bank of Barbados, January.

Worrell, DeLisle, 1993. "The economies of the English-speaking Caribbean since 1960," in *Democracy in the Caribbean: Political, Economic and Social Perspectives*, edited by Jorge I. Domíguez, Robert A. Pastor and DeLisle Worrell. Baltimore and London: Johns Hopkins University Press.

Worrell, DeLisle. 1992. *Economic Policies in Small Open Economies: Prospects for the Caribbean*. London: Commonwealth Secretariat.
Worrell, DeLisle. 1990. "The Caribbean," in *Latin American Adjustment: How Much Has Happened?* edited by John Williamson. Washington, DC: The Institute for International Economics.
Worrell, DeLisle. 1989. "Comparative experience of Caribbean countries," in *Development in Suspense*, edited by George Beckford and Norman Girvan. Kingston, Jamaica: Friedrich Ebert Stiftung.
Worrell, DeLisle. 1987. *Small Island Economies: Structure and Performance in the English-speaking Caribbean Since 1970*. New York: Praeger.
Worrell, DeLisle. 1984. "Central America and the Caribbean," in *Adjustment Crisis in the Third World*, edited by R. Feinberg and V. Kallab. London: Transaction Books.
Worrell, DeLisle. 1980. "External influences and domestic policies: the economies of Barbados and Jamaica in the 1970s," *Social and Economic Studies*, December, Vol. 30, no. 4, pp.134–155.
Worrell, DeLisle and Compton Bourne (eds). 1989. *Economic Adjustment Policies for Small Nations: Theory and Experience in the English-speaking Caribbean*. New York: Praeger Publishers.
Worrell, DeLisle, Shane Lowe and Simon Naitram. 2013. "Growth forecasts for foreign exchange constrained economies," *Journal of Business, Finance and Economics in Emerging Economies*, Vol. 8, no. 1.

3 Selected Country Experiences

Barbados from the end of World War II

Barbados is the easternmost Caribbean island, with a population of slightly less than 300,000, and a GDP of about US$4.5 billion. The country has been transformed from an economy based on the export of sugar and a society with a small wealthy elite and a working population mired in poverty in 1946, to a modern middle class society based on tourism today, with a population that enjoys a standard of living comparable with that in advanced economies. In the late 1940s the island already boasted levels of literacy that were in the region of 80 per cent of the population, but by all other indicators, the country was among the worst performers in the Caribbean: life expectancy at birth was about 50 years, the incidence of maternal mortality, childhood malnutrition, low birth weight and other health indicators were among the poorest; overcrowding and poor housing were commonplace, the majority of the labour force had employment only during the five months of the sugar harvest, and there were few opportunities for the employment of women.

The main drivers of economic activity during these seven decades shifted over three periods whose boundaries are defined according to the main sources of foreign earnings, in an economy that has fuelled by exports of goods and services from its beginnings in the seventeenth century. Cane sugar was the only significant export until the mid-1960s, with sugar production reaching its all-time peak in the decade and a half from 1950. Sugar production declined sharply from the late 1960s, at a time when a significant export of clothing and other light manufacturing developed, together with the beginnings of popular tourism, thanks to the introduction of passenger jets, which made resort tourism affordable for middle income North Americans and Europeans. The emergence of manufacturing activity was important, because the workforce was mainly female, opening widespread employment opportunities for women for the first time. In addition to providing job opportunities for both sexes, tourism has trickle-down income effects that are pervasive, through entertainment, cultural, security and transportation, as well as bars, restaurants and other services (see Figure 3.1).

DOI: 10.4324/9781003247609-4

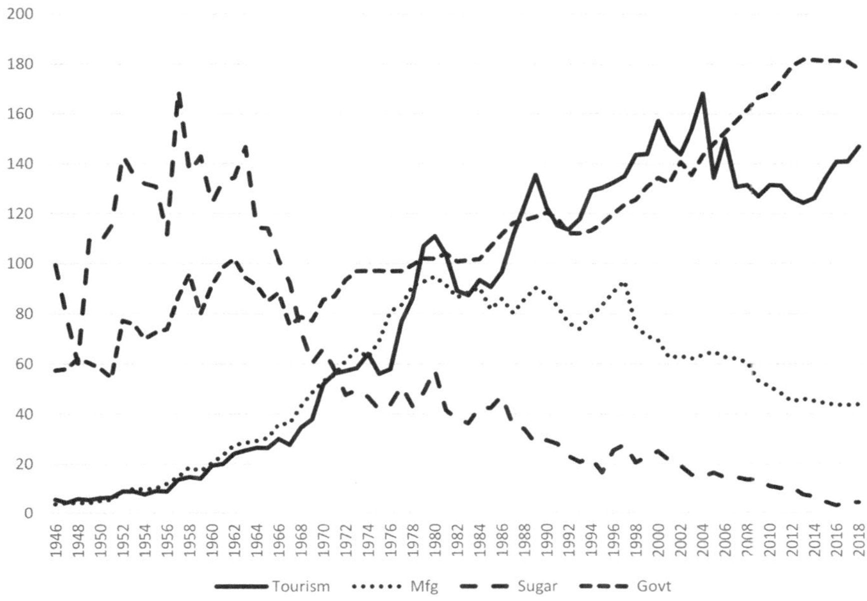

Figure 3.1 Barbados: Real GDP, BDS$m
Source: Author's calculations, Central Bank of Barbados data.

During the 1980s the Barbados economy was more diversified than it has been before or since, with sugar exports still of importance, now in third place behind tourism and manufacturing. Over the course of the decade Barbados lost most of its garment industry to Trinidad, where a currency devaluation had lowered labour costs, but the country had successfully switched to data processing for export, which sustained the industrial sector for much of the next decade. However, Barbados lost most of those data processing firms to cheaper competition from the Far East and elsewhere, and industry has been on a slow decline since the turn of the millennium. Meanwhile sugar production has dwindled to nothing, so that today more than two-thirds of the country's foreign earnings come from the dominant tourist industry.

We may therefore distinguish three periods in the social and economic development of Barbados in the post-War period: from 1946 to the early 1960s there was a period when economic activity was driven mainly by sugar exports. From the mid-1960s to the late 1990s, we see an economy with three significant sources of foreign earnings, mainly sugar exports at the beginning of the period, through to the 1970s when manufacturing and tourism overtook sugar and ending with tourism the main earner, with data processing still a major source of employment and foreign earnings. Since 2000 or thereabouts, data processing has all but disappeared, and exports of rum, household chemicals and other items are a minor source of foreign currency, leaving tourism as the mainstay of economic activity in what remains a foreign currency-driven economy. The story of how the economy evolved, and the main factors that affected the outcomes, is told in six studies, from which highlights are taken in what follows.

Saunders and Worrell (1981) was a study of the efficiency of public services, comparing expenditures on health, education and other services, as well as Government's capital expenditures against the delivery of services and the building of infrastructure. Data on educational achievement at primary, secondary and tertiary levels, and on hospitalisations, mortality and morbidity, housing conditions and other social conditions were evaluated against corresponding Government spending, and major capital works and expenditures were identified and discussed. It is the only study of this kind that has been undertaken in Barbados. It could not be replicated today, because the performance data for education, health and the delivery of other services is no longer produced, an example of the extent to which productivity in the public services has declined in Barbados. The paper finds that:

> The extensive development of Barbados' social and economic infrastructure in the post-war period has resulted from increases in the scope of Government activity, rather from any major shift in emphasis. Education and health still dominate Government spending, as they did in 1946, and social services, broadly defined, are as important now as they were then. Educational and health services have been enlarged and their quality improved; serious attention was given to improving the housing stock, and facilities and benefits for senior citizens have been upgraded. A great deal of attention has been paid to economic infrastructure. The harbour and airport have been modernised, water services have been extended and high service standards maintained; road maintenance has been adequate. Government enterprises have not been profitable on the whole, but budget allocations for their support have accounted for only a modest part of Government's spending.
>
> The costs of sustaining the machinery of Government, and of maintaining law and order, have been contained. Administrative costs have declined in relation to the size of the Government budget, and the national debt has been so managed that service costs have remained comparatively low. The relative costs of maintaining law and order have declined and although it does not seem that crime has increased, facilities seem to have deteriorated as a result.
>
> (Saunders and Worrell, 1981, p. 71)

Such was the degree of fiscal prudence and Government productivity in 1981.

Worrell (1982) is a volume of essays on the Barbados economy between 1946 and 1980 which remains the most comprehensive source of economic data for Barbados for that period. Among the book's conclusions were that increasing costs of investment goods appear to have inhibited investment: investment was relatively high, but it produced disappointing growth. The analysis of savings and investment revealed patterns consistent with the thesis that foreign exchange, rather than domestic saving, was the limit on investment. The single episode of money creation, recorded in 1976, had no adverse impact on the balance of payments; periods of high balance of payments volatility between 1955 and 1960 and between 1966 and 1977 were mainly due to terms of trade fluctuations. With respect to public finance, Government focussed on infrastructure building, including a deep water harbour, roads, a new airport terminal, a new general hospital, schools, establishment of a campus of the regional university, and water and gas distribution. Government's current account savings financed one-third of capital expenditure. The study documented improvements in job quality, increases in wages, and the provision of jobs for women. Significant increases in labour productivity were recorded. Foreign prices accounted for 70 per cent of inflation during the period.

Worrell (1996) was an assessment of the economy on the 30th anniversary of independence, by which time many weaknesses in Government policy and in the leadership of both the public and private sectors had begun to emerge. The study listed the factors that drove progress including the attention and resources devoted to education by Government and by households; the contributions of foreign direct investment, the opening up of resort tourism as a result of the introduction of commercial jet transport, and the introduction of household mortgage loans, which enabled a transformation of housing standards. In addition, Barbados benefitted from spill-overs from the oil boom in Trinidad in the 1970s; that country became an important source of tourists, especially in the summer, when hotel occupancy is low, as well as a source of foreign investment, in industry, finance and commercial activity. The country also benefitted from migration, with immigrants providing new skills in finance and other areas, and emigration providing an outlet that helped to alleviate previously high unemployment levels. On the distaff side, Government tax and other incentives for investment were found to be inadequate and arbitrary. In addition, there was an unresolved tension between the public's perception of the tax burden, compared to the adequacy of the provision of public services. A general sentiment persisted that the population was not getting value for the tax dollar. Wage increases unrelated to productivity were undermining the viability of many businesses, and contributing to a deterioration in fiscal management, from exemplary standards of prudence in the 1960s and 1970s. Futile attempts to increase self-sufficiency in agriculture and other consumer goods had the potential to impoverish the country, as did Government promotion of housing and other nontradable activities, if they crowded out essential public services such as health, education and law and order, or were financed by money creation, because they would impair the nation's attractiveness to foreign investors and create excess pressure on the foreign exchange market.

By this time sugar exports had declined to trivial proportions, a tragedy attributed to the failure to adopt new technologies and to diversify outputs and markets. As a result, the profitability of agriculture had declined so badly that farms could not compete with real estate development for the use of land. Government tried in vain to stop the alienation of agricultural land by legislation, but the laws were invalidated by economic necessity, as farms were sold as a last resort in the face of imminent bankruptcy. With the precipitate decline in sugar agriculture came the irretrievable loss of centuries of accumulated expertise, and the end of any real hope of revival. The study expanded on the story of the manufacturing sector, which had its early roots in food processing, then progressing to garments, mainly for export to Trinidad and Tobago. However; labour productivity failed to keep up with labour costs and the direction of trade in garments was reversed. The study chronicles the relaxation of earlier fiscal discipline, beginning in 1985, leading to high foreign borrowing which triggered a balance of payments crisis in 1991. The persistence of a high public sector borrowing requirement frustrated interest rate policy, as Government reacted against rising domestic interest premiums driven by their own demands on financial resources. Government made productive investments in infrastructure, but state-owned commercial ventures all fell into insolvency.

Twenty years later I began my review of 50 years of Barbados' independence (Worrell, 2016) with the remark that that event was a way station on a journey that began earlier, rather than a radical new departure. By 2016 the Human Development Index was available to provide a measure of the quality of life in Barbados, along with other indicators (data on housing and indices of competitiveness) which were used to evaluate the performance of the economy and the quality of life. Barbados had achieved a quality of life comparable with advanced economies, but the most transformative changes in health and per capita income were recorded before 1966, the year of independence. More modest gains had been made over the years since independence, in large part through strengthening the island's competitive advantage in quality tourism, and in the export of fine rums. Against these were examples of failure, in manufacturing (except for a handful of high quality products), and the collapse of sugar agriculture. The efficiency of public services had declined, and there was a failing consensus on the tax burden and social provisions. Changes in the social structure meant that the current balance between taxation and the provision of free public services was outdated and wasteful. Public services were overstaffed, poorly skilled and had low productivity. In general, the economy was plagued by inefficient use of technology, and labour costs were outrunning worker productivity. The Government needed to address the urgent necessity for public sector reform, to build a capacity to devise and implement appropriate strategies for incentivizing investment, and promoting alternative energy and the potential of cultural industries.

The self-published Worrell (2017) documented the failings of Government policy in the wake of the 2013 General Election, which left Barbados with a weak Government, an ineffective and temporising Prime Minister and a tenuous majority of a single seat in the Parliament. Faced with an unsustainable fiscal deficit and a precipitate decline in foreign reserves Government failed to implement the organisational changes in the public sector that would have led to increased productivity, a reduction in the wages bill and significant reductions in transfers to state-owned enterprises. Instead, expenditures on wages, purchases and transfers were frozen, resulting in low morale in the public service, neglected maintenance and the accumulation of arrears by Government and state-owned enterprises.

The burden of adjustment to reduce the fiscal deficit and slow the accumulation of debt was placed mainly on additional taxation. The ratio of Government revenue to GDP rose to a historic high of 29 per cent in 2016. Even so, expenditures on Government current operations remained in excess of receipts, by almost five per cent of GDP.

Failure to address low productivity in the public service halted private investment and eroded Barbados' international competitiveness. Several projects in tourism, construction and the energy sectors were delayed, in some cases by years, and other projects were abandoned. In every one of these cases investors had identified profitable ventures which they were able to finance and execute without official support, but they were unable to secure timely permissions of one kind or another from official institutions. Levels of public sector productivity that were low by international standards had eroded Barbados' international competitiveness ranking, as reported in the World Economic Forum's "Global Competitiveness Report 2017" (World Economic Forum, 2017). Barbados had slipped badly in the rankings because of the large budget deficit and the rising debt levels, the increasing burden of Government regulation, the growing inefficiency of the legal system, wasteful spending by Government and concern about possible bias in decisions of Government and officials.

The Government's failure to implement its own strategy meant that deficits continued to be unsustainably large and the ratio of debt-to-GDP continued to rise. The 2013 adjustment was sufficient to arrest the precipitate fall in foreign reserves witnessed in that year, but the Central Bank continued to lose foreign reserves in subsequent years, when the Bank should have been accumulating reserves to repair the losses of 2013. To make matters worse, the combination of poor indicators – high debt, large deficit, falling foreign reserves, slow economic growth and delayed investment – eroded investor confidence, which was reflected in the loss of investment grade for Barbados' debt, followed by a series of further downgrades and a persistent negative outlook for the future of the economy. With the loss of the investment grade Barbados effectively lost access to international financial markets. Barbados bond issues are small by international standards and were of interest generally only to investors who buy investment grade securities with a good interest rate when they are first issued, and hold them to maturity.

The downgrade of Barbados Government securities aggravated Government's financing problems. Commercial banks and private domestic investors were increasingly reluctant to lend to Government, even though up to that time there had never been a late payment on any Government obligation, much less any impairment of the principal amount invested. Investors' reluctance shifted the burden of financing Government onto the Central Bank of Barbados. The Bank recycled some surplus funds that commercial banks deposited with Central Bank, but these were insufficient and Central Bank created new money to the extent of 3.5 per cent of GDP for Government finance in 2015 and again in 2016. This monetary injection, in Barbados dollars, ultimately led to a demand for more imports, which had to be paid for in foreign currency. Central Bank funding of Government's deficit was the main factor behind the decline in foreign reserves in 2014, 2015 and 2016.

Declining productivity in the public sector was a drag on the recovery of the economy. The economic revival was led by tourism, a sector in which Barbados is internationally very competitive. Arrival numbers recovered in 2010 and 2011, along with the rest of the Caribbean, but faltered in the next three years, while Caribbean growth gathered pace. The year 2015 proved to be pivotal for Barbados' tourism, with a 14 per cent increase in arrivals, an all-time high for a single year, after which Barbados' tourism continued to outpace the rest of the Caribbean, but at about half the record 2015 rate, up until 2019. The revival is attributable to private investment in hotels, upgrades, refurbishment and the development of support and ancillary services.

Apart from an extension of berthing facilities for cruise ships at the Bridgetown port, none of the new hotels or other tourism related projects announced by Government was brought to fruition. On the contrary, several tourism projects, including two large hotels, were delayed in Government administrative or legal processes of one kind or another. Moreover, the slide in public sector productivity over the past decade had lowered the average for the economy as a whole.

Worrell (2021a) brought the story of Barbados' economic performance since 1946 up to date to 2018. The study included a new analysis of investment, growth and productivity, observing that investment was much more productive in the three decades from 1950, than it became thereafter.

> A factor which would have contributed to the low productivity of investment in the 2000s was the fact that much of the surge in investment at that time was on account of a boom in foreign purchases of second homes in Barbados, in contrast to investment in manufacturing and tourism in earlier periods.
>
> (Worrell, 2021a, p. 308)

The economy was judged to have been in the doldrums since 2008, with an increasing burden of largely inappropriate taxation, Government regulations that blocked potential investment, Government tax and other incentives that distorted tourism services away from the top quality segment where Barbados has its competitive advantage, insufficient and inefficient public investment, poor public administration and a failure to adopt new organisational practices and systems for good governance in the twenty-first century.

The economies of the Eastern Caribbean Currency Union since 1980

The Eastern Caribbean Currency Union comprises the countries of Antigua and Barbuda, Dominica, St Kitts-Nevis, St Lucia and St Vincent and the Grenadines, together with the British dependencies of Anguilla and Montserrat. They have a combined population of 651,000 and a GDP of US$6 billion. The countries of the ECCU are all ranked in the second of four groups in the HDI, that is, countries with High Human Development. This category includes Belize, the Dominican Republic, Jamaica and Trinidad and Tobago in the Caribbean, Brazil, China and Mexico, and other small countries such as Seychelles, Fiji and Maldives. The Bahamas and Barbados are the only Caribbean countries (apart from the UK dependencies) that enjoy a Very High level of human development, comparable to that enjoyed in North America and Europe.

The countries of the ECCU maintained an HDI advantage over the Caribbean average over the past two decades. In 2000 the ECCU already stood well above the Caribbean average, with a gap of ten per cent between the lowest score for an ECCU member country (St Vincent and the Grenadines) and the average. However, other Caribbean countries improved more than the ECCU did, narrowing the advantage enjoyed by the lowest-scoring ECCU country (now Dominica) to six per cent in 2018.

The economies of the ECCU have handsomely out-performed other Caribbean countries and SIDS since 1980 (Figure 3.2), with GDP increases to 2018 between 25 and 35 per cent, compared to gains of less than 20 per cent for the Caribbean and for SIDS. St Kitts-Nevis and St Vincent and the Grenadines were consistently among the best performers. GDP per capita rose strongly in Dominica and Antigua and Barbuda in the 1980s, but the growth rate slowed in Dominica after 2000, and in Antigua and Barbuda GDP per head has not increased since 2010. After faltering in 1981 and 1982 GDP per capita in St Lucia recovered to keep pace with the leaders for the rest of the 1980s. However, growth slowed thereafter, for the rest of the period. GDP per capita grew steadily in Grenada throughout the entire period, with only occasional lapses (early 1980s, 1992–93, 2004–05 and 2009–10).

Tourism is now the main source of foreign exchange in every ECCU country except Dominica, where it is a close second to industry (construction and public utilities). Tourism's share of GDP has continued to rise in St Kitts-Nevis, St Lucia and Dominica. It was also a rising percentage in Grenada

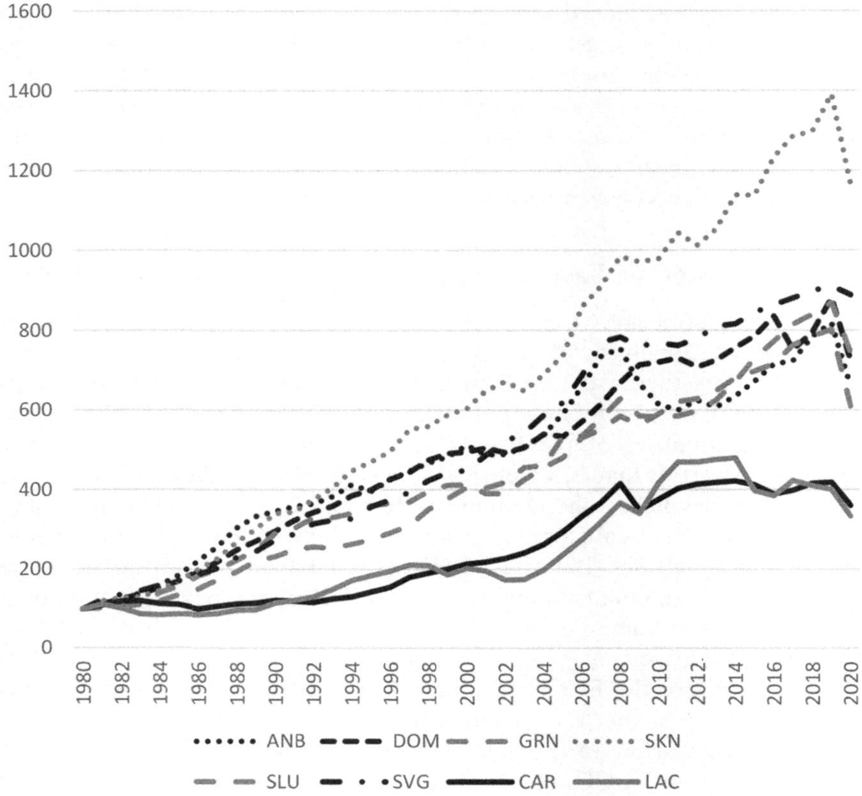

Figure 3.2 ECCU and comparators, GDP per capita, indices
Source: World Bank, 2022.

and St Vincent and the Grenadines until the early 2000s, but its share in those two countries has not increased since. Construction and public utility services have supplemented tourism as a major source of foreign exchange and a major impetus for the growth of ECCU economies. In three countries – St Kitts-Nevis, Antigua and Barbuda and Dominica – successful programmes to attract investment as a way to accelerate eligibility for citizenship were an important motivation for foreign currency inflows that are reflected in a boost to the construction sector and increased demand for public utility services. Agriculture, which was the largest sector in Dominica in the 1970s, and was also of significance in Grenada, St Vincent and the Grenadines and St Lucia at that time, has now declined to relative insignificance everywhere except in Dominica, where it ranks third in importance as a source of foreign exchange, with foreign earnings that are about one-third the amount of the investment inflows.

The fallacy of the assumption that large current account deficits in the balance of external payments are unsustainable in all circumstances is demonstrated by the ECCU experience. Current account deficits as large as 30 per cent of the region's GDP were recorded, with no depletion of the foreign reserves of the Eastern Caribbean Central Bank (ECCB). The deficit for the region remained in excess of 20 per cent of GDP in successive years from 2006 to 2009, and it remained over ten per cent from 1997 to 2013, financed by foreign direct investment for the most part, supplemented by much smaller amounts of external borrowing. This fact accounts for the observation that there was no depletion of foreign reserves, and that large current account deficits were sustained, with no risk of a devaluation of the currency, over this period (Figure 3.3).

The movement in the ECCB's foreign reserves bears testimony to the region's resilience to external shocks. In the 25 years prior to 2019 there were only three years when the ECCB has recorded a significant decline in the foreign reserves: 1996, 2005 and 2008. In 1996 the decline is attributed to the effects of Hurricane Luis; 2005 saw the passage of two destructive hurricanes, Ivan and Emily, and the decline in 2008 reflects the impact of the global recession. In every case the recovery in reserve levels was remarkably swift, with foreign reserves higher than before the shock within a year. The exception to this pattern has been the unprecedented series of shocks since 2018, with the ongoing economic crisis caused by the COVID-19 pandemic following on the heels of two devastating hurricanes, Maria and Irma.

The swift recovery of reserves after the hurricane shocks is, in large part, due to the financial and material inflows that usually follow on the incidence of natural disasters, by way of relief funds, supplies and transfers, settlement of insurance claims, and reconstruction and rehabilitation activity. The fact

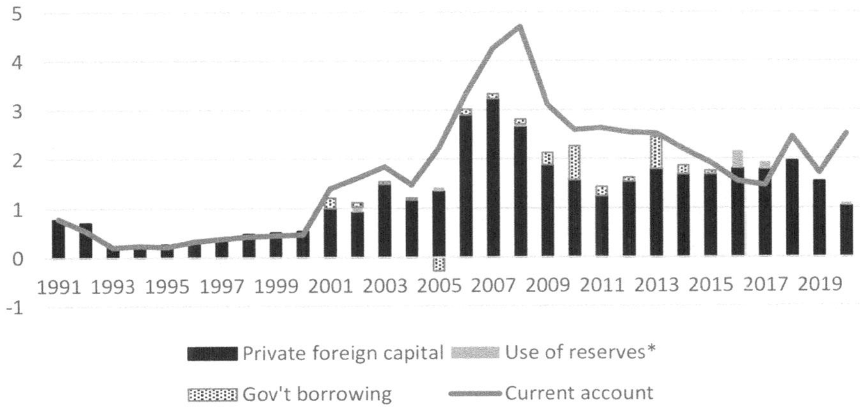

Figure 3.3 ECCU: Financing of the current account, % of GDP
*Amounts (max EC$0.35b) too small to appear on the chart
Source: Eastern Caribbean Central Bank, 2022.

that the ECCU operates a foreign reserves pool provides an additional shock absorber, with respect to the impact of external shocks on the balance of payments. Reserve pooling appears to have helped to alleviate the impact of the Global Recession, which depressed current account inflows in St Kitts-Nevis and St Lucia more noticeably than for other ECCU member countries. Foreign receipts in St Lucia did not recover until 2015, but early gains by St Kitts-Nevis would have aided the overall recovery in reserves. The impact of the shock would also have been minimised because these two countries were the only ECCU members where current account inflows fell at the time of the global recession.

Economic transformation in the Dominican Republic came with political stability and the development of tourism

The Dominican Republic, with a population of 11 million and a GDP of US $79 billion, shares the island of Hispaniola in the Greater Antilles with Haiti. Worrell (1991) chronicles the economy's development from 1966, following a period of political instability, with civil war and depression in 1968 briefly interrupting the rehabilitation of the country's economy. The years from 1970 to 1973 saw strong expansion, based on traditional exports (sugar, supplemented by coffee, cacao, bauxite) and a build-up of foreign reserves, thanks to overall surpluses on the external accounts and small fiscal deficits, which did not occasion excessive money creation at any time during these years. The period from 1974 to 1981 saw a slowdown in growth, even though production of sugar and ferronickel rose; the proximate causes were adverse terms of trade changes. External balance was maintained, and foreign reserves remained adequate. The years 1982 to 1985 saw major disequilibrium in the wake of the second oil crisis, with terms of trade losses, declines in sugar exports and capital flight. Even though fiscal policy remained tight, there was a downward spiral of exchange rate depreciation and high inflation.

Rapid transformation of the economy began around 1985, based on investment in tourism and the establishment of free trade zones which attracted a considerable export manufacturing industry. Porzo and Giraldi (2020) takes up the story from 1990. A decade of macroeconomic stability in the 1990s ended with a major failure of three domestic banks, leading to capital flight and devaluation in 2003. External balance was restored with the help of an IMF standby agreement in 2005, and growth resumed steadily thereafter. The story of the transformation of the foreign earning sectors of the Dominican economy since 1990 is told in Chapter 4.

Trinidad and Tobago – economic management in the petroleum-dependent economy

Worrell (2018) assessed the economic prospects for Trinidad and Tobago, the insular Caribbean's only major oil-exporter, at the end of the second decade of the new millennium. The common challenge of oil-dependent economies since the early 1970s has been the management of this very remunerative commodity in a world in which its prices are extremely volatile. Petroleum exporters must develop strategies which allow them to deploy bonanzas to finance investment for long-term returns when prices rise, and to moderate fiscal expenditure during the price boom so that unsustainable deficits do not emerge during the bust. Governments in Trinidad and Tobago have had modest success in this regard since 1970, mainly in the early years.

Oil production in Trinidad has been in decline since peaking in 1978, and the throughput of the island's oil refineries, which at the time exceeded the export of crude oil in volume and value, had been falling since 1970. (Tobago, a tourism-driven economy, produces no oil.) In 1973, when the Organization of Oil-Producing Countries (OPEC) first imposed oil boycotts, causing a spike in world oil prices, the Government of Trinidad and Tobago invested part of the windfall in large scale industry. The industrial hub established at the time at Point Lisas was the kernel of an industrial complex that grew to a level that transformed Trinidad and Tobago into a regional economic powerhouse with a manufacturing sector that contributed 11 per cent to GDP by 1990. Although manufacturing continued to grow, its contribution fell to six per cent by 2000, as surging oil prices caused ballooning of the petroleum sector from the late 1990s through to a peak in 2008. Some part of this windfall was set aside in a Heritage Fund, which grew to the equivalent of 23 per cent of GDP in 2014, just before oil prices tumbled from around US$100 per barrel. The period of the oil bonanza in the 2000s witnessed a considerable increase in Government expenditure, equally distributed between investment and consumption. Government consumption left an unsustainable fiscal deficit once oil prices fell, a deficit which remained problematic despite drawdowns from the Heritage Fund and cuts in infrastructure spending. Government did respond to the early signs when deficits first appeared in 2008, cutting expenditures in 2009 and 2010. However, the cuts were not sustained, the public sector borrowing requirement remained too high, the foreign exchange market tightened and foreign reserves fell by one-third between 2015 and 2018.

Henry (2021) is a mine of information on Trinidad's industrial development over this period. The 1970 petroleum-related industrial initiative saw the establishment of an ammonia plant in 1975, a fertiliser plant in 1976 and steel fabrication in 1977, all initially by state enterprise. The 1980s saw the peak of state ownership, as fiscal deficits grew ever larger, with the decline in world oil prices. The year 1986 saw an economic adjustment programme that was accompanied by a devaluation of the local currency, an act which simultaneously boosted the local currency tax revenues – mostly from oil and related fees and taxes – and cut real aggregate spending in the economy through inflation of local currency prices. In 1993 all controls on foreign currency transactions were removed, a move which was not consequential, a reflection of the pervasiveness of informal exchange transactions.

The late 1990s spike in oil prices turned the economy around, and new projects between 1997 and 2000 included major investment in the production and export of liquefied natural gas (LNG). The 2000s saw expansion in exports of oils, gas and methanol, and a period of great economic prosperity. The 2008 collapse of oil prices and the global recession brought an end to 15 years of economic expansion. Energy-related production accounts for 40 per cent of Trinidad and Tobago's GDP, including the production of natural gas, ammonia, urea (a fertiliser) and methanol. In addition, exploration services, mostly for natural gas, added to energy-related GDP. The closure of the last remaining refinery in 2018 saw the end of exports of refined oil, the largest export item in 1970. Foreign reserves, not including the Heritage Fund, peaked in 2014 at US$11.5 billion. The economy became increasingly dollarized: foreign currency deposits of US$1 billion in 2001 were already 50 per cent of all deposits; since then foreign currency deposits have grown more than four times, while local currency deposits have remained static. The Trinidad and Tobago economy has been in decline since 2014 because of low energy prices and lack of investment in industrial capacity.

Belize

Belize shares the Caribbean's dependence on tourism, but exports of sugar, fruits, clothing and other manufactured goods are also of importance. Belize is a Central American country with a population of 0.4 million and a GDP of US$1.9 billion. At the time of independence in 1981 tourism was already the main source of foreign exchange and the main driver of the economy, reflected in the service sector's 42 per cent contribution to GDP (Bulmer-Thomas, 2021). By 2018, the services sector (which also includes wholesale, retail, government and other services, all nontradable activities, which depend largely on tourism and other foreign currency inflows) had grown to 74 per cent of GDP. Agriculture and other primary activities fell from 27 per cent to 12 per cent, while secondary activity (manufacturing) fell from 31 to 14 per cent. Belize recorded respectable growth of 4.3 per cent per annum in the four decades since independence; with an increasing population, the per capita annual growth averaged 1.5 per cent per year. The three decades from 1981 to 2010 witnessed steady expansion in real GDP, but since then the economy has stagnated. Overall, growth has been consistently above the average for the Caribbean (Worrell, 2021b).

Thanks to its land borders with Mexico, Guatemala and Honduras, Belize attracts significant migration from these and other nearby Central American countries, attracted by Belize's more stable society and politics, and somewhat more prosperous economy and better living standards. Belize is ranked higher in the Human Development Index than El Salvador, Guatemala, Honduras and Nicaragua, and the Mexican provinces that share a border with Belize are among that country's poorest. The levels of indigence in Belize are relatively low, at about ten per cent of the population. The foreign-born

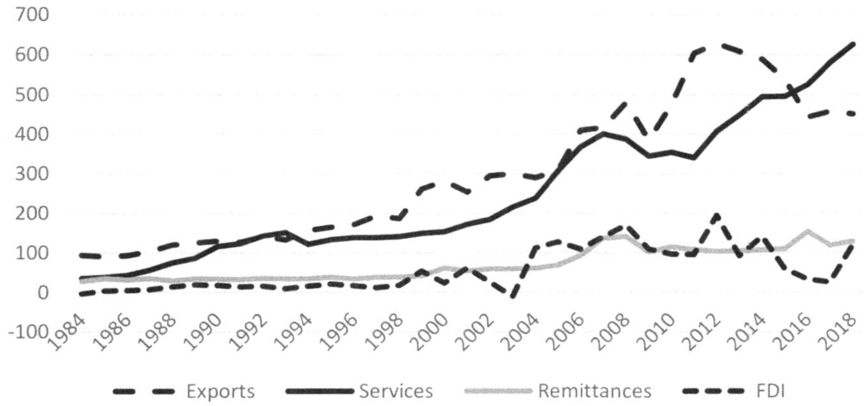

Figure 3.4 Belize: Sources of Foreign Exchange, US$m
Source: ECLAC, 2020.

population is 15 per cent of the total, of which 80 per cent are from the Central American region. They are employed mainly in agriculture. As elsewhere in the Caribbean, manufacturing and tourism have opened opportunities for female employment, with female participation rates rising from 25 per cent at independence to 53 per cent, a figure that remains low by the standards of the rest of the Caribbean. Immigration and the rise in female participation have meant that overall rates of unemployment have remained in the region of ten per cent for the past three decades. An additional factor was a slowdown in emigration from Belize, mainly to North America. About 40,000 Belizeans migrated to the US and elsewhere during the 1980s; that figure fell to about 25,000 in the 1990s, with the tightening of US immigration regulations and controls, and it has fallen further to about 20,000 since the turn of the century. The unchanged exchange rate peg to the US dollar has so far been a secure anchor for macroeconomic policy, and successive administrations have managed fiscal policies to mitigate expansion in total expenditure in the economy rising to levels that might have depleted foreign reserves and forced a depreciation of the local currency. A small overall balance of payments deficit in 2004 was reversed the next year, and a surplus was maintained on the fiscal current account, a prudent measure that reflected the use of borrowed funds for fixed capital formation. A large overall fiscal deficit in the 2015/16 Fiscal Year was gradually reduced each year until 2019.

Cuba

Cuba, the largest island nation in the Caribbean, has a population of 11 million and a GDP of US$100 million. Its experience reflects an unfortunate combination of geo-political victimisation and bad economic management. Once virtually a colony of the USA, the revolution of 1958 brought economic and social changes that have been of lasting benefit to the population. Health and educational achievements have been outstanding: life expectancy of 79 years, mean years of schooling of 12 years and expected years of schooling of 14 years have lifted Cuba into the second tier of countries in the Human Development Index (High Human Development) in spite of the country's comparatively low GDP per capita. Adult literacy is virtually universal, and the national income is spread much more equitably across the population than is typical for the Caribbean.

Unfortunately, that equitable distribution is at a level of income that reflects a shared misery and pessimism about their future prospects which pervades the population. The Cuban Revolution owes its durability to the early patronage of the Soviet Union, which provided an assured market for sugar exports in exchange for supplies of fuel and supported the Cuban economy with transfers and equipment to enable the country to play a leading role in the liberation struggles in Africa. Soviet support acted as a counterweight to the effects of the US blockade of Cuba, but Cuba adopted a Soviet Socialist system of economic management which gave advantage to collective consumption and the provision of public goods, and severely limited the availability and quality of private consumables. In the 1980s, now considered the Golden Years of that era, standards of housing, and the variety and quality of automobiles, household appliances, cultural and entertainment services, and other consumables was well below what was on offer elsewhere in the Caribbean.

The collapse of the Soviet Union in 1989 dealt the Cuban economy and society a shock from which it has not yet recovered. The economy contracted by 35 per cent in the following three years, depressing living standards, and the loss of the country's main trading partner had lasting effects on production and exports. A depressed economy inevitably bred disaffection which might have provoked the Cuban authorities to respond by imitating the strategy which the Chinese had embarked on ten years earlier, one of cautious relaxation of the iron grip of the state bureaucracy on all commercial activity. A relaxation of the US economic boycott at this point would have been an enlightened policy under the circumstances, opening opportunities and providing incentives and inducements for a liberalisation of the Cuban economy, driven by the need for the Government to satisfy the material aspirations of Cubans themselves. Sadly, the US Government has persisted with coercive policies, which ironically have fuelled nationalist sentiment and strengthened the hand of hard-liners in the Cuban administration.

The recent economic history of Cuba is eloquently told by Feinberg (2021). Although some health and educational gains have been eroded since 1990, the delivery of these services remains "impressive", and Cuba ranks fourth in Latin America in the HDI rankings, after Chile, Uruguay and Costa Rica, but ahead of the Dominican Republic, Jamaica, El Salvador, Guatemala and Nicaragua. Female participation in the labour force has increased markedly, and the economic situation of the black population has improved, relative to the white population. This is partly a result of the emigration of the white population, and partly due to black migration from the poorer eastern provinces of Cuba. Levels of personal safety are very high, and it is safe to walk anywhere, even at night. However, industrial production in many sectors remains below 1989 levels and the sugar harvest is "a shadow of its once proud self". The Government is described as "grossly inefficient" and public servants are poorly paid, with an average monthly wage of US$50 per month.[1] The business climate is unattractive and the balance of external payments is chronically in deficit.

A guarded liberalisation process was announced in guidelines (*Lineamientos*) issued in 2011, after a lengthy process which produced a document laced with contradictions, but which nevertheless led to a flowering of restaurants, bread and breakfast accommodation, taxi services and other small enterprises that by 2017 provided an estimated 40 per cent of all employment. The door for private foreign direct investment had been opened selectively in 2009, and in 2014 the Government under Raul Castro, Fidel's brother and successor, offered expanded tax and other incentives. However, state participation in joint ventures was stipulated for most investment, the process of approval remains long and complicated, there is a lack of due process and the outcome of applications is uncertain. Other disincentives are the poor domestic infrastructure and the fact that, though profit repatriation and other payments are assured, their timing may be delayed because of foreign currency shortages. The disincentives have worked against Cuba's competitive advantages: an educated workforce, unions that follow state guidance, stable political institutions and an outstanding degree of personal security. As a result, the FDI inflow has been disappointing.

Raul Castro's lasting legacy has been to broaden Cuba's commercial networks, with trade of US$1 billion or more with Venezuela (the largest by some distance, thanks to oil imports), China, Spain and Canada, and significant trade with Mexico, Brazil, Russia, Italy, Germany and France. Migrants' remittances are now the largest source of foreign exchange by far. They include transfers from the export of skilled labour of medical workers and other professionals. Tourism is the other major source of foreign currency. Arrivals rose from 2.1 million in 2007 to a peak of 4.7 million in 2017 and 2018. Cuba now has a stock of 60,000 hotel rooms of which 57,000 are in the desirable four and five star categories. Fifty per cent of all accommodation is bed and breakfast establishments, an important segment of the private enterprise sector which at its peak in 2017 provided 40 per cent of all employment.

In 2017 the ongoing tension between reformists and promoters of state control tilted towards the latter, and the reform process was frozen. The Diaz-Canel-led administration which succeeded Raul Castro in 2018 is disinclined to take new initiatives, and the tourism sector has been hobbled by a renewal of the US boycott. Once more, a bloated, burdensome and inefficient bureaucracy is able to put the blame on the US boycott rather than address its own poor performance and lack of vision. Among the opportunities which have gone abegging are the potential of renewable energy, which currently provides only four per cent of generating capacity, and activity in the Mariel port, which remains very underutilised. A modern makeover of the organisation and delivery of public services, and a carefully regulated liberalisation of commerce, including relaxation of joint venture stipulations, would go a long way to reviving economic activity and improving the quality of the lives of Cubans.

Iceland

The trend in Iceland's real GDP is shown in Figure 3.5. The resilience of the economy brought the country unscathed through the banking crisis brought on by the global financial crisis of 2008. Real output rose continuously from 1960, with only three interruptions, in 1966–68, 1991–93 and 2008–2010. In 2019, just before the onset of the COVID-19 pandemic, the economy was nine times larger than it was in 1960. The first downturn saw real output fall by seven per cent from 1966 to 1968; in took two years after that to return to the 1968 level. The next downturn was less severe, with output in 1993 falling three per cent below 1991. It took just one year for the economy to recover the lost ground. The big challenge came with the banking crisis in 2008. Iceland was the country worst affected by the global financial crisis which followed the dramatic collapse of Lehman Brothers in September 2008, measured by the impact relative to the size of its economy. It took all of five years to recover the level of output the economy recorded in 2008.

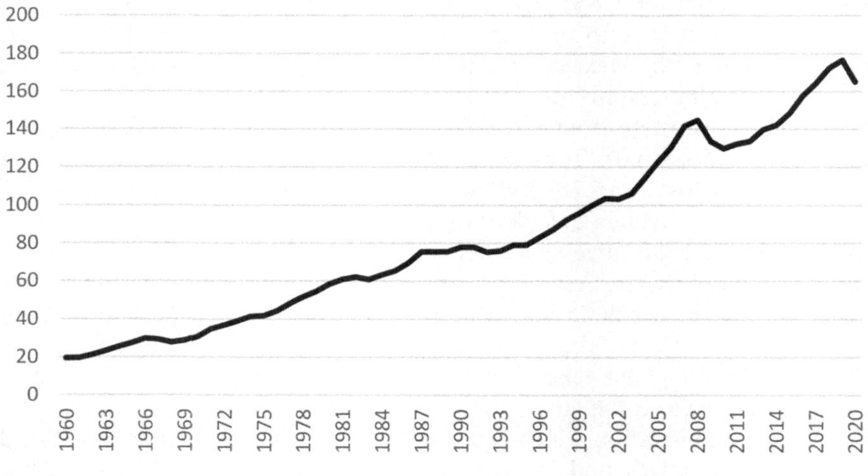

Figure 3.5 Iceland: Real GDP, index on 2000 base year
Source: IMF, 2007.

GDP doubled in the 15 years after 1960 and doubled again between 1975 and 1995. By 2008, just before the impact of the financial crisis, real GDP had grown by another 80 per cent. The collapse of Icelandic banks and the associated crisis caused an 11 per cent economic contraction by the time GDP bottomed out in 2010, but a swift climb back resulted in real income in 2019 which had more than doubled since 1995, the third time since 1960 that this had been achieved.

The main drivers of Iceland's growth were exports and tourism. In 1976 foreign earnings from exports were twice the receipts from tourism and other traded services, with exports of fish accounting for three quarters of exports. Exports of fish increased rapidly between 1970 and 1990, with a brief interruption from 1983 to 1985, after which the value of fish and fishmeal products increased very little. Other exports, mainly aluminium products (thanks to Iceland's abundant thermal energy supply),[2] sustained the growth of exports. Exports in 2018 were three times what they were in 2000.

Meanwhile tourism had grown from being the junior partner, with half the earnings of exports in the mid-1970s, to overtake the total of all exports in 2016. Receipts from tourism and other services grew by two and a half times over the decade to 1986, and doubled to 2000. A period of more rapid growth followed, with peak receipts in 2018 six and a half times what they were at the turn of the century. Most recent data show tourism as the main foreign currency earner, with 42 per cent of the total, followed by aluminium products and fish products, both with about 17 per cent (US International Trade Administration, 2019).

Foreign direct investment and other foreign finance was in the range of US $0.1–0.2 billion per year until the early 1990s. In the second half of that decade inflows rose sharply, to US$0.8 billion by 2000. After a three-year slump, foreign finance jumped to US$2 billion in 2004, with a similar level of inflows in 2005. This proved to be the beginning of a period of wild fluctuations, lasting until 2017. There were very large net outflows for the next three years, followed by a big increase, with the total rising to US$12.3 billion in 2008, the year when the insolvency of the Icelandic banks became apparent.

As late as 2007 there was little warning of the impending crisis. The International Monetary Fund's Staff Report of that year (IMF, 2007) saw "some signs of slowing" in the growth of GDP, following three years of rapid expansion, but they judged that "the banking sector appears well-placed to withstand significant credit and market shocks" (IMF, 2007, p. 1). This assessment was based on a positive review of Iceland's financial stability framework and banks' liquidity and asset position. Iceland's market access was thought to be assured by the "the diversification of funding sources", and the available support from the Nordic financial network (IMF, 2007, p. 14).

The stark outline of the magnitude and implications of the banking crisis that emerged in 2008 are summarised in the IMF Staff Report that was issued to provide the justification for the Fund's decision to support Iceland's adjustment to the crisis with a two-year financing arrangement in the amount of US$2.1 billion, equivalent to 16 per cent of GDP.

> Iceland's economy is in the midst of a banking crisis of extraordinary proportions that is expected to lead to a deep recession, a sharp rise in the fiscal deficit, and a dramatic surge in public sector debt, reflecting a very high fiscal cost of restructuring the banking system. The virtual collapse of the on-shore foreign exchange market poses a serious and immediate risk to the economy considering its very high import dependence.
>
> (IMF, 2008, p. 1)

The key to the success of the adjustment programme was the stated commitment to "ensuring medium-term fiscal sustainability". In the short run capital controls were employed to help stem capital flight, in an attempt to halt the free fall of the currency. The third element of the strategy was a comprehensive bank restructuring strategy, centred on "measures to ensure fair value of assets [and] maximise asset recovery", bearing in mind the need to settle "claims by depositors and other creditors in a fair, collaborative, and best-effort manner" in order to restore access to international capital markets.

The crucial importance of fiscal adjustment to the recovery from the economic losses of the banking crisis is evident from Figure 3.6. Export and tourism earnings were unaffected by the bank failures, but available foreign currency was drastically cut by the very large reversal of foreign financial inflows. Government cut its current expenditures by eight per cent between 2008 and 2012, measured in constant dollars. This put a drag on private consumption, reinforcing the effects of a drastic devaluation of the kronor, which lost half its value in US dollars in 2009. Aggregate expenditure contracted, and imports fell by more than one-third from 2007 to 2009. Fiscal restraint was maintained all the way to 2016, with government expenditure in

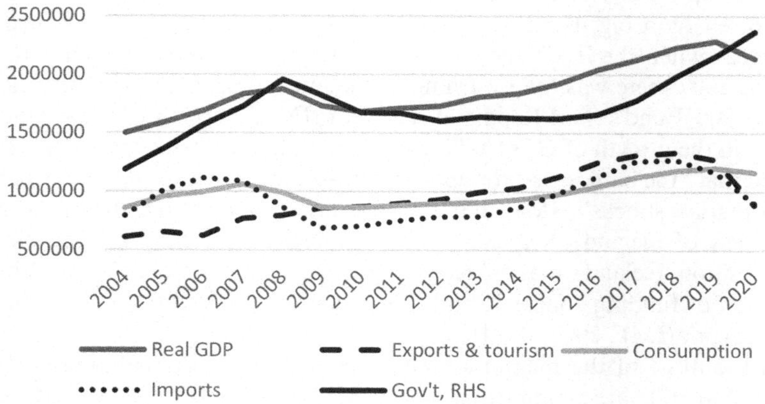

Figure 3.6 Iceland: the banking crisis, constant US$m
Source: IMF, 2008.

that year no higher than it was in 2012, in constant dollars. Tight fiscal policies cemented the rebalancing of aggregate expenditure and imports, and was the major factor in rebuilding the country's foreign reserves and stabilising the value of the kronor; in 2019, just before the onset of the COVID-19 pandemic, the US dollar in value local currency was virtually the same as in 2008, at 121 kronor to the dollar. Thanks to the fiscal restraint, the economic recovery which began in 2012, and which lifted GDP in constant dollars past the 2008 pre-crisis peak by 2014, was led entirely by exports. Fiscal policies were loosened only from 2017 onwards, by which time the economy was once more on a sustainable path of foreign currency-led growth, with foreign reserves at historic highs and a stable currency.

Mauritius

Mauritius' remarkable economic improvement in well-being came as a result of tourism, clothing and textile exports and small fiscal deficits since 1987. The Mauritius economy has grown rapidly since 1973 after a period of economic stagnation which saw no increase in real GDP between 1963 and 1972. The main driver in the 1970s was the export of sugar, with foreign currency earnings in 1980 which were five times larger than a decade earlier. However foreign earnings from sugar stagnated in the 1980s. The new engine of growth until the mid-1990s was clothing and textile manufacturing, which grew rapidly with the establishment of export processing zones in the early 1980s. Manufacturing exports faltered somewhat after 1996, but in the meantime the tourism industry was growing in importance. Earnings from tourism rose from insignificance in the 1980s to the equivalent of 55 per cent of receipts from manufacturing in 1996, and tourism revenues accelerated from that time onward, while export receipts from manufacturing stagnated. Although manufacturing recovered in the early 2000s, the sector was overtaken by tourism in 2007. Tourism revenues peaked in 2014 and fell away somewhat thereafter, but in 2019, just before the onset of COVID-19, tourism earnings were 36 per cent higher than for manufacturing (Figure 3.7). Sugar exports in 2019 yielded just 23 per cent of receipts from manufacturing. Overall, the economy stumbled briefly at the time of the global energy price inflation of the early eighties, but thereafter growth was remarkably resilient in the face of the global slowdowns in the early nineties and in 2008–09, thanks to exports and tourist earnings.

The main challenge to economic growth and external stability was manifest in large deficits of the public sector in the period between 1977 and 1983. The deficit widened from sustainable levels of no more than three per cent of GDP in the 1960s and early 1970s, to 6.3 per cent in 1974. Efforts to correct the situation in the next two years were not sustained, and the deficit widened to 8.4 per cent in 1977, bottoming out at almost 13 per cent in 1981 (Figure 3.8). The inevitable result was pressure on the foreign currency market, and the value of the rupee had depreciated 264 per cent by the time the fiscal

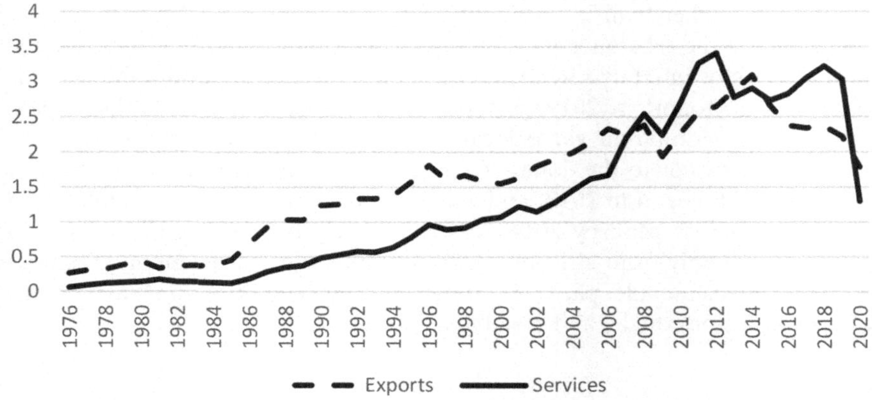

Figure 3.7 Mauritius: foreign currency inflows, US$b
Source: IMF, n.d.

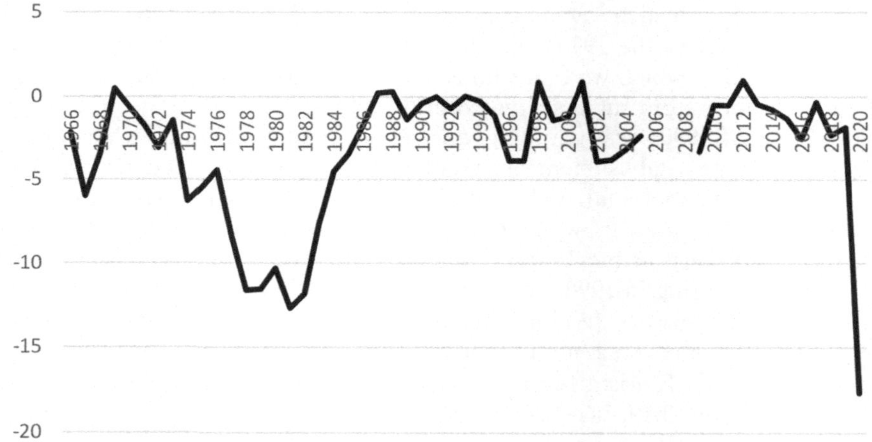

Figure 3.8 Mauritius: fiscal balance, % of GDP
Source: IMF, n.d.

deficit was brought under control in 1984. The public sector accounts were lifted into a small surplus in 1987, and the public finances remained within sustainable bounds thereafter.

In spite of the renewed fiscal discipline, confidence in the maintenance of fiscal prudence had been lost, and the rupee continued to depreciate, even though an ongoing build-up of foreign reserves suggested that there was no pressure on the foreign currency market from the mid-1980s onward. At the height of the fiscally-induced balance of payments crisis foreign reserves were so low that they were sufficient to cover only about one month's imports. Reserves recovered to seven months of cover by 1991, and averaged five

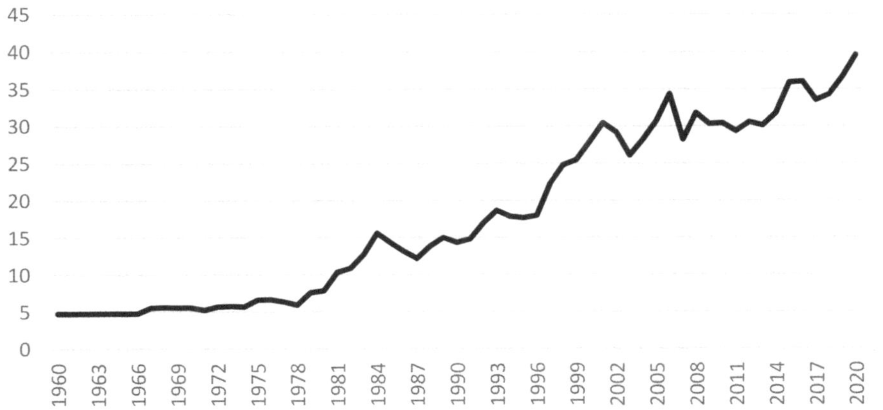

Figure 3.9 Mauritius: exchange rate, rupees per US$
Source: IMF, n.d.

months for the rest of that decade and the next, but the rupee was down 50 per cent by 2000 and a further nine per cent by 2010. There was a large build-up of foreign reserves, to levels that would serve to finance almost two years' worth of imports by the end of 2020, but the rupee continued to fall in value, by another 30 per cent (Figure 3.9).

The extent of the gain in the HDI for Mauritius (Chapter 2) suggests that the country has been efficient in the use of the resources provided by the strong and sustained growth of GDP over the course of four decades. Supporting evidence is provided by data on life expectancy at birth, which has increased from 71 for females and 64 for males in 1983 to 78 and 71, respectively, in 2020. Educational indicators such as the number of pupils per teacher in primary schools (18 in 2020) and improvements in education performance confirm that there have been significant gains in average well-being in Mauritius.[3]

Notes

1 The quotations are from Feinberg (2021).
2 The production of aluminium is very energy-intensive.
3 Mauritius, Government of, 1990, 2020.

References

Bulmer-Thomas, Victor. 2021. "Belize," in *Handbook of Caribbean Economies*, edited by Robert Looney. Abingdon: Routledge.

Eastern Caribbean Central Bank. 2022. "DashboardDatas | Eastern Caribbean Central Bank." eccb-centralbank.org.

ECLAC. 2020. "Yearbook of Statistics." Santiago: United Nations Economic Commission for Latin America and the Caribbean.

Feinberg, Richard E. 2021. "The Cuban economy: Socialist stagnation with Caribbean characteristics," in *Handbook of Caribbean Economies*, edited by Robert Looney. Abingdon: Routledge.

Henry, Lester. 2021. "Trinidad and Tobago," in *Handbook of Caribbean Economies*, edited by Robert Looney. Abingdon: Routledge.

IMF. n.d. "International Financial Statistics – At a Glance." *IMF Data*.

IMF. 2007. "Iceland: 2007 Article IV Consultation," *Staff Report*. August 29.

IMF. 2008. "Iceland: Request for Stand-by Arrangement," *Staff Report*. November 25.

Mauritius, Government of. 1990, 2020. "Annual Digest of Statistics." Port Louis.

Porzo, Susan and Antonio Giraldi. 2020. "The Dominican Republic," in *Handbook of Caribbean Economies*, edited by Robert Looney. Abingdon: Routledge.

Saunders, Muriel and DeLisle Worrell. 1981. "Government expenditure in Barbados, 1946–79," *Central Bank of Barbados Quarterly Report*, June.

US International Trade Administration. 2019. "Iceland – Market Overview." www.export.gov.

World Bank. 2022. "World Development Indicators." www.worldbank.org.

World Economic Forum. 2017. "Global Competitiveness Report." Geneva.

Worrell, DeLisle. 2021a. "Development and underperformance in the Barbados economy, 1946–2018," in *Handbook of Caribbean Economies*, edited by Robert Looney. Abingdon: Routledge.

Worrell, DeLisle. 2021b. "Economic policies for prosperity and stability: Thoughts on the future for Belize." The Inaugural Gian Gandhi Memorial Lecture, University of Belize, February 25.

Worrell, DeLisle. 2018. "Economic prospects for Trinidad and Tobago". Working Paper, Economic Prospects for Trinidad and Tobago, October.

Worrell, DeLisle. 2017. "The Barbados Economy – the Road to Prosperity," available at www.ssrn.com.

Worrell, DeLisle. 2016. "The economy at fifty," in *Barbados: Fifty Years of Independence*, edited by Trevor A. Carmichael. Kingston and Miami: Ian Randle Publishers.

Worrell, DeLisle. 1996. "Barbados at thirty: the economy," in *Barbados: Thirty Years of Independence*, edited by Trevor Carmichael. Kingston and Miami: Ian Randle Publishers.

Worrell, DeLisle. 1991. "Economic policy in the Dominican Republic since 1966," in *The Latin American Debt*, edited by Antonio Jorge. London: Palgrave Macmillan.

Worrell, DeLisle (ed). 1982. "The Economy of Barbados, 1946–1980," Central Bank of Barbados.

4 The Sources of Foreign Exchange in Caribbean and Central American Countries

This chapter deals with Caribbean and Central American experiences with sectors that earn foreign exchange. The Caribbean is known internationally as a leading international tourism resort destination, and some countries (The Bahamas, Barbados, Jamaica and Cuba) do earn most of their foreign currency from tourism. Tourism is also a major source of foreign earnings for a group of Caribbean countries, including the Dominican Republic, which boast manufacturing and agricultural production exports of equal or greater importance than tourism. Agriculture, which was once the region's leading export sector, remains of significance, mainly in the mainland countries, and minerals and international business services are major sources of foreign earnings for some countries. In addition to exports, tourism and other traded services, foreign investment, government borrowing and remittances are major sources of foreign exchange; the factors affecting these inflows are also discussed. In this chapter we review the landscape with regard to sources of foreign exchange, and discuss the factors which explain the mix of production evidenced across the region.

In the 1950s the Caribbean and Central America were all mainly agricultural exporters, with only a handful of mineral exporters. Their comparative advantages were seen as endowments of oil, bauxite, nickel and other minerals, and the availability of abundant supplies of cheap labour with easily acquired skills in the production of sugar cane, bananas, coffee and other crops. Significant new opportunities opened up with provision of tax incentives to manufacturers of clothing and other easily transportable items in the 1950s and 1960s, to take advantage of the available low cost labour to manufacture these items in the Caribbean for export to the US and elsewhere. The model was established by the legislature of Puerto Rico, which in May 1947 passed legislation abolishing corporation taxes, in a successful drive to attract US firms to the island. Thanks to this programme, which came to be known as Operation Bootstrap, the growth engine of the Puerto Rican economy shifted from agriculture to industry, with an immediate jump in the quality of life for the island's workforce.

The startling effects of Operation Bootstrap attracted widespread attention and many imitators, countries which introduced tax holiday regimes in an

DOI: 10.4324/9781003247609-5

effort to reap similar benefits. This ignited a debate which rages to this day about the impact of tax and other fiscal incentives on the location of investment and production. However, what perceptive economists understood from the inception of the programme was that it was the wage differential between agriculture and manufacturing which was crucial in making it attractive for US and other manufacturers to locate production in offshore locations for export back to the US. Operation Bootstrap awakened investors to the fact that this reservoir of labour existed at wages which were significantly lower than in the US, but the tax relief per se, though welcome, has not been shown to have been a decisive factor.

Among the first to recognise and to popularise the benefits of offshoring of manufacturing was the Caribbean economist and Nobel Laureate, Arthur Lewis. That is unsurprising because his seminal work (Lewis, 1954) had at its core the transformational benefit of the transfer of unskilled agricultural labour to more productive industrial activity. Offshoring was a natural extension, allowing access to cheaper labour abroad as a means of extending the benefits to be had from the switch from agriculture to industry. There are potential benefits for investors, workers and consumers; labour earns substantially more than agriculture, entrepreneurs earn higher profits from the use of cheaper labour, and it is usually possible to share some of the margins with consumers, in the form of price reductions.

Starting with the Puerto Rican success, light manufacturing began to appear throughout the Caribbean and Central America, displacing agriculture in Puerto Rico and elsewhere to a greater or lesser extent. The benefits derived by countries varied, in part as a result of how incentive policies were implemented. It can be argued that fiscal incentives became unnecessary once manufacturers recognised that there was a labour reservoir in the region waiting to be tapped. However, instead of dispensing with incentives after an initial period, most governments in the region added to the incentive regimes, and fortified them with tariffs and other restrictions and stipulations, in efforts to stimulate manufacturing for home consumption, rather than for export. In contrast to competitive export manufacturing, the protective regimes eroded actually diminished local well-being, because domestic consumers were faced with more expensive local items, often of indifferent quality.

The switch of labour from agriculture to export manufacturing brought with it a marked improvement in material well-being for the countries of Central America and the Caribbean. Among the benefits were the provision of job opportunities for women, and the provision of permanent employment for all workers, as opposed to the episodic and seasonal nature of most agricultural jobs. In addition, over time the manufacturing sector served to draw up the average wage level, including in agriculture. It became increasingly difficult to attract labour to low paid, seasonal work in agriculture now that there were better alternatives on offer, and agricultural firms were challenged to respond by investing to raise productivity in agriculture to support higher wage levels. Sadly, much of agriculture failed to rise to the challenge.

Experiences of industrial transformation have varied across the region. In cases where import substitution and production for the local market were a focus, little remains of the efforts that were initiated in the 1960s and 1970s; these producers have almost all been driven out by better, cheaper imports. Of companies that focussed on the export market, most are nowadays in services such as telemarketing and customer service, rather than the production of physical products. A major factor has been the success of the industrialisation drive in lifting wages and living standards, eroding the wage advantage which the Caribbean previously enjoyed in clothing and other light manufacturing.

It was technical change in the form of the introduction of commercial jet aircraft that made for the commercial exploitation of the tourist potential of the Caribbean and of Central American countries such as Costa Rica and Belize. Until the 1960s travel to Caribbean resorts was the preserve of the wealthy, including, famously, the first President of the United States when he was still a young man. Visitors travelled with a retinue of assistants and attendants and stayed in private accommodation, for the most part. They travelled by ship, for extended stays. Apart from notorious exceptions such as Havana, Cuba, tourist activity created little local employment and generated limited income.

That all changed when the large middle class in Europe and North America could afford to fly to the Caribbean for a short holiday, an especially attractive proposition in the winter months. The tourism industry quickly came to prominence across the Caribbean, taking labour away from both agriculture and manufacturing. Wages in tourism are somewhat higher than for manufacturing on average, but what gives tourism a greater edge is the variety and flexibility of employment opportunities, and the myriad spin-offs and supporting activities, formal and informal, that the tourist industry provides. With just a handful of exceptions, government tax and incentive policies have played no decisive role in the rapid growth of tourism in the Caribbean and Central America.

A fourth major source which has emerged for many countries in the region is workers' remittances. They are the largest source of foreign exchange for Haiti and El Salvador, and they account for one quarter to one third of all foreign inflows for Jamaica, Guatemala, the Dominican Republic and Nicaragua. This phenomenon is part of a global trend, and represents an alternative to production for export which can, like exports, serve to raise domestic living standards. The social costs of over-dependence on remittances, as in the cases of Haiti and El Salvador, are of serious concern, however, though they are beyond the scope of our expertise.

Trinidad and Tobago is the only country in the Caribbean that exports mainly petroleum products. Oil production began in Trinidad in the early 1900s, but by the 1950s Trinidad was mainly a processing centre for Venezuelan crude. The composition of Trinidad's exports has changed radically since the 1960s. First came the production of offshore oil and gas; then in the 1970s a far-sighted Government, led by Eric Williams, the path-breaking economic historian, invested much of the windfall from a steep rise in oil prices to create large scale export manufacturing capacity, including petroleum products and steel fabrication. Subsequent private investment in the production of methanol, urea and other petroleum products have resulted in a switch away from refinery operations, with the closure of the last operating refinery in 2018.

There is one other foreign currency engine which is of importance to the smallest territories in the region, most of them UK dependencies. The domiciling of international business and financial services is the principal source of foreign exchange and economic activity in the Cayman Islands, the British Virgin Islands, the Turks and Caicos Islands and Bermuda. Such services are now of declining importance in the Bahamas and Barbados, where they once offered promise of significant contributions to foreign earnings.

Foreign direct investment is another vital and continuing source of foreign currency in the Caribbean and Central America, as in all other SOEs. As we have explained elsewhere, the import content of investment in the SOE is as high as for consumption, if not higher. Therefore, foreign currency finance is needed for all investment to cover these import requirements. If there is no foreign finance of that import requirement, either directly or through the banking system, consumer imports will be displaced or there will be a drawdown of foreign reserves. A healthy inflow of foreign direct investment is therefore desirable, and an indicator of the competitiveness of the economy.

Government foreign borrowing is a more ambiguous indicator of economic health and good management of government finances. Foreign funding for infrastructure and for public utilities and other public services are a positive indicator, providing they do not drive the servicing of the external debt to levels which impair the country's credit rating. However, general-purpose external borrowing has proved problematic more often than not, increasing debt service costs to finance current public expenditure, and leaving the economy with no lasting increase in productive capacity or any gain in competitive advantage.

Chapter 4 tells the stories of changing production structures in the foreign earnings sectors of countries, and in foreign finance, in the Caribbean and Central America, and charts the manner in which the changes came about and the main factors influencing these developments. In doing so, we explore the associated themes of wages and labour productivity, inflation, migration into and out of the region and the exploitation of natural resources.

The sources of foreign exchange inflows in Central America and the Caribbean

The sectors and activities discussed in this chapter are tourism, other services such as data processing, call centres and international business services, exports of clothing, processed food and other manufacturing, mineral and other primary extractive industry exports and remittances. The Bahamas,

Barbados and the countries of the Eastern Caribbean Currency Union derive most of their foreign earnings from tourism and related activities. In the late 2010s the industry accounted for between half and two-thirds of the foreign exchange inflows in these countries. No other activity supplied as much as 15 per cent of the total. Tourism was also the largest contributor to inflows in Cuba and Jamaica. In Cuba, exports of manufactured goods was second in importance, about 60 per cent of the revenues from tourism. In Jamaica foreign workers' remittances yielded almost as much foreign currency as did tourism, each with about a third of foreign currency inflows (see Table 4.1).

The Dominican Republic, along with three Central American countries (Costa Rica, Nicaragua and Panama) are mainly exporters of manufactured goods such as pharmaceuticals and medical equipment. Tourism is second in importance in Costa Rica, the Dominican Republic and Panama, and it also makes a small contribution (less than ten per cent of inflows) in Nicaragua, a country where remittances are second in importance, with about half the foreign currency contribution of exports.

Exports of bananas, sugar, coffee, fruits and other agricultural products are the largest sources of foreign earnings for Guatemala and Honduras, followed by workers' remittances. In Guatemala, exports are about half of all inflows, with remittances about one-third; in Honduras, exports contribute two-thirds, and remittances about one-fifth. Tourism makes a small contribution in both countries (less than ten per cent).

Table 4.1 Sources of foreign currency inflows (% of total)

	Tourism	*Exports*	*Other Services*	*Remittances*	*Direct Investment*	*All other*
Bahamas	62	14	4	5	14	1
Barbados	56	11	10	3	8	12
Costa Rica	16	47	19	4	12	2
Cuba	47	29		13	11	0
DR	25	36	24	5	8	2
El Salvador	8	35	42	10	3	2
Guatemala	7	49	4	33	5	2
Haiti	0	22	0	68	8	2
Honduras	6	64	3	19	7	1
Jamaica	33	15	6	31	5	10
Nicaragua	7	55	10	22	5	1
Panama	16	45	12	3	15	9
Trinidad-Tobago	4	86	2	1	3	4

Source: ECLAC, 2020.

Trinidad and Tobago is the only country in this region which exports petroleum and related products, accounting for approaching 90 per cent of inflows, although in the early 2020s Guyana is poised to become the second oil exporter. During the period of our analysis that country has been an exporter of agricultural products for the most part, along with some manufactured goods. Remittances are as important as exports as a source of foreign currency for the country.

There are two countries for which remittances have become the main source of foreign currency, El Salvador and Haiti, tragically in both cases as a result of social and political instability, with high levels of insecurity of person and property. El Salvador derives about one third of inflows from exports, mainly of garments, but the garment industry in Haiti has largely collapsed.

International business services, including legal, accounting, insurance, finance and marketing, are now of importance mainly in the Cayman Islands, Bermuda and the smaller UK dependencies in the Caribbean. Relentless international political pressure from the Group of Twenty nations,[1] born of their unwillingness or incapacity to deal with internal distributional problems, has largely driven The Bahamas from the market, and stymied efforts by Barbados, the Netherlands Antilles and others to establish the capacity to provide these services, despite their competitive advantages of language, geography, high levels of education, good communications and international networks. Although some vestigial activities remain, international business services have now been "reshored" to Delaware, South Dakota and other states of the US, and to Luxembourg, Monaco and other European locations, as well as to London and New York, where niches in market regulations create artificial opportunities in activities known to those specialising in these areas.

Tourism

Worrell (2021) provides a comprehensive assessment of tourism performance in the Caribbean in the five decades since 1970. The study is based on data published by the Caribbean Tourism Organisation, covering all the insular Caribbean, from the largest islands of Cuba and Hispaniola (shared between Haiti and the Dominican Republic) to tiny Montserrat (population 6,000), and including all language and ethnic groups and dependencies and individual resorts as well as independent countries. The Mexican resorts of Cancún and Cozumel are members, as is Bermuda in the Atlantic, all well-known tourism destinations. Guyana, the French *departmente* of Guyane and Suriname on the northern coast of South America, which aspire to build on their considerable eco-tourism potential, as yet unrealised, are also members, and are included in the study.

There is a great variety of resort tourist experiences on offer in these Caribbean destinations, from undifferentiated tropical resorts offering services no different from what might be found anywhere in the tropics, to value-added destinations which offer high quality services, countries focusing on eco-tourism and sports tourism, boutique resorts offering unique experiences, and special cases, like the Virgin Islands and the Grenadines, whose specialty is yachting. These are not exclusive categories, and the larger destinations will offer a variety; the classification is based on what contributes the overwhelming proportion of tourism revenues.

Resort tourism in the Caribbean and elsewhere in the tropics took off with the introduction of passenger jet transport in the 1960s, and the Caribbean as a whole has kept pace with global growth in the industry ever since. The strategies employed to sustain growth over five decades were varied, and were driven by private initiative for the most part. Two notable exceptions were Cancún in Mexico, and Aruba's switch from oil refining in the mid-1980s:

> In Aruba, the failure of the oil refinery that had been the mainstay of the economy until the early 1980s left Government the urgent task of promoting an alternative with the capacity to quickly become the bedrock of continuing economic prosperity. Tourism was the obvious choice, and official policy initiatives were successful in attracting large-scale hotel investments, thanks to which arrivals more than doubled within five years of the start of the initiative. By 2018 Aruba had become the seventh largest Caribbean destination, by arrivals (and sixth largest, by accommodation).
>
> The development of Cancún was the result of a Mexican Government initiative to diversify the economy by developing the tourist potential of the Caribbean coast. In the early 1990s the Bank of Mexico, the central bank, provided finance for massive investment in roads, an international airport and other infrastructure, attracting investment to make Cancún the Caribbean's third largest destination, after the Dominican Republic and Cuba.
>
> (Worrell, 2021, p. 65)

Two periods of very rapid growth of Caribbean tourism were identified: from 1985 to 2000 and from 2010 to 2016. The competitiveness of Caribbean countries is assessed, based on observation and comparison of changes in market share and changes in relative prices of tourism services. I started with the premise that there are two strategies – which may be combined – for gaining market share in competitive markets: you may improve the quality of your offering sufficiently to move upmarket, maintaining your market share by attracting the more affluent customers who are happy to pay the higher prices you must charge to ensure favourable net revenues; and/or you may offer richer experiences, such as sports facilities or cultural and entertainment services, that allow you to gain market share at prevailing prices for your quality of product. In either case the success of your strategy will be signalled by a relative price which increases or remains unchanged, together with a market share which also increases or remains unchanged. In an analysis of the two periods of high growth based on a reduced sample of 21 observations, the results for the Caribbean using this process of evaluation shows something of a mixed bag: during the period 1985–2000 (nine observations) five countries showed improved competitiveness via quality improvement, while the remaining four lost market share. In the more recent period two countries improved market share through quality improvement, two lost market share and eight adjusted prices downward to hold on to their market share. The general conclusion of the study was that countries where tourism is the main source of foreign exchange had creditable performances, and the larger destination such as Cancún and the Dominican Republic also did well. The successful strategies were characterised by flexible responses to market changes, an emphasis on quality and the appeal of the individual destinations, and a history of adaptation to changing opportunities.

Exports of manufactured and agricultural products in selected Caribbean and Central American countries.

The Dominican Republic and Cuba are the only independent countries in the insular Caribbean which have a significant export sector, contributing respectively 36 and 29 per cent per cent of all foreign currency inflows in the late 2010s. Agricultural exports have declined to insignificance in the smaller islands, and exports of rum, other beverages and a handful of niche market products yield around ten per cent per cent of foreign currency inflows, if that. The analysis in this section focusses on the Dominican Republic and Cuba, together with the countries of Central America: Costa Rica, El Salvador, Guatemala, Honduras, Nicaragua and Panama. The contribution of exports in these countries ranges from Cuba's 29 per cent per cent to 64 per cent per cent for Honduras.

Except for Cuba and El Salvador, exports are the largest contributor to foreign exchange flows for these countries. Services, mainly tourism, haves now become the main foreign exchange earner for Cuba, while for El Salvador remittances now contribute 42 per cent per cent of inflows, compared with 35 per cent per cent for exports. Six countries – all except Guatemala and Honduras – export mainly manufactured products. Costa Rica, Cuba and Panama export medical products and supplies. They are the largest export item in Cuba and Costa Rica, and second to garments exports in Panama. Garments are also the main manufactured export item in the Dominican Republic, El Salvador, Guatemala and Nicaragua. The Dominican Republic, El Salvador and Nicaragua export electrical cables and other electrical supplies. Cigars from Cuba and the Dominican Republic, and beverages and processed food from Guatemala, Honduras and Panama are among the largest export items from the region (see Table 4.2). The contribution of manufactured exports to foreign exchange in five of these six countries ranges from ten per cent per cent (El Salvador, a reflection of the dominance of remittances) to 26 per cent per cent for Nicaragua. The extent of Cuba's dependence on tourism is reflected in the fact that even though exports of manufactured goods are second in importance, their foreign exchange contribution is only seven per cent.

Guatemala and Honduras are the countries where exports continue to be mainly traditional agricultural staples, bananas and coffee in both countries, along with sugar in Guatemala and seafood and fruit in Honduras. Bananas are also exported from Costa Rica and the Dominican Republic, and coffee and sugar from El Salvador and Nicaragua. Seafood is exported from Cuba, Honduras and Nicaragua.

The Dominican Republic (22 per cent), Cuba (21 per cent), Guatemala (20 per cent) and Costa Rica (12 per cent) were the countries with the largest share of the total manufacturing output of the eight countries in our analysis in 2018. The Dominican Republic registered the fastest growth of manufacturing over the past three decades, more than tripling output since 1990, thanks to very rapid growth in the 1990s. The establishment of free trade zones attracted foreign investment from the late 1980s, and a decade of political stability cemented the gains (see Chapter 3). The Dominican Republic increased its share of manufacturing value added over the three decades to 2018 by eight percentage points, from 14 per cent per cent in 1990. Manufacturing output in Costa Rica and Guatemala in 2018 was about twice what it was in 1990, sufficient for an increase of one and two percentage points, respectively. In Cuba, the loss of its major trading partner following the collapse of the Soviet Union resulted in a decline of one third of its manufacturing output between 1990 and 1993. Although there was a slow climb back over the next two decades, by 2015 output was just 36 per cent over where it stood in 1990, and output has since declined by nine percentage points. In 1990 Cuba's contribution to total manufacturing output was the highest among the eight countries at 30 per cent; by 2018 it had lost nine percentage points of

Table 4.2 Exports of manufacturing and agriculture

Percentage of foreign currency inflows			
Country	*Exports*	*Manufacturing*	*Agriculture*
Costa Rica	47	16	9
Cuba	29	7	1
DR	36	12	2
Guatemala	47	6	12
Honduras	64	14	32
Nicaragua	55	26	16
Panama	45	24	0
El Salvador	35	10	2

Source: ECLAC Statiscal Yearbook, 2020.

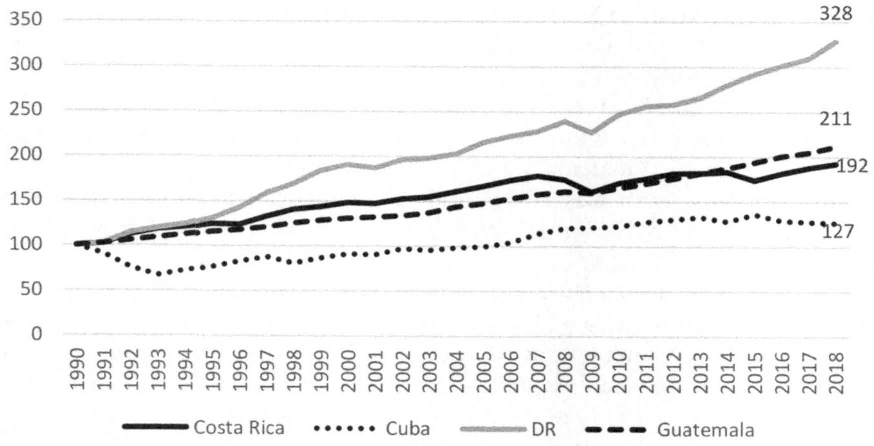

Figure 4.1 Manufacturing value added, index
Source: ECLAC, 2020.

market share, to be pipped at the post by the Dominican Republic (see Figure 4.1).

Guatemala (26 per cent of the total for countries in this sample) and the Dominican Republic (20 per cent) were the leading producers of agricultural products, followed by Costa Rica, Cuba and Honduras, all with 12 per cent in 2018. The Dominican Republic was again the top performer, with output not far short of three times what it had been in 1990. There was an especially rapid expansion of agricultural output in the last decade, with value added in the sector increasing by two-thirds between 2008 and 2018. The country's share in total agricultural output in our sample jumped seven percentage points from 1990. Honduras shows a similar pattern of rapid expansion in the most recent decade, a 50 per cent increase in this case, good for a gain of four percentage points in market share. Costa Rica and Guatemala both recorded agricultural output that more than doubled over the past three decades. Output growth did accelerate from around 2010, but less markedly than for the Dominican Republic and Honduras. Costa Rica and Guatemala gained two and five percentage points of market share, respectively, over the entire period. All countries gained market share at the expense of Cuba, where the loss of its market in the USSR, the main purchaser of the country's sugar exports, had an even more severe impact on agriculture than it did on manufacturing; agricultural output fell by 50 per cent between 1990 and 1994. Since then increases have been small and growth has been slow and erratic. By 2018 value added in agriculture in Cuba was only three-quarters of what it had been in 1990 (see Figure 4.2).

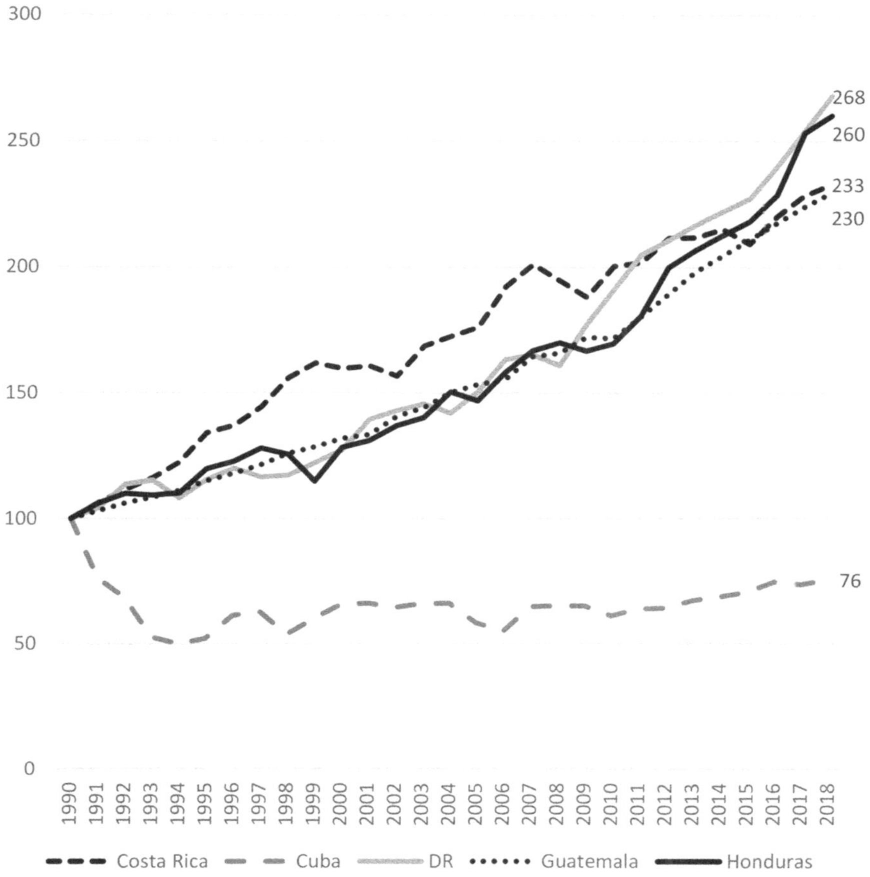

Figure 4.2 Agricultural value added, index
Source: ECLAC, 2020.

International business and financial services

Worrell and Lowe (2011a, 2011b) list the main international business and financial services (IBFS) centres in the Caribbean as Aruba, The Bahamas, Barbados, Bermuda, Netherlands Antilles and St Kitts-Nevis. The decline in this activity in the independent countries on the list was already evident: the 40-odd international banks operating in Barbados around the turn of the century, mainly in treasury management, had by then all closed, as a result of regulatory uncertainties in Canada, the home country of most of the institutions set up in Barbados. The UK dependencies accounted for most of the IBFS business in the Caribbean, the region with the largest share of this activity, about 60 per cent of the global total. Global balances in small financial centres, though significant for the local economies, were less than ten per cent of total cross-border assets. Investments from Bermuda, which had by far the largest individual share, were 1.5 per cent of the world total; Cayman Islands, with the largest share of liabilities, accounted for about five per cent of the world total. The Caribbean has significant comparative advantages of language, economic and political stability, climate and geography, communications and business, financial, trading and cultural links, which are the real foundation for its attractiveness as a location of activities such as marketing, customer relations, legal services, accounting services, brokerage and other specialised services. The main players boast a well-educated labour force with sophisticated skills and experience, and a modern urbane culture which many find congenial.

Unfortunately, the potential this seemed to offer for the development of competitive international financial centres has now been lost to all but a handful of UK dependencies, thanks to a combination of mindless and counter-productive international regulations and a failure by independent countries to develop strategies that were adapted to the realities of international relations. The UK dependencies have been much more successful in this regard, balancing resources devoted to compliance with an even greater emphasis on efficient business facilitation and acquisition of top quality expertise. Competitive IBFS sectors might have been developed to supplement tourism and other sources of foreign earnings by offering compelling opportunities for profitable business, if necessary under the protective regulatory scrutiny of regulators from the Group of Twenty countries. Maintenance of a stable, low inflation economy and the free circulation of the US dollar and other international currencies might also have enhanced their appeal. The remaining euro-currency, private banking and asset management activities of IBFS providers in The Bahamas and Barbados have now mostly disappeared. Bermuda accounts for the lion's share of captive insurance (a form of self-insurance by very large companies), while investment services, including mutual funds, hedge funds, company services, trust and other services are to be found in the Cayman Islands and the British Virgin Islands for the most part.

The Trinidad and Tobago experience illustrates the difficulty emerging market economies have in managing oil wealth

Trinidad and Tobago has had the benefit of far-sighted leadership that has sought, during periods when oil prices afforded the country unexpectedly large foreign earnings, to divert a substantial part of the windfall to diversify the country's productive capacity, and to invest another large portion with a view to the long-term investment needs of the economy. Despite successive governments' best efforts, however, the economy has been unable to avoid violent swings in economic activity that mirror the movements of oil prices, devaluation of domestic money, bouts of high inflation, repeated crises of public finance and the damaging impact of the oil sector on the output of other export sectors.

The pattern of Trinidad and Tobago's exports corresponds remarkably well with the evolution of world oil prices. Exports fell in the early 1980s as oil prices fell, stagnating for a decade and registering little growth until the late 1990s. In 1998 the value of exports was 17 per cent less than in 1980. However, the following year saw the start of a dramatic rise in world oil prices to a peak of US$93 per barrel in 2008, by which time Trinidad and Tobago's exports had multiplied almost seven times from the 1999 value. The remarkable match of exports and oil prices continued through the dramatic fall in 2009 and 2010, and the equally rapid, but temporary resurgence of oil prices, topping out over US$100 per barrel in the next two years, with the oil prices and Trinidad and Tobago's exports in free fall in 2015 and 2016 (see Figure 4.3).

The large investments in manufacturing capacity and infrastructure in Trinidad in the 1970s and again in the early 1990s (see Chapter 3) were overshadowed by the massive swings in oil revenues, and there is little evidence that the diversification of exports has increased the economy's resilience in the face of oil price fluctuations. Part of the reason may be that many of the new investments were in petroleum-related industries. It is also the case that rising oil prices lifted wages throughout the economy, reducing the profitability of agriculture and hastening the demise of the sugar industry (the last operating sugar manufacturing facility, Usine St Madeleine, was closed in 2006). This commonly-observed phenomenon, which has come to be known as Dutch Disease, was in fact first identified by the British economist Dudley Seers in Trinidad (Seers, 1964). The consequence is that the main source of the foreign currency which fuels this SOE remains earnings from the export of oil and

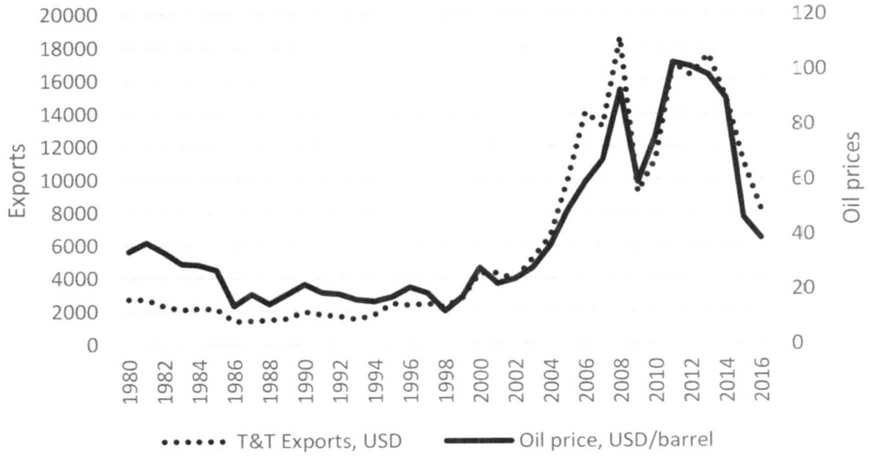

Figure 4.3 T&T exports & world oil prices
Source: ECLAC, 2020.

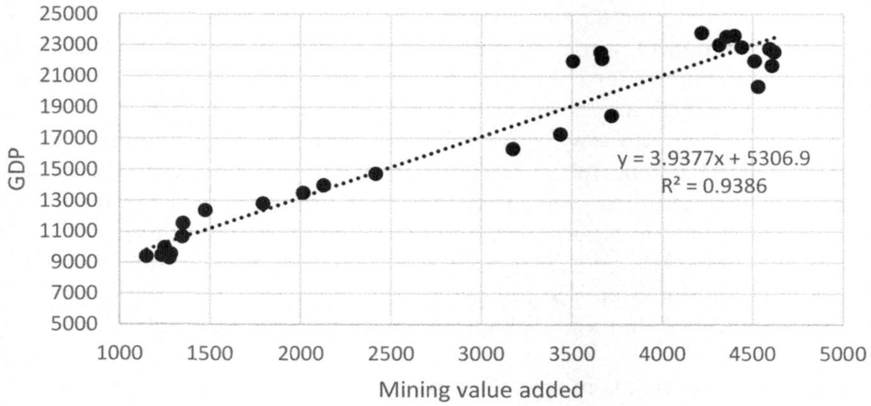

Figure 4.4 T&T correlation of GDP with mining value added, US$m
Source: ECLAC, 2020.

related products whose prices vary with the international price of oil. This is evidenced by the correlation between value added in the mining sector and overall GDP over the past three decades (see Figure 4.4).

Foreign currency remittances

The countries which derive more than ten per cent of all foreign currency inflows from remittances are, with the sole exception of the Dominican Republic, those with the lowest incomes per head, measured in terms of purchasing power. They are, in descending order of purchasing power per head in US dollars, Guyana (9,455), Jamaica (9,319), Cuba (8,621), Guatemala (8,494), El Salvador (8,359), Honduras (5,308), Nicaragua (5,284) and Haiti (1,709). The Dominican Republic, with 24 per cent of foreign currency from remittances, has the highest per capita income of this group by some distance (17,591), well ahead of Barbados (14,936), where remittances are only two per cent of inflows.

There are two forces, both related to income, which have pushed up remittances from modest proportions (around ten per cent of foreign currency in 1980, except for Haiti), to 20 per cent or higher in most cases. One factor is the relatively slow growth of real per capita incomes in these countries in the last four decades, and the consequent paucity of local employment opportunities, leading to continuous large-scale emigration. The migration pressure has continued despite increasing hostility in many receiving countries, pressure that has been aggravated by social, economic and political instability, and a general sense of insecurity. Cuba and Haiti are special cases at opposite ends of the spectrum. The US blockade and the survival of an inefficient Soviet-style bureaucracy, arguably and ironically fortified by unrelenting US hostility, has stifled emigration opportunities for Cubans, while natural disasters, widespread insecurity and endemic political crises have driven Haitian migration to persistently high levels.

In Barbados and countries with higher per capita incomes, emigration has continued, but at much more modest levels, and involving higher skills and more reliance on formal channels. The overseas populations of these countries are generally of longer standing abroad, and the households they leave behind are not, for the most part, dependent on remittances for the daily necessities of life. Regular monthly cash transfers have become quite rare, and transfers are much more likely to be in kind, sent as gifts at Christmastime or for special occasions. Many long-term emigrants also build retirement homes in their countries of birth or elsewhere in the region, bringing with them pensions and related income, which are now much more significant sources (though typically below ten per cent of the total) than are remittances.

In contrast, the per capita incomes of many families in countries where remittances are high do rely on these inflows to pay the monthly bills, pay rent, buy groceries, cover the costs of schooling, and other necessities. In Haiti such transfers are the main source of income for those households lucky enough to receive them, and El Salvador receives more money from remittances each year than the country earns from the export of garments and other exports. In Jamaica remittances bring in about as much foreign currency as does tourism, while in Honduras, Guatemala and Nicaragua remittances are second in importance to exports of agricultural and manufactured products, with contributions of 20 per cent or more of foreign currency inflows.

Remittances now provide almost seven of every ten dollars of foreign currency in Haiti. In 1980, when the country still exported clothing and other products, remittances were already in the region of 40 percent; political uncertainties in the 1990s drove the proportion to 74 per cent in 1995, and it has remained at that level of contribution ever since. Remittances are around 40 per cent of foreign inflows in El Salvador, about five points ahead of exports, the other major source. Starting at less than ten per cent in the early 1980s, the contribution of remittances rose steeply to 47 per cent in 1992. Remittances have contributed between 40 and 50 per cent of inflows since then, except for three years from 1996, when the contribution fell to average a little over 30 per cent.

The contribution of remittances in Jamaica rose erratically in the 1980s, from about ten per cent to about 20 per cent. The contribution fell back to a little over ten per cent in the early 1990s, thanks in some part to capital inflows associated with a relaxation to some degree in what had previously been a highly distorting regime of exchange controls. However, disappointing economic growth over the ensuing two decades is reflected in a persistent rise in the remittances contribution, to 36 per cent in 2010. That contribution has remained above 30 per cent for the remainder of the period. In a similar fashion to El Salvador, remittance inflows in Nicaragua grew more rapidly than imports for most of the 1980s, from around ten per cent in the early years to 1991, a year in which they contributed 47 per cent of total inflows. The value of remittances fell sharply in the following years, back to nine per cent of total in 1994. The flow of remittances recovered over the 1990s decade, and since 1998 the increases kept pace with exports in most years. As a result, the contribution of remittances held steady between 20 and 30 per cent (see Figure 4.5).

The contributions of remittances in the Dominican Republic, Guatemala and Honduras have all shown gradual increases, from around ten per cent in the early 1980s to the start of the 2000s decade. Since 2010 their contribution has remained unchanged for Guatemala at about 30 per cent, and a little over 20 per cent for the Dominican Republic. (Recent data for Honduras is not available.) Limited data for Cuba show remittances contributing about one-sixth of foreign currency in most years.

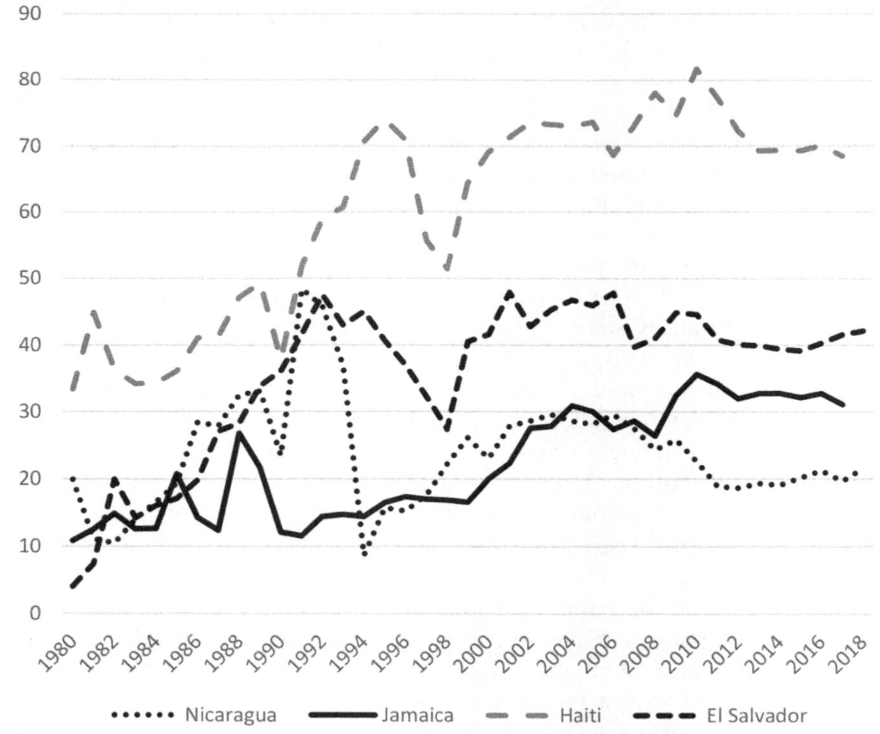

Figure 4.5 Ratio of remittances to foreign currency inflows, %
Source: ECLAC, 2020.

Foreign direct investment in Central America and the Caribbean

Central America and the Caribbean attracted little foreign direct investment in the 1980s. The regional total did not reach US$1 billion any year during that decade, and there was one year (1987) when a small net outflow was recorded. The anaemic investment performance was evident everywhere, in the tourism-driven economies as well as manufacturing and agricultural exporters, including Trinidad and Tobago, the region's significant oil exporter. Political turmoil in Panama led to a loss of foreign investment of over US$1 billion in 1987 and 1988, with a major impact on regional FDI (see Figure 4.6).

Foreign direct investment picked up in the 1990s; the major contributions were from Panama, with the handover of the Canal administration to the local authorities and the restoration of political stability, and from Trinidad and Tobago, where a recovery of oil prices fuelled a new round of investment in the energy sector and related industries. The year 1997 saw an FDI peak in both countries, US$1.3 billion for Panama and US$1 billion for Trinidad and Tobago, reflected in investment ratios of 12 and 17 per cent respectively (see Figure 4.7). Foreign investment in these two countries retreated in the years following, but regional totals were boosted by a one-year peak in FDI for El Salvador in 1998 (US$1.1 billion for an 11 per cent ratio of FDI to GDP) and a more sustained surge in FDI in the Dominican Republic, peaking at US$1.3 billion (six per cent of GDP) in 1999, and continuing at about US$1 billion for the next three years. The overall FDI to GDP ratio, at 4.3 per cent for the selected regional countries, fell to 2.5 per cent in 2002, with FDI in Panama falling to just US$100 million.

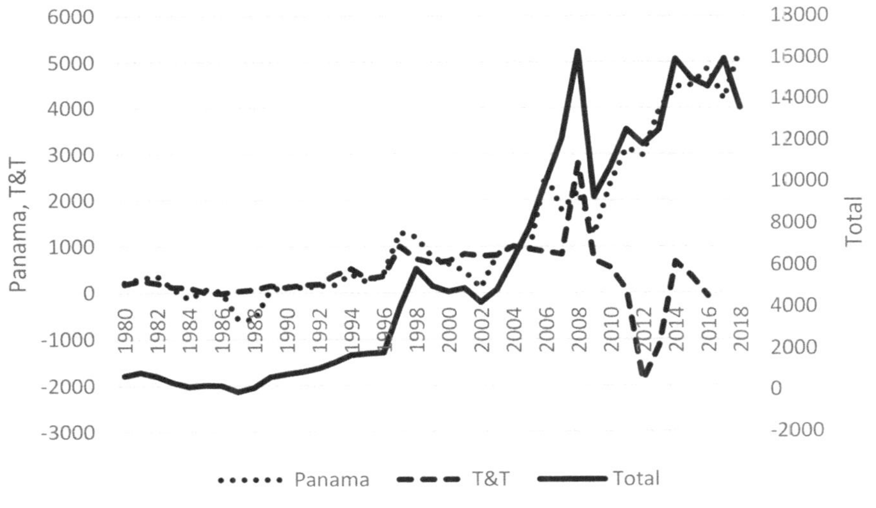

Figure 4.6 FDI, US$m
Source: ECLAC, 2020.

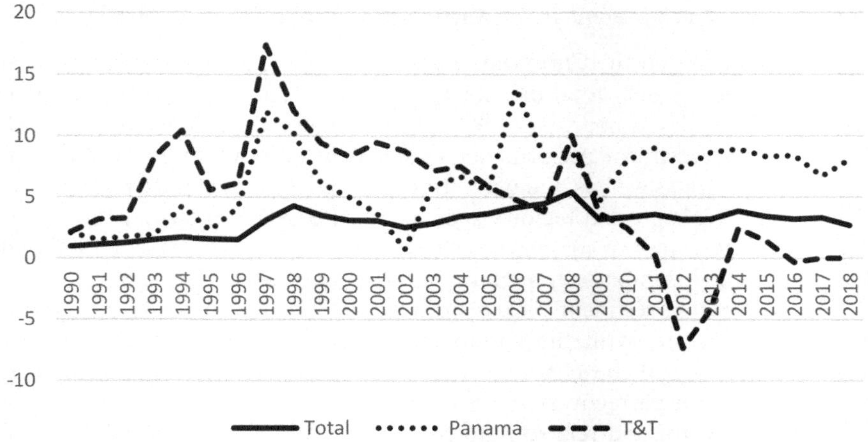

Figure 4.7 FDI ratio to GDP, %
Source: ECLAC, 2020.

There was a remarkable recovery after 2002, with investment rising to a peak of US$16 billion, 5.4 per cent of GDP. Thanks to the global financial crisis, FDI fell by over 40 per cent in 2009, and the peak level was not seen again until 2014. No country escaped the adverse impact of the crisis on FDI in 2009; for many low levels of FDI were being recorded three years later, and countries such as The Bahamas, Barbados, El Salvador and Trinidad and Tobago never recovered to the levels seen in the five years prior to the crisis.

The regional recovery in FDI levels was again led by Panama, along with Costa Rica and the Dominican Republic, countries which all recorded levels of FDI exceeding the 2008 total towards the end of the 2010s decade. However, the FDI ratio for the region as a whole in 2018 (2.7 per cent), and for Panama (8.1 per cent), Costa Rica (4.6 per cent) and the Dominican Republic (three per cent) were all below the 2008 peak.

Note

1 The Group of Twenty is an intergovernmental forum of 19 of the world's largest countries, plus the European Union, which facilitates international cooperation on economic and financial matters.

References

ECLAC. 2020. "Statistical Yearbook," Santiago: United Nations Economic Commission for Latin America and the Caribbean.

Lewis, W. Arthur. 1954. "Economic development with unlimited supplies of labour," *The Manchester School of Economic and Social Studies*, Vol. 22, no. 2, pp.139–191.

Seers, Dudley. 1964. "The Mechanism of an Open Petroleum Economy," *Social and Economic Studies*, Vol.13, no. 2, pp. 233–242.

Worrell, DeLisle. 2021. "The Caribbean holds its own in global tourism competition," in *Handbook of Caribbean Economies*, edited by Robert Looney. Abingdon: Routledge.

Worrell, DeLisle and Shane Lowe. 2011a. "International business and financial services centres in the Caribbean," *Economic Review*. Central Bank of Barbados, June.

Worrell, DeLisle and Shane Lowe. 2011b. "Priorities for international financial reform, From a Caribbean perspective," *Working Paper*. Central Bank of Barbados, December.

5 Economic Integration in the Caribbean

This chapter makes the argument that there exists a single Caribbean economy, which has a fluid definition, and therefore policies are effective only if they make a difference to economic agents within this regional space. The boundaries of "The Caribbean" differ depending whether the topic is tourism, culture, finance or natural resources. For economic purposes the Caribbean also includes the diaspora. Brooklyn is the most inclusive Caribbean city in the world, with neighbourhoods that blend Caribbean people of all languages, origins and ethnicities. The Caribbean diaspora are scattered across the globe, with major concentrations in North America and the UK. Overseas communities are an important market for Caribbean cultural production, a window of opportunity for upward mobility and a fount of remittances and other inward transfers.

Unfortunately, the decision-making structures of the Caribbean do not correspond to these economic realities. Governments and regulators are all national, and this creates frictions which have been a major obstacle to the formulation and implementation of policies to advance the region's economic prosperity. This chapter reviews the history of Caribbean regional integration since the end of the colonial era. There have been a handful of success stories, but the general picture is one of the repeated failure of most initiatives.

The chapter draws lessons from more than 50 years of experience during which time many, various and often repeated efforts to build influential regional institutions have all failed. Those that have not entirely collapsed have been subject to national capture or have become mere cyphers, form with little substance. This has left a major vacuum in the Caribbean's economic and financial relationships with the wider world, and it has also been a source of harmful tensions within the region. Both in terms of regional productivity and competitiveness, and in the enhancement of livelihoods, the failure of regional governance has been costly for the Caribbean.

At the end of World War II Caribbean economies were still largely defined by their colonial relationships. Puerto Rico and the US Virgin Islands (USVI) were quasi-colonies of the US, and the US Government and US interests exercised a decisive influence on economic activity and economic policy in the largest islands, Cuba and Hispaniola. Guadeloupe, Martinique and French

DOI: 10.4324/9781003247609-6

Guyana together with the French islands in the Indian Ocean (Reunion and Mayotte) became a single overseas department of metropolitan France; the Netherlands recovered their colonies of Aruba, Bonaire, Curacao, St Maarten and Dutch Guyana; and most of the rest of the Caribbean remained British colonies, except for islands off the Caribbean coast of Central and South America. Trading, commerce and finance flowed largely along channels defined by those relationships. The countries of the region were specialist agricultural exporters, producing and selling sugar, bananas, coffee and other primary goods to the metropolitan country at the centre of the empire to which they belonged.

The giant presence of the US economy overlay the colonial relationships with other imperial powers. US military bases were dotted across the Caribbean, creating their own infrastructure of roads, ports, airports and utilities, affording income and employment to a wide range of formal and informal service providers. The US dollar was already the common currency of the Caribbean, even though the British colonies used domestic currencies tied to the pound sterling, the Dutch colonies used florins and guilders and the franc was in circulation in the French-speaking islands. US investment in the Panama Canal, in the sugar industry in Cuba and in oil refining in the southern Caribbean boosted economies and created employment opportunities that provoked considerable migration within the region. There were also long-standing trading relationships between ports in eastern Canada and in New England that exported foodstuff to the Caribbean.

The tidal wave of independence sentiment that swept the globe in the 1950s and 1960s produced noticeable changes in the arrangements of Caribbean governance and political interchange both within the region and with the rest of the world. In this chapter we explore the economic effects of changed political arrangements, and of national policies and regional and international agreements. There is distinct evidence of a Caribbean nation, defined by the nature and scope of economic and financial arrangements, which is emerging under the broken facade of unsuccessful integration schemes and trade agreements.

Human development in the Caribbean in the late 1940s

Bulmer-Thomas (2012) provides summary data on national income per capita in the early 1950s, along with comparisons between the Caribbean and other regions of the world (Tables 5.1 and 5.2). In 1950 the average for the Caribbean was only a quarter the average income for North America, one-third that for Oceania and half that for Western Europe, which was still recovering from the devastation of the World War II. Levels for individual islands or groups ranged from a high of US$1,157 for the Dutch Antilles to a low of US $83 for Haiti. The high income levels for the Dutch Antilles and for Trinidad and Tobago, which was third in the income rankings, were derived from the oil industry. They both refined Venezuelan crude oil, and Trinidad also

Table 5.1 National income per head, Caribbean

	National income per head	*Year*
Dutch Antilles	1157	1957
Puerto Rico	455	1954
T&T	332	1954
Cuba	279	1954
Guyana	262	1954
DR	255	1954
Suriname	239	1954
Fr Guyana	228	1955
Jamaica	221	1954
Barbados	209	1954
Belize	180	1946
Windward Is	128	1954
Leeward Is	126	1954
Haiti	83	1955

Source: Bulmer-Thomas (2012, Table 10.1, p. 261).

Table 5.2 Caribbean comparators

	Caribbean/other regions, 1950, %
World	111.5
W. Europe	52.8
Asia	378.5
Latam	89.5
N America	25.3
Oceania	31.1
Africa	260.4

Source: Bulmer-Thomas (2012, Table 10.1, p. 263).

exported locally produced crude. Puerto Rico owed its second place in the income rank to the success of Operation Bootstrap, the industrialisation strategy that brought US firms to take advantage of lower wage costs compared to the mainland (see Chapter 3). The main sugar-producing territories – Cuba, Guyana, the Dominican Republic, Jamaica and Barbados – were significantly less well off, while the banana-producing Lesser Antilles had even lower average incomes.

The low standards of living in the 1940s were reflected in health statistics. Life expectancy in the Caribbean ranged from a low of 45 and 49 years (male and female respectively) for Belize, to no more than 53 and 56 for Trinidad and Tobago, at a time when the white population of the US was registering life expectancy of 64 years for males and 70 years for females (Table 5.3). Rates of infant and maternal mortality were high, as was the incidence of infant malnutrition and low birth rate.

The exception to this unpromising picture was education. Thanks to the prevalence of free primary education Barbados enjoyed an adult literacy rate of 93 per cent in 1946, and rates for the English-speaking Caribbean were in the high seventies (as a percentage of the adult population), except for Dominica (65 per cent) and St Lucia (55 per cent).

Although the quality of life was far below North America and a devastated Europe, average incomes were much higher than for Africa and Asia. Life expectancy was higher than for Guatemala and Mauritius, both with life expectancies below 40 years in the 1940. Educational achievement in the Caribbean also compared favourably with the rest of the developing world.

There was little by way of economic linkages across the Caribbean in the late 1940s and 1950s. Trade and finance followed north-south patterns that had been characteristic of the region for centuries. The region's exports were destined mainly for the European countries to which they were linked by history, language and culture and, for Cuba, the Dominican Republic and Puerto Rico, to the US. The US was the main supplier of imports, with the European countries in second place, each country's trading partner as for exports. The financial sectors were integrated to a degree within language

Table 5.3 Life expectancy in the Caribbean, 1940s

	Male	*Female*
B'dos	49	53
BG (Guyana)	49	52
BH (Belize)	45	49
Leewards	50	55
T&T	53	56
Ja	51	55
Guatemala, 1939–41	36	37
Mauritius, 1942–6	32	34
Netherlands, 1937–40	66	67
NZ, 1934–8	65	68
Panama, 1941–3	51	53
US, whites	64	70
US, non-whites	56	50

Source: Bureau of Statistics, Jamaica (1950).

groups, by virtue of common links to a trading partner in Europe or North America. British and Canadian banks opened branches in all the English-speaking countries, and so did insurance companies. Following their lead, local insurance companies and some commercial companies spread their operations within the English-speaking area. These companies and the colonial services of the European countries offered some limited opportunities for migration within the language groups, for teachers, policemen and public service workers. Such emigration as there was, was mainly driven by economic opportunities, in the absence of official incentives. Trinidad's oil industry and the refineries of Aruba and Curacao attracted migrants from the south eastern Caribbean, and a large US naval base at Chaguaramas also generated formal and informal job opportunities which attracted workers from neighbouring countries to Trinidad. There was no significant intra-regional trade; neighbouring countries did trade small amounts of fruits and fresh produce, and most Caribbean ports featured colourful wharf-side markets in which these products were sold, but their contribution to countries' that were essentially commodity exporters was of little importance.

Trade patterns in the late 1940s

Comprehensive data provided by Bulmer-Thomas (2012) show the composition and direction of exports from all language groups in the Caribbean, including all the islands, Belize in Central America and the Guyanas on the northern littoral of South America. Exports of sugar and its by-products (molasses and rum), bananas, coffee, cacao and other agricultural products accounted for 75 per cent or greater of exports from most of the Caribbean. Exceptions included Trinidad and Tobago where exports of petroleum accounted for two-thirds of foreign earnings, with sugar providing another 13 percent; Suriname, with 60 per cent of export earnings from bauxite; and Guyana, where bauxite exports equivalent to 18 per cent of foreign earnings supplemented sugar exports, which were over 50 per cent. At this time Cuba was the only Caribbean country with a substantial tourist industry, based on the famed entertainments of the capital, Havana. Exports were directed mainly to what Bulmer-Thomas terms the "core" countries in Europe and North America, the UK, France, the Netherlands, the US and Canada. These were also the countries from which the Caribbean sourced all imports. Whereas exports were limited to a handful of items, imports covered the full range from basic foods such as wheat flour, rice and canned foods, through clothing and household appliances and supplies, to vehicles, equipment and fuels. Imports also included some products produced in the Caribbean, such as sugar, which were refined in the core countries for re-export to the Caribbean. Correcting this exploitative bias, termed the "Muscovado Bias" by economists of the Caribbean "Plantation Economy" school, was an obvious target of the policies of Caribbean economists in the early years of Caribbean Independence movements (Best and Levitt, 2009).

The Caribbean in the anti-colonial era, 1946–1960

The economic fortunes of Caribbean nations in the intermediate aftermath of the World War II were defined, as they have always been since the arrival of Europeans, by the politics of the relationships with the core countries. The economies of Cuba, Haiti, the Dominican Republic and Puerto Rico were linked to the US economy, in a two-way trading relationship. They exported almost exclusively to the US, from which they obtained their import requirements. Only Puerto Rico was formally incorporated into the US, in a special dependent relationship which affords the Puerto Ricans US citizenship but denies them representation in the US Congress, but the other three at this time featured autocratic governments that were under the tutelage of the US Government. The Bahamas also had a close two-way relationship with the US, thanks to the country's close proximity to the US state of Florida, even though the islands were at that time still a British colony.

Belize, the Guyanas and the Lesser Antilles, the small islands that define the eastern boundary of the Caribbean Sea, were colonies of the UK, France and the Netherlands Antilles. The colonial relationship determined the direction of their agricultural exports to the colonial centre and, in the case of the UK colonies, also to Canada, with which the English-speaking countries had long-standing trade and financial ties. Like the larger Caribbean countries, this group imported mostly from the US, as well as Canada, which were also the sources of much of the region's foreign direct investment. In contrast to agriculture, petroleum and bauxite exports were directed mainly to North America.

This period, prior to the assertion of their sovereignty by Cuba, Haiti and the Dominican Republic, and the independence of the Caribbean colonies of the European nations, witnessed the most transformative gains in the livelihoods of Caribbean populations. Rates of economic growth in the 1950s and 1960s were generally twice as high as in subsequent decades, life expectancies at birth rose from about 50 years to the mid-60s, and substantial gains were made in adult literacy rates, in those countries which had not already achieved full adult literacy in 1946. In most of the Caribbean there was only a tiny middle class in the 1940s, comprising artisans, shopkeepers, teachers, policemen and a small public service; by the 1960s a considerable middle income workforce was engaged in manufacturing and tourism, thanks to the skills which these occupations required.

The aftermath of the failure of the Federation of the British West Indies, 1958–62

It is against this economic background that economists evaluated the short-lived Federation of the British West Indies, after its failure in 1962. The Federation was considered the way forward for the British colonies in the Caribbean, at a time when European colonial empires were collapsing all around the world. In the Caribbean the process was contentious but not violent, and in Guyana, the only country in which violence did break out, the conflict was among the colonials, not with Britain. The governance of the colonies was gradually transferred from London, in a process which saw responsibilities transferred incrementally to local administrations. However, it was thought that the individual countries were too small to form viable economic entities, and that the only way to fully transfer sovereignty without compromising future economic prospects was as a single federal nation. I shall argue that, in retrospect, this was not far from the truth, but for rather different reasons than was believed at the time.

I began my undergraduate studies at the University of the West Indies (UWI) in September 1964, two years after the fateful Jamaican referendum which led to the dissolution of the Federation and the establishment of the independent nation of Jamaica. The ensuing decade was one of fertile economic debate at the University, which produced a flowering of research which the UWI has not subsequently been able to match, in quantity or lasting impact on regional thinking. The prevailing opinion, which I shared, was that the failure of the Federation was rooted in its evident irrelevance to the lives, livelihoods and life chances of the populations of any of its member countries. The argument that persuaded a majority of Jamaicans to vote to leave the Federation was based on a fear that resources were being drained from their country to support the struggling economies of the much smaller islands of the Eastern Caribbean, even though, in fact, those populations saw no evidence of such benefit.

The conclusion that was drawn was that efforts should be redoubled to establish regional integration on the basis of a sound economic foundation. In response an ambitious research project was established to explore economic possibilities and propose a strategy for the integration of trade and production, taking advantage of opportunities for vertical integration to increase value added in the region (Brewster and Thomas, 1967). The criteria for identifying the sectors that offered the greatest potential for integration included: the size and growth of the regional market for the product, the range of production possibilities in the region, the contribution that the sector might make to a switch away from low-skilled agriculture, the nature and extent of linkages with other industry, the proportion of local value added in final output and the sector's potential contribution to total output. The authors of the study conducted a regional industrial programming exercise based on regional demand for industrial products, per capita import demand (using data from Jamaica and Trinidad and Tobago, the region's largest economies), and using a cut-off based on a minimum feasible scale of production. They estimated the potential final demand for base materials which have the greatest potential for linkages. Their recommendation was for a development process which is initially geared to the regional market, protected by external trade policy, to lift regional productive capacity to a level of production and skill that would provide a platform for international competition, opening the way for exports. The study indicated that production of food products with high elasticity of demand, and of base materials with high potential for linkages, offered the richest potential for establishing this foundation for competitive industrial development in the region.

The authors evidently intended their study as one element in a more extensive strategy for the economic development of the Caribbean. They acknowledged the "extremely narrow scope" (Brewster and Thomas, 1967, p. 14) for trade creation of the type their study focused on. Its importance was for its potential to strengthen economic ties across the region, as a way of ensuring that the economic benefits of industrialization were widely shared. Their objective was also to address the fact that the attempt elsewhere in the Caribbean to imitate Puerto Rico's Operation Bootstrap (Chapter 3) by providing fiscal incentives and other inducements had failed to attract a volume of manufacturing to cities like Kingston, Jamaica, sufficient to absorb enough labour to lower unemployment and raise productivity in agriculture. The study envisaged further research on the potential for export of manufactured goods.

This landmark study received little attention from policy makers of countries which by this time were focussed narrowly on local economic activity and the management of national budgets. Leaders of Government and business remained committed to economic regionalism in principle, but even though a formal treaty was concluded in 1973 for the establishment of a Caribbean Economic Community (CARICOM) at the Chaguaramas Conference Centre in Trinidad – the site of what was formerly the southernmost US naval base in the Caribbean and so chosen for its symbolic significance – little of substance has come of the good intentions that motivated the treaty. The chronically underfunded secretariat was located in Guyana, economically and politically among the smallest and weakest of the member countries despite its size and natural resources. (The economy's size will increase by 50 per cent or more with the recent start of oil exports, but it will still be far smaller than the economies of Trinidad and Tobago and Jamaica.) Guyana also has poor telecommunications and weak transportation links with the rest of the region, especially the countries in the western Caribbean (Jamaica, The Bahamas and Belize). Furthermore, CARICOM has no executive powers; it acts only as secretariat and facilitator, but all decisions taken by the Heads of Government depend on individual members for their implementation.

After nearly two decades of frustration, with only patchy implementation of the regional free trade area, the very first step in the integration process, the Heads of Government of CARICOM countries set up a special West Indian Commission, chaired by Sir Shridath Ramphal, Secretary-General of the Commonwealth, and one of the Caribbean's leading statesmen, to assemble documentation, consult widely with people at all levels within the region, issue a status report and recommend reforms to make CARICOM an effective instrument of economic integration. I served as the Commission's

Director of Studies, and much of the research conducted for the Commission was published in Worrell and Farrell (1994), which is discussed in Chapter 11. A central recommendation was for the formation of a monetary union, with a Caribbean currency pegged irrevocably to the US dollar, supported by foreign reserves protected by fiscal and balance of payments funding limits imposed by a Caribbean Monetary Authority. Supplementary studies explored the implications of the common currency rules for government finances, employment, debt and adjustment policies. Suggestions were made for the institutional structure of the monetary authority and the process of transition to the common currency.

The Ramphal Commission's report *Time for Action* (1992) evaluated progress with implementation of the Treaty of Chaguaramas, which envisaged a single economic market of five million people. Intra-regional trade had increased from five per cent of total trade in 1967 to ten per cent in 1981, but had declined afterward. CARICOM's Common External Tariff was in effect in eight states with 92 per cent of the region's population. The CARICOM Multilateral Credit Facility, a regional clearing arrangement that allowed for regional payments in local currency with quarterly net settlements in US dollars, had failed after less than five years of operation, and US dollars were needed for all regional payments once more. An Oils and Fats Agreement for regional trading in edible oils had also failed. Strangely, in the face of such weakness, the CARICOM Heads of Government had set even more lofty ambitions for the region in the Grande Anse Declaration, signed in Grenada in 1989. The ostensible objective was now a single market, with financial integration and monetary union added to the objectives. The Commission registered comprehensive failure to follow through on treaty commitments, which it attributed to the facts that regional arrangements lack a direct democratic content, and that the civil services of member countries lacked personnel, expertise, budget and motivation for the implementation of regional initiatives. The Commission's recommendations included free convertibility of regional currencies, freedom of movement of labour throughout the region, full implementation of the Common External Tariff, tripartite consultations between governments, labour and management representatives, the establishment of development banks to provide equity and new regional governance structures, including establishing three posts of CARICOM Commissioner, on the model of the European Union.

The Ramphal Commission marked the last credible effort to revive CARICOM as a functional entity that influenced policy and economic performance in any of its member countries. A token secretariat still exists, with its main function to arrange meetings of the heads of Government of the members and a variety of consultative bodies. These meetings are valuable, because they are the catalyst for the growth within the region of professional and personal linkages and networks on environmental, energy-related, educational, judicial, economic and social issues. However, while these networks are useful for information sharing, they have no fixed budgets, no permanent staff, and no administrative or executive functions.

In the 30 years since the Commission issued its report there have been numerous studies and reports on aspects of regional integration. The most recent is Hall and Chuck-a-Sang (2022), a volume whose main value is to provide a brief but comprehensive summary of the frustrating history of efforts for regional economic integration.

My own contributions to the post-Commission literature included Worrell (1991) which analysed the coordination of fiscal policies between countries participating in a monetary union, using simulations for four members of CARICOM – Barbados, Guyana, Jamaica and Trinidad and Tobago. The simulations were to inform the use of fiscal tools to balance external payments and stabilise the exchange rate, thereby creating the conditions for deepening the monetary union. The target for the simulations was to secure adequate levels of foreign reserves, along with significant GDP growth and inflation that was no higher than world inflation. Policy tools that were used in the simulation included the ratio of income taxes to national income, the ratio of expenditure taxes rate to GDP, and the ratio of total Government expenditure to GDP. Barbados, Jamaica and Trinidad and Tobago were judged to have had feasible but costly options for stabilising external payments, but Guyana did not, and the study concluded that the local currency could be expected to depreciate further. With respect to the overall prospects for CARICOM, the study concluded that divergent growth and inflation are tolerable within limits, provided the GDP in all four countries were trending in the same direction. Fiscal uniformity is difficult to achieve even in unitary states, and it was not necessary to align tax and expenditure policies everywhere within the region. A practical and effective alternative would be to harmonise policies among countries in a measured but consistent way, over time.

Worrell (1998) shows why the liberalisation of exchange markets among CARICOM countries is impractical in the absence of a common regime for all participants with respect to transactions in US dollars. Everywhere within the region there was a preference for saving in US dollars, to protect values against the possibility of devaluation of local currencies. However, some CARICOM member countries retained limitations of one kind or another on unrequited transfers (those for which there was no purchase of goods or services). If those limits were removed for transfers to CARICOM members which had no such limitations, this would provide an obvious indirect avenue for savers to evade limitations on conversions to US currency. The paper also listed other barriers to financial integration within the region, including differences in the structure of the corporation tax, poor information about investment opportunities, limited investment opportunities in traditional activities, the high risks associated with innovative activities, legal and administrative inefficiencies and pervasive uncertainty about the exchange rates of all regional currencies except those of the Bahamas and the Eastern Caribbean Currency Union.

There have been efforts, even more feeble than CARICOM, to provide a more inclusive framework of regional cooperation, with membership of non-English-speaking independent nations in the Caribbean, and CARICOM itself has expanded to include Creole and French-speaking Haiti and multilingual Suriname, which uses Dutch as the official language. The most all-embracing is the Association of Caribbean States (ACS), a vestigial organisation with headquarters in Port-of-Spain, Trinidad, which embraces the insular Caribbean as well as countries on the littoral in Central and South America. The ACS is little known, even in the Caribbean. CARIFORUM, the other wider regional association, is an artificial construct, consisting of CARICOM and the Dominican Republic, for the sole purpose of interfacing with the European Union, which treats the group as a single unit.

The earlier concept of regional integration, reflected in Brewster and Thomas (1967), as a strategy for enhancing the Caribbean's competitiveness in the wider world has now all been lost. The idea of building a competitive Caribbean manufacturing sector as a platform for penetrating world markets faced formidable obstacles of long-standing large-scale investment in production, transportation, finance and other services geared towards raw material exports to traditional markets in the Northern Hemisphere, obstacles which were never addressed. The fragmentation of their individual industrial development policies doomed the efforts of most small CARICOM member countries, which might have stood some chance of success had there been sufficient resources devoted to building an integrated regional production capability.

The region's economic fortunes were made worse by the atrophy of existing cooperative institutions for the production of sugar, rum and other by-products. At the height of Caribbean sugar production in the 1950s and 1960s the English-speaking countries boasted regional organisations and cooperative arrangements for the production, marketing, financing, research and development of sugar and its by-products, a collective treasury of experience and expertise, which, with enlightened leadership in the industry and in official circles, might have transformed Caribbean agriculture into a competitive activity, with the use of modern technologies.

The international competitive success of the Caribbean, which rests mainly with tourism, owes little to official policy, and nothing to regional cooperative efforts. The influential Caribbean Tourism Organisation, an authoritative source of data on tourism in the region, is funded mainly by private sector members. There is no comparable institution for other exports of goods and services.

Ironically, the Caribbean has become more integrated socially, culturally and, on a sub-regional basis, economically, at the same time that the official institutions have lost their credibility. The region has developed a small but remunerative cultural industry that fuels economic activity of Caribbean people in ways which economic statistics do not record. The region boasts an entertainment industry whose competitiveness is attested to by luminaries in music, sport, literature and art, and by festivals and events that attract attention worldwide. These all provide income flows which contribute to the well-being of Caribbean populations through a variety of channels, by practitioners who travel frequently and who may or may not reside in the Caribbean.

Opportunities for migration within the region, to the mutual benefit of sending and receiving countries, have grown in response to employment opportunities, even though the limited and impossibly bureaucratic formal arrangements for intra-regional migration have proven completely ineffective. The costs and productivity of immigrant labour for construction and agriculture in the region's better-performing economies is so superior to what is available locally that companies can offer affordable prices only with the help of immigrant labour, which pervades these industries, the limitations of official policies notwithstanding.

There has been an intensification of financial integration within the Caribbean (Worrell and Jhinkoo, 2009). The financial systems of regional member countries were already integrated in 1946, thanks to the regional spread of British and Canadian banks, as well as insurance companies with branches across the regional, some headquartered in the UK and Canada, but several of regional provenance. Worrell and Jhinkoo used measures of financial integration – the incidence of cross-border ownership, evidence of arbitrage on regional stock exchanges, the ratio of intra-regional bank balances to the total outstanding, and evidence of convergence of interest rates of member countries of CARICOM – to provide an assessment of the strengthening of financial integration in recent decades. Every one of the indicators shows evidence of financial deepening: the largest Caribbean firms have networks covering many countries, the stock exchanges of Jamaica and Trinidad and Tobago (the only ones still active) show evidence that the prices of obligations of firms that are traded in both markets are consistent, and there appears to be some interest rate convergence among countries that have maintained fixed pegs to the US dollar. The evidence suggests that financial links are stronger between neighbours than for more distant CARICOM member countries.

Economies in the shadow of an economic giant

The facts of geography dictate that the Caribbean has an America destiny, and the economic weight of the US makes it inevitable that the region's economic fortunes depend on the nature of its relationships with that country. The Caribbean is tightly bound to USA and Canada by trade, tourism, finance, business services, investment and capital flows, migration, language, cultural affinity and history. The US is the focal point of Caribbean convergence, of interest rates and prices (Worrell, 1993). The evolution of the relationship is a process that has proceeded at varying speeds, depending on history and institutional arrangements. Not surprisingly, given the differences in size, the Caribbean has had little agency in shaping the terms of the relationship. It may however be argued that the Caribbean has not used the unequal relationship to its best advantage because of the pursuit of futile attempts to resist American influence, rather than find ways to take advantage of the relationship to further the goals of the Caribbean people.

The most wrong-headed aspect of this policy has been the insistence of all Caribbean nations on maintaining separate local currencies, with freedom to determine their values in terms of the US dollar, and to pursue independent monetary policies. This has never been an option for economies as small as those of the Caribbean, even if they were successful in forming a monetary union. The persistence of discussion of exchange rate options for Caribbean countries (and other SOEs) is evidence of cognitive dissonance in intellectual and policy circles, internationally, a subject to which we turn our attention in Chapter 14. The reality is that maintenance of an irretrievable peg to the US dollar is the policy which enables Caribbean economies to secure the best terms of trade for the exchange of the products and services it sells internationally for the imports that sustain the region's economies. My own proposal for a Caribbean currency union (Worrell, 1994) recognised this reality, and proposed that the union be set up with institutional arrangements to ensure that the regional currency would be pegged to the US dollar by means of a store of foreign reserves fed by open market operations by the regional central bank whenever necessary. More recently, with the abandonment of the regional monetary integration project, I have advocated for the full dollarisation of the regional economies, a prospect which now appears inevitable, even if governments choose to continue to drag their feet (Worrell, 2021a).

The 1990s saw a surge in interest in bilateral and multilateral free trade areas. Worrell (1992), evaluated the probable impact of a CARICOM free trade agreement with US, concluding that such an agreement would not materially affect the challenges and opportunities of Caribbean economies. The analysis was based on the estimated gains from removal of tariffs on Caribbean textiles, plus gains from lower inflation in the Caribbean as a result of lower tariffs on imports. The Caribbean was already highly penetrated by US exports and effective rates of protection in the Caribbean were already low and falling. The challenges facing Caribbean exporters had nothing to do with market access; the main problem was that productivity increases were not keeping pace with increases in real incomes. External economic linkages of CARICOM countries were already mainly with the US, through tourism and other export services, the use of the US dollar for all regional and external pricing and international transfers, and the fact that interest rates and banking and financial markets were linked to the US market.

Worrell (1993) recommended that the Caribbean take action to influence US-Caribbean relationship to the region's best advantage, rather than trying to swim against the tide. The paper suggested that particular emphasis be given to effective regional representation at the World Trade Organization, the Pan American Health Organization, the Interamerican Development Bank and others. However, these initiatives were of secondary importance compared with the economic benefits that would follow from policies to increase competitiveness, raise productivity and peg exchange rates to the US dollar in order to gain credibility for domestic policy. The study concluded that economic links between the Caribbean and North America remain strong under all circumstances. The Caribbean has options for negotiation, despite the constraints of relative size, with respect to non-trade barriers for specific products, managing the monopoly power of US companies, and with the negotiation of environmental policies and other externalities. The convergence of prices and interest rates on US benchmarks is a benefit because it fosters Caribbean economic integration. In contrast economic links between the Caribbean and Latin America remain very weak, and there is no activity that offers much prospect for deepening that relationship.

The Caribbean and the rest of the world

The impact of the growth of highly competitive Chinese exports to world markets has had a profound effect on Caribbean economies, though imports bought directly from China and Chinese investment have been modest, compared with investment and imports from North America and Europe. Worrell (2021b) estimates that "the purchase of more affordable products from China has afforded the Caribbean additional imports of the order of five to ten per cent, compared with what the same money would have bought from alternative sources" (Worrell, 2021b, p. 689). This is the best estimate that can be made of the order of magnitude of the impact, because most of these Chinese-made goods were imported indirectly from American, European or other sources. The estimate also took into account products from these sources that use Chinese-made components. In addition, the superior productivity of Chinese firms has dramatically reduced the cost of solar photo-voltaic and wind power sources, making of the abundant sunshine and reliable trade winds of the Caribbean a new natural resource that is, in the long term, more valuable than fossil fuels, because supplies are inexhaustible (Worrell, 2018). Chinese investments in the Caribbean have been few but they have major potential economic impact. They include a large hotel complex in The Bahamas, a major expansion in the Kingston port to take advantage of transshipment business from the recently widened Panama Canal, and a highway linking the tourist resorts of the northern coast of Jamaica with the capital, Kingston.

The assessment – the unrecognised Caribbean nation

What emerges from an overview of Caribbean economies today is a picture of exceptional achievement by the people of the region in virtually every field of human endeavour, and the achievement of levels of living in the region that, with few exceptions, are not far short of those typical of countries in Europe and North America. In contrast, the landscape of policy and governance is one of unrelieved failure to attain the often lofty intentions of the region's independent nation-states. The results of this dichotomy are reflected in the fact that few of the region's overachievers make their homes in the Caribbean, and their contributions to the Caribbean, in its widest sense, are under-reported as a result.

In order to fully appreciate the sources of improvements in Caribbean well-being, it is helpful to think of the Caribbean as including the diaspora, up to now mainly in North America and Europe, but increasingly spreading to the Middle East, Asia and elsewhere. It is not only that the diaspora already contribute in measurable ways to Caribbean economies, through remittances and the incomes of retirees; perhaps even more important are the unmeasured benefits, through the provision by the diaspora of accommodation and other services in kind to residents and travellers from the Caribbean, and the novel and informal channels of international commerce from the region which the diaspora makes possible.

The diaspora is also perhaps the most powerful instrument of integration of the Caribbean nation. Its global centre is New York City, and the borough of Brooklyn in particular, the largest urban concentration of Caribbean people from all language groups. It therefore offers a richer blend of Caribbean cultures, including music, festivals, cuisine, art and literature, than may be found anywhere in the Caribbean region. The Caribbean diaspora is the economic driver that ensures the longevity of the Trinidad Carnival, and similar street festivals throughout the region. The diaspora is the main market for cultural practitioners who make a living from their skills, and for many foods and other products from the region.

This wider concept of the Caribbean nation also turns on its head the concept of the "brain drain", the emigration from the region of a majority of its best minds. Rather than as a loss to the region, the brain drain proves to be a rich source of skills and experience, providing opportunities for advancement and enrichment of knowledge and skills, way beyond what is available in their small Caribbean homelands. The homeland benefits in many ways, through the market opportunities which the more affluent diaspora can provide, and through the transfers of skills which returning emigrants bring with them. So far, limited networks of cooperation have developed, through joint ventures between residents and emigrants, and forward-looking firms in the Caribbean have recruited from the diaspora for top executive positions, with good results.

Sadly, misguided migration policy and non-recognition of the ways in which the diaspora is integral to the Caribbean economy are issues in which the region's policy makers have shown a lack of vision, and a failure to recognise an opportunity with major economic potential. In contrast to the progressive private sector, the Caribbean public sector is most reluctant to recruit from the diaspora, and, on the few occasions that they do reach out, the poor remuneration on offer in Caribbean public services means they can seldom attract and retain the services of candidates of high calibre who have mastered their craft to internationally competitive levels. The problem of uncompetitive public sector remuneration, particularly acute at executive levels, is one which will not be addressed without thorough-going reform of the organisation and staffing of Caribbean public services.

Policies that facilitate the widening and strengthening of links between the Caribbean and its diaspora, including the removal of tariffs on telecommunications, promoting exchange programmes with health and educational institutions, negotiating visa-free travel, and the elimination of obsolete stipulations restricting the recruitment from abroad, could be used to enhance benefits to the region from engagement with the diaspora. The diaspora could be the catalyst for productivity increases in the public and private sectors; emigration is a useful vent for relieving pressures for job creation and a source of motivation for ambitious young people, eager to achieve mastery of their chosen field; emigration also provides local educational authorities with benchmarks for evaluating the quality of their graduates, because those who fall short of the requirements for the international market will find they have only the limited opportunities the local market offers.

Migration may offer a practical way to fund social insurance schemes for an aging population; opening a competitive international market to the local workforce should increase productivity and real wages, with a corresponding improvement in yields from the social security contribution. At the same time, a large proportion of retirees will be returning locals who will invariably be recipients of benefits from abroad, and will have neither the entitlement nor need to call on the domestic scheme.

These observations are intended only to give a flavour of what is possible, given the talents, natural endowments, international networks and resources of skills and knowledge available to Caribbean countries that could make the Caribbean nation, in its widest sense, a world leader in the quality of lifestyles of its peoples. Much of the raw material for the realization of a new era of regional prosperity is already in evidence. What is lacking, in the leadership of business, government, the media and academia, is a practical vision of the policies, organisational, administrative and regulatory institutions, and research, knowledge and communication that is needed to make a coherent regional strategy of the unquestionable potential of the Caribbean and its peoples.

References

Best, Lloyd and Kari Levitt. 2009. *Essays on the Plantation Economy.* Kingston, Jamaica: University of the West Indies Press.

Brewster, Havelock and Clive Thomas. 1967. *The Dynamics of West Indian Integration.* Kingston Jamaica: Institute of Social and Economic Research, University of the West Indies.

Bulmer-Thomas, Victor. 2012. *The Economic History of the Caribbean since the Napoleonic Wars.* Cambridge: Cambridge University Press.

Bureau of Statistics, Jamaica. 1950. "West Indian Census 1946, Part A: General Report on the Census of Population," Kingston, July 11.

Hall, Kenneth and Myrtle Chuck-a-Sang (eds). 2022. *Caribbean Integration.* Georgetown, Guyana: The Integrationist.

West Indian Commission, The. 1992. *Time for Action: The Report of the Commission.* Black Rock, Barbados: The Commission.

Worrell, DeLisle. 2021a. "The time has come to permanently retire all our Caribbean currencies," *Studies in Applied Economics*, no. 179, April.

Worrell, DeLisle. 2021b. "Measuring China's economic impact in the Caribbean," *Global Discourse: An Interdisciplinary Journal of Current Affairs.* Vol. 11, no. 4, pp. 679–692.

Worrell, DeLisle. 2018. Inaugural Confucius Institute Lecture. The University of the West Indies, Cave Hill, Barbados, January.

Worrell, DeLisle. 1998. "Capital market integration: Capital controls and exchange rate stability," *Social and Economic Studies.* Vol. 47, nos. 2 & 3.

Worrell, DeLisle. 1994. "A common currency for the Caribbean," in *Caribbean Monetary Integration*, edited by Terrence Farrell and DeLisle Worrell. Port-of-Spain, Trinidad: Caribbean Information Systems and Services.

Worrell, DeLisle. 1993. "Economic integration with unequal partners: The Caribbean and North America," *Working Paper.* Washington, D.C.: Woodrow Wilson International Center for Scholars.

Worrell, DeLisle. 1992. "US-Caricom free trade," in *The Premise and the Promise: Free Trade in the Americas*, by Sylvia Saborio and Contributors. Washington, DC: The Overseas Development Council.

Worrell, DeLisle. 1991. "National fiscal policy and regional economic cooperation in the Caribbean," in *Public Finance with Several Levels of Government*, edited by Remy Prudhomme. The Hague: International Institute of Public Finance.

Worrell, DeLisle and Terrence Farrell. 1994. *Caribbean Monetary Integration.* Port of Spain, Trinidad: Caribbean Information Systems and Services.

Worrell, DeLisle and Julia Jhinkoo. 2009. "Financial integration in the Caribbean," *Working Paper.* St Augustine, Trinidad: Caribbean Centre for Money and Finance, December.

Section B

Monetary, Fiscal, Financial and Exchange Rate Policy in the Small Open Economy

The most consequential policy failures in SOEs in the past 50 years have been the result of faulty economic analysis, based on misapprehensions about how these economies work. The conventional wisdom, reflected in the analyses and reports of the IMF, the most widely known and quoted source of macroeconomic policy advice, is that SOEs should be managed in the same manner and using the same tools as all other economies: with monetary policy aimed to control the rate of inflation, an exchange rate that equilibrates the supply and demand for foreign exchange, and a fiscal policy whose effects on the macroeconomy are neutral over the economic cycle. The chapters in this section are a capsule of my research establishing that these views are based on a misrepresentation of the economic reality of modern SOEs.

In the modern era, starting in the late 1960s, business, social and familial ties across national borders have intensified to the point where capital controls cannot be employed to ration cross-border financial flows. Since then, SOEs have been unable to sustain an independent exchange rate policy through intervention by the monetary authority on the foreign exchange market. This is because the local currency in the SOE is an inferior money: the country's exports and imports are all priced in foreign currency, mainly US dollars, and increases in the US dollar price of local currency is the main source of domestic price inflation. There is therefore an overwhelming preference for US dollars by financial savers. As a result, there is a chronic unsatisfied demand for foreign exchange, and the exchange rate never stabilises unless the local currency is locked into a fixed value in terms of US dollars (or euros, for small countries in the neighbourhood of the European Union). If that is the case, domestic savers who have no access to foreign savings at the prevailing exchange rate will be content to maintain local currency savings, confident that when they come to deploy those savings, their value will not have been eroded by depreciation in the value of domestic currency. However, if they are not confident of the durability of the peg, savers will use every avenue to convert savings to foreign currency. The consequence is that the exchange rate of the SOE is effectively pegged, and the scope for monetary policy is very limited.

DOI: 10.4324/9781003247609-7

With the exchange rate pegged to the US dollar (or the euro), the domestic interest rate in the SOE is determined as the comparable US rate plus the country risk premium. If the central bank intervenes to lower domestic rates, for example by issuing public debt, there will be an outflow of funds: companies would borrow local currency in preference to more expensive trade credit, and companies and wealthy individuals will have an incentive to hold working balances in foreign currency. Conversely, should the central bank buy government debt in an effort to raise interest rates, we should expect an inflow of finance, all others things being equal. Countervailing cross-border financial flows are set in motion, in either case, which nullify the intended effect of the central bank initiative.

However, the reaction to central bank intervention is typically more complicated and the responses asymmetrical. All too often, central bank's purchases of government debt cause an outflow of finance rather than the expected inflow. That happens whenever the market believes that the public sector deficit is too large to be sustained, and that there is a risk that any gain from the interest margin over foreign rates may be wiped out by an imminent devaluation of domestic money. In effect, the risk-adjusted return on investment falls because the central bank's action confirms market apprehensions and increases the country risk premium by more than the expected marginal return.

The practical implication of these circumstances is that policy makers in SOEs do not have the policy choices that are assumed by the conventional model, and summarised in the well-known Mundell-Fleming trilemma. This thesis states that policy makers can sustain a fixed peg and an independent monetary policy only by limiting cross border financial flows. If the policy maker lacks the tools to inhibit cross-border financial flows, they should allow the exchange rate to find its market level and use interest rates as the tool to manage financial flows. However, for reasons just explained the market for foreign exchange will not settle until the entire amount of domestic savings is converted to foreign currency at a rate so low that it drives domestic inflation to a level which severely depresses real domestic income.

The above circumstances are what is meant when one refers to structural features which render the conventional suite of policies for stabilising the economy and controlling inflation ineffective in the small open economy. The policy tools which remain, and which will be shown to be effective, are the allocation and management of government expenditure, taxation policy, government borrowing and the management of public debt.

A more fundamental challenge for macroeconomic policy is the design of economic strategies to stimulate faster growth of the economy. The economics literature suggests that growth potential may depend on the endowment of human and natural resources, the extent of training and skills, the assimilation of new technology and other factors that affect the use and productivity of the available land, labour and financial resources. It is evident that government policies will affect growth in significant ways, whatever the nature, size and role of the government. The elements of the policy mix, the relationships between them, and the factors that make for faster and slower growth are complex and their effects controversial. The practice in recent decades has been to boil these down to recommendations on legislative reform and the liberalisation of markets for products, labour and finance.

What is important, for our argument, is to recognise that government's expenditure, taxation and financial policies will have a major – perhaps decisive – impact on economic growth, which will usually be their most consequential impact on the material well-being of the population. Fiscal policy, defined in this way, should at one and the same time be designed to stimulate the sustained growth of the economy in the longer term, while ensuring a balance of foreign currency inflows and outflows in the shorter term. Monetary policy has a subsidiary role to play in this exercise, and the policy-maker has to bear in mind that short-term economic and financial instability is a factor which may inhibit investment and reduce growth potential in the longer term. Successful stabilisation policy can be a stimulus to long-term growth.

We shall unpack this multi-faceted relationship between macroeconomic policy, sustainable economic growth and economic stabilisation in stages in Sections B and C of this volume. The chapters in Section B provide the framework for understanding the economic structures of the SOE, how they are different from large economies that can be more self-sustaining, what are the variables that are critical for investment and stable, sustainable growth and how government policies may impact the outcome. The discussion in this section also covers the implications of size for openness, production diversification and international competitiveness, and how policy should be calibrated in the SOE. Chapter 6 sets out the theoretical framework, and shows how it compares with conventional frameworks. Chapter 7 explains the use of fiscal policy to manage aggregate demand and lend predictability to exchange rate expectations. Chapter 8 addresses the impact of fiscal policy on competitiveness and growth. Chapter 9 expands on the role of monetary policy in the SOE. The importance of financial stability and its relation to economic growth is the burden of Chapter 10. Chapter 11 is devoted to a discussion of currency unions, the pros and cons of full dollarisation and the ways in which digital money is changing the financial landscape.

6 A Policy Model for Stabilization and Growth in the Small Open Economy (SOE)

This chapter presents a behavioural model which incorporates the distinguishing features of small open economies (SOEs): their growth depends on investment in the capacity to produce internationally competitive tradable goods and services, sold abroad at ruling world prices; there is no substitutability between the tradables they sell to earn foreign exchange, the imports they need to sustain production and lifestyles, and government services and other nontradables; and their financial markets cannot be insulated from the international financial markets which enable their external commerce, the lifeblood of their economies. The key to successful policies for stable growth and long-term prosperity in SOEs is fiscal policy designed to manage aggregate demand with a view to external balance and a stable exchange rate, while at the same time deploying tax, expenditure and government borrowing policies to sustain and improve international competitiveness. In this chapter the effectiveness of this strategy is brought to light with the use of the SOE-specific model, and its conclusions are compared with conventional wisdom.

Despite decades-long efforts to increase their appeal and acceptance, programmes of financial assistance offered by the IMF are regarded with suspicion, even fear, by most of the Fund's member countries. Perhaps the most disliked feature of the standard suite of IMF conditionalities is that the exchange rate should be managed flexibly, instead of being anchored on the US dollar or other internationally acceptable currency. The reason for this recommendation, which is inappropriate for the small open economy, lies with a crucial weakness in the economic model which is at the heart of standard IMF analysis. This weakness, pointed out by Agénor and Montiel (2008), requires a modification of the standard model, with the introduction of a specification providing for three goods – exports, imports and nontraded goods. The present chapter describes a three-goods model, with structural equations for output and prices, the balance of payments, finance and investment, and the accounts of the public sector. The model is articulated to highlight the tools available to policy makers, including government's tax, expenditure and financing policies, interest and exchange rate policies, and direct intervention in the trade, labour and financial markets. We evaluate the impact of each policy on economic

DOI: 10.4324/9781003247609-8

outcomes, and deduce what are the most effective tools for growth and stabilisation in small open economies.

What people care about is their material well-being

Economists are aware that GDP growth is not really reflective of the quality of life in any society. For many years the GDP was the only metric we had of the economy as a whole that was widely available for all countries. However, for the past three decades we have had a superior measure, published every year for all countries, in the form of the *Human Development Index* (HDI). Economic policy should aim to improve the material well-being of the population, and the HDI is the best measure of material well-being we have, so that needs to be the indicator by which the success of economic policy is gauged.

The real per capita GDP is one of three elements in the HDI; the reported GDP figure is adjusted for the fact that the same income purchases different amounts of any basket of goods in different countries. Beyond the impact of economic policies on the real GDP per capita at purchasing power parity, the policy maker needs to take account of the impact of policies on educational achievement and on health services, the two other elements of the HDI (see Chapter 17).

The model presented in this chapter is behavioural. Every economy is the aggregate of the production and exchange of all goods and services among the population and with the rest of the world. How much is produced and the prices at which exchange takes place depend on the behaviour of economic agents and the factors that motivate that behaviour. The objective of economic policy should be to influence the behaviour of economic agents in ways that result in an improved quality of life.

The model presented in this chapter does not intend to represent market equilibrium of any kind. Modern economies operate by fixed price contracts, explicit or implicit, of varying lengths. The price of bananas in the supermarket should be considered an implicit contract to sell the product at the advertised price so long as that price is displayed. Very little business in a modern economy is conducted in markets where negotiations between agents with equal economic power and with full information about the product by all parties, produces an agreed price. We do not need to employ concepts of markets and equilibrium in the construction of the model described in this chapter. Instead we try to describe the way economic agents actually behave, as may be observed in day to day activity.

An intuitive summary of the model

How do we improve the material well-being of the population of an SOE? By enhancing the economy's capacity to produce internationally competitive goods and services to be sold to provide foreign currency income, while at the same time monitoring health outcomes and educational achievements to ensure there is improvement in both. The foreign currency income allows the population to purchase the range and variety of imports a modern SOE needs for consumption and investment.

We will return to the health and educational elements when we come to discuss the tools available to the policy maker for achieving and maintaining a prosperous economy. Ours is an economic model, to elaborate on policies to grow real GDP; the relationships between government expenditure and health and education are direct, and there is not much that an economist can contribute to their evaluation, other than from the point of view of value for money. The relationship between economic policy and the growth of real income, in contrast, is the subject of ongoing controversy and debate among economists and economic policy makers. That relationship needs therefore to be fully elaborated.

The key to growth in an SOE is to nurture and develop the products and services in which the country has an established international competitive advantage and to follow up selectively on clues as to coming activities which show promise for sales to foreigners, given the society's endowments. International competitiveness is the key that unlocks the potential for the growth of exports, tourism and other services. The SOE is an atomistic producer of any product or service offered to the rest of the world. It may sell an unlimited amount at the ruling international price, and it will do so, up to the point where marginal sellers fail to make a profit sufficient to keep them in business. The way to increase sales and foreign currency earnings is by increasing the productivity of labour and other domestic factors, and by adding value to established products that are being sold competitively at ruling world prices.

We should dispense with two common misperceptions before moving on. Competitiveness is about giving value for money; it is not about price. The reason wealthy US customers purchase German and Japanese luxury cars in preference to domestic brands, notwithstanding the price, is that they believe they are getting better value for money. Most consumers will purchase the most expensive cell phone they can afford, not the cheapest on offer, for the same reason. The notion that a lower price makes a product – or an economy – more competitive is as erroneous as it is pervasive.

A second common misapprehension is that SOEs may increase foreign earnings by diversifying their economies away from traditional exports and tourism. This is almost never a realistic option, for obvious reasons. If exporters and providers of tourist and other services cannot succeed in the international markets they know well, the chances of successfully making inroads with unfamiliar products and services in the face of established competition are low. The key to continuing growth of faltering foreign exchange sectors is investment in productivity increases and value enhancement. Healthy and growing foreign currency sectors can provide the resources for exploration of ancillary activities and new directions for exports. In time these may grow to importance, and official policy in support of selective initiatives of this kind is fully justified. However, to suggest that any such investments will offer a new major stream of foreign earnings within the medium term is unrealistic in most circumstances.

The investment equation is central to the economic model, particularly investment in the tradable sector, because investment in increasing labour productivity in the tradable sector, and in widening the market appeal of tradables, increases the supply of growth-enhancing foreign currency. The observation of full capacity in tourism, exports and other foreign earning sectors is a signal that attracts potential investors. Whether their interest materialises into actual investment depends on the cost of inputs, unit labour costs, labour productivity and finance costs, all things which determine whether the investor's return will be competitive with alternative uses of his funds. In addition, the investor is always betting on an uncertain future, so he values low inflation and stable labour and financial markets, things which help to minimise investment risks.

Next we move on to output of tradables, the bulk of which will be exported. The world will buy as much as the SOE can supply of products and services that are appropriately priced for the quality they offer. That amount, with the existing capacity of hotel accommodation and available production facilities, depends on labour, material and finance costs. The amount produced of tradables is fully determined on the supply side.

In contrast, the amount that is produced of nontradable services, such as the distribution of consumer goods, construction and personal services, depends on the producers' expectations of what domestic consumers will set out to purchase in the coming financial year, and how much they can afford to pay for each item or unit of service. Producers set a target output, explicit in the budgets of larger and better organised firms, implicit for most small enterprises and sole proprietors, and prices are advertised in expectation that all that is produced can be sold at that price.

The price that is set depends on the amount to be supplied and costs for labour, supplies and finance to supply that output. If the projected demand is very high it may be necessary to hire extra staff, buy additional equipment, extend working hours or take other measures to ramp up production, all of which will incur additional cost. Conversely, weakening demand may lead to layoffs and idling of equipment, in order to cut costs and secure the continuing viability of the business. In this way, the amount actually produced and sold is determined by both demand and supply. Notice that this realistic behavioural relationship does not require any appeal to notions of markets or equilibrium.

Our next task is to find out whether the external accounts will be in balance with the expected levels of investment and output. The principal inflows are tourist spending, revenue from the sale of exports and foreign finance for investment. Tourist spending and export receipts are derived directly from the output of tradables, multiplied by the established international prices (in US dollars) at which these products and services are sold. The foreign finance for investment, as we shall explain later, is equal to the value of equipment, materials and other imported inputs for investment projects. Other inflows that are of major significance in some countries are workers' remittances and income of retirees who have lived and worked abroad.

External payments will be in balance if these inflows are sufficient to pay for imports which consumers are expected to purchase and which producers will require, as well as to cover service costs on foreign loans and accumulated foreign investment.

If inflows are larger than outflows, the surplus accrues to the country, usually via the central bank (where there is one) in the form of foreign reserves, which are invested with the Federal Reserve Bank of New York, on deposit or for investment in obligations of the US Treasury. The anomaly that SOEs so often celebrate the volume of foreign currency they lend to the US Government, surpluses that would be better employed in creating additional export capacity, is one of the great puzzles of economics. In reality, those funds would be more productively employed in investment in tradables, apart from a minimum amount needed to maintain stability in the market for US dollars.

In the event that inflows of foreign currency fall short of payments for imports, foreign debt service and other outflows by a substantial amount or over several successive years, economic policy makers in SOEs need to take action. In such cases there is a danger that the country's foreign reserves held with the US Federal Reserve will eventually be exhausted, no matter how large they might be. What is more, any unexpectedly large fall in reserves creates apprehension about the value of the local currency among agents in the foreign exchange market; in these circumstances, the defensive financial strategies which banks, investors and international companies adopt add to the pressure on the foreign exchange market. This attracts the attention of speculators who see a sure thing in betting against the local currency. The inevitable result is to exhaust the foreign reserve stockpile, much sooner than the economic circumstances warrant.

The way to avert this sequence of events is to take decisive fiscal action no matter the source of the shock that caused the foreign reserves to fall in the first place. The fiscal contraction, by way of tax increases, cuts in expenditure – less additional foreign borrowing if the country's external credit rating is strong – must be sufficient to fully restore the level of foreign reserves through a large enough cut in imports. It is wise to make the calculation under pessimistic assumptions; if things turn out as expected, there will then be some extra fiscal space to ramp up tradable investment directly or through incentives to private investors. This course of action immediately stabilises foreign currency markets, which is essential if policy makers are to avoid uncertainty and contentious foreign exchange behaviour which ultimately cause a sacrifice of investment and economic growth.

We need now to consider which fiscal tools to employ, and what magnitude of fiscal contraction is called for. The ways in which government taxation, spending and financing affect the economy's appetite for aggregate expenditure and imports are complex, and in practice the fiscal strategy must be executed via a process of action, review and assessment, with corrective measures as necessary. Factual information on progress to the stabilisation goals should be provided to the public at regular intervals, to reassure market agents that adjustment is being diligently pursued and that balance can be restored to the external accounts within the stated time frame.

This procyclical fiscal approach seems much harsher than the standard prescription. In fact, it is not. The reality for the SOE is that imports have to be accommodated to the available foreign exchange if the country is to avoid impairing its growth potential. If the country borrows to finance consumption imports from whatever source, whether from the IMF, other international financial institutions or private markets, it does not add to its capacity to service the new debt. In the short run, debt-financed countercyclical policy will be used to pay for consumer imports for the most part. It will be impossible to ramp up government investment in the short run, and in any case, the places where the foreign currency shortages are showing up will be supermarkets, petrol stations and other consumer distribution services, not in demand for inputs for investment.

The great value of a procyclical policy response to an adverse shock is that it relieves foreign currency market pressure and stabilises expectations, thereby nipping in the bud any incentive for defensive stances against the local currency. Once market agents are reassured that the fiscal adjustments are sufficient to restore external balance, the central bank can fend off speculation against the domestic currency by supportive monetary policy. With the passage of time, the fiscal corset may be loosened by ramping up government investment in infrastructure, skills enhancement and other activities that increase the country's international competitiveness, and by strengthening incentives for private investment in the tradable sector. If, on the other hand, government fails to act decisively to cut aggregate demand and consumer imports in the short run, uncertainty about the exchange rate, capital flight and speculation may result in devaluation, inflation, and economic and financial instability, circumstances which will prejudice the prospects for public and private investment in the medium term.

A similar sequence of events and circumstances will usually characterise shocks caused by natural disasters, except that no procyclical fiscal policy is needed because the disaster will have destroyed sources of income and the capacity to import. However, just as in the case of procyclical responses to other shocks, the initial import contraction is followed by foreign investment inflows for reconstruction and rehabilitation.

The link between fiscal policy and the balance of payments via aggregate spending and imports provides us with guidelines for the conduct of fiscal policy. In effect, the public sector needs to design its strategy to accommodate to the private sector's intended spending, so as to ensure that aggregate spending and imports do not exceed expected inflows of foreign currency. Government does have influence over private spending, through taxes, spending and the impact of its domestic borrowing on the country's interest rate premium, so in preparing the public sector budget, the forecast of aggregate expenditure needs to take account of any policy changes. The forecast, thus amended, should then be used to determine whether the fiscal stance should be neutral or contractionary. Should this exercise throw up a need for further adjustment, a second iteration of the aggregate forecast will be needed, and further rounds, until the budget is consistent with a projected balance in the external accounts.

The fiscal-balance of payments relationship also provides us with a practical measure of fiscal space. In foreign currency markets everywhere, there is usually an understanding of what is the value of local currency in terms of the relevant international currency, and what level of foreign reserves the central bank needs to maintain in order to keep the rate stable in that vicinity. It used to be thought that the equivalent of three months' worth of imports was an adequate level, and many countries do target this as a minimum level still, even though many others insist on a much higher minimum. Whatever is the market sentiment on the minimum level of foreign reserves, that data can be used to measure how much space the public sector has for expansion. The available fiscal space is defined by the impact of any government expansion on aggregate expenditure and imports, thereby depleting the foreign reserves. So long as government proceeds in an orderly and predictable way, fiscal expansion is possible until foreign reserves fall to a level equivalent to three months of imports, or whatever level is accepted as the minimum locally.

The final set of relationships needed for this (policy maker's) version of the model have to do with the behaviour of the financial sector. Some of the most damaging effects of fiscal expansion result from the financing of the public sector, particularly when expansion is financed by lending of local currency by the central bank. Fiscal expansion that is financed by prudent foreign borrowing by countries with good credit may be beneficial, particularly if the proceeds are used to improve the country's competitiveness. Fiscal expansion that is financed by the issue of marketable local currency instruments may not be a problem for a government that has plenty of fiscal space. Banks in most SOEs have idle funds placed with the central bank at below market returns, funds which they are happy to lend to government at prevailing interest rates. The use of these previously idle financial savings may provoke an increase in aggregate spending and imports, but there is a surplus of foreign exchange (our definition of fiscal space) to accommodate the additional demand. The corollary, naturally, is that local market borrowing cannot be sustained if there is insufficient fiscal space. Forecasts can be made, using the model suggested in this chapter, to determine the circumstances of any country.

The model in detail

Investment creates the capacity to produce more goods and services, especially tradables, and the equipment and new technologies that allow local producers to supply them more productively, thereby growing the national income. The investment equation is the key relationship for the economy's sustained growth. What motivates the decision to invest? Investors' interest is piqued in the tradable sectors if there is persistent full capacity. If hotels are always full, bars, restaurants and other tourist facilities and attractions booming, financiers with an interest in tourism will take a closer look. Much the same is true for exports of manufactured goods and agricultural exports when markets show potential for expansion. Whether a decision is taken to go ahead with a new project depends on the expected costs of production, as well as the economic, social and political environment. The potential investor will usually research the government's macroeconomic policies, the available infrastructure of roads, transport, ports, airports, public utilities and services. Investors will also be more forthcoming in countries with stable social and political systems and institutions. The success of government's policies for economic stability is reflected in the balance of payments and the resulting movements of foreign reserves. Successful policies will maintain an adequate level of foreign reserves, and downward pressure on the foreign exchange market is a warning sign. The policy makers may try to alleviate that pressure by raising the premium on domestic interest rates or by allowing the currency to depreciate. To ensure early detection of *exchange market pressure* (emp) a composite index is used, with weighted values of a decline in foreign reserves (when that happens), increases in the domestic interest premium and depreciations in the value of the local currency. Where available, the other social, economic and political influences may be captured by a qualitative index such as the *Global Competitiveness Index* (GCI).

The principal cost factors that will determine the profitability of the new investment venture are the *unit labour cost* (ulc), the cost of machines, equipment, building materials and other inputs, all of which are imported (SOEs do not have the capacity to produce this variety of products at internationally competitive prices) at the international price, p_t. The benchmark against which the investor will assess the profitability of the investment is assumed to be the foreign interest rate, r_f, the opportunity cost of the investment.

The potential investor in nontradables such as public transport and electricity generation and distribution faces similar costs, and has the same concerns about macroeconomic, social and political stability. However, whether there is a need for new capacity in the nontradable sector depends on the growth of potential demand, the sources of that growth, and whether it can be sustained. Herein lies the crucial difference between the motivation for investment in the tradable and nontradable sectors: full capacity in the tradable sector, if persistent, is a clear signal that the potential investor can earn a competitive return, so long as he can match (or better) the costs of the highest-cost producer who remains in business. There is infinite demand for the output internationally. In contrast, the potential investor in nontradables has to worry whether the demand for the product will be sustained. She will go ahead only if she has confident expectations that future aggregate demand will provide adequate sales to justify the investment. The composite investment equation presented below, covering both types of investment, includes both expected aggregate expenditure (which motivates nontradable investment) and a capacity variable for investment in tradables.

$$i = f_1(-xcap_t(-1),\ a^*,\ p_t,\ ulc,\ r_f,\ emp,\ GCI) \qquad (6.1)$$

Where:

- i: investment;
- $-xcap_t(-1)$: full capacity variable for tradables, the negative of excess capacity;
- a^*: aggregate expenditure, expected;
- p_t: price of imported inputs, which are tradable by definition;
- ulc: unit labour costs;
- r_f: the foreign interest rate, the opportunity cost of investment;
- emp: exchange market pressure variable, a weighted average of foreign reserve losses, domestic interest rate premium increases and exchange rate deterioration;
- GCI: the Global Competitiveness Index, or similar indicator of (non-price) competition.

The output of *tradables* is determined on the supply side: the producer in the SOE can sell to the limit of their capacity, so long as they are profitable at ruling international prices.

$$q_t = f_2(p_t,\ ulc,\ r) \qquad (6.2)$$

The costs of production are those anticipated in the investment equation, plus the cost of working capital for the business, provided by banks at the domestic interest rate, r. The new variables are:

- q_t: the output of tradable goods and services;
- r: the domestic interest rate, the cost of working capital.

Producers of *nontradable* goods and services will budget to produce a monthly, quarterly or annual output based on the previous year's sales, their product quality and marketing strategy, the expected growth of the market, and the company's target share of that market.

$$q_n = f_3(a^*,\ q_n(-1)) \qquad (6.3)$$

where:

- q_n: output of non tradables.

As this is, in conventional terms, a demand equation, some may question why there is no relative price term in the equation. However, in this model the alternative goods are tradables and imports, neither of which can be substituted for nontradables, by definition. A rise in the relative price of tradables may indeed reduce the demand for nontradables, but it will do so through a rise in domestic inflation, which will reduce domestic purchasing power, and the amount of nontradables that can be afforded. Relative price changes have an income effect, but no substitution effect.

The budgeted output will be offered for sale at a price which provides normal profitability with the cost elements previously mentioned for the production of tradables; typically in SOEs wage costs are uniform across all sectors, when account is taken of productivity differentials.

$$p_n = f_4(q_n, p_t, ulc, r) \tag{6.4}$$

where:

- p_n: the price of nontradables.

The remaining behavioural equations are for *imports* and *government revenue.* The import equation is:

$$m = f_5(a) \tag{6.5}$$

where:

- m: imports, in real terms.

There is no relative price term because in an SOE there are no locally produced substitutes that can be supplied at prices to compete with imports of equivalent products.

The government revenue will rise or fall with the nominal national income, Y, and changes in tax rates, tx_i:

$$Rev = f_6(Y, tx_i) \tag{6.6}$$

where:

- Y: nominal national income;
- tx_i: tax rates, $i = 1, 2, 3, \ldots$

Identities and balance equations

The total national output (real GDP) is the sum of the production of tradables and nontradables:

$$q = q_t + q_n$$

The price level is the weighted average of the prices of tradables (the world price) and the price of nontradables, using output weights:

$$p = p_t.(q_t/q) + p_n.(q_n/q)$$

National income is the value of national product:

$$Y = p.q$$

The foreign reserve movements reflect the external balance: when inflows exceed outflows the reserves increase, and vice versa:

$$\Delta FXR = p_t(x - m) + FDI + B_f$$

where:

- Δ: change in the variable;
- *FXR*: foreign exchange reserves;
- *x*: exports of goods and tourist and other services sold abroad;
- *FDI*: foreign direct investment;
- B_f: foreign borrowing by the public sector.

To a useful approximation, all tradables produced are exported:

$$x = q_t$$

The fiscal balance, *FISC*, is:

$$FISC = Rev - G_c - G_k$$

where:

- G_c, G_k: government current and capital expenditure.

Without much, if any, loss of generality, we assume that the only circumstance that occasions an increase in base money that is not the result of an increase in foreign reserves is a fiscal deficit that cannot be financed by foreign borrowing or by the issue of domestic debt to the private sector:

$$\Delta MB = -(FISC - B_f - B_d)$$

where:

- *MB*: base money;
- B_d: new issues of domestic debt, net of redemptions.

The reason we may ignore the possibility of money creation for lending to banks or other financial institutions is that these institutions would never have a reason to borrow from central bank in the normal course of business. Debits that arise from overnight items in course of settlement are covered by banks' reserve balances with the central bank, while liquidity deficits of longer duration will be financed from abroad, rather than paying the central bank's penal discount rate. In practice, banks in emergent markets and developing countries more often than not find themselves with idle liquidity, over and above the reserve stipulations of the monetary authority.

Aggregate expenditure a (in real terms) is the sum of output and the real value of newly created money, $\Delta MB/p$:

$$a = q + \Delta MB/p$$

This is a simplification, which assumes that an extra dollar of income has the same effect on the decision to spend as does an additional dollar of wealth. That is probably not the case, but it is not unreasonable to suppose that the difference that a more sophisticated representation would produce is not significant in the aggregate.

Readers who are familiar with more conventional models of the balance of payments will notice the absence of an exchange rate variable in this model. The reason is that the model abstracts from the effects of capital flight and the related uncertainties associated with currency depreciation purely for clarity of exposition. In practice, these flows will invariably overwhelm any effect that the exchange rate will have on the current account.

To illustrate, let us introduce the exchange rate variable and restate the balance of payments equation in local currency:

$$\Delta FXR_d = e.p_t(x - m) + e.FDI + e.B_f - e.\Delta NFA$$

The exchange rate, e, converts all values to domestic currency (FXR_d is the domestic value equivalent of the foreign reserves) to be compatible with the rest of the model. Notice the introduction of a new variable, the change in the net foreign assets of the private sector (ΔNFA), to take account of capital flight. If there is a deficit on the current account of the balance of payments, the fall in the value of local currency worsens the overall balance, measured in local currency, while seeming to leave the current account unaffected in foreign currency. However, we now have to incorporate the effect of exchange rate volatility on NFA, as well as the impact of exchange rate depreciation on the volume of imports, which will have become less affordable. The current account may improve, not because of an increase in exports but because the fall in domestic purchasing power resulting from devaluation-induced inflation depresses the volume of imports, reflecting a contractionary real income effect, rather than an expansionary (counter-cyclical) relative price effect. Moreover, the inevitable capital flight which accompanies devaluation means that foreign reserves will decline in spite of the improvement in the current account. We do not need to explore these circumstances further, because we advocate an economic strategy which stabilises the balance of payments by anchoring on the exchange rate, which, if it changes at all, will do so in a predictable manner, thereby avoiding capital flight.

A second reason to omit the exchange rate is that we have established that the growth rate of the SOE depends on expansion of tradable output, up to capacity limits which are constantly pushed back by investment in new capacity and higher productivity. The output of tradables is unaffected by changes in the value of local currency, except possibly negatively, if labour market instability following a devaluation leads to a loss of productivity (Equation 6.2). Investment is also unaffected by a loss of value of local currency, except negatively if there is destabilising exchange market pressure (Equation 6.1).

Our model omits a savings variable as well. The reason is that there is an infinite supply of finance for investment which yields an internationally competitive rate of return in any sector of the economy. In the identity

$$i = s + FDI/p_t + B_f/p_t$$

domestic saving s is a residual; all other variables in the identity are determined separately: investment by Equation 1, *FDI* by private investors in search of a competitive rate of return, and borrowing by government. This is the real value of savings that will actually be realised. There is no reason to expect that value to be equal to what savers wanted to save. Desired savings s^* may be represented by

$$s^* = f_7(y) \tag{6.7}$$

where:

- For convenience we assume $y = q$.

Consider the case where the real value of the amount people wish to save exceeds the amount required to finance all the investment that is included in i in the identity above. If a new project is undertaken with the excess savings, the imports needed for that project will have to be paid for by purchasing foreign exchange from the central bank, as per the balance of payments identity. That has the effect of transferring that amount to the category of foreign savings, with an equivalent reduction in foreign reserves. In effect, the excess of domestic savings is used to purchase previously accumulated foreign funding for the additional investment. *Ex post* it is the increase in *FDI* which finances the additional investment, except for the purely local expenditure that the investment may involve.

There is a further consideration relating to the efficient use of the excess saving. Any projected use of this financing is for investment projects which are below the minimum threshold of internationally competitive rates of return. That is why foreign investors have not taken them up. There are exceptions, where domestic investors have local knowledge not yet available internationally, and other circumstances which may be categorised as market failure, where such investments are indeed competitive, even though that is not generally recognised. Also, there are innovations and new productive directions, including environmentally sustainable investments, where international financial markets do not adequately price in social returns. In these circumstances the additional investment is fully justified, but it remains the case that the domestic savers who seek to employ their surpluses in these directions will have to source foreign exchange for imports, and that will be reflected in an increase in *FDI* or foreign borrowing, *ex post*. Following a similar logic it can be seen that government borrowing *Bf* will finance the import requirements of public sector investment.

The available tools for the SOE policy maker

The tools available in the model above are changes in tax rates and tax structure (tx_i), government expenditures (G_c, G_k), and foreign borrowing (B_f) by Government. These tools offer ample scope for the design of strategies for sustained growth and economic stability in all circumstances.

Growth-oriented fiscal policy involves stimulating investment and productivity in the tradable sectors of the economy. The specifics must be tailored to each economy's structure of production and economic circumstances, but some generalisations may be offered, based on Equations 6.1 and 6.2. The variables that can be influenced by government policies may include *ulc*, *EMP*, and a range of socio-political and infrastructural variables, including the efficiency of public administration and the delivery of public services. Tax incentives and government support for the adoption and adaptation of new production and organisational technologies are important for raising unit labour productivity. The tax system as a whole should be biased in favour of foreign-exchange earning activities, including incentives for reinvestment, product upgrades, enhancement and marketing. SOEs should embrace the concept of the *entrepreneurial state* (see Chapter 14), drawing on the experiences of the Asian Tigers. Immigration policies can also contribute significantly to the improvement in labour productivity, providing a way to better align varying levels of skills needed in an economy where living standards are rising, with the endowments and expected wages in the host country.

A summary of the tools available to government to improve the material well-being of the population appears as Exhibit A.

Exhibit A. Fiscal Tools and Their Effects on Material Well-being

Tax systems that are biased in favour of tradables => investment in tradables, enhanced competitiveness, higher productivity

Government investment in infrastructure, public utilities, transport and communications => investment, enhanced competitiveness, higher productivity

Expenditure on upgrades to health and education systems => investment, improvement in the HDI score
State entrepreneurship (Mazzucato) => investment in tradables, upskilling, technology adaptation and adoption
Expenditures to address challenges of inequality and the environment => investment, improved well-being
Expenditure to ensure and maintain a framework for social and political stability => investment, improved well-being
Public service efficiency and effectiveness, and public sector accountability via timely publication of audited annual reports => investment, improvements in material wellbeing
Achievement of macroeconomic stability, over the course of international economic cycles => investment, enhanced competitiveness

The *Global Competitiveness Index* offers a convenient way to summarise the overall impact of government policies on a country's international competitiveness. It combines the strength of the institutional framework, the quality of infrastructure, the macroeconomic environment, the country's health and educational services, the efficiency of the markets for goods and labour, the development of financial markets, the readiness to absorb new technologies, the size of the market, the sophistication of business practices, and the evidence of innovation. There are several items under each heading; for example, the 21 items under the heading of "institutional framework" include property rights protection, judicial independence, the strength of auditing and reporting standards and similar items. A score is awarded for each item and the country is ranked for that item based on that score. The individual items are aggregated to provide a score for each category and then an overall score, which allows countries to be ranked internationally and compared with peers and close competitors. Tax policies, expenditure priorities, state entrepreneurship, social investments and government capital projects can all be evaluated in light of the impact they are intended to have and all the items which are expected to improve as a result.

This is an appropriate point to remind ourselves of the importance of securing gains in health and education, as critical objectives in the design of fiscal policies, because they feature in the measure of well-being employed in this book. Government's annual budget should be prepared with a view to staying on course for achieving medium budgetary targets, because it is only in the medium term that changes in the quality of health and education, as well as other factors that contribute to the well-being of the society, will appear. As we shall see in Chapter 17, the elements that contribute to society's material betterment are many and multilayered. That must not deter us from always focusing on some crucial indicators at every stage in the design of fiscal policy. It is the only way to address the dissonance between economic performance and the quality of life, a dissonance which is the source of widespread disaffection worldwide.

How to use fiscal tools to stabilise the economy

Policy makers in the SOE can use Equations 6.2 to 6.6 to design, implement and monitor strategies to stabilise the economy on an ongoing basis, to inform markets and support predictable behaviour in tranquil times, and to detect and address potential economic challenges at an early stage. The balance of payments identity is the place to start; the level of foreign reserves, which should be reported daily to the economic policy team, is an immediate, up-to-the-minute signal of overall surpluses and deficits in the market in foreign currency. By observing it continuously, making allowances for seasonalities and special occurrences such as debt servicing, policy makers can detect underlying trends, and compare actual outcomes with expectations. A regular monitoring and decision meeting of the policy team, on a monthly basis, is able to detect deviations from expected foreign reserve levels at an early stage, assess the reasons for the discrepancy, decide if and when corrective policies are warranted, and recommend on the size of adjustment. In crisis situations more frequent meetings will be necessary.

The balance of payments gives information for the direction and speed of adjustment, as well as the mix of policy tools in the overall strategy. Consider the circumstance when foreign reserves are well in excess of expectations. Conventional wisdom is that the authorities should take no corrective action and allow foreign reserves to accumulate without limit. However, foreign reserves are a low-interest loan to the US government, and a build-up beyond what is needed for daily and seasonal fluctuations, and to reassure foreign currency markets of the soundness of local currency, may not be optimal if the unexpected windfall can be put to more productive use, such as investment in tradables. The factors that would have to be taken into account include whether the windfall persists or is likely to be reversed, the time that would be necessary to prepare productive investment projects as an alternative use of the funds and whether the investment would be by way of direct government investment or incentives for the private sector, which would use up the foreign currency surplus indirectly, via imports.

In the alternative case where an unexpected fall in foreign reserves is deemed to require a reduction in imports, either because the fall is large and likely to persist, or out of an abundance of caution, the balance of payments identity will give a working estimate of the reduction to be aimed for. Judgments can also be made whether additional foreign borrowing is warranted to alleviate the burden of contraction, depending on the capacity to service additional debt, under pessimistic assumptions about the economic forecast.

The reduction in aggregate expenditure needed to achieve any desired contraction in imports is derived from Equation 6.5. A useful way to design a package of fiscal measures sufficient to secure the cut in aggregate expenditure is to begin with the monetary base. If the entire amount were to be cut purely by a reduction in the money supply, what size of reduction in the fiscal deficit would be necessary to reduce ΔMB by that amount? There are other possibilities, however: tax rates may be adjusted, and expenditure programmes may be postponed or abandoned. To the extent that expenditure and tax measures impact directly on aggregate expenditure, the burden of overall fiscal contraction and on the money supply is reduced.

A role for monetary policy

Monetary policies cannot match the power of the fiscal tools. Domestic interest rates cannot deviate radically from the international rate, r_f. The country risk premium, the difference between the domestic and international rates, is proportional to the cost of foreign exchange transactions c_x, and it widens dramatically when there is apprehension about the value of the local currency, which we represent with the *emp* variable:

$$r - r_f = f_7(c_x, emp) \qquad (6.8)$$

In a scenario where the economic policy team detects a need for adjustment, there is imminent danger of increasing market pressure.

Monetary measures do have the advantage of speed. The central bank may intervene aggressively on the treasury bill market to drive up interest rates, with instant impact on other rates. However, in circumstances where *emp* has increased, a large increase in interest will be seen as an act of desperation, and will trigger capital flight. This is where slow-acting but powerful fiscal measures come into play. A fully articulated adjustment package, explaining the nature of the problem, describing the fiscal package which is being implemented and showing that it is an adequate response, will reassure agents in the foreign currency market that the value of the local currency is protected, especially if the government's decision and monitoring framework is known and widely understood. That relieves the exchange market pressure, and a modest increase in the premium on holding local currency, via central bank intervention on the treasury bill market, will provide an additional incentive to resist the temptation for capital flight, during the period when the impact of fiscal policy has not yet materialised. Other, more direct interventions such as global credit limits ordered by the central bank, have also proved helpful in these circumstances, so long as they are timed to expire when the fiscal measures are expected to take full effect.

Fiscal and monetary coordination is essential

The treasury, the revenue authorities, the government debt managers, the economic forecasters and the monetary and financial authorities must work together on all aspects of the economic policy exercise, including budgeting and forecasting, target setting, the design of economic strategies for economic prosperity (in the long run) and stabilisation (short term), policy implementation, monitoring, correction and redesign if necessary. This allows the policy makers to depend on the great power of fiscal adjustment, reinforced by quick-acting monetary policy. Both arms of policy play crucial roles: without simultaneous announcement of sufficient fiscal adjustment, monetary policy fails; equally, in the absence of quick-acting monetary policy, the external financial situation may have deteriorated badly by the time that fiscal measures take effect, and an adjustment package that should have been adequate will need to be reinforced.

The economic policy team should monitor both short-term stability targets and longer term targets for improvement in national well-being within the single decision-making framework. In tranquil times, monitoring should be done on a monthly basis, with course corrections made quarterly in line with stability targets, and annually, to stay on course to hit the targets for improved well-being. When risks of economic dislocations arise, more frequent monitoring becomes necessary.

The need for coordinated monetary and fiscal policy has increasingly been recognised. The arguments in favour of coordination are strong in all countries. Uncertainty is the bane of all economic decision making and of all economic policy. Whenever there appears to be a disjuncture between the fiscal and monetary stance in any country, financial markets, prices and output and investment decisions are thrown into disarray. The fractures may not be apparent in tranquil times, but they surface inevitably during times of economic difficulty.

There is an additional reason why the notion of central bank policy to independently target inflation has no credibility in SOEs. Everyday experience, supported by theory and empirical evidence, makes it obvious that inflation is mainly driven by international prices.[1] While bad monetary policies are observed to drive high inflation, mainly through depreciation in the value of local currency, there is nothing that the central bank can do to reduce local inflation below international inflation, even with appropriate monetary measures. What is more, fiscal dominance is inevitable. In the event of an excessive fiscal deficit, if the monetary authority is unable to create money, there is build-up of government arrears, a deterioration of government services, ballooning of informal markets, including for foreign currency, and capital flight – in a word, an adjustment process that is disorderly and worsens the country's international risk profile.

A digression on exchange controls, credit and trade restrictions, wage policies and other interventions

Not included in the suite of policies analysed in this chapter are any measures which stipulate or limit the volume of transactions or the prices at which exchanges take place. The reason is grounded in the principle which was offered in Chapter 1, that policies are effective only if all the economic agents involved are able to accept the outcome. With a few exceptions, and mainly in the short term, policies which purport to compel economic agents to behave in ways they do not think to be in their interest will not have the desired effect. To illustrate, we consider some commonly advocated policies.

It is commonplace, even in today's world of internet banking and electronic payments, to encounter the view that countries with durable exchange rate pegs have maintained the link to their anchor currency by limiting foreign currency outflows with the use of exchange controls. However, as far back as the 1970s the monetary authorities in Guyana, Jamaica and Trinidad and Tobago gave us examples of the lasting harm that attempts to ration the use of foreign exchange have on inflation and on the long-term prospects for growth. The story of the comprehensive failure of these countries' so-called foreign exchange budgeting is told in some detail in Worrell (1987). The interventionist approach to macroeconomic policy – which was not limited to the foreign exchanges – marked the start of the divergence between Guyana and Jamaica on the one hand, and the better performing economies of the eastern Caribbean on the other.

Even more limited restrictions on the use of foreign exchange have proven ineffective in limiting the demand. The exchange controls in effect in Barbados and countries of the ECCU applied only to one way financial transfers, excluding all imports, and were mainly employed to smooth out lumpy payment outflows. However, the Barbadian authorities discovered in 1991 that even these less obtrusive interventions failed in a crisis situation. With an unsustainable fiscal deficit in the wake of the 1991 election, and an administration reluctant to take decisive corrective action, the foreign exchange markets were suddenly drained of supply, and Central Bank foreign currency sales quickly exhausted reserves that were previously thought adequate, albeit barely so. How did this massive financial outflow take place with no reference to the central bank, which maintained surveillance of all unrequited financial outflows? The answer lay with the defensive action of importing companies. With the imminent threat of a devaluation, merchants paid off their US dollar trade credits, borrowing on their local currency overdrafts to buy foreign currency to do so. In effect, motor car distributors and other importers replaced foreign financing of their inventory with local currency, to protect themselves and their customers against the inflation that would have resulted, had there been a devaluation. There was no central bank control over the switch, since the payments related to import trade, and the Barbadian authorities had always avoided controls on the use of foreign exchange for imports.

In the years since 1991, electronic payments have almost completely replaced cash except for small payments, payments in poor countries and for illicit payments. Opportunities for defensive actions in the face of any looming foreign currency shortage are now very widely available in small countries that have modern economies; tightening controls in these circumstances aggravates the foreign exchange shortage, since so many have access to foreign exchange through a variety of nonbank electronic transfer systems.

The value of the local currency cannot be protected by exchange controls; the controls will fail, precisely in the circumstances when they are needed. In tranquil times, in the absence of balance of payments shocks and with sustainable fiscal budgets, the local currency of any SOE doesn't change much, in relation to the US dollar, the euro or other international currency which matters most to the population. This is a frequent observation in IMF Staff Reports on SOEs, occasioning accusations of central bank intervention, and provoking denials of active intervention by central banks. The central banks are innocent; they play a passive role, supplying foreign exchange at a more or less constant rate to take care of overnight shortages and seasonalities. We know the central banks are innocent because their intervention succeeds only in tranquil times; whenever the market experiences unexpected shortages, the bank is obliged to allow the rate to slip, officially or on informal markets, for fear of exhausting its war chest of foreign reserves.

A second measure for which it is difficult to find a justification are selective credit controls, which stipulate how much should be lent for agriculture, industry, consumer durables or any other sector. Credit has to be allocated to trustworthy borrowers with sound business plans, a track record which attests to their financial management skill, and an actual or projected income stream sufficient to service new debt. If the government wishes to promote any activity, measures should be put in place to ensure that those involved meet the credit-worthiness criteria. Banks are not at liberty to lend to those who do not meet the criteria, under the rules set by international banking supervisory bodies.

Caps on total credit may be of some value in the short run, as part of a comprehensive package of adjustment measures. An example was the use of a global credit cap, lasting six months, which was imposed on the Barbados banking system as an element of the adjustment package which secured IMF financial support in 1991. However, it is more difficult to find justification for the use of credit caps as the main tool of adjustment, as has been suggested during periods of very rapid acceleration. The challenge of designing credit caps to take some steam out of credit booms is one of determining where on the credit cycle the financial market sits, in real time. That makes it difficult to decide when to intervene and by how much to limit the expansion. There is a further consideration: unless the authorities succeed in persuading both banks and borrowers that it is not in their best long-term interest to borrow and lend at this time, all that the credit cap will do is to divert lending to informal markets. The central bank should instead direct its attention to explaining to borrowers and lenders the inevitable consequences of their intemperate actions. The bank's success depends on its ability to persuade market players that it is in their interests to take the long view, and tighten their guidelines for credit approval. Only when a consensus has been achieved between banks and the central bank should the central bank issue an instruction to put the guidelines into effect. Without such an instruction, individual banks might have an incentive to cheat, to boost profitability and increase the value of their franchise in securities markets. Equally, to impose the guidelines before all banks are convinced of the necessity for them risks driving credit into the informal market. The central bank has a role to inform and give guidance to the market; the bank can expect to be successful in this effort to the extent that it is able to convince market agents to change their behaviour, on the merits of its arguments. If, as too often happens, the central bank issues new guidelines in an effort to compel the banks to limit credit when they can see no reason to do so, there is a strong motivation to move the credit beyond the regulatory perimeter. It may take a few months to set up arrangements, during which interval the controls may appear to be working, but that apparent success is a an illusion.

Trade controls and import rationing are a third example of interventionist policies that were once in common use. They have proved a universal failure, resulting in price distortions, artificial scarcities and inefficiencies of production, consumption and distribution. They have almost completely disappeared from the policy agenda, everywhere.

A fourth area of policy concern, which is not treated with in this chapter, has to do with the determination of wages. The relationship between wage increases and labour productivity is a vital element in maintaining the SOE's international competitiveness. There is, consequently, justification in arguing for official policy guidance on wages. However, it is difficult to generalise as to how this might best be done, as circumstances, labour market practices and institutions, and the climate of industrial relationships vary so much among countries.

Economic policy makers have a clear responsibility to provide all agents in the labour market with timely data on wages, inflation and the productivity trends in key sectors, to inform wage negotiations. It is important, to ensure credibility, that such data be provided regularly, on a pre-announced schedule. It is essential that government set the example in the public sector, of wage increases that are aligned with improvements in productivity. In addition, a framework of consultation on the economy, with the participation of trade and business organisations, workers' representatives and economic policy makers, can be helpful in providing a framework for labour market stability and wages that do not run ahead of productivity.

That seems to be as far as we may go with generalisations about wage determination. The factors that enter into that equation include the rate of growth of tradable output, the relative productivities of various sectors, including the public sector, the size of the public sector relative to the economy, the distribution of income, where the country sits on the HDI scale, and other factors such as the extent of female participation in the labour force.

In addition, the impact of migration on the labour market of the SOE may be substantial. Emigration has a positive impact on average incomes in many countries, thanks mainly to workers' remittances, but also, at higher levels of skill and enterprise, because it offers scope for advancement when one exceeds the limits offered by the local economy. In SOEs that are in the top quartile of the HDI, immigration is frequently the main source of supply for lower skill levels of the labour force. In all these cases, migration puts upward pressure on wages, in complex ways. In many SOEs migrants' remittances are in the top three foreign currency inflows; in these cases it may be that household incomes benefit sufficiently to increase the effective minimum wage at which it makes sense to seek work rather than work in the home. Construction booms in countries across the globe attract immigrants from other countries where levels of unemployment are high and wages low, relative to those in the host countries. Equally, a predominance of immigrant workers in many countries reflects a shortage of lower skilled labour as a domestic labour force with higher levels of skill seek jobs at home or abroad, which allow them to be as productive as they can be.

The wage levels that emerge from this mix of economic and institutional factors is important for the growth and well-being of the society. Understandably, economic policy makers are motived to influence the evolution of wages so as to avoid rises in unit labour costs that undermine productivity, while at the same time sustaining and improving on average real wages to ensure there is no impairment of well-being. It is difficult to see how policy makers can go beyond moral suasion with full information on economic variables and credible projections of prospects. It is then up to agents in the labour market, including the government itself, to negotiate wage increases that do not damage, but rather enhance, future prospects. Experiences with attempts to reduce this process to a formula, for example through wage indexation, have not been encouraging. Ad hoc negotiations between fully informed partners are messy, and are not guaranteed of a sensible outcome, but they at least open the possibility that skillfull negotiators will produce a number that all parties are able to live with.

Why does the IMF get it wrong?

The basic IMF financial programming model has no growth engine. It is, in essence, a monetary model of price determination and economic fluctuations. The structure of investment, competitiveness, capacity building, and sectoral real growth does not appear in the standard IMF analysis. In general, there are three possible approaches to explaining the factors that influence changes in GDP: via the determination of what is produced, which is the approach taken in this chapter; via the income earned by the factors of production; or via the elements of aggregate expenditure, which is the approach used by the IMF.

The IMF's choice of approach is consequential, because it renders the institution blind to the structural peculiarities of the SOE, in particular the fact that tradables, nontradables and imports are distinct nonintersecting commodity bundles. In the aggregate there is no substitutability among the three baskets in the SOE. Staycations offer a large measure of relief to the hotel sector in the US and China which are clearly not SOEs, but not in

Jamaica or Kenya, which are. When the local prices of imported goods rise in the SOE, either because of international inflation or depreciation of local currency, consumers face shortages because there are no affordable local substitutes available in quantity, as there would be in a large relatively closed economy. Governments of SOEs and developing economies worldwide have discovered that compensating for a failing agricultural export sector by employing displaced labour in public services, or even trying to produce for local consumption, inevitably fatally impairs the country's growth potential and prospects, because foreign exchange reserves have to be depleted to finance the import needs of the newly employed workers and the additional imported inputs for production. In the SOE local sales cannot substitute for lost exports, there are no affordable local substitutes for imports that locals can no longer afford to buy, and those who lose their jobs in export industries cannot find employment in nontradable sectors because of the foreign exchange constraint.

The methodologies used for IMF forecasts do not recognise these realities of the SOE, and the implications they have for export growth and diversification, import substitution, exchange rate policy and potential growth. As far as one can tell, the IMF's country growth forecasts, issued twice a year, are based on a combination of *ad hoc* estimates, backstopped by models which incorporate an implicit assumption that domestic products, exports and imports are all perfect substitutes. That no doubt accounts for the fact that the immediate growth forecasts, which are heavily biased towards the *ad hoc*, garner all the public attention whenever a new version of the IMF's *World Economic Outlook* is issued. The longer term forecasts, which probably owe more to the economic model used by the Fund, have less credibility and are less interesting.

In contrast, the model presented in this book provides a medium-term forecast that can be fully justified by the assumptions made about trends in international prices and interest rates, local productivity and fiscal policies. Within this framework, policies can be designed to target medium term objectives, related to the improvement of national well-being, as well as to keep the economy stable in the short run. Policy makers can then track progress with respect to investment, exports, fiscal balances, health and educational services, the development of public utilities and infrastructure – that is to say, all the factors that really matter for improving the well-being of the population – comparing their forecasts against actual performance continuously. They can use the model to evaluate divergences between performance on growth, prices, foreign reserves, exports of goods and services, fiscal balances and other target variables. Depending on the source of the divergence, an appropriate policy response can be designed. If, for example, the divergence is as a result of an unexpected external shock of the magnitude of the COVID-19 pandemic, projections for foreign earnings will have to be drastically revised downwards, prejudicing the achievement of targets for improving material well-being in the medium and long term. Using the relationships of the model, the authorities can make estimates of the lower trajectories for the target variables, with current policies in place, before going on to explore policy changes that would serve to improve the prospects. At the end of this exercise policy makers are in a position to offer a convincing strategy for the way forward, showing the short- and long-term impact of the pandemic, the new policies which are being implemented, what are the expected results of the new policies, over what time period they are likely to appear, and what external factors and imponderables, such as oil prices, pose risks that have to remain the subject of constant scrutiny.

The treatment of inflation in the IMF approach is a self-evident weakness. It is not possible to close the external financial account in any modern economy, and it therefore follows that changes in the money supply of any country will have an impact outside of the domestic economy, via the financial account. If an SOE which issues its own local currency increases the supply of that currency, and if that increase were to provoke an increase in aggregate spending, there might be some upward pressure on the price of nontradables (Equations 6.3 and 6.4), but the larger impact would be on the demand for imports (Equation 6.5). That, in turn, leads to a fall in foreign reserves, and eventually to a depreciation of the exchange rate. However, even though inflation in this case has its roots in monetary expansion, it cannot be tempered through monetary contraction, once there has been a depreciation of the exchange rate. To assign an inflation target to the central bank is to set the bank up for failure: in the first place, the target for domestic inflation cannot be lower than the international inflation rate because of the dominance of imports and exports, so the SOE's inflation rate has an unknown minimum value. Secondly, inflation appears via a depreciation of the exchange rate, which cannot be arrested with the use of monetary policy alone.

Our model provides a practical measure of fiscal space which can be used to define fiscal sustainability, replacing the IMF's flawed Debt Sustainability Analysis (DSA). A relationship may be established between money creation to finance a fiscal deficit, ΔMB, and the level of foreign reserves, using Equation 6.5, the identity for aggregate expenditure and the external balance identity. Using this relationship the authorities may estimate the amount of money creation that reduces the foreign reserves to the minimum which is considered adequate to protect the value of the local currency. This estimate is a good indicator of fiscal space for any country whose external credit is rated below investment grade. Such countries cannot expand fiscal deficits beyond this point, because they will be unable to secure market finance, and any further borrowing from the monetary authority will unsettle foreign exchange markets and risk devaluation and economic instability. This provides a practical measure of the extent of fiscal space, with a threshold which, if breached, imperils the country's targets for economic stability and, by extension, economic growth and general well-being.

Our model can also be used to debunk the fallacy that increases in domestic saving can be a spur to faster economic growth. It is no accident that no domestic savings variable appears in Equation 6.1. There is abundant foreign finance available for internationally competitive investment projects in SOEs, should there be insufficient domestic savings available. What is more, only a small percentage of the available savings in local currency can be for investment projects, because of the high import content of such projects. Imports of machinery, equipment, construction materials, fuels and supplies for the project have to be paid for in foreign currency which local currency savers will need to purchase from banks, depleting the net foreign assets of the country, which are in effect accumulated foreign savings.

Retrospective on the evolution of the model

The model presented in this chapter has evolved over the course of four decades; a review of that process will illustrate the sources of many of the insights that are incorporated into the current version, as well as some of the modules that can be built out to expand on the behavioural relationships, areas where further research is required and what we have learned from the dead ends encountered along the way.

An early exploration of exchange rate policy (Worrell, 1980) analysed the effects of relative price changes on inflation and the balance of trade, with less than full employment and wage rigidity and with inefficient co-operating factors. The paper discussed the real balance effect, export incentives arising from devaluation, the role of expectations, and the effects of lags in wage and price adjustment. The conclusions were that it would be important to estimate the impact of exchange rate changes on the distribution of income and the exports of manufactured goods, as well as the resulting acceleration of inflation. Policy makers were advised to "be mindful of the dislocation and instability which accompany changes in the [exchange rate] regime or the numeraire" (Worrell, 1980, p. 151). The degree of trade concentration and the development of financial markets were mentioned as important considerations in the exchange rate decision. The impact of devaluation on the climate of industrial relations and "the limits to the government's powers of coercion" were also to be taken into account.

Four observations were made in Worrell (1982): 1) the fact that domestic savings did not appear to be a constraint on growth in Barbados was not surprising, since foreign savings, which are abundant, were a perfect substitute for domestic savings; 2) production was faltering in the manufacturing sector because wage increases were higher than was justified by the increases in productivity and enhancement in product quality. In retrospect it can be seen that wages in manufacturing were being pulled up by the faster growth of wages in tourism and other services, as well as by (ultimately unsustainable) increases in public sector wages; 3) tariff protection resulted in fewer jobs and less growth than the economy is capable of because resources were diverted from expanding capacity in growth-enhancing exports to import substitutes which were less affordable than the imports they replaced; 4) exporters could not secure additional sales by lowering their prices because they supplied such a small slice of the markets to which they sold. Devaluation was characterised as an attempt to force the entire community to subsidise employment in marginal exports.

Holder and Worrell (1985) is an elegant early presentation of the complete model, tailored to focus on the impact of exchange rate changes, wage policies and monetary expansion on inflation. It offers a good intuitive explanation of the equations which is still convincing. Empirical tests were conducted for Barbados, Jamaica and Trinidad and Tobago. The findings were that foreign prices account for one-third of total inflation; exchange rate changes and import tariffs had effects similar effects to foreign prices; domestic interest rate increases were inflationary in Barbados only, and wage inflation was evident only in Jamaica; no monetary expansion effects were detected.

Two papers published in 1989 analysed the effects of tax policy and tax incentives on production and the distribution of income in Barbados. Worrell (1989a) finds strong bias in favour of investment in agricultural machinery in the corporation tax system, and a weak bias in favour of manufactured goods, but the "tentative" overall conclusion is that the tax structure is not a leading factor in investment decisions. An analysis of the tax system in Worrell (1989b) shows that although the system is supposedly designed to provide incentives for investment, especially in exports and import substitutes for the CARICOM market, there is not much actual import substitution because of the small size of this market. The costs of local production are so high that production of import substitutes doesn't yield a competitive rate of return, even behind tariff protection. The income tax system had a progressive impact on incomes even though contributions to the national social security scheme reduced its progressivity.

Papers in the book *Financing development in the Commonwealth Caribbean* (Worrell, Bourne and Dodhia, 1991) focussed on more effective use of domestic saving and increasing government savings. Over the three decades prior to publication of the studies, the savings ratio rose in Barbados, but fell in Guyana, Jamaica and Trinidad and Tobago, with government dissaving in Guyana. In Barbados government and private savings and foreign investment were all vigorous in the 1960s and 1970s, but FDI and total investment declined in the 1980s. The common characteristics for attracting foreign investment to the Caribbean were non-economic: they included their democratic systems, their proximity to the US, the fact that English is the native language and cultural links to investors' home countries.

The volume edited by Wen and Sengupta (1991) made an important contribution to the understanding of competitiveness. "Natural competitiveness" (Wen and Sengupta, 1991, p. 2) was defined as the comparative advantage which any country has by virtue of its resource endowment. Governments may improve on natural competitiveness by upskilling of the labour force and by a variety of other incentives. The cost factors affecting the extent to which a country realises and improves on its natural comparative advantage include domestic unit labour costs, and the costs and reliability of power, transport and materials supply. The unit labour cost may be lowered by means of increases in labour productivity, containing increases in real wages, and exchange rate policy. In addition, competitiveness may be enhanced by non-price factors, such as securing a reputation for quality, branding and the uniqueness of its product offerings.

A fully articulated version of the model appears in Worrell (1992). It includes production dualism (tradables and nontradables), capital mobility, limits to import substitution, endogenous exchange rate adjustment, and endogenous money, wage and price formation. This model also includes an investment equation for tradables which sets future capacity limits for tradable production, and it elaborates on the labour market and wages formation, and on financial market reactions to monetary stimulus. This study also attempts a richer fiscal structure to capture the many-layered effects of fiscal adjustment policies on output, aggregate demand, investment incentives, government investment, and relative prices. However, it proved impossible to estimate the model in its full complexity, and the forecasts for 1991–1995 for Barbados, the Dominican Republic, Guyana, Jamaica and Trinidad and Tobago were based on a simplification not dissimilar from what appears in this chapter.

Worrell (1993a) provides a survey of investment in all the English and French speaking countries of the Caribbean, as well as the Dominican Republic, Puerto Rico and Suriname. There are also empirical estimates of the determination of investment for Barbados, Jamaica, and Trinidad and Tobago. Investment in the Caribbean is relatively high, but the foreign contribution is low, less than ten per cent of the total. Observations about the data included a weakening in the 1980s, incremental capital to output ratios generally in the range of one to three, and the fact that overall investment was heavily concentrated in nontradables, although foreign investors showed a preference for export industries. Factors affecting foreign investment discussed in the paper included social and political stability, infrastructure, public utilities, health, education, real wages, natural resources, history and language. No effect of relative wages on foreign investment was detected in pooled data for Barbados, the Dominican Republic, Jamaica and Trinidad and Tobago. Other observations were that tax incentives seemed to have no measurable effect; there was a noticeable accelerator effect for investment in nontradables in Trinidad and Tobago only; government investment acted as catalyst for private investment; rising interest rates were an inhibiting factor for all investment; and increases in the relative price of tradables stimulated investment in that sector.

Worrell (1993b) presents a theoretical model of the small open economy and derives conditions for internal and external balance. The paper shows that to achieve economic equilibrium one needs to shift the internal balance schedule and the external balance by using changes in the money supply, output of exports, capital flows or changes in foreign reserves, because the relative price effects are weak. In any case, it is hardly possible to alter relative prices: the derivatives of relative prices with respect to nominal exchange rate changes, changes in foreign prices, changes in the money supply and changes in the response time of nontradable to tradable price changes are derived; it is shown that the effects may be perverse, and in any case they are insignificant. "If monetary expansion leads to a depreciation of the exchange rate we may expect a fall in output in the long run, whatever happens in the short run" (Worrell, 1993b, p. 159). "In some circumstances the exchange rate is endogenous... If the reserve loss is large the currency depreciates at a rate determined by market expectations." (Worrell, 1993b, Worrell, 1993b, p. 159). Depreciation in response to a fiscal deficit is determined by "the additional import demand, the additional output, and the adverse effects of uncertainty" (Worrell, 1993b, p. 160). With respect to investment "the most dependable source of long-term growth lies in the tradable sector" (Worrell, 1993b, p. 16). Assuming non-quantifiable factors are favourable, investment in tradables is a function of expected relative prices, their variance, and actual relative prices. "Investment may be expected in sectors where a competitive edge can be sustained in the face of international competition, and the volume of investment will depend on relative prices." "The increase in productivity must be sufficient to overcome the depressing effects of real wage increases on output" (Worrell, 1993b, p. 162).

Worrell (1994) is a literature survey of the macroeconomics of small developing economies from which inferences are drawn, including the following: "It is usually more effective to change the real exchange rate by using fiscal and monetary policy, and to use the nominal exchange rate as an anchor for expectations" (Worrell, 1994, p. 101); "Exchange rate policy is not particularly useful in small open economies, even when the fundamentals of the external environment have changed" because of imperfect information and moral hazard (Worrell, 1994, p. 102); "... nontariff trade barriers encourage rent seeking and distort market signals" (Worrell, 1994, p. 104); "... in open economies, savings and investment are not congruent ... Investment in a competitive economy is never constrained by saving, thanks to the international mobility of capital" (Worrell, 1994, p. 107). Inferences about policies to stimulate growth include the promotion of research and development, the adaptation and adoption of new technology, spreading of new knowledge and human capital development. Trade liberalisation is a possible stimulus to growth but the relationship is complex. External debt is not a constraint, though the real rate of interest may be: for any rate of growth the real interest rate determines the ratio of external to internal finance. In circumstances where there is foreign currency shortage the rate of investment may fall. Fiscal policy emerges as the cornerstone of the economic strategy for the small economy.

Worrell (1997) offers a high level comparison of the explicit or implicit models underpinning models in use for policy formulation and discussion, including by the IMF and World Bank. Real growth is exogenous in the IMF

Polak model,[2] and nominal growth is determined by the money supply. The World Bank uses a savings-investment-growth model, with no consideration of external finance or trade. Neither model includes consideration of the determining features of policy outcomes in Caribbean economies, i.e. the limited possibilities for diversification of production, the reality that investment in tradables is the binding growth constraint, the fact that foreign prices largely determine domestic inflation, and that there is no predictable relationship between the nominal and real exchange rate.

Worrell and Craigwell (1997) is a collected volume which includes two unconventional approaches to the modelling of the economy. The Watson-Teelucksingh model uses the expenditure approach, with equations for consumption and investment, government revenue (expenditure is exogenous), money demand, the public sector borrowing requirement, exports, imports, labour and employment. This model is not intended for discussion of economic policy issues. McClean (1997) uses a monetary model of prices, output, and the balance of payments to demonstrate that the actual adjusts to the desired monetary stock in a labour-surplus, fixed exchange rate small open economy; he deduces that monetary policy should be dedicated to management of the balance of external payments, a conclusion that is consistent with our own.

Two papers have to do with the design of tax policy for growth. Worrell et al. (2012) and Worrell (2014) show that the Barbados value added tax, introduced in 1997, increased administrative costs as a percentage of indirect tax revenue collected, rendered the overall tax system less equitable, and discriminated against the tourism sector, the country's principal source of foreign exchange. Every one of those outcomes has a negative impact on investment in tourism, earnings of foreign currency and the well-being of the population of the country.

Worrell (2021) uses the Barbados experience to put the model (investment is the key to growth and savings is not a constraint) through its paces, concluding that official policies are required to provide support for innovation, to improve the efficiency of the public sector, and to support small and medium enterprises in order to accelerate the growth rate. The economy should be stabilised with the use of fiscal policy. The orthodox policy suite does not work because money is endogenous.

The central features of SOEs that drive the approach to economic policy presented in this chapter are amply illustrated by these studies: the absence of substitutability among exportables, importables and nontradables; the fact that the drivers of inflation and interest rates are principally external; the fact that growth and stabilisation depend on expansion in foreign currency inflows and on how available foreign currency is employed. In addition, these papers contain insights and observations that deserve to be explored in greater depth in future research.

One such topic is the impact of exchange rate depreciation on the distribution of income. Income shifts from those earning or holding assets in local currency, to holders of foreign currency and foreign assets. Also, to the extent that wage reaction lags devaluation-induced inflation, there is a transfer from wage-earners to owners of capital in the export sector. Some analysts see this as providing an incentive for new investment in tradables and others expect an increase in overtime and other measures to fully exploit existing capacity in the near term. However, both these expectations will probably be disappointed whenever there is any unplanned exchange rate depreciation, because of uncertainty about future exchange rate changes and labour market instability. Casual empiricism suggests that the redistributional effects of exchange rate depreciation are unambiguously negative.

A related issue is the equivalence of exchange rate and tariffs, and the fact that, when they are deployed in an attempt to protect local farmers and manufacturers, all domestic consumers are taxed in order to subsidise marginal exporters and noncompetitive import substitution.

Wage determination and the structure and functioning of labour markets in open economies are an aspect of the economic structure which remains undeveloped in this model. Some issues which are deserving of research are the relationship between real wages, productivity and technology, the impact of unionisation, the differences in wage-productivity relationships in tourism, manufacturing and agriculture, and the labour market consequences of the size and efficiency of the labour force in the public sector. In addition, improvements in communications and transport technologies now provide new possibilities for wage spill-overs from abroad, while improved access to education can open possibilities for emigration if the domestic labour market does not provide suitable employment opportunities.

Concluding remarks

All too often, the celebration of the completion of a successful IMF-supported economic adjustment programme is not reflected in the sentiment of a majority of the population who will have witnessed no improvement in the quality of their lives, nor do they have encouraging prospects for the future. Fiscal sustainability will usually have been achieved, but a depreciated exchange rate, a catastrophic decline in government investment in infrastructure and expenditure on public services, health and education, would all have impaired the well-being of the population. These growth-inhibiting costs of adjustment are not inevitable. The fault lies with the poor design of fiscal policy, the result of an economic policy framework which is not squarely focussed on material well-being, and the international competitiveness, tradables investment and sustained growth which provides the financial resources for improvements in well-being in the medium and long run. The use of a suitably structured and focussed macroeconomic model and framework of policy-making opens the way to tailored design of fiscal policy for the SOE, one which measures success in terms of the well-being of the population.

Notes

1 Introducing a notion of a target for "core" inflation that excludes the most influential items in the consumer basket implies that marginal items are the "core", which, apart from the obvious contradiction, undermines the credibility of the monetary authority.
2 So called after the author of the early IMF Paper (Polak, 1957) in which the financial programming approach was first proposed.

References

Agénor, Pierre-Richard and Peter J. Montiel. 2008. *Development Macroeconomics*, Princeton and Oxford: Princeton University Press.

Holder, Carlos and DeLisle Worrell. 1985. "A model of price formation for small economies: Three Caribbean examples," *Journal of Development Economics*, Vol. 18, pp. 411–428.

McClean, Wendell A. 1997. "Monetary dynamics in Barbados: the evidence from cointegration analysis and error correction modelling." In *Macroeconomics and Finance in the Caribbean: Quantitative Analyses*, edited by DeLisle Worrell and Roland Craigwell. St Augustine, Trinidad: Caribbean Centre for Monetary Studies.

Polak, J.J. 1957. "Monetary analysis of income formation and payments problems," *Staff Papers*. International Monetary Fund, Vol. 6, no. 1, pp. 1–50.

Watson, Patrick K. and Sonia Teelucksingh. 1997. "Macroeconomic modelling and cointegration in a small sampling framework (with application to Trinidad and Tobago," in *Macroeconomics and Finance in the Caribbean: Quantitative Analyses*, edited by DeLisle Worrell and Roland Craigwell. St Augustine, Trinidad: Caribbean Centre for Monetary Studies.

Wen, Yin-Kann and Jayshree Sengupta (eds). 1991. *Increasing the International Competitiveness of Exports from Caribbean Countries*. Washington, DC: The World Bank.

Worrell, DeLisle. 2021. "An alternative policy approach to growth and stabilization in small open economies." in *Handbook of Caribbean Economies*, edited by Robert E. Looney. New York: Routledge.

Worrell, DeLisle. 2014. "How the VAT hurts tourism," *Policy Paper*. Central Bank of Barbados, July 7.

Worrell, DeLisle. 1997. "Economic policy and Caribbean economic performance," *Annual Research Review*. Central Bank of Barbados, July.

Worrell, DeLisle. 1994. "Macroeconomics and small developing economies: A policy-maker's perspective," in *Economics in a Changing World*: Volume 4, edited by Edmar Bacha for the International Economic Association. London: Macmillan.

Worrell, DeLisle. 1993a. "Investment in the Caribbean," *Social and Economic Studies*, Vol. 42, nos. 2 & 3, p. 21.

Worrell, DeLisle. 1993b. "Economic adjustment and growth in small developing countries," in *Open Economy Macroeconomics*, edited by Helmut Frisch and Andreas Wortgotter. London: Macmillan.

Worrell, DeLisle. 1992. *Economic Policies in Small Open Economies: Prospects for the Caribbean*. London: Commonwealth Secretariat.

Worrell, DeLisle. 1989a. "The tax system of Barbados," *Bulletin for International Fiscal Documentation*, October.

Worrell, DeLisle. 1989b. "Comparative experience of Caribbean countries," in *Development in Suspense*, edited by George Beckford and Norman Girvan. Kingston, Jamaica: Friedrich Ebert Stiftung.

Worrell, DeLisle. 1987. *Small Island Economies: Structure and Performance in the English-speaking Caribbean Since 1970*. New York: Praeger.

Worrell, DeLisle. 1982. "Industrial policies and economic growth," *Working Paper*. Central Bank of Barbados.

Worrell, DeLisle. 1980. "Exchange rate policies for LDCs." *Social and Economic Studies*, Vol. 29, nos. 2–3, June/September.

Worrell, DeLisle, Compton Bourne and Dinesh Dohdia (eds). 1991. *Financing Development in the Commonwealth Caribbean*. London: Macmillan.

Worrell, DeLisle and Roland Craigwell. 1997. *Macroeconomics and Finance in the Caribbean: Quantitative Analyses*. St Augustine, Trinidad: Caribbean Centre for Monetary Studies.

Worrell, DeLisle, Tracy Maynard, ChrystolThomas and Michelle Doyle-Lowe. 2012. "A review of the VAT system in Barbados," *Central Bank of Barbados Economic Review*, Vol. 38, no. 2, December.

7 Targeting the Exchange Rate using Fiscal Policy to Adjust Aggregate Expenditure

The domestic currencies of small open economies are of limited usefulness unless their value is assured in terms of a currency that is used in international trade. The SOE sells competitive products and services on the world market to earn income with which to import everything it needs for domestic consumption and investment. The local currency of the SOE is of no interest to overseas buyers, either for purchases or sales; local currency is therefore not useful to locals either, unless it can always be freely exchanged into the preferred international trading currency at a predictable price.

This circumstance negates the basic assumption upon which conventional views of exchange rate management are based, that is, that changes in the price at which the local currency is traded for the US dollar (or other benchmark currency) will serve to balance the demand and supply of dollars: if the dollar becomes more expensive, locals will switch to purchasing local goods and services, reducing the demand for dollars, and vice versa when the price of the dollar falls. Since the SOE produces a trivial amount of a very few of the importables it needs, that is not an option.

The challenge for the SOE is to assure agents in the foreign currency market of the security of the exchange rate under all circumstances and in the face of any shock, whether from natural disaster, high fuel prices, unsustainable fiscal deficits, credit booms or any other domestic or external source. It will usually not be possible to increase the inflows of foreign currency in every one of these cases by external borrowing or raising interest rates to attract portfolio investment; indeed attempts to raise interest rates to borrow invariably send the wrong signal to the market, confirming apprehensions about a depreciation of the exchange rate. The adjustment in times of pressure on the exchange rate must be on the demand side, to reduce aggregate demand and imports by an amount which the foreign exchange market deems sufficient to relieve the exchange market pressure. This chapter explains how fiscal policy can be used to adjust the demand for foreign currency to ensure that, whenever it runs ahead of the available supply, that demand is reduced by a suitable amount to restore balance. The tools that Government uses for this purpose are the size of the fiscal deficit and the means by which the deficit is

DOI: 10.4324/9781003247609-9

financed. This chapter explains how these tools may be employed to maintain a stable external balance over the economic cycle.

This chapter presents a unique approach to the management of the exchange rate, one which I believe to be the only credible way to stabilise the exchange rate of any open economy. Professor John Hicks, in discussing the adjustment process in labour markets, popularised the distinction between "fixed price" and "flex price" markets.[1] The common assumption in much of economics is that markets fall into the latter category, and that prices adjust to clear the market. However, in modern markets prices are not adjusted continuously in response to current market conditions, and there is an element of rigidity which may lead to temporary gluts and shortages, destabilising the market. In most markets it is possible to minimise price instability by warehousing stocks to augment supply where and when necessary. That is what central banks attempt to do by holding reserves of foreign currency. The challenge addressed by the approach advocated in this book is that of ensuring that the monetary authority maintains an adequate war chest of foreign reserves under all circumstances. That allows the US dollar value of the domestic currency to be controlled through market intervention at the unchanging rate, at all times and in all circumstances.

On the face of it, the foreign currency market is a flex price market, and in tranquil times it usually acts that way. The interbank foreign exchange market takes care of most inflows and outflows on a daily basis, buying foreign currency from the monetary authority to cover needs the system cannot meet and selling surpluses over the system's needs. However, consider what happens when excess pressure of demand for foreign exchange emerges, because of concern about the size and financing of the public sector deficit, a sharp increase in the international prices of imported commodities or a collapse of foreign investment inflows to the country. Doubts arise about the adequacy of the country's foreign reserves, no matter how large they are, and everyone takes defensive measures: those who can switch to foreign currency deposits, companies borrow locally to pay off foreign currency trade credits and other foreign obligations, and everyone stockpiles foreign currency. Whatever action the monetary authority takes only heightens apprehension about a large devaluation of the local currency and high inflation. That is so whether the central bank sells foreign currency from its reserves, raises domestic interest rates, imposes limits on foreign transfers or allows the exchange to depreciate. What ensues is typically a deep devaluation and a period of uncertainty, high inflation and low investment.

If instead the foreign exchange market is treated as a fixed price market, policy makers in the open economy may avoid this instability and its possible long term damage to investment and growth prospects by cutting aggregate demand to relieve the excess foreign currency pressure, using tax policy, government expenditure and government borrowing strategy. The appropriate mix of tax, spending and borrowing depends on the source of the excess pressure.

While it is intuitive that foreign exchange market shocks that were caused by fiscal excess in the first place should be addressed by fiscal adjustment, the argument can be made that it is preferable to address external shocks with a combination of foreign currency sales, exchange rate adjustment and interest rate adjustment, particularly if the shock is a temporary one. This approach is unrealistic in practice, because it presumes the government and foreign exchange agents have information in advance about the source, magnitude and duration of the shock and the pervasiveness of the domestic impact of the shock itself, and that they are agreed on the exchange and interest rate policies that should be adopted in response.

In contrast, decisive, timely fiscal correction removes many levels of uncertainty and maintains a favourable investment climate. Close collaboration and joint programme design by the fiscal and treasury managers and the monetary authority is essential. Institutional arrangements for discussions with representatives of commerce and labour and a good communications strategy are also important.

Officials reduce uncertainty with the help of a macroeconomic forecast, incorporating the impact of the shock, the measures proposed to compensate for its impact and the expected outcomes for growth, employment, inflation, the exchange rate and the levels of foreign exchange. The importance of this forecast is as a benchmark against which to evaluate both the magnitude of the impact of the shock and the effectiveness of the policy responses, and as a guide for adjustments as required to stay on target. The forecast is vital, providing a reference against which policy makers can measure the distance between the actual outcomes and their expectations, and from which they may deduce the magnitude of any corrective measures needed to keep the economy on course.

Monetary and exchange rate policies may be employed to complement fiscal policy within this framework. Tax and expenditure measures will take some time to bite, and in the meantime temporary credit limits, foreign currency sales and interest rate changes may be used to relieve some pressure on the foreign currency market. Once a package of fiscal adjustments has been announced, markets may not be especially alarmed by some decline in foreign exchange, and a larger domestic interest premium may serve to attenuate capital flight as the threat of a large devaluation recedes.

The process of ongoing monitoring, evaluation and appropriate adjustment is essential to maintain the credibility of government policy and reduce the uncertainty that motivates market agents to take defensive actions to the detriment of macroeconomic performance.

It is against this background that this chapter proposes that small open economies set targets for the exchange rate, in terms of the US dollar, euro or other international currency, and adopt frameworks of fiscal and monetary coordination that enable the use of fiscal policies to modulate the demand for foreign exchange to the expected supply. This is not just the preferred approach to external balance and macroeconomic stability for small open economies; it is the only option that avoids investment uncertainties that prejudice the capacity for future growth.

The great advantage of the fixed-price approach to the foreign exchange market is that it allows for the fluid functioning of the interbank foreign exchange market. Banks can buy and sell foreign exchange at the ruling exchange rate, confident in the knowledge that they can purchase foreign currency from the central bank at that rate, at any time. The central bank always has an adequate reserve stock of foreign currency, because whenever a large or persistent call on foreign reserves is detected, timely fiscal adjustments are made to reduce the demand for imports by a sufficient amount to accommodate to the available foreign currency inflows. The secure exchange rate pegs of The Bahamas, Bermuda, the Cayman Islands and the Eastern Caribbean Currency Union have survived for decades without serious challenge, not because of exchange controls, which are token where they exist, but because the central banks and monetary authorities have maintained ample foreign reserves in all circumstances, thanks to a variety of mechanisms which ensure there is never any domestic money creation in response to foreign exchange market pressure. In the cases of Barbados and Belize, where the exchange rate has come under threat periodically, decisive fiscal contraction was the tool used to protect the exchange rate peg in every case.

The approach proposed here is also applicable to countries which have exchange rates which are managed by the monetary authorities, and are subject to change. Exchange rates in such countries are especially sensitive to shocks, real or suspected, which make it very difficult to engineer an orderly evolution of the exchange rate, along the authorities' chosen path. Rather than accumulate excessive stockpiles of foreign reserves, finance which might be better employed to invest to accelerate competitiveness and growth, the authorities in such countries would be better advised to set up a framework for managing the demand for foreign currency, using fiscal and monetary policy.

Modifying the IMF model to reflect the SOE foreign currency market

Agénor (2004) offers a useful starting point for demonstrating how acknowledging the fact that exports, imports and nontradables are not substitutes in production or spending modifies the conventional analysis of balance of payments adjustment policy. Figure 7.1, which is adapted from Agénor (2004, p. 372), shows the combinations of the exchange rate and the level of foreign reserves which are consistent with the balance of external payments and receipts, *BB*, and with a balance between the supply of money and the demand for credit, *MM*. The exchange rate appreciates as we move along the horizontal axis. If we assume, as does the conventional analysis, that depreciation of the exchange rate causes import substitution (and increased foreign earnings, if exporters have market power and can price internationally in the domestic currency), then the *BB* schedule slopes upward to the left:

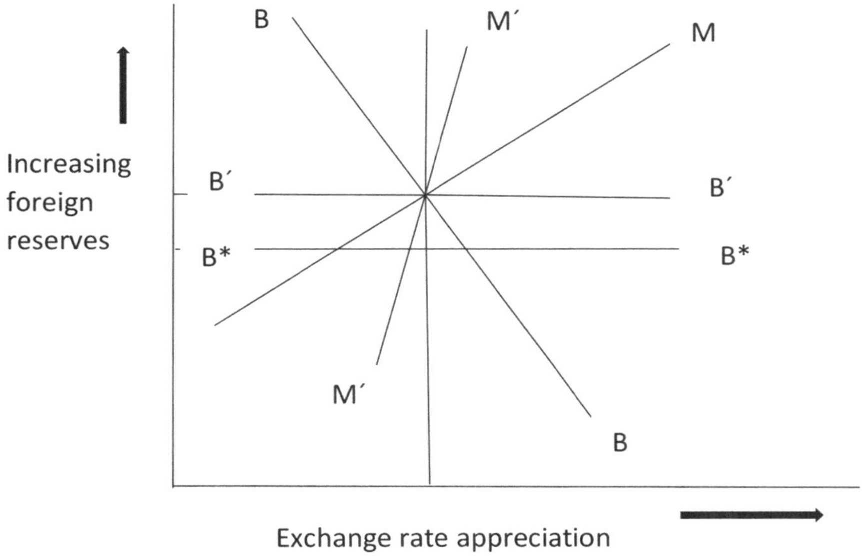

Figure 7.1 The IMF framework modified
Source: Agénor (2004, p. 372).

depreciation economises on the use of foreign exchange (and stimulates additional foreign earnings), leading to an accumulation of foreign reserves. However, in the absence of substitution effects the schedule becomes horizontal, as shown by *B'B'*; changes in the exchange rate have no effect on imports, exports or the level of foreign reserves. Indeed, the level of foreign reserves may fall (e.g. to *B*B**), as a result of capital flight. There may be some improvement in the current account, to the extent that inflation erodes domestic purchasing power and depresses the volume of imports, but the impact will be small, compared to the flight of capital.

The *MM* schedule shows the combinations of exchange rate changes and changes in foreign reserves that are consistent with the internal balance of money and expenditure. An increase in foreign reserves represents incoming foreign currency which is not needed to pay for imports or for any other outward financial transfers. Instead the foreign currency is sold to the central bank for local currency, which adds to the domestic money supply. The slope of the *MM* schedule reflects an assumption that the effects on aggregate spending and imports are relatively small, compared with the increase in foreign reserves, so that there is a tendency for the exchange rate to appreciate. There is some question about the effects of the impact of a foreign reserve-induced increase in the money supply in banking systems which feature chronic surpluses of liquid funds, and where bank finance is readily available to established credit-worthy companies from foreign sources, should there be a shortage of funds on the local market. The evidence suggests that domestic credit is fully determined on the demand side, in which case there is little or no impact of increased money supply on expenditure, so long as the source of the money expansion is foreign reserve accumulation. In this case *MM* does slope upward to the right as shown, but the real balance effects are weak, as reflected in a shift to *M'M'*.

Because of weak price effects, therefore, the conventional framework for analysing balance of payments provides no guidance for managing the demand for foreign exchange. For that we need relationships between fiscal policy and aggregate expenditure (Figure 7.2) and between expenditure and the demand for foreign exchange, Figure 7.3. The choices of taxation, expenditure and financing in the fiscal package which will determine the effect on spending cannot be easily summarised; Figure 7.2 simplifies for expository purposes by representing only the impact of money creation in the overall fiscal package, neglecting tax and expenditure effects for the moment. Working backwards from Figure 7.3, the authorities can estimate the reduction of imports ($-\Delta m$) needed to correct for the balance of payments shock, and devise a fiscal adjustment programme ($-\Delta b$) sufficient to reduce aggregate spending ($-\Delta a$) by enough to secure the necessary reduction.

Guidelines for the design of fiscal policy

The content of the fiscal package will depend on the source of the shortages in the foreign currency market. While we cannot make generalisations for all countries, it is possible to offer high-level guidelines for the shape of the fiscal

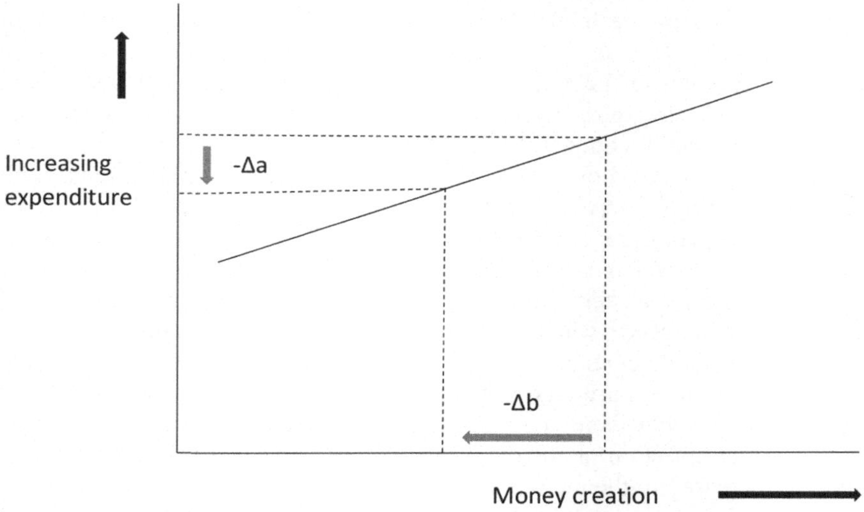

Figure 7.2 Money supply and aggregate expenditure
Source: Author's construction.

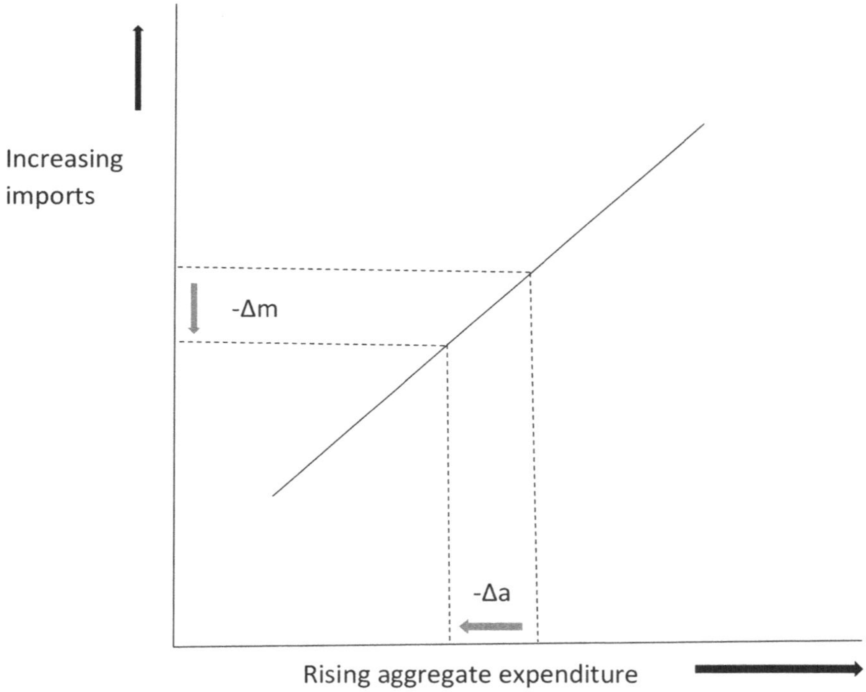

Figure 7.3 Aggregate expenditure and imports
Source: Author's construction.

policy envelope in response to balance of payments problems which are frequently reported.

A particularly difficult structural problem, affecting both competitiveness and stability, is a secular decline in public sector productivity. This has been the bane of public sector performance in much of the English-speaking Caribbean in the past four decades. The decline is not easy to quantify, because part of the evidence of that decline is the fall-off of the quality and quantity of published data on all aspects of Caribbean economies. Whereas in the 1970s there was a wealth of data produced by government agencies on health, education, housing conditions, access to public utilities and other concrete measures of performance against which to compare expenditure in these categories, comparable data is now hard to find, despite the revolution in compilation and communications technology. However, evidence of poor public sector performance abounds in the deterioration of infrastructure, lack of maintenance of government property, the glacial pace of administrative processes, long delays in the administration of justice and every other area of public sector activity. Throughout the region projects and programmes are announced but not implemented, so there is now widespread cynicism about every new initiative.

The decline in public sector performance is hugely consequential: years of poor policy design and administrative inefficiency have left the majority of Caribbean countries with little or no fiscal space, limiting their access to international finance and their ability to respond to new challenges. To the extent that Caribbean Governments have been unable to arrest the productivity decline, they are themselves responsible for much of the vulnerability of which everyone complains.

This problem has been recognised since the 1980s, but "reforms" of the organisation and structure of tax systems and the public sector more generally have only served to accelerate the decline. The introduction of the vaunted value added tax in Jamaica, The Bahamas, Barbados and other service-oriented economies is an example; economics offers no objective way of measuring value added in services and as a result the so-called VAT becomes an excessively high sales tax on goods and services. Other examples of "reforms" which have depressed productivity abound, including public-private partnerships where government provides all the finance and services all debt, the politicisation of state corporations set up ostensibly to operate on a quasi-commercial basis, and heavy but futile use of private consultants instead of building needed capacity in the public sector.

A clear sign that countries have turned the corner on public sector performance would be the timely publication of comprehensive data on health, education, crime, public utilities, housing, sanitation, social services and all other aspects of public sector performance. In order to restore their credibility, state corporations, government departments and government agencies should publish timely annual reports and accounts, with adequate analysis for informed readers to assess their performance. This information is essential to develop a multi-year fiscal reform programme and track its implementation against hard measures of performance.

A second possible source of balance of payments difficulty is an international shock such as the COVID-19 pandemic. The challenge in this case is twofold: to re-order government priorities to make room for a substantial increase in the allocation for health for an immediate emergency response, and to build a stronger public health system that has the capacity to respond more quickly to future pandemics (Charumilind et al, 2020); and secondly, to trim all other government expenditure to fit within a reduced envelope of finance, comprising reduced revenues thanks to the hit to GDP, borrowing from international financial institutions, and whatever other borrowing the country's credit-worthiness allows. The differing pandemic responses in various countries serve to illustrate the effect of public sector efficiency on the resilience of countries in the face of any shock. The more efficient governments were those that were able to quickly mobilise resources to ensure they tracked the spread of the disease, equipping themselves with the capacity to make a deliberate choice about their strategy for suppression. The less efficient governments remained at the mercy of the spread of COVID-19, engaged in an ongoing struggle to avoid overwhelming their health services.

Spill-overs from the international economy are a third category of shock to the balance of payments of the SOE. In this case the appropriate response would be an across the board cut in expenditure and/or a tax rate increase that does not affect the distribution of income. This generalisation would be tweaked to accommodate government's capital projects, some of which might be postponed while others are kept on schedule.

Election cycles are typically among the most problematic of destabilising shocks. The obvious corrective is to reverse all election-related expenditure immediately after the new (or re-elected) administration takes office, and plan and implement a strategy to replace the lost income and employment by government investment and other spending to increase competitiveness and output capacity. On the rare occasions when a strategy along these lines was implemented, the temporary widening of the fiscal and balance of payments deficits was quickly reversed, and there was no slowdown in the economy. The aftermath of the 1982 election in Barbados is a case in point (Worrell, 1987). However, a case like this is a rarity, at least in the Caribbean. One problem is that the post-election cuts needed to reassure foreign currency markets that enough spending power has been subtracted may be larger than the pre-election stimulus. The new leadership may lack the confidence or the political capital to follow through on the deep cuts that are required. We have an example of this, again for Barbados, in the incomplete adjustment programme in the wake of the 2013 election. A second problem arises on the labour market. The unemployed who secure pre-election jobs are largely people with low levels of skill and often not well adjusted to the disciplines of the workplace. They are unlikely to secure jobs in the post-election programme for investment and competitiveness because of their low productivity. This is a social engineering challenge to which Caribbean governments have not yet addressed themselves.

SOEs must accept that there is nothing they can do to moderate the impact of inflation on the international prices of food and fuel, and they should be clear on this matter in the design of policy and in how policy is communicated to the public. The case against subsidising imported food and fuel is easily made: the money for the subsidies has to be taken from tax receipts, so in effect consumers are simply paying higher taxes instead of higher prices. Alternatively, some other spending priority must be cut to make way for the subsidy. The alternative of gradually eliminating the subsidy in favour of increasing income support for the most vulnerable is more socially acceptable, in most circumstances.

Another category of balance of payments shock arises from rapid inflation in property prices, often supported by a boom in credit. Regulatory policies such as setting minimum down payments and tighter risk management benchmarks are the preferred tools in this situation, although they have proved problematic in application. A central question that confronts the policy maker is to know when to take action. Booms are explosive events, which go rapidly from small clouds on the horizon to become raging hurricanes. Typically the first signs of a credit boom are innocuous, increases that seem to be nothing out of the ordinary. However, in contrast to similar episodes that would previously have been observed, on this occasion the next report reveals a situation that is already so alarming that intervention risks increasing uncertainty in the market, causing some agents to panic, precipitating a crash. The regulator is caught on the horns of a dilemma: should they intervene and risk the possibility of a crash, or should they wait in the hope that the surge will run out of stream? Only after the event will they know whether they have made the right decision. We have no record of the number of occasions when forbearance was the correct decision; we only know about the times when the decision to intervene was made only in the maelstrom of a full-blown crisis. The uninitiated assumes that no-one was paying attention earlier; that is seldom the case.

A different kind of adjustment problem arises where the property price inflation is the result of purchases from abroad, as in the cases of Barbados in the mid-2000s and more recently in some countries of the ECCU. These inflows cause a large surge of foreign currency inflows, which are followed by a "sudden stop", when the inflows came to an abrupt end, and foreign currency is no longer so very abundant. In this case, the challenge is to moderate the impact of the surge in FDI on spending and imports, to accumulate part of the foreign currency bonanza in the form of foreign reserves. The helps to avoid a fiscally induced bust, in order to sustain the external balance once the heavy inflow of FDI has subsided.

Is there an equilibrium exchange rate?

The appeal of a managed, predictable value of local currency in terms of the US dollar, the euro or other currency used in international trade and finance is unquestionable. The challenge which SOEs face is one of supporting the value of the local currency with foreign reserves that will be adequate even in emergencies, and doing so at reasonable cost. We have shown a way to achieve this objective through the use of fiscal adjustment to counter the balance of payments effects of all shocks, whatever their source or nature. By ensuring that foreign currency outflows are always moderated in line with inflows, the foreign reserve stocks are protected from capital flight and speculation that could compromise the central bank's ability to support the value of local currency by intervention at the anchor rate. This approach has the virtue that the exchange rate is managed via the interbank market, with no need for quantitative limits, caps or other non-market interventions.

Our approach to exchange rate management also has the merit that it achieves internal and external balance. In fact, external balance is attained by using fiscal tools to achieve internal balance, at a level of aggregate expenditure which is consistent with external balance. We do not need to think of these balances as being in equilibrium, even in a dynamic sense. Instead, the fiscal tools are calibrated to affect the behaviour of consumers, investors, lenders and all other economic agents in ways that lead to the desired outcomes. There are monitors on the outcomes so that the authorities can collect data to make adjustments where necessary to stay on course.

As is reflected in the discussion in the previous section, fiscal tools are varied and flexible, and strategies may be tailored to the circumstances by calibrating each tool to fit into the overall picture. The tools also have the advantage that they comprise actions which are directly within the government's purview – that is, direct spending – and actions which are designed to affect the behaviour of actors in the private sector, which offers even greater flexibility. This wealth of options for the custom design of fiscal policy cannot be captured by a single indicator, so it is not surprising that fiscal multipliers and other such indicators do not yield much insight into the strategy for any individual case.

The fiscal policy approach to exchange rate management contrasts with all other approaches, including my own early work on exchange rates. A review of selected papers from this literature uncovers the ongoing frustrations of policy makers over their inability to stabilise exchange rates and reduce the inflation and uncertainty that volatile rates engender, using any of the commonly recommended exchange rate strategies.

Worrell (1982) compared the exchange rates of Barbados and Jamaica with hypothetical rates based on a trade-and-tourism weighted basket of currencies, concluding the basket was an inferior option: the basket-linked rates were just as volatile as the actual rates, and levels of uncertainty were higher, which would have implied higher foreign currency conversion costs. Bourne, Cox, Solis and Worrell (1985) set out to come up with a recommendation for a common exchange rate strategy that would promote the growth of intra-regional trade within the Caribbean Community (CARICOM). In this they were not successful, perhaps because they found that exchange rate changes had no discernible relative price effects. Worrell (1985) was an ambitious effort to derive an index of real exchange rate changes that took account of real balance effects as well as trade elasticities. The index was computed for Barbados for the period 1962–82. Harriott and Worrell (1997) estimated equilibrium real exchange rates using two alternative methods for Barbados, Colombia, Costa Rica, the Dominican Republic, Guyana, Honduras, Jamaica, Mexico, Trinidad and Tobago and Venezuela. The first test used a single equation model offered by Sebastian Edwards in 1989 based on a structural VAR for the period 1972–92. The results were compared with an intuitive method based on three factors: the growth of each economy over several consecutive years, whether the country achieved a low inflation rate during the growth periods and whether a small deficit or surplus was recorded on the balance of external payments. The only general observation for all countries was that "real exchange changes are not an effective stimulant to growth in any country" (Harriott and Worrell, 1997, p. 15).

Worrell (1992) included an exhaustive taxonomy of exchange rate policies (Worrell, 1992, pp. 28–43), ending with the recommendation that "Policy makers in small open economies... should set a target for the exchange rate to be attained by suitable monetary and fiscal policies" (Worrell, 1992, p. 42). This book also makes the following observations: devaluation increases competitiveness to the extent that it drives a wedge between the price of tradables and the cost of domestic factors of production; to succeed in stabilising the balance of payments, devaluation should be reinforced with fiscal and monetary policies; investment in the tradable sector determines the country's potential growth; fixed exchange rates are prone to crisis, which can force disorderly adjustment, with devaluation, informal markets and wage-price spirals. The study marked the first recognition that the key to stabilising the external accounts lay with the management of aggregate demand.

Worrell, Marshall and Smith (2000) is a study of the political and economic drivers of exchange rate policy in the English-speaking Caribbean, based on case studies and empirical tests with pooled data for the exchange rate, the exchange regime (pegged or floating), the volatility of the rate and the relative price of nontradables (the real exchange rate). The study provides a potted history of exchange rate changes for the 1980s to 1997. The case studies are the sterling devaluation of 1967; the switch from pegging to sterling to the US dollar at various times over the years 1973–1976; the Jamaica 1977 crawling peg; Jamaica's 1983 exchange rate auction system; the Trinidad and Tobago 1985 devaluation to improve the fiscal balance; the Antigua 1986 experience, when the country's membership of the Eastern Caribbean Monetary Union (ECCU) was a source of credibility; the Guyana 1987 devaluation and economic restructuring; Jamaica's introduction of the floating rate in 1990; Barbados' 1992 adjustment programme which was anchored on the exchange rate; the Grenada 1991 fiscal adjustment, which, like Antigua's earlier experience, took place within the constraints of the ECCU. The empirical tests included the following economic explanatory variables: the change in world tourism arrivals, the US Treasury bill rate, consumer price inflation (CPI) as ratio to US CPI, cumulative inflation, the balance of payments less short term capital, aggregate domestic spending, short term capital, the import cover, the share of agriculture and services in GDP, the US GDP, an index of openness, the broad money supply and gross domestic capital formation. The political explanatory variables included were a trade union dummy, a chamber of commerce dummy, a stable party system dummy, the number of parties in parliament, and the number of years to the next general election. The general conclusions include the observation that the exchange rate strategy is "not solely – perhaps not mainly – driven mainly by economic conditions" (Worrell, Marshall and Smith, 2000, p. 43). The economic factors may have had greater effect on exchange rate volatility and the real exchange rate than on the nominal rate, while monetary union has made for a durable fixed exchange rate among the ECCU countries. This comprehensive study served to demonstrate the practical difficulties in the way of designing an exchange rate strategy to attain stability and growth objectives.

Against this background, more recent papers expand on systems for managing the exchange rate through containing aggregate expenditure, using fiscal policy. A critical feature of the framework is joint policy design and implementation by the central bank and the fiscal authorities:

> In the real world of information asymmetries, uncertain expectations and changeable preferences, it is not enough to create an autonomous and publicly accountable central bank. In addition, the central bank and the treasury must work together on the design, implementation, monitoring and, when necessary, the revision of macroeconomic policy, and on providing the public with information on ongoing economic developments and interpretation of the macroeconomic strategy.
>
> (Worrell, 2000, abstract)

Worrell, Codrington, Craigwell and Greenidge (2006) is a study of the institutional arrangements for exchange rate targeting in Barbados, using mainly fiscal tools. "Monetary policy played only a small role in the adjustment process, but the Central Bank of Barbados was at the centre of the design and management of the economic adjustment programme" (Worrell, Codrington, Craigwell and Greenidge, 2006, p. 82). Worrell, Craigwell and Mitchell (2008) tested the proposition that a country with a long-term exchange rate peg will maintain uncovered interest parity, using daily foreign currency trading data for Barbados. The study concludes that inflows and outflows were consistent with uncovered interest parity. This result is important, because it implies there is little scope for independent management of the interest rate. Worrell, Moore and Beckles (2018) explores the empirical evidence on the non-substitutability of exports, imports and nontradables, as well as the impact of exchange rate volatility on growth and the HDI score of a selection of SOEs: ".... we should expect to see an inverse relationship, however weak, between the volatility of the exchange rate and the country's HDI score. That is indeed what we observe" (Worrell, Moore and Beckles, 2018, p. 198).

This review of Caribbean experience goes a long way to explaining why the notion of an equilibrium value of the exchange rate which balances the demand and supply for foreign exchange, and the use of the exchange rate tool to stimulate growth, are notions which have no currency in the region. Both theory and experience attest to the difficulty of managing the rate, the dire consequences of allowing the foreign currency market to seek a rate that clears the market, and the futility of using devaluation as a tool to stimulate exports and growth in the SOE. These studies also introduce the approach to managing the exchange rate using fiscal policy.

Defining fiscal space

We may employ the relationship between the fiscal balance and the balance on external payments and receipts – with given tax, expenditure and government financing policies – to measure the discretionary space available for government expansion. Starting from a tranquil economic situation, where fiscal and monetary policies enjoy public credibility and the exchange rate is stable, the room available for expansionary fiscal policy is defined by the excess of foreign exchange reserves over the minimum that the market considers adequate to defend the exchange rate. Government may use that entire amount to buy time for other measures to take effect or to spend on targeted adjustment spending, provided such expansion is embedded in a fiscal package that maintains the credibility of the overall government strategy. The overall strategy must be considered sufficient to limit the loss of foreign reserves to no more than the surplus over the minimum needed to reassure agents in the foreign currency market of the adequacy of the foreign reserve stock.

This approach to defining fiscal space is proposed in Belgrave, LaCorbiniere, Worrell and Applewhaite (2011), where it is used to measure the fiscal space available to the Government of Barbados over the previous four decades. Starting with the observation that the overall balance of external payments, reflected in changes in the level of foreign reserves is the most proximate signal of fiscal sustainability, the study determined the limit for expansionary policy by stressing the fiscal balance and observing the impact on the external balance, using a macroeconomic model structured along the lines of Chapter 6. Fiscal deficits in Barbados were unsustainable in the late 1980s and early 1990s, leading up to the 1991/1992 economic crisis and its immediate aftermath. This approach to defining fiscal space was refined and applied to seven Caribbean countries in Worrell et al (2015). The risk that the sovereign will have insufficient foreign reserves in any future contingency was estimated on the basis of the estimated impact of marginal government spending on the demand for foreign exchange, taking account of any wealth effects of the public sector borrowing requirement and the way it is financed.

The relationship which measures the fiscal space may be derived from the balance of payments and aggregate expenditure identities and the import equation in Chapter 6. The expression is:

$$\Delta FXR/p = p_t x - p_t f_5[q - (FISC - B_f - B_d)/p] + FDI + B_f \tag{7.1}$$

The change in foreign reserves ΔFXR is equal to the difference between total inflows comprising export receipts x, foreign direct investment FDI and foreign borrowing by government B_f, and outflows for imports, given by the expression $p_t f_5[q - (FISC - B_f - B_d)/p]$, all values being expressed in real terms. The expression in square brackets is a more articulated version of Equation 6.5 (which expresses the propensity to import based on aggregate expenditure). Aggregate spending is the sum of output q and money creation. Money creation is the amount of the fiscal deficit ($-FISC$) which is not financed by local (B_d) or foreign borrowing (B_f). Using the model of Chapter 6, an estimate of the amount of space for discretionary fiscal spending can be made, assuming unchanged borrowing strategies. The fiscal space is the amount of money creation that can be accommodated before foreign reserves fall to the minimum level which the market finds acceptable.

Barbados, 2013: incomplete balance of payments stabilisation

The macroeconomic policy framework described in this book was employed in the design of an adjustment strategy in response to a precipitate decline in foreign reserves in Barbados in the wake of a general election in 2013. In a classic case of the election cycle, the fiscal deficit doubled from the previous year to 8.5 per cent in 2012, climbing further to 11 per cent in the election year. By May 2013, in the immediate aftermath of the election, the Central Bank of Barbados informed the Prime Minister and the Minister of Finance that its daily foreign exchange monitor had detected a rate of decline in the foreign reserves that, if not arrested, would have undermined confidence in the Bank's ability to defend the peg. The high-level macroeconomic management committee, chaired jointly by the Minister of Finance and the Central Bank Governor (myself) drew up a package of fiscal measures designed to restore the foreign reserve levels of January 2013, which were considered more than adequate. The package was agreed by Cabinet and discussed with the Social Partners, and a contractionary budget was passed in the Parliament in June 2013. No interest rate change was thought necessary because the large stock of foreign reserves offered a comfortable margin over minimum levels. Also, to the extent that the rapidity of the foreign exchange loss reflected defensive strategies adopted because of a fear of devaluation, it was expected that the budget announcement would have reassured the market and moderated the slide.

However, as may be seen from Figure 7.4, which reproduces the Central Bank's daily foreign reserves monitor, the June budget had no discernible effect on the rate of foreign reserve loss. A second set of contractionary measures was decided upon and adopted in October. As year-end approached the foreign reserve stock had fallen to levels which the authorities deemed unacceptably low, and a decision was made to float a large US dollar bond, partly to retire outstanding high-interest debt, but also to provide an extra amount to boost foreign reserves. However, the attempt at liability management was unsuccessful, because international markets were rattled by the continuing foreign reserve slide, and the Government's failure to demonstrate a decisive commitment to an adequate adjustment strategy in the absence of IMF oversight. An agreement with the IMF would have been very difficult at this time, because the IMF staff was insistent that a depreciation of the exchange rate was a necessary element of any package which they were prepared to take to their Board. With foreign reserves still more than adequate, to have entered into discussions with the IMF in these circumstances might have undermined confidence and aggravated the foreign reserve loss, prejudicing the success of the fiscal adjustment strategy. In the event, a foreign loan was secured, though at less favourable terms than the Government might have

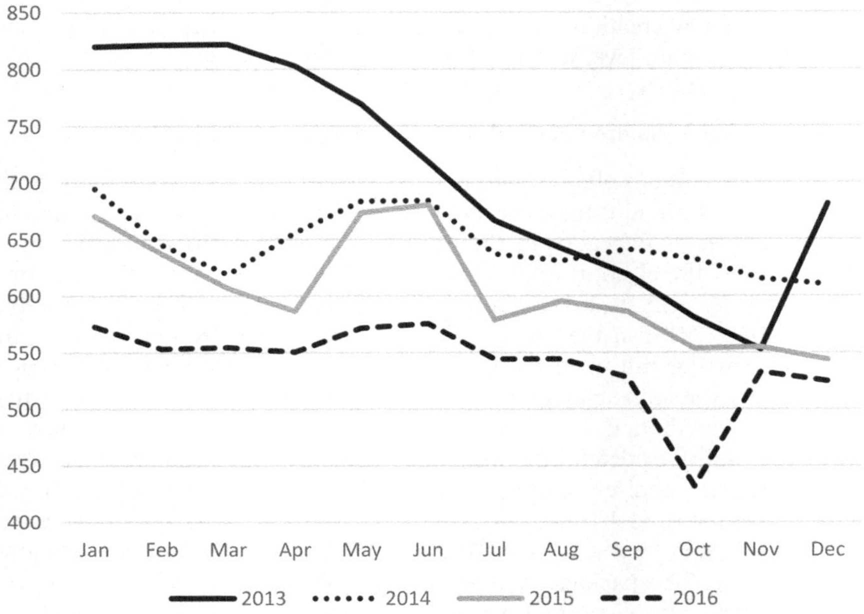

Figure 7.4 Barbados international liquidity, US$m
Source: Author's construction.

wished. This attenuated the year-end reserve loss, to the equivalent of four weeks of imports of goods and services. At the end of 2013 foreign reserves were considered more than adequate, at the equivalent of a little more than 15 weeks.

The fiscal measures took full effect in 2014, and the foreign reserves monitor shows that the familiar seasonal patterns of fluctuations re-emerged over the course of that year. The adjustment strategy must be considered a qualified success, however. There was a further decline in foreign reserves in 2014, albeit of only the equivalent of one week of imports. More critically, fiscal strategies failed to boost incentives to the extent needed to stimulate investment in increased export and tourism capacity, improved productivity and quality enhancement. As a result, foreign currency inflows never recovered enough to repair the losses incurred through the priming of the pump for the 2013 election.

Fiscal policies for development and stabilisation: Caribbean experiences

The crucial impact of government policy on the quality of life is unquestioned, and the experiences of North America and Europe in the 1950s and 1960s are testimony of that. The Caribbean experienced gains during this period as a result of the extension of health, educational and social services, gains in real income per head and the growth of the middle class. However, gains have been much harder won in the three most recent decades. Most countries have made progress, but there are a few which have seen no noticeable improvement in the well-being of citizens since the 1970s, and nowhere have gains been as rapid as in the previous three decades. For the most part the circumstances of Caribbean countries are not dissimilar: apart from Trinidad and Tobago, the only established international oil exporter, they power their economies with proceeds from tourism, other services and exports of agricultural and manufactured goods. Arguably, fiscal policies were a major factor both in the recent slowdown in development gains, as well as the disparity of outcomes of different countries. In this section we offer some examples.

Worrell (1987, Chapter 9) offers a summary assessment of economic adjustment policies in the English-speaking Caribbean in the 1970s and early 1980s. Conservative financial policies, especially with respect to the government budget, were judged to have produced the most favourable outcomes, but there was little success with policies to increase the supply of goods and services. Relative price changes had little effect. The value of prompt, early adjustment was brought home by the observation that those countries which did not succeed in restoring external balance after the first oil price shock had no good policy options for coping with volatile commodity prices and high interest rates in the early 1980s. Jamaica and Guyana, the countries that were expected to be star performers because of their relatively abundant natural resources, turned out to be among the worst performers. A central factor was the extensive use in both countries of non-market interventionist policies such as rationing of foreign exchange sales by the central bank, directing banks to meet quotas for lending to manufacturers and agricultural enterprises, and similar policies. These interventions left importers, banks, borrowers and the general public frustrated in carrying out what, from their perspectives, were reasonable, legitimate and necessary transactions. The result was a proliferation of informal markets, including an informal market for foreign currency where the US dollar was traded at a large premium over the rate offered by the central bank. In time, such a large proportion of transactions was shifted to informal markets that devaluation became inevitable. Currency devaluation under these circumstances had lasting effects, causing high inflation that reduced most real incomes, eroding the value of domestic savings and the incentive to save, and creating financial and labour market volatility which deterred foreign investors and widened the country's risk premium.

While arguing that "we are rather more confident about policies for stabilisation than about policies for growth", Worrell (1992, p. 3) showed how adjustment policies could be improved on by fuller articulation of fiscal policy. The case for fiscal management to secure external balance was made, including the value of assured external balance in lending credibility to the overall fiscal stance. Other useful observations were that financial and economic markets often need guidance, particularly when there is apprehension about economic fundamentals. The monetary, financial and fiscal authorities are best equipped to provide that guidance, thanks to their staffs of economists and financial analysts who are constantly monitoring the pulse of the economy. Formal and informal channels of coordination between the private and public sectors are useful, and it is essential that the authorities establish channels of public information which are regular, well-informed and documented, and insightful, providing sound analysis that is presented in a way that is appealing and persuasive. The informal press conference, the off-the-cuff remark and the cryptic tweet are the opposite of what is required.

Public sector reform

There is a wealth of data to support the conclusion that the productivity of Caribbean public services has been in decline at least since the 1980s. Comprehensive region-wide data on all relevant indices do not exist, but there are documented declines in health, educational and public security indicators for individual countries. We have witnessed chronic lack of water supply (Barbados), failure of affordable drug procurement systems (Jamaica) and widespread accumulation of arrears of payment in all countries. Equally, the persistence of the problem of low productivity is attested to by the repeated efforts for public sector reform that have been an objective of practically every new government administration in the Caribbean in the last four decades.

In Barbados by the mid-1990s "public opinion [had] become increasingly exasperated by examples of poor quality in some government services" (Worrell, 1996, p. 20), partly because public sector wage policy had eroded the premium on skills in the public sector. Twenty years later the problem was more acute: there was now evidence of "low levels of productivity in the delivery of public services" (Worrell, 2016).

Countries have taken initiatives and devised strategies for public sector reform over five decades, with little success. Starting in the early 1970s Jamaica embarked on a series of public service reforms which continues to the present. An assessment of the reforms up to 2002 appears in Tindigarukayo (2004). The seven programmes the study identifies over three decades failed to reach their objectives because, according to the author, public service salaries throughout remained too low to attract high calibre personnel; external funding agencies were too involved in the design of the reform strategies; there was a lack of integration between those who were responsible for policy design and those who were tasked with implementation; and an "informal system" frustrated the operation of many policy innovations.

The Caribbean tax reform programmes did not lack for high-level expertise, thanks to the support of international financial institutions and the donor agencies of leading advanced countries. A prime example was the Jamaica tax reform programme of the mid-1980s, which was based on a comprehensive suite of empirical analyses of the tax system and the estimated impact of the proposed reforms (Alm, 1985; Alm and Bahl, 1985; Bird and Miller, 1989;

McLure, 1986; Moussavian, 1984; Thirsk, 1984; Wasylenko, 1986, 1987; Wozny, 1985). No comprehensive assessment of that programme has been done *ex post* but it is evident that the fiscal reforms did not contribute sufficiently to the stabilisation of external payments, which remained in disequilibrium until the 2000s. Also, Tindigarukayo's (2004) bird's-eye view assessment included the 1980s tax reform as one of the seven reform packages, all of which were judged to have been failures.

A recent analysis of the Jamaica public sector reforms over the period 2013–2019, when the country completed adjustment programmes with IMF support which are considered successful, found that on average 75 per cent of the reforms were completed, a creditable performance (Bowen, Salmon, Brown and Serju-Thomas, 2021). However, the reforms appear to have had little impact on the Jamaican economy's anaemic growth rate, which rose from an average of 0.6 per cent 2000–2013, to a disappointing 0.9 per cent on average since that time. The authors of the study speculate that the reform package was not sufficiently ambitious in scope, and that they imply that the reforms may not have been well managed.

A major public sector reform programme was undertaken in the Eastern Caribbean Currency Union (ECCU) in the middle 1980s. An interim evaluation of the project (Worrell, Belchere and Coolidge, 1987) found that the major factors in the effectiveness of public policy formulation and implementation were the expertise of senior management of the public service and the commitment of governments to the economic strategy. Commitment came from a conviction of the necessity and benefits of the agreed strategy. The senior management in the countries with the most successful policies "insisted that the new policies be tailored to local realities, they gave guidance as to the priorities, and they went out of their way to ensure general support for the programmes. Without a core of energetic and talented officials, fiscal reform programs have little chance of success" (Worrell, Belchere and Coolidge, 1987, p. 71). In addition, fostering discussion and public information about the fiscal system and the proposed changes created a favourable environment for the receptivity of the reforms. Cross-fertilisation of ideas on financial management, including with the wider Caribbean, proved helpful, but more needed to be done. A scarcity of skilled middle level executives was a concern, and the empirical and technical foundations of policy needed to be beefed up. The early promise of these 1980s ECCU reforms has not been fulfilled, and the region suffers from public sector disabilities in equal measure with the rest of the Caribbean.

Although the 1991 IMF-supported adjustment programme in Barbados has been judged a success (Worrell, Codrington, Craigwell and Greenidge, 2006), it failed to reverse the secular downtrend in public sector productivity and the quality of public services which had become evident in the late 1980s. The programme was successful in that it restored the balance of external payments at the fixed exchange rate, thanks to a sharp reduction in the fiscal deficit and supporting temporary credit restrictions which expired after six months. However, the suite of policy reforms on which much of the supporting finance (loans from the Interamerican Development Bank, the Caribbean Development Bank and other official sources) was conditioned was spottily implemented. It is now largely forgotten, but the 1991 Standby Agreement with the IMF, supported by other international financial institutions, was abandoned mid-way in the three-year span, largely because of failure to complete structural reforms. The Government could have afforded to forego the remaining finance under the programme, because the swingeing fiscal cuts in 1991 reduced the 1992 import bill by something of the order of 20 per cent, restoring external balance with such decisiveness that the threat of devaluation had completely receded within a year of the approval of IMF support. The most useful innovations by Government in the 1990s were the establishment of a productivity council, which, though very under-resourced, has produced what little in-depth research exists on this topic for Barbados, and the Social Partnership, which has degenerated over the period of its existence into a vehicle for political posturing, with no relevance to the formulation and implementation of policy. Much more damaging was the failure to institute any of the structures for financial control, timely reporting on performance, professional management and publication of reports by Government departments and agencies, and by state corporations. In the absence of this framework, there are no benchmarks against which to measure public sector performance, and no way for the parliament and the people to hold public servants accountable. In Barbados, as elsewhere in the Caribbean and beyond, what passes for accountability and transparency is little more than political theatre.

Sadly, Barbadians have not learned from the 1991 experience, and the IMF-supported Extended Fund Arrangement of 2018 again failed to address a basic requirement for public sector transparency, that is, timely publication of performance reports, together with financial statements, by every major entity within the public sector. Public tolerance of this dereliction is surprising in view of the abundant evidence of major deterioration in educational achievement, services at the public hospital, the administration of justice, the water supply system, the road surfaces throughout the island, the efficiency of tax administration, the bureaucratic nightmares involved in licensing and obtaining regulatory permission, the neglect of maintenance of public property and a litany of other failures.

It is thanks to this public tolerance of public sector inefficiency that the Barbados Government chose to restructure its debt, as part of the package of measures agreed with the IMF under the Extended Fund Facility in 2018. In discussions of national debt, the concern is usually with US dollar debt; the often-quoted rules of thumb for debt limits are almost always in respect of foreign debt. At the time of the 2018 agreement with the IMF the ratio of US dollar debt to Barbados GDP was no more than 28 per cent, as reported by the Central Bank of Barbados. That is an extraordinarily low figure by international comparison, hardly reason to seek IMF financial assistance. The loss of foreign reserves which precipitated the appeal by the newly-elected Government was caused by excessive lending to Government by the Central Bank, in local currency, which boosted aggregate demand and imports. The bulk of the overall debt, reported by the Bank at 149 per cent of GDP, was in domestic currency, mainly owed to the public sector itself (the Central Bank and the National Insurance Fund).

Additional evidence of declining public sector performance in selected Caribbean countries may be found in the *Global Competitiveness Report* (World Economic Forum, 2018). For Barbados there was a noticeable fall in the index score for all public institutions, in the quality of roads, infrastructure, the port and airport, and in life expectancy, infant mortality and the net primary school enrolment rate over the five years to 2017.

The Caribbean experience with policies to stimulate development in the last four decades has yielded little measurable success. The main contribution to competitiveness in The Bahamas, Barbados, Belize and the countries of the Eastern Caribbean Currency Union was the maintenance of macroeconomic stability, evidenced by the enduring nature of their exchange rate pegs to the US dollar. The economic development plans and strategies of individual countries were never followed up by concrete action at a national level, and development banks, technical and financial support and tax incentives have all turned out to be of little effect, no doubt because they were never situated within an internally consistent, fully articulated and monitored strategy. Perhaps the most significant dereliction, however, has been the unrelieved decline in the productivity of the public sector and the quality of public services, across the English-speaking Caribbean. Bureaucratic inefficiencies are now the most pervasive drag on investment in the region.

Note

1 See Marcello, 2009.

References

Agénor, Pierre-Richard. 2004. *The Economics of Adjustment and Growth*. Cambridge, Massachusetts: Harvard University Press.

Alm, James. 1985. "Payroll taxes and contributions in Jamaica," *Working Paper*. Syracuse, NY: Metropolitan Studies Program, Syracuse University, March.

Alm. James and Roy Bahl. 1985. "Evaluation of the structure of the Jamaican individual income tax," *Working Paper*. Syracuse, NY: Metropolitan Studies Program, Syracuse University, New York, October.

Belgrave, Anton, Jason LaCorbiniere, Delisle Worrell and Denisa Applewhaite. 2011. "Fiscal sustainability in an open economy with an exchange rate peg. The reform of indirect taxes in Jamaica," *Working Paper*, Syracuse, NY: Metropolitan Studies Program, Syracuse University, March.

Bird, Richard and Barbara Miller. 1989. "The incidence of indirect taxes on low income households in Jamaica," *Economic Development and Cultural Change*, Vol. 37 no. 2, January.

Bourne, Compton, Winston Cox, Felix Solis and DeLisle Worrell. 1985. "Exchange Rate Policy within the Caribbean Community," *Working Papers.* Central Bank of Barbados, pp. 154–241.

Bowen, Brooke-Anne, Dwayne Salmon, Donya Brown, and Prudence Serju-Thomas. 2012. "Assessing Jamaica's Growth Enhancing Reforms," *Bank of Jamaica Discussion Paper*, September.

Charumilind, Sarun, Matt Craven, JessicaLamb, and Matt Wilson. 2020. "Preventing future waves of COVID-19," *McKinsey and Company.*

Edwards, Sebastian. 1989. *Real Exchange Rates, Devaluation and Adjustment: Exchange Policy in Developing Countries.* Cambridge, MA: MIT Press.

Harriott, Kenton and DeLisle Worrell. 1997. "Estimating equilibrium real exchange rates: a menu approach," *Working Paper.* Central Bank of Barbados.

Marcello, Cecco. 2009. "Hicks's notion and use of the concepts of fix-price and flex-price," published online by Cambridge University Press, 29 June.

McLure, Charles. 1986. "Private sector capital investment and the company tax," *Working Paper.* Syracuse, NY: Metropolitan Studies Program, Syracuse University, March.

Moussavian, Mohammad. 1984. "The structure of protection in the Jamaican manufacturing sector," *Working Paper.* Syracuse, NY: Metropolitan Studies Program, Syracuse University, November.

Thirsk, James. 1984. "Jamaican tax incentive," *Working Paper.* Syracuse, NY: Metropolitan Studies Program, Syracuse University, August.

Tindigarukayo, Jimmy Kazaara. 2004. "An assessment of public service reforms in Jamaica," *Social and Economic Studies.* Vol. 53, no. 3, pp. 81–109.

Wasylenko, Michael. 1986. "The distribution of the tax burden in Jamaica: pre-1985 reform," *Working Paper*, Syracuse, NY: Metropolitan Studies Program, Syracuse University, August.

Wasylenko, Michael. 1987. "Tax burden in Jamaica before and after tax reform," *Working Paper*, Syracuse, NY: Metropolitan Studies Program, Syracuse University, October.

World Economic Forum. 2018. *Global competitiveness report.* Geneva, Switzerland: World Economic Forum.

Worrell, DeLisle. 2016. "The economy at fifty," in *Barbados: Fifty Years of Independence*, edited by Trevor A. Carmichael. Kingston and Miami: Ian Randle Publishers.

Worrell, DeLisle, Harold Codrington, Roland Craigwell and Kevin Greenidge. 2006. "Economic Resilience with an Exchange Rate Peg: The Barbados Experience 1985–9," in Lino Briguglio, Gordon Cordina and Eliawony J. Kisanga, *Building the Economic Resilience of Small States.* Malta: University of Malta and Commonwealth Secretariat.

Worrell, DeLisle. 1996. "Barbados at thirty: the economy," in *Barbados: Thirty Years of Independence*, edited by Trevor Carmichael. Kingston, Jamaica: Ian Randle Publishers.

Worrell, DeLisle. 1992. *Economic Policies in Small Open Economies: Prospects for the Caribbean.* London, Commonwealth Secretariat.

Worrell, DeLisle. 1987. *Small Island Economies: Structure and Performance in the English-speaking Caribbean Since 1970.* New York: Praeger.

Worrell, DeLisle. 1985. "Indice de los efectos de las variaciones cambiarias en las equenas economias abiertas," *Monetaria*, July–September.

Worrell, DeLisle. 1982. "The impact of floating exchange rates on Barbados and Jamaica," in *The International Monetary System: Choices for the Future*, edited by Michael Connolly. New York: Praeger.

Worrell, DeLisle, William Belchere and Jacqueline Coolidge. 1987. *An interim evaluation of the public management and policy project*. Bala Cynwyd, PA: Wharton Econometrics.

Worrell, DeLisle, Harold Codrington, Roland Craigwell and Kevin Greenidge. 2006. "Economic resilience with an exchange rate peg: The Barbados experience 1985–9," in *Building the Economic Resilience of Small States*, edited by Lino Briguglio, Gordon Cordina and Eliawony J. Kisanga. Malta: University of Malta and Commonwealth Secretariat.

Worrell, DeLisle, Roland Craigwell and Travis Mitchell. 2008. "A small foreign exchange market with a long-term peg – Barbados," *Applied Financial Economics*, Vol. 18, no. 8, pp. 673–682.

Worrell, DeLisle, Don Marshall and Nicole Smith. 2000. "The political economy of exchange rate policy in the Caribbean," *Working Paper*. Washington DC: Inter-American Development Bank, June.

Worrell, DeLisle, Winston Moore and Jamila Beckles. 2018. "A new approach to exchange rate management in small open financially integrated economies," in *Handbook of Small States – Economic, Social and Environmental Issues*, edited by Lino Briguglio. New York: Routledge.

Worrell, DeLisle et al. 2015. "Fiscal Sustainability and Debt in Small Open Economies: An Application to the Caribbean," St Augustine, Trinidad: Caribbean Centre for Money and Finance. Available at https://ssrn.com/abstract=2759391.

Wozny, James. 1985. "The taxation of corporate income in Jamaica," *Working Paper*. Syracuse, NY: Metropolitan Studies Program, Syracuse University, September.

8 International Competitiveness with an Exchange Rate Anchor

It is helpful to begin by distinguishing between price competition and non-price competition. Price competition is the act of offering a lower price in the hope of attracting a large number of customers, enough to yield the seller more revenue than they would have secured by selling at the same price as competitors. It is a form of competition which is not open to any small producer in a large market. Small sellers in big markets find other ways of attracting customers at the prevailing market price, by offering better quality, more efficient service, extra inducements or a more attractive or convenient sales environment. This logic applies to countries and exports as much as it does to individuals and companies. It is therefore surprising, and difficult to understand, why so much of the analysis of production and output in small open economies is concerned with prices and exchange rates. It can never be the case that a small economy can attract additional foreign currency by offering exports of goods and services to the international market at lower than the ruling price for the quality of product or service that is on offer. Rather, the potential customer will consider the lower price as *prima facie* evidence of poor quality, because why would the seller give the buyer a share of their returns when, because there is no shortage of buyers for the small amount they have on offer, they would have no difficulty disposing of their entire output at the market price? In any case, the selling prices for most goods and services sold internationally are quoted in US dollars; the seller's challenge is to produce profitably at the ruling US dollar price for the quality of good or service on offer.

The focus for small open economies, therefore, is to increase foreign earnings by maintaining and strengthening non-price competition. That is the fundamental basis for growth in these economies because, as we have previously established, increasing foreign currency inflows provides the wherewithal to acquire the imports needed to lift the society's well-being. The selling price plays no part in output determination, and the exchange rate anchor provides a favourable environment for investment in exports. Nothing can be done to mitigate volatility in international prices, but the exchange rate anchor ensures that the adverse effects of any exogenous fluctuations are not aggravated by exchange rate uncertainty.

DOI: 10.4324/9781003247609-10

The growth strategy which emerges from this perspective bears little resemblance to most of conventional debate, and many of the apparent puzzles of actual economic performance turn out not to be puzzles at all. The nominal exchange rate, the real effective exchange rate, however measured, the evolution of the rate and how the rate is managed – none of them has any effect on the potential growth rate, so long as the rate evolves in a stable, incremental fashion, if it moves at all. Instability – exchange rate, macroeconomic, political or social – is the enemy of investment, increasing uncertainty, driving up risk premiums and, in the limit, deterring investment altogether (Pindyck, 1991).

This chapter discusses how the SOE may devise a growth strategy to increase investment by stimulating international competitiveness. It is an articulation of the elements on the right hand side of the investment equation, Equation 6.1:

$$i = f_1(-xcap_t(-1),\ a^*,\ p_t,\ ulc,\ r_f,\ emp,\ GCI)$$

The variables over which domestic policy makers have command are the unit labour cost, *ulc*, the exchange market pressure, *emp*, and the competitiveness measure, *GCI*. Policies to ensure there is no negative external market pressure were the subject of Chapter 7. This chapter discusses strategies to ensure that wages do not outrun labour productivity and push up costs, and non-price measures that will sustain and improve external competitiveness.

Measures of international competitiveness

In their book *Competitiveness, convergence and international specialization*, Dollar and Wolff observe "It is always possible to compete internationally through a devalued currency and lower wages. Clearly this is not what is meant by competitiveness" (Dollar and Wolff, 1993, p. 13). Competitiveness is defined instead as higher output than other countries per unit of capital and labour. The elements of increased competitiveness are investment in more productive technology and increases in labour productivity at every level of technological sophistication. In frictionless international markets where producers, consumers and traders are all fully informed, and where the factors of production are immobile, classical theory shows that countries export where their competitive advantage is greatest. Typically in SOEs, there is a large gap in comparative advantage between tourism and a handful of exports that provide 80 per cent or more of foreign earnings, on the one hand, and all other production. Enhancing competitiveness means stimulating investment in more efficient technologies and increased labour productivity in these already well-established activities.

Competitiveness is many faceted, involving aspects such as marketing and branding in addition to productivity and adopting new technology. A number of indices together may be used to offer a comprehensive evaluation of a country's competitiveness. Firstly, a comparison of trends in the country's share of the regional or international market for each of its exports (of goods and tourism and other services), with the trends in the relative prices compared with the average of competitors, can be a very revealing indicator of successful competition (Worrell, 2021). A 2x2 evaluation matrix can be set up as in Figure 8.1, in which the greatest successes in international competition are to be found in Cell *B1*, where a country gains market share for its exports even though the average price of those exports has risen relative to the competition. This indicates that quality has been added to the product, and as a result customers are happy to pay higher prices. Next in the hierarchy of success are those countries whose exports are found in Cell *B2*: market share has increased, but the country did not get the added benefit of higher prices relative to the competition. This may be cause for concern if exporters are investing insufficiently in quality improvements, product enhancements and other strategies which add value to their product. That is the only way to increase average returns, since the unit price of the product or service is set in US dollars, and is the same for all suppliers, for each quality of the product. Exporters who find themselves in Cell *B2* should evaluate their strategies, and their governments should revisit incentives for these activities to ensure they are not in danger of losing market share. There is often a temptation for cash-strapped hotels, agricultural and manufacturing exporters to offer products and services at discount if they have excess capacity. This is seldom advisable; if the industry is in an international slump, as is being experienced during the COVID-19 pandemic, there is no business to lure away from competitors; on the other hand, if the enterprise's productivity has fallen behind its competitors at home or abroad, lowering prices to maintain volumes will worsen profitability, and the company will eventually lose market share. Countries in Column A are losing market share; they will need to determine whether they

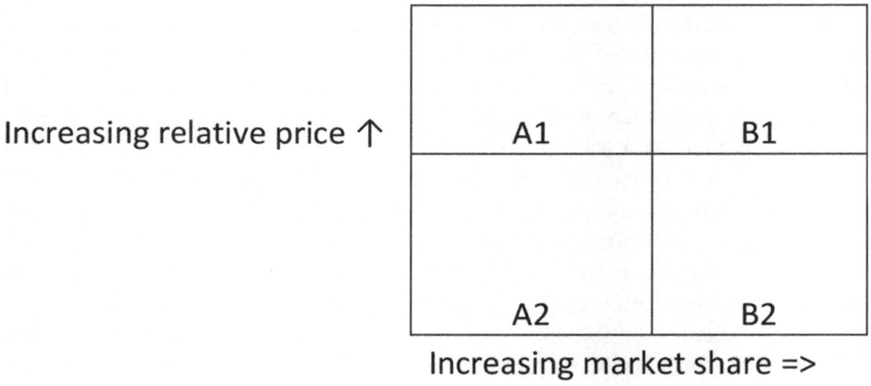

Figure 8.1 Matrix of relative prices and market share
Source: Author's construction.

have comparative advantages such as production and marketing expertise, export networks and established specialised markets and other tangible and intangible assets which they can leverage to acquire resources to recover and maintain market share. Their governments should make informed judgments as to the nature and amount of incentives and assistance to offer, conditional on the achievement of specific performance targets.

In Worrell, Boamah and Campbell (1996) my colleagues and I attempted an empirical study of exports and tourism that explicitly took account of some quality differences. We recognised that a country is more competitive if it produces more output for any input of capital and labour; that price is an indicator of quality when products are similar; and that non-price competition – advertising, branding, loyalty programmes, packaging for market appeal – are the levers most often used for gaining market share. SOEs like Barbados compete on costs, not product prices; costs include transport costs, which are governed by economies of scale. Other factors affecting competitiveness include institutional, cultural and historical associations, and government interventions that affect wages and rates of return. We computed the relative price by sector in Barbados relative to competitors for sugar, manufacturing, tourism and all other exports, making a quality modification for tourism (the percentage of accommodation in the top quality) and we compared the relative price in each sector with a relative wage index to compute competitiveness indices for each activity.

A second and complementary approach to the measurement of competitiveness is by use of measures of labour and total factor productivity for exports, tourism and other traded services. An upward trend indicates that the country is maintaining its competitiveness, particularly if gains are at a faster pace than for close competitors. Conversely, stagnant levels of output per worker, or a falling trend, are warning signals which call for a policy response to maintain competitiveness. Worrell (1995) used productivity data to assess Barbados' competitiveness relative to Caribbean rivals, concluding that the country lost ground in tourism and exports in the 1980s. Labour productivity increased in Barbados, but not as fast as for Jamaica and Trinidad and Tobago; competition increased, including new entrants, most importantly the Dominican Republic and Aruba; and Barbados had been slow to adopt advances in process and organisational technology.

In recent years a powerful, comprehensive index has become available which incorporates a range of environmental factors affecting competitiveness and a country's appeal to investors: the *Global Competitiveness Index*, GCI (World Economic Forum, 2019). The GCI, which in 2019 contained information on 144 countries, ranks countries according to indices relating to the institutions of government and civil society, transport infrastructure, coverage of electricity and water supply, telecommunications usage, life expectancy, schooling, training and skills, measures of domestic market competitiveness, trade openness, labour market indicators, the range of financial services available, the soundness of banks, business regulation, business culture, the diversity of the workforce, the volume of research undertaken, buyer sophistication and many others. These are aggregated into an overall index, which also takes account of GDP, inflation, the national debt and the openness of the economy. The strength of this index is its comprehensiveness, the balance of factors included, and the fact that it is available for a wide cross-section of countries.

A comprehensive assessment of Barbados' international competitiveness appears in Worrell and Lowe (2014). The factors included were the GCI rankings, broken down; Barbados' share of Caribbean markets for tourism, agriculture, mining, manufacturing, international business and financial services; Barbados' centrality to the global banking system, relative to other small international business and financial services centres; skills endowment, infrastructure, other non-price factors; trends by sector re unit labour costs and real output per worker; and relative price elasticities for tourism and tradable services. The results suggested that Barbados was competitive both regionally and globally, ranking ahead of its peers in key areas such as the strength of its institutions and the quality of its health care and primary and higher education. In addition, despite some declines in tourism post the global recession in 2008/9, the island had maintained market share in most of its key foreign exchange earning sectors, while seeing improved price competitiveness of its internationally-traded goods and services over the previous decade.

Policy tools for increasing international competitiveness

Armed with a realistic notion of competitiveness and practical measures for tracking competitive success, we address the question of the toolkit which economic policy makers may use to improve competitiveness. Early insight into the possibilities may be found in Worrell (1988): "The best way of approaching the future is to make the most of the knowledge you have accumulated in the past" (Worrell, 1988, p. 25). In that essay the essence of my thoughts on a successful strategy for expanding the foreign exchange earning sectors of the economy emerges in embryo.

> What products and services, of those … already produce[d], can [the country] contrive to sell at internationally competitive prices? And what new products and services embody resources and skills that [the country] already possess[es], which may enable [it] to steal a march on the competition?
>
> (Worrell, 1988, p. 25)

I suggested a corporatist approach, devised and implemented jointly by Government and the private sector. I argued that Government must pick winners, and the financial sector was seen as having the responsibility to reward performance and weed out inefficiency.

Worrell (1993) argued that the most effective macroeconomic policy for stimulating investment in small open economies is to curb aggregate demand to reduce the profitability of the nontradable sectors; the profitability of tradable sectors is unaffected, since that depends on international prices, and is therefore unaffected by domestic demand. Corporate tax relief should be targeted to the tradable sector, accompanied by incentives for non-price competition and investment in productivity, such as research and development, market development, improved quality, adoption of new technology, and process modernisation. Tariff exemptions should be provided for inputs to the tradable sector, but quantitative restrictions are a useless tax on consumers. With respect to finance, "… if a firm cannot secure adequate finance with a little effort its project is probably not viable" (Worrell, 1993, p. 47); state financial institutions should be strictly wholesalers; and special fiscal incentives are needed for venture capital.

Designing tax systems to stimulate competitiveness

The experience of the English-speaking Caribbean over the past four decades offers some insights for the design of policies that can have a positive effect on the after-tax rate of return in the SOE. In the first place, the primacy of foreign exchange for the development of the economy provides justification for a sliding scale of corporate taxation, with the lowest marginal tax rates for enterprises which earn 100 per cent of revenues from tourism or exports. This biases investment towards the most productive activities, in terms of their potential to accelerate economic growth.

Secondly, a low general border tax is advisable; the incentive to evade a small tax is not great, insufficient to fund the growth of a culture of tax evasion and the informal institutional network that characterises cross-border transactions throughout the Caribbean. Cost-benefit analysis would probably reveal that the administrative costs of the complex border taxation regimes of Caribbean countries and the costs of policing their operation outweigh the diminishing revenue from import duties. Such an analysis would involve adding up the costs of detailed customs manuals with thousands of items and hundreds of schedules, the time consuming inspection and processing of cargoes at the borders and the attendant warehousing, congestion and security costs. In contrast, a universal five per cent import duty would be simple to apply, and would not provide sufficient rents to fund the tax evasion infrastructure. The arguments for import duties to stimulate domestic production do not hold water in SOEs: there are no competitively-priced domestic substitutes for all but a handful of imports. The import duties are a tax on consumers. Both consumers and government revenues (net of costs of administering the border tax) would benefit from substituting a low uniform import tariff; consumers would enjoy lower prices on imported items, and government might actually record higher receipts, net of collection costs. Importantly, in terms of its effect on competitiveness, a low uniform import tax would reduce input costs for tourism and exports, and with it, the need for a regime of exemptions, with its attendant distortions, controversies and rent-seeking behaviour.

A third recommendation, based on Caribbean experience, is for a modest final sales tax on goods and services of around 10 per cent, with the exception of books, pharmaceuticals and educational and healthcare products. Such a tax would probably yield more net revenue than the currently fashionable so-called value-added taxes in the Caribbean. The value-added tax (VAT) on services turns out to be in effect a final tax, because, unlike manufacturing, services industries do not add value to raw materials or other inputs. This means that the full amount of the tax is added to the final price of the service, and whatever refund the seller might claim for VAT paid on electricity, laundry services, etc, is retained by the seller. More damaging is the fact that the VAT is biased *against* tourism; for those countries that impose a VAT, the tax adds to the price of a visitor's holiday, compared to rivals in competing VAT-free countries which offer a similar visitor experience at comparable US dollar prices.

A tax system comprising a general sales tax, a graduated corporation tax and a low import tax removes most of the incentives to seek special regimes of tax incentives for growth-enhancing investment. Much proverbial ink has been spilt in debates over the importance of tax incentive regimes, including by the present author (Worrell, 1989). A reasoned summary of the state of play would be that no persuasive evidence exists of the benefits of tax incentives in almost all countries. By removing any strong motive for seeking such exemptions, a reform of Caribbean taxation systems along the lines suggested would make the tax system more predictable and transparent. Overall, the costs of tax administration would be reduced with no loss of revenue, and with a significant gain in efficiency and productivity, and a bias in favour of tourism and exports would be restored. Security and enforcement resources that the revenue authority would no longer need could be released for deployment elsewhere.

State entrepreneurship is essential for competitiveness in a dynamic world

In her insightful and influential book *The Entrepreneurial State*, Mariana Mazzucato (2013) popularised the notion of the state as an active collaborator with the private sector in a national strategy for economic development in a world of dynamic competition. She argues persuasively, using historical examples in societies with every type of political and institutional structure, that the investments in technological innovation which are essential for maintaining international competitiveness in an ever-changing world have always been the result of joint public-private action on a mutually understood national strategy.

> The book comprehensively debunks the myth of a lumbering, bureaucratic state versus a dynamic, innovative private sector. In a series of case

studies – from IT, biotech, nanotech to today's emerging green tech – Professor Mazzucato shows that the opposite is true: the private sector only finds the courage to invest after an entrepreneurial state has made the high-risk investments. In an intensely researched chapter, she reveals that every technology that makes the iPhone so 'smart' was government funded: the Internet, GPS, its touch-screen display and the voice-activated Siri. Mazzucato also controversially argues that in the history of modern capitalism the state has not only fixed market failures, but has also actively shaped and created markets. In doing so, it sometimes wins and sometimes fails.

(from the promotional material for the book)

In a subsequent elaboration on the role of the state in the growth process, Mazzucato and Jacobs (2016) offered the following key insights for rethinking capitalism:

- Markets are best understood as the outcomes of interactions between economic agents and institutions, public and private. Endowments, motivation, culture, legal structures constrain these outcomes.
- Competition among companies selling identical products on a single market is an unhelpful characterisation of the economy. Many of the most important markets are oligopolistic, and economies of scale and network effects are pervasive. There is persistent heterogeneity in firm characteristics and their reaction to market circumstances. Evolutionary economics has shown heterogeneity to be a long-run feature of economic systems.
- Ownership and governance structures differ in ways that help to determine outcomes. Maximising shareholder value is neither universal nor the most successful of strategies.
- Investments in technological and organisational innovation, both public and private, are the driving force behind economic growth and development. This is the primary source of increases in productivity and the resulting rises in living standards.
- For development we need firms with risk-taking management cultures; incentives which reward long-term perspectives; public banks which steer finance to long-term projects, leverage private capital and stimulate multiplier effects; and tax policies to provide incentives for long-term investment.
- Innovation needs well-funded public research and strong industrial policies that set the direction and pace of innovation.
- The creation of wealth is a collaborative public-private process, because it requires law and order, infrastructure, energy, water and waste disposal, education, health and social care, all services which do not offer a competitive private return.

- Government plays a critical role in creating expectations of future growth and animating Keynes' "animal spirits", the intangible motivation for investment and innovation.
- Taxation promotes growth to the extent that it is used productively by an active public sector.
- Redistributive policies which reduce inequality have a positive effect on growth. Rising wage pressures can be an incentive for greater productivity.
- Environmentally friendly investment, organisation and production processes are essential to assure future sustainability.

Small open economies should filter these insights through the lens of their economic structures and the feasible options for maintaining competitiveness in a world of rapid change. Governments should pick winners, but intelligently and realistically, with feet planted on solid ground. The best place to start is by leveraging existing skills, knowledge, experience and networks, retooling, repositioning and modifying products, services, processes and organisation to take advantage of emerging opportunities (Worrell, 1988). The Caribbean sugar industry can be used as an illustration. The cultivation of sugar cane has shrunk throughout the Caribbean, and most of the insular Caribbean no longer exports sugar or products from the cultivation of the cane. This is a major tragedy: not only was sugar the most sophisticated and versatile industry the Caribbean has ever known; but also, without sugar as a reliable anchor, domestic agriculture is no longer internationally competitive. Throughout the region, former sugar lands lie idle and neglected, defacing the landscape with scrub and unsightly brush.

That the outcome could have been different is suggested by the exception, the one product of sugar cane with which the Caribbean (and Central America) has had outstanding success: the export of high quality, aged and branded rum. Unlike the rest of the sugar industry players, rum producers in the 1980s anticipated the emergence of a global market, and, through a variety of innovative strategies, adopted new technologies of production and organisation, married with the mystique of centuries-old equipment and techniques, and built a prominent presence on the world market. This story of Caribbean rums remains to be told, but it stands in stark contrast with what has befallen the rest of the sugar industry. The achievements of rum producers suggest that the sugar industry's demise was not inevitable; had Caribbean governments been visionary and entrepreneurial, they might well have collaborated actively with the sugar industry in adapting to the loss of privileged marketing arrangements for sugar in the way that countries like Mauritius were able to do. Had that been the case, the Caribbean would now boast a vibrant sugar industry, specialising in the production of brown table sugars, liquid sugar, fertiliser, special oils for perfumery and other uses, and industrial alcohols (including gasoline additives), as well as molasses for use in the production of rum. In addition, sugar factories could provide a contribution to the renewable supply of electricity, through co-generation during the processing of the sugar harvest, using bagasse, a by-product of sugar, as fuel.

Government needs to devise a comprehensive, internally cohesive and consistent strategy for maintaining and enhancing competitiveness in close collaboration with the private sector. The strategy should be fully articulated with long-term and intermediate goals, quantified to the fullest extent possible; it should be published in a form that is at once substantive and comprehensible by the general public, with performance markers that people care about, such as the growth of exports, tourism, employment and average incomes. Care should be taken, and active leadership is required, to persuade the general population of the merits of the chosen strategy, and to minimise coercive elements by use of a persuasive data-driven communications strategy.

The competitiveness-enhancing strategy will need to nudge producers in new directions, a process that few countries have been able to manage successfully. Government disposes of the largest complement of economists and statisticians and an extensive network of overseas embassies and agencies which can be used to provide data and information on which to ground the economic strategy. Data should be shared, on an ongoing basis, with the private sector, universities and think tanks, to be used in preparing technical studies on the wide variety of issues and considerations which are the building blocks of a national economic strategy. This process produces a national economic strategy which is informed and realistic: all the technologies will be established, accessible and affordable; investors will be keen to participate, because the projects in which they are interested will have had the input of knowledgeable, experienced professionals; and workers and the general public will build confidence in the strategy as it begins to deliver jobs, a higher quality of education, better health services and a wider range of affordable goods and services. This is an ideal which is never fully realised in practice, but experience in East Asia and elsewhere suggests that a successful national economic strategy is elusive if the main elements are not in place: a solid base of fully documented, authoritative analytical studies, including by independent non-governmental groups; inputs from practicing businessmen, traders and financial institutions; and an ongoing process of active consultation with representative bodies of all stakeholders.

There are a few examples of successful state entrepreneurship in the sample of 41 countries surveyed in Section A. Aruba is perhaps the most outstanding, with the establishment of the framework for a switch from the refining of Venezuelan crude oil, no longer a profitable business by the mid-1980s, to tourism as the mainstay of the economy. The establishment of an industrial park for the production of steel, fertilisers and other industrial products in Trinidad and Tobago in the 1970s providing the country with a source of foreign earnings to supplement oil exports was another example of successful state enterprise. Cancún was developed into a major tourist resort through an initiative by the Mexican government, and the Government of Mauritius is credited with the establishment of industrial parks that provided the basis for a substantial export manufacturing industry (see Chapter 4).

Investment and the quality of infrastructure and public services

There is little argument that investment in roads, ports, airports and other transport and communications infrastructure is a vital catalyst for investment. The same is true for the supply of electricity, water, sanitation and other essential services. If there is the possibility of exploiting a natural resource, a potential investor may choose to install these facilities and services, but they will expect a higher share of returns in exchange. However, all too often the investor is put off by the lack of critical infrastructure, and much output has been lost because of intermittent power cuts and unreliable public utility services.

The difficult issues are the rate at which government invests in infrastructure and public utilities, the sources of finance, the role private firms can or should play and the choice of projects which ought to be included in the public investment package. The sustainability of current fiscal policy determines the outer limit of public investment spending. In practice, an otherwise desirable capital works programme will have to be modified whenever that is necessary to restore the external balance, and that will in turn call for a recalibration of future capital works.

Factors which affect the decision on the rate of investment in public works, public utilities and public services include the starting point, the time horizon, the implementation capacity and the availability of appropriate finance on terms that the country can afford. There will be many paths from the existing network of transport and communications infrastructure, electricity generation, water and sanitation coverage, etc, towards goals that may be set five, ten or 30 years ahead. Assumptions will have to be made about technologies to be used, how technology might evolve, the changes in the world economy and international prices; the economic feasibility of alternative realistic options will have to be explored; and environmental and other non-economic factors must be brought to bear in evaluating the various options.

A plan has to be made for the financing of the economic strategy over the various time horizons of the component projects. It is good fiscal practice to generate a small contribution to the capital works budget from fiscal savings, something of the order of two per cent. That saving is mainly for stabilisation purposes, to hold current expenditure in tranquil times below spending, to create space to weather the immediate impact of an unexpected drop in revenue. In such circumstances, government may compensate for the revenue loss by calling a moratorium on some major capital works, to avoid abrupt cuts in the wages bill or a burgeoning fiscal deficit. Fiscal savings are not necessary for public sector investment by credit-worthy governments, because they have unlimited access to foreign funds on the basis of government's guarantee. The public investment strategy and the foreign debt strategy are interrelated.

There is another range of choices with respect to private sector involvement in the provision of public utilities, public services and infrastructure. Experiences in many countries over all of modern history suggest that the privatisation of services which are essential to the maintenance of civilised society leads to capture of the commons by sectional interests, and should be avoided. Recent experiments with military contractors, privately-run prisons, and the proliferation of private security substitutes for deficient policing have confirmed that these services should be fully provided by the public sector. This leaves a wide range of choices for private participation in health, education, public transportation, road construction, the operation of ports and airports, and many more. A few observations can be made, based on real life experiences. Long-term decisions on private participation should be made strictly in accordance with the public sector investment strategy, resisting the temptation to secure foreign finance for short-term adjustment programmes by opportunistic decisions on private participation. The strategy should take advantage of possibilities which private participants can provide, which would otherwise be beyond reach. The best example is long-term leases of ports and airports to international companies with global networks for moving freight and passengers. Exclusive reliance on private providers of public transport is seldom optimal; the poor are saddled with services that are inadequate, inconvenient and often dangerous, and workers in the industry are seldom afforded standard labour market protections and facilities. Less than universal coverage of primary education is undesirable; the wealthy may choose to opt out in favour of private schools, but society has an obligation to provide all citizens with the basic skills to be productive.

The choice of investment projects has to be made with a view to achieving national goals in a future which is more and more obscure, the further out your projections go. SOEs have limited human and financial resources at their disposal, and investment projects are lumpy and with a long life, over which time the world will change in ways that are not now foreseen. Such economies are well-advised to anchor public investment on established technologies, leaving bets on emerging technologies to countries with the resources to explore many options at the same time. A current example is to be found in country strategies for renewable energy. The only established renewable technologies for generating electricity are hydro, solar and wind. These are all variable power sources; there is, to date, no renewable source of base power for stabilising electric grids that does not involve internal combustion. For most countries this means that a target of producing 100 per cent renewables is not within reach.

The coverage and quality of educational, health, sanitation and security services, and the strength of civil society institutions, are among other elements that make for an attractive climate for investment. Worldwide, coverage of education and health has increased appreciably in a majority of countries, but there has been little perceived improvement in the investment climate in parallel, which suggests that a general decline in the quality of services across the board has wiped out any potential gains. Challenges that face the Caribbean include reversing the decline in average educational achievement at primary, secondary and tertiary levels; modernising health systems to counter the rising incidence of non-communicable diseases, better cope with health emergencies and promote healthy lifestyles; the upgrading of police services; and the modernisation of sanitation and waste disposal systems.

Public sector efficiency and the investment decision

The speed, predictability, pertinence and courtesy which characterise public services are factors which always rank highly in surveys of businesses, large and small. The skills and organisational requirements for managing a modern economy are of a very high order. The public services should have the capacity to devise, design and mobilise the society and implement a national economic strategy for implementation jointly by the public and private sectors, with adequate phasing, monitoring and collaborative institutions for course correction as and when needed. What is needed are public services which are slimmer, much more skillful and collegial, and with the capacity to employ new technologies to achieve swift and practical improvements in productivity and provide favourable experiences for everyone who does business with government. The public services should be headed by experts with an international reputation who are able to determine national priorities for the use of the financial and human resources available to the government and to the society as a whole.

Compared to what is required, public sectors in the Caribbean are well below minimum requirements and are falling further away from a gold standard in spite of numerous fiscal reform efforts over five decades. There is an unresolved and long-standing tension between the people's elected representatives who staff the cabinet that sits at the apex of public decision making, and the career public workers who have the expertise to design and implement feasible policies. The sum of the people's aspirations, reflected in political manifestos, always far exceeds what available material, financial and human resources can provide within a time frame that matches electors' expectations. An impartial public service of the quality outlined in the previous paragraphs can provide the cabinet with a selection of feasible options which can actually be accomplished within the current budget and a rolling five-year growth strategy. Sadly, no Caribbean country has an institutional structure which is up to the task. The reality that economic strategies in the Caribbean, both those which are articulated in published documents and the majority that have to be inferred, are politicians' aspirations rather than feasible strategies, means that failure to implement is inevitable.

The lack of suitable analytical tools

The wrong-headedness of public economic policy in the Caribbean – and in many other SOEs – is evident. Central banks target domestic inflation, knowing full well that the main sources of inflation are the prices of food and fuel, both of which are imported; governments commit to replace food imports with domestically produced substitutes which, if they can be produced locally – most cannot – cannot be cultivated and marketed at prices that the average wage-earner could afford; governments commit to diversifying their economies from tourism, agriculture and light manufacturing into no-one knows what; in the Caribbean there is a strong demand for intra-regional migration of low-skilled workers, which remains illegal, while regional leaders bemoan the scant interest in regional work certificates for those with tertiary education for which there is no demand. Numerous other examples may be cited.

The unfortunate fact is that, seven decades of Caribbean investment in tertiary education and a proliferation of universities, colleges and specialised institutes notwithstanding, economic policy makers have no practical guidance on the design of strategies that answer to the region's circumstances and needs. The same appears true for SOEs worldwide. In contrast to the avalanche of studies on the effects of climate change on small island developing countries (SIDS), macroeconomic interest in the SOE appears to have evaporated since the 1980s.

The absence of thinking and analysis from the perspective of the SOE is hugely consequential: it is at the root of poor policy design for countries in this category, and it trivialises their interventions on the global stage, at the United Nations, the International Monetary Fund and elsewhere. Small nations' participation in global fora gives them voice; to make most of such opportunities, presentations should offer novel perspectives and practical proposals, founded on data and analysis. Speeches should command attention because they raise issues, considerations and consequences which have not been previously brought to attention, in place of the familiar litany of complaints and requests for extra assistance.

The SOE best leverages its membership of global institutions by the cogency and persuasiveness of their contributions at major events. The most influential contributions are those which make the audience sit up and take notice because of some important fact, circumstance or consequence of which they might previously have been unaware. One of the few examples of what is possible is the contribution of the Islands and Small States Institute of the University of Malta to the explanation of the widely different performance of SOEs in similar circumstances and with similar resource constraints, which range from Iceland (population 367,000) ranking Number 4 in the world in the Human Development Index, to Guinea-Bissau (population 2 million) at Number 175 of 189 countries (Briguglio, Cordina and Kisanga, 2006; UNDP, 2020). While admitting that small countries are exposed to a broadly similar range of vulnerabilities, the book explores factors which have made for greater resilience in the face of shocks which all have encountered.

A summing up

The analysis of this chapter goes a long way in explaining the varieties of performance of economies which depend for their growth on exports of goods and services whose prices are in no way affected by their contribution to global supply. Their competitiveness is defined by their productivity, the attractiveness and stability of the social, economic and political environment they offer to potential investors, the quality of domestic infrastructure and the quality and appeal of the products and services they sell. Their success is measured by their ability to maintain and improve their shares of international markets. The overall design of the tax system influences the country's overall competitiveness, as does the efficiency with which the public sector conducts the people's business. It is not a good idea for the state to get into a slanging match with the private sector, nor is it useful to impose limits or give instructions which the private sector has no motive to comply with, particularly when such directives cause them to lose money or market share. The most successful growth strategies are to be found where an entrepreneurial government develops strategies for competitiveness in close collaboration with an entrepreneurial private sector, with the public sector effectively exercising its responsibilities for social security, equity, poverty alleviation and environmental sustainability. Affecting all aspects of policy is the availability – or lack thereof – of analytical tools and perspectives fashioned to the circumstances and needs of SOEs.

References

Briguglio, Lino, Gordon Cordina and Eliawony J. Kisanga. 2006. *Building the Economic Resilience of Small States.* Malta and London, UK: University of Malta and Commonwealth Secretariat.

Dollar, David and Eduard Wolff. 1993. *Competitiveness, Convergence and International Specialisation*' Cambridge, Massachusetts: MIT Press.

Mazzucato, Mariana. 2013. *The Entrepreneurial State: Debunking Public vs. Private Sector Myths.* London: Anthem Press.

Mazzucato, Mariana and Michael Jacobs (eds). 2016. *Rethinking Capitalism: Economics and Policy for Inclusive and Sustainable Growth.* Hoboken, NJ: Wiley Blackwell.

Pindyck, Robert. 1991. "Irreversibility, uncertainty, and investment," *Journal of Economic Literature*, Vol. XXIX, no. 3, September.

United Nations Development Programme. 2020. "Human Development Report," New York: UNDP.

World Economic Forum. 2019. "Global Competitiveness Index," Geneva, Switzerland: The Forum.

Worrell, DeLisle. 2021. "The Caribbean holds its own in global tourism competition," in *Handbook of Caribbean Economies*, edited by Robert Looney. Milton Park, UK: Routledge.

Worrell, DeLisle. 1995. "Open market operations in small open economies with fixed and flexible exchange rates," *Social and Economic Studies*, Vol. 44, Special Issue.

Worrell, DeLisle. 1993. "Investment, trade and finance in small states," *Bulletin of Eastern Caribbean Affairs*, Vol. 18, no. 1, March.

Worrell, DeLisle. 1989. "The tax system of Barbados," *Bulletin for International Fiscal Documentation*, October.

Worrell, DeLisle. 1988. "Foundations of a new export drive," *Barbados Sugar Review*, no. 57, June.

Worrell, DeLisle and Shane Lowe. 2014. "Barbados' international competitiveness," *Working Paper*, Central Bank of Barbados. January.

Worrell, DeLisle, Daniel Boamah and Trevor Campbell. 1996. "The price competitiveness of Barbados' exports," *Central Bank of Barbados Economic Review*, Vol. XXIII, no. 1, pp. 12–32.

9 The Uses of Monetary Policy in SOEs

In this chapter we describe how monetary policy can play a supporting role, albeit an effective and crucial one, in a framework of macroeconomic stabilisation in SOEs. Monetary policy tools are important because they are quick-acting, in contrast to fiscal tools, which are powerful but slow to take effect. A coordinated approach to economic shocks, deploying simultaneously fiscal tools sufficient to restore external balance and monetary tools to calm financial markets, offers the best chance of successful adjustment. The fiscal tools alone may not work, because capital flight may have worsened the situation to such an extent by the time they begin to bite, that measures which were considered adequate months earlier are hopelessly inadequate. This can bring on a downward spiral which imposes punishing adjustment costs. Equally, a modest interest premium increase may be sufficient to dissuade cautious but rate-sensitive investors not to move funds offshore, but only if they are reassured that a fiscal package adequate to restore external balance has been put in place.

The monetary authority can perform a second important economic service by offering guidance to the financial markets through interest rate policy, moral suasion and information sharing. Through these measures the central bank may help to reduce the volatility of interest rates and exchange rates, improve the perceived climate of risk in the country, and increase the country's attractiveness to new investors. In this chapter we expand on the possibilities of monetary policy in both of these important roles, and contrast this approach to the conventional view of the objectives and use of monetary instruments.

The version of the interest parity condition shown in Chapter 6 (Equation 6.8) provides a helpful frame for our discussion:

$$r - r_f = f_8(c_x, emp)$$

The equation expresses the domestic interest premium, $r - r_f$, as a function of the costs of exchanging local and foreign currency, c_x, with a widening of that premium when there is exchange market pressure, *emp*. In response to a shock which creates pressure on the foreign exchange market, monetary policy

DOI: 10.4324/9781003247609-11

should be used to raise the domestic interest rate to offer a sufficient extra premium on holding domestic currency to remove any motivation on the part of market agents to aggravate the pressure by taking defensive positions in foreign currency. They will understand that such action will be costly so long as appropriate fiscal action has been taken to completely eliminate the exchange market pressure. That will be the case only if the fiscal authorities have a reputation for prudence and there is an effective framework for economic management which monitors performance and makes timely adjustment to keep the remedial policies on target.

The equation also shows how the monetary authority may give guidance to the financial sector to ensure an orderly evolution of the domestic interest rate in line with long-term trends in the foreign interest rate. Every well-structured monetary authority will have a team of economists and financial experts whose task it is to monitor international interest rates, among other things. They will have available to them the best data and analysis on the factors driving international rates and they are better equipped than any other financial institution to make informed judgements about the interest rate forecast. Through intervention to keep the domestic interest rate in line with the best forecast on a predictable schedule, the monetary authority can reduce volatility in local rates, making adjustments to the local rate only when changes in the international rate seem likely to persist.

In the next section of this chapter we describe a framework for central bank intervention in an open auction of three-month treasury bills as the tool for monetary policy to secure the above objectives, that is, to secure an orderly evolution of domestic interest rates that follows the trends and longer term cycles of international rates, and to support fiscal adjustment when there is need to adjust to economic shocks, whether of domestic or external origin.

A framework for the conduct of monetary policy in the SOE

Worrell (1997a) offers guidance on the conduct of monetary policy in the SOE based on a comparisons among the central banks of CARICOM countries. The Central Bank of Barbados, with its use of a market-friendly approach to monetary policy, was offered as the role model for monetary policy. Tools employed included moral suasion, signalling via the discount rate, intervention at the treasury bill auction, offering government bonds for sale under repurchase agreements and pricing of new bonds issued by Government. In addition, at the time of writing the Bank also set interest rates on household deposits at commercial banks, making changes as needed to keep them in line with international trends. Controls were used as a last resort, and only after consultation with banks and financial institutions, with a view to persuading them of the logic of the intervention. The Central Bank was sensitive to the practical limits to public policy, and never attempted to force banks' hands against their stated interests. The paper argued that the Central Bank needed to be the price leader in the financial market because it was the only institution with a staff of economic and financial experts capable of providing informed judgement about the economic fundamentals. By and large Central Bank non-price interventions had failed to secure the intended objectives. Lending rate stipulations and credit ceilings did not have any noticeable effects, while consumer credit controls were distortionary, diverting borrowers from banks to retailers and non-banks. The exception was a temporary hold on new credit in 1991, which had served to contain expenditure during the second half of the year when measures for fiscal contraction (which had been implemented mid-year) were gradually beginning to bite.

A contrast was drawn with the Jamaican experience in the early 1990s at a time when the exchange market was liberalised. The Bank of Jamaica attempted to tighten the money supply via open market operations, but instead the high interest rates on offer attracted a large but volatile influx of short-term funds. The Bank was trapped into a high interest regime from which it was unable subsequently to escape: whenever conditions warranted a monetary ease the fall in interest rates provoked a financial outflow which starved the domestic financial market of liquidity. The independent use of monetary policy was inflationary in the first instance, and it has since been a deterrent to fixed investment, especially in agriculture. The Jamaican experience is typical of outcomes in floating exchange rate countries. The failure to anchor the exchange rate with suitable fiscal measures prejudiced the success of the Jamaican adjustment. The essay advised that "Central banks should adjust in line with private sector adjustment plans, in circumstances where macroeconomic stabilisation and adjustment are achieved via fiscal policy" and that "Fiscal policy must be appropriate and sufficient" (Worrell, 1997a, p. 53).

A more recent paper (Worrell, Doyle-Lowe, Belgrave, Downes and Guy, 2012) was the basis for completing the transition to market-based monetary policy in Barbados, with the removal of stipulations on deposit interest in 2013. The paper found that trends in the foreign rate and perceived needs for an inflow of foreign finance were the main factors motivating interest rate policy over the 1966 to 2011 period; the Barbados country risk premium was affected by the amount of domestic free liquidity, the public sector borrowing requirement and the rate of domestic inflation. Interest adjustment was market driven, via the open financial account. Empirical tests provided evidence that the logic of Equation 6.8 was a faithful representation of the working of the financial market.

The Barbados experience shows that an active short-term money market is not essential for the operation of monetary policy through the use of market-determined interest rates. In the absence of such a market the Central Bank of Barbados conducted monetary policy through intervention at the treasury bill auction when necessary to change interest on three-month bills, which was the main policy instrument. Guidance for the longer term was offered by way of a notional yield curve, built through the periodic issue of longer-term government bonds at rates which, in the Bank's judgment, best reflected future trends in foreign interest rates. Whether the Bank's expectations were in line with market expectations became apparent from the appetite for new long-term issues, and the notional curve could be adjusted accordingly with subsequent issues.

The central bank was able to adjust short-term interest rates consistent with the current fiscal policy stance and the balance of external payments through intervention, and give guidance as to expectations via the notional yield curve, in the absence of active trading in short- term financial instruments, and without the need for open market purchases and sales by the central bank. Two circumstances make this possible. Firstly, the frequency of the treasury bill auction, a necessity for efficient management of government's cash flow, means that interest rates can be influenced in whatever direction the central bank wishes by consistent pressure in that direction in successive auctions, until a change of sufficient magnitude is attained. Secondly, so long as the exchange rate anchor is secure, the banks' appetite for free unremunerated domestic liquidity is unaffected by interest rate changes of the order that can be effected without creating alarm about economic fundamentals. Various reasons have been suggested for banks' nonchalance about the level of free reserves: Saxegaard (2006) found that Nigerian data suggested that a plausible explanation might lie with the fact that the banks' deposit liabilities in that country – and presumably other developing countries – were more volatile than in more advanced countries. In order to avoid the costs of insuring against this volatility or over-reliance on thin local money markets and expensive foreign borrowing (supposing they had access to foreign markets), banks hold enough free liquidity in local currency to cover the range of the ins and outs of deposit variation. Alternatively, it may be that the banks are sufficiently profitable with their existing asset/liability profile and see no way to expand their local currency loan portfolio to creditworthy local customers, including the public sector. The banking systems of SOEs typically comprise only a few institutions, which see no benefit in engaging in price competition for credits, including to the public sector. These circumstances make for predictable liquidity forecasting by the central bank, which can temper its intervention accordingly. In tranquil times the proportion of deposits held in unremunerated liquid form remains unchanged, and banks will respond to central bank interventions by adjusting the bid rate at the treasury bill auction – which is the reaction that the central bank wishes to see – rather than using free liquidity to keep the rate constant. In the face of any shock, the situation is no different: the proportion of unremunerated liquidity can be expected to be unchanged, provided that the policy response to the shock is a fiscal adjustment of sufficient magnitude to protect the exchange rate anchor. The central bank may then use the treasury bill auction, once the fiscal programme has been legislated, to provide supporting monetary adjustment.

Khemraj (2014) provides an elegant description of the workings of monetary policy in an SOE in the absence of an exchange rate anchor. His point of departure is the fact that central banks in SOEs have to hold foreign reserves, irrespective of the exchange rate regime, in order to guard against instability and to maintain credibility in the economic strategy. In the short term, foreign accumulation can drain domestic liquidity (as the central bank competes with banks for the available supply); in the longer term inflows of foreign currency which are bought by the central bank (from the proceeds of exports and foreign borrowing) will add to the pool of domestic liquidity. Domestic interest rates are determined by how large this domestic liquidity pool is, relative to the local currency demand for credit by credit-worthy borrowers. Mopping up this excess by open market operations is best regarded as compensating banks for holding excess cash in domestic currency, to avoid a depreciation of the local currency. Excess reserves (in local currency held with the central bank) do not cause banks to lend more in local currency. Instead they seek investments in foreign currency if the domestic interest premium is thought to be insufficient. This action has the potential to trigger an exchange rate depreciation, which has inflationary consequences. Monetary policy affects inflation through the exchange rate channel: if domestic interest rates are set at a level which offers banks adequate compensation on their excess liquidity, the exchange rate is unchanged and inflation remains at the international rate. However, if domestic interest does not provide a sufficient return on local currency holdings, the exchange rate depreciates, aggravating the impact of international inflation on the domestic economy. Just as in the case of the SOE with an exchange rate anchor, it is the change in the exchange rate which produces inflationary effects. If the central bank is able to ensure that the domestic interest rate is sufficiently attractive to maintain liquid balances in domestic rather than foreign currency, the change in interest rates has no effect on domestic inflation. In the end, the best inflation outcome on offer is in the case of an unchanged exchange rate. In effect the central bank is burdened with the task of anchoring the exchange rate, in this case with the use of interest rate policy rather than through sales from its foreign reserve stock.

In sum, whether or not the exchange rate is anchored on an international currency, monetary policy is useful only as support for fiscal adjustment in the face of shocks. With or without the exchange rate anchor, changes in interest rates must be employed to deter destabilising switches from domestic to foreign financial assets. Intervention by the central bank in the treasury bill auction is a market-friendly way of influencing the interest rate, which offers the best chance of success in arresting exchange rate speculation and defensive moves against local currency asset holding. This instrument is available everywhere that government issues marketable short-term debt, even where there is no active money market, and even when there is a chronic excess of liquid funds in the banking system.

The channels of monetary policy influence

The widespread endorsement of inflation targeting by central banks does not reflect a consensus among macroeconomists about the channels along which monetary impulses run, or about whether money affects output or prices. In a paper on the channels of monetary transmission Mishkin (1996) listed seven possible results of monetary expansion, all affecting real income. (His paper was not concerned only with small or developing countries.) Monetary expansion might provoke a decline in the real interest rate, which could stimulate business decisions on investment, housing and expenditure on consumer durables, resulting in increases in real income. A second channel might be through the effect of the fall in the real interest rate on the exchange rate, a depreciation which could stimulate exports. A possible third channel was via equity prices, which might stimulate investment by increasing the market value of firms relative to the replacement value of their capital. A fourth possibility was that inflation in equity prices might stimulate consumption demand because equity holders found that they were wealthier than expected. The fifth lending channel, via the impact of increased bank funding on loans and investment, was said to be of declining importance worldwide. The sixth possibility was that the increase in wealth might improve the creditworthiness of firms, leading to more lending and investment. The seventh possibility was that the increased money supply might lead to expectations of higher inflation and a reduction in the real value of firms' outstanding liabilities, opening space for an expansion of credit.

Beyond empirical questions of which if any of these channels are of importance in any country, we must consider the time frame over which any of these effects will play themselves out. The realisation of new investment is not instantaneous, and any expected increases in real output capacity will manifest themselves only in future time periods. It is very likely that aggressive monetary expansion will result in expansion in domestic expenditures that run ahead of domestic production capacity, causing inflation in the short run. In the case of SOEs, this excess demand is reflected in an import surge and an increase in exchange market pressure; the proximate cause of inflation will be a depreciation of the exchange rate.

Two implications emerge from this discussion: one, that the focus on the inflationary effects of monetary expansion, rather than real output effects, is warranted in the short run, even if there may be increases in output in the longer term; secondly, that inflationary effects of monetary expansion will not appear in the SOE unless and until the exchange rate depreciates. This is true even though the expenditure on nontradables is typically much larger than domestic spending on tradables, because there is usually enough spare capacity in nontradable activities to ramp up production in response to additional demand, and therefore prices are not affected until it becomes necessary to restock imported final and intermediate goods. Swift and decisive fiscal action to put the brakes on expenditure before foreign reserves are depleted and a depreciation of the domestic currency becomes inevitable can eliminate the risk of inflation.

A further ambiguity arises with respect to the symmetry of monetary policy effects. Let us focus on the interest-exchange rate channel, since that is of most concern to the monetary authority in the SOE, and let us accept that the target is to keep domestic inflation at the level of international inflation. Intervention by the central bank to ease the monetary stance by lowering the treasury bill rate is intended to stimulate expenditure in the short run (and output and investment in the longer term), leading to an increased demand for imports and pressure on the exchange market that might cause the rate to depreciate, leading to an acceleration of inflation. Of greater interest is what we might expect when the central bank intervenes to temper a rate of inflation which exceeds its target. In this case the intention is to reduce aggregate spending and curtail imports, but this will achieve slower inflation only if the exchange rate appreciates. Here we need to factor in market expectations; the exchange rate will appreciate as expected only if there are confident expectations of a sustained surplus in the future supply of foreign currency. If that is not the case, the attempt to arrest accelerating inflation may have perverse effects, through increasing market uncertainty.

This discussion reinforces the primacy of fiscal policy in the adjustment strategy. In order to provide reassurance about future inflows of foreign currency, government must convince the foreign exchange market that the fiscal stance will contain expenditure and imports in the short run, and that there is sufficient stimulus for investment in the long term to ensure a continuing increase in foreign currency inflows.

Yet another imponderable is the magnitude of the elasticities of expenditure responses to interest rate changes. Marginal changes in the policy rate, which are preferred because they do not risk upsetting market expectations, will typically elicit no measurable expenditure response. There are plausible explanations as to why this might be, including information costs, transactions costs and exchange rate uncertainty. Also, the demand for household mortgages and consumer durables typically is affected only when interest rate changes are large enough to impact the proportion of income that must be devoted to servicing costs. Worrell (1985) estimated "zones of inertia" within which there was no perceptible responses to interest rate changes in Barbados and Jamaica. The consequence of this discontinuity is that responses to monetary impulses are lumpy, with no discernible reaction until successive changes in interest rates cumulate to a sufficient threshold. This is an additional argument for limiting the ambition of monetary policy to keeping domestic interest rates on the international trend line, rather than as a tool for demand management.

Another unresolved question which receives scant attention in monetary policy discussions is the differing elasticities of response to interest rate changes by producers and consumers. This is especially consequential with respect to bank credit. Except in markets where active short-term money markets are a crucial link in the transmission process, the monetary impulse impacts spending mainly through bank credit. Arguably, the immediate impact of changes in the cost of bank credit is manifested in producers' costs, much sooner than any impact on consumer spending appears. A rise in the loan rate is directly reflected in the costs of firms' working capital, whereas consumers will typically not react unless successive increases cause them to postpone discretionary purchases and consider renegotiating their mortgages. The implication is that attempts to tighten the money supply by raising interest rates may have the perverse effect of aggravating inflation through effects from the cost side if the impact on finance costs is pervasive.

Monetary instruments and money markets

Even as the orthodoxy of flexible exchange rates and inflation targeting took hold at the IMF and elsewhere in the 1990s, there were doubts about its relevance to economies where there were no active short-term money and exchange markets. An exhaustive survey of the challenges to monetary policy in shallow markets (Iden, Laurens and Swaray, 2003) recognised the problems in implementing market-oriented monetary policies: an asset price channel was absent because of lack of a market where short-term financial assets were actively traded and the widespread use of controls on the current and capital account of the balance of payments, which weakened the exchange rate effects. Monetary authorities in the wide sample of emerging market and developing countries sampled showed a strong preference for targeting the monetary base or the exchange rate, intervening so often and so forcefully that such short-term markets as did exist yielded no reliable price information. Base money forecasts were subject to wide margins of error, and were not employed to guide policy in a sufficiently flexible manner with monitoring and adjustments to keep the money supply on target. The authors thought that the requirements for open-market type operations – an active interbank market and a capacity for sufficiently reliable liquidity forecasting – were beyond the reach of some countries at the time, and they therefore suggested a hierarchy in the use of monetary tools. Countries where the required market mechanisms did not exist were obliged to depend on changes in bank reserve requirements, and the provision of deposit, credit and refinancing facilities on demand to banks as the tools of monetary policy. They should take steps to move to the next stage, to join the group of countries which were fostering the development of an active interbank market in local and foreign exchange liquidity. The study envisaged that SOEs would continue to use non-market tools along with intervention on the interbank market jointly in their toolbox, and it was envisaged that a fully diversified short-term market in local and foreign currency was unlikely to develop in such economies, because of the low volume and limited range of financial institutions and instruments, a perspective which has proved to have been realistic. The countries discussed in the study – the Eastern Caribbean Currency Union, the Democratic Republic of the Congo, Egypt, the Kyrgyz Republic, Malta, The Gambia, Tunisia, Uganda, Ukraine, Vanuatu and Zambia – covered the spectrum of emerging market and developing country experience and the full range of monetary and exchange rate strategies, but they were all less than satisfied with their ability to achieve the objectives of their monetary policies.

In a decade of offering technical advice on monetary policy to countries in Africa, Asia-Pacific, the Caribbean and Europe, I encountered the practical challenges in applying policies to target the supply of money in countries at different stages of development and in varying economic circumstances. The obstacles that frustrated the achievement of monetary objectives ranged from systems that featured a single commercial bank in the Comoros and São Tomé, through deficiencies in data and technical liquidity forecasting capacity in Haiti, Papua New Guinea and Bosnia-Herzegovina, to fiscal excesses which robbed the interbank market of suitable collateral for lending in Pakistan, Sri Lanka, Ghana and the Caribbean. Targets for the supply of money were sometimes achieved, though more often they were not, but it was rare to be able to point to any obvious successes in attaining ultimate inflation, exchange rate or output targets.

Meanwhile, the orthodoxy with respect to monetary policy has coalesced around flexible exchange rate regimes, with monetary policy assigned the task of hitting a target for the rate of inflation. The gravitation towards flexible rates was more out of a sense that central banks did not have the capability to manage the exchange rate, rather than a conviction that foreign currency markets met the efficiency criteria for discovering the equilibrium rate that would equate the demand and supply of foreign currency in any economy. The inevitable consequence has been an ongoing debate and discussion about the prevalence of central bank intervention affecting foreign currency liquidity – often empirical studies use data on foreign currency transactions, but unsterilised local currency injections will also affect the foreign currency market – and the puzzling but very common observation that the exchange rates of SOEs remain unchanged for extended periods of time in the absence of any active intervention whatsoever on the part of the central bank.

We have now reached a point where the orthodox view admits of the value of foreign exchange intervention (Hofman et al, 2020): the paper observes that foreign exchange intervention is "a widely-used policy instrument among inflation-targeting E[merging] M[arket] E[conomy] central banks" (Hofman et al, 2020, p. 4). They refer to recent studies which suggest that the benefits of exchange rate flexibility may be overstated in the presence of currency mismatches, endogenous financial risks and US dollar invoicing of trade, which is characteristic of all SOE foreign transactions. The case for intervention is strongest in the presence of large currency mismatches or underdeveloped markets; further, although in theory interventions could inhibit the development of short-term financial markets, it is not clear that this actually is of any importance, and the negative impact on the credibility of the policy framework may be smaller than is often assumed, according to the findings of the study, which includes a comprehensive survey of recent orthodox research and opinion.

Excess bank liquidity and the impact of monetary initiatives

Because the bank credit channel is the principal – often the only – channel through which monetary policy affects expenditure and prices in the SOE, the widely observed phenomenon of a chronic excess of holdings of liquid reserves with the central bank, at zero or below-market interest, may rob monetary initiatives of their effectiveness. Increases in reserve requirements have no effect: small increases will not make much of a dent in the excess, and there will be no impact on the supply of credit; but the increase cannot be large enough to eliminate the full amount of the excess in most circumstances, because the free reserves are not evenly distributed among banks, and small banks may be pushed over the edge into bankruptcy. In the case of market-based monetary policy, central bank intervention to tighten liquidity will either be so prolonged as to be ineffective, or it will require a change in the policy rate that is so large that it will unsettle the liquid funds market, especially the demand for foreign exchange. As a result, the reasons for excess reserves and their implications for monetary policy have been a constant preoccupation in monetary policy discussions relating to SOEs.

A working hypothesis, reflected in Worrell (1985) and Worrell (1997a) is that, in fixed exchange rate systems, there is a level of unremunerated local currency reserves with which bank are content, because, given their levels of local currency deposits, the demand for credit-worthy borrowers, the availability of liquid financial assets of sufficient quality and currency conversion costs, the net benefit from any of the available options for significantly reducing excess reserves is less than the costs that would be incurred. For example, acquiring foreign assets will incur exchange costs, either from having to purchase foreign exchange on the interbank market, or, if the bank uses its own foreign currency purchases from tourists and exporters, an opportunity cost, equal to the margin it would have earned of sale of that foreign exchange to importers. In the model of Worrell (1985), adjustment in reserve holdings enters into the consideration, along with changes in deposit and loan rates, in response to any exogenous change. Worrell (1997c) tests working hypotheses about how banks' appetite for treasury bills and the offer rates for loans and deposits respond to changes in the level of excess reserves. Worrell (1997b) surveys research on bank behaviour and draws implications for monetary policy from the characteristics of Caribbean banking systems in light of what is known about bank behaviour in imperfect markets. The study suggests that, because the increasing returns to scale and credit markets in the Caribbean are so small, banks may widen spreads in response to an increase in the policy rate, or they might keep their rates unchanged for prime customers, while raising premiums for less preferred customers. Also, interest rate functions are evidently discontinuous with no responses for incremental changes. These features mean that some increases in base money end up in excess reserves, because there is no credit demand response to a fall in the interest rate. Banking markets in the Caribbean are oligopolistic, and this might make for some sluggishness in responses to policy, especially where information channels are less than ideal and levels of trust are low. The study concludes that reactions to changes in the policy interest rate have consequences that are hard to predict and that the best monetary policy might be the least active.

The challenges of inflation targeting

The basic tenet of inflation targeting – that monetary policy may be employed to achieve a target inflation rate – is untenable in SOEs, because inflation is mostly imported. The widespread adoption of inflation targeting frameworks by central banks around the world, including many SOEs, surprising though it may be, cannot alter that fact. Any policy strategy based on flexible exchange rates for SOEs faces the intractable problem that, in the absence of a credible value of local currency in terms of internationally accepted money, there is no anchor for expectations. In a world of imperfect information, with the need to devise and implement forward-looking economic strategies, the economic and financial environment is then subject to instability resulting from news, rumours and misinformation.

The literature identifies other challenges to a single-minded focus on inflation by the central bank, including risks to the financial system from currency mismatches when the exchange rate is volatile, and the fact that, for SOEs as well as for many large countries, all external transactions are priced in US dollars. This reality is baked into all realistic models of the SOE, and the fact that the economics community is only now waking up to reality is symptomatic of how poorly exchange rate theory is understood.

The basic challenge of using orthodox models for the analysis of monetary policy, whether the models are neo-Keynsian, neo-classical or, as claimed by Hofman et al (2020) post-Keynsian, is that they depend on a notion of an equilibrium exchange rate. For much of the 1980s I was associated with the late John Williamson of the Peterson Institute, one of the leaders in the search for a real life analogue for the theoretical equilibrium exchange rate which could be employed for practical policy formulation. It must now be admitted that that search has ended in failure. The common observation is that expectations coalesce around whatever exchange rate persists for an extended period of time until some shock displaces the rate. Except in the case of a country whose major export is oil or some other internationally-traded commodity, in which case the new level will reflect the price of that commodity, the exchange rate settles nowhere near where economists or the business and financial community expects it to be.

References

Hofman, David J., Marcos Chamon, Pragyan Deb, Thomas Harjes, Umang Rawat and Itaru Yamamoto. 2020. “Intervention under inflation targeting – when could it make sense?” *Working Paper*. Washington, DC: International Monetary Fund, January.

Iden, George, Bernard J. Laurens and Stephen Swaray. 2003. “Challenges to monetary policy in shallow markets,” *Seminar Paper*. Washington, DC: International Monetary Fund, August.

Khemraj, Tarron. 2014. *Money, Banking and the Foreign Exchange Market in Emerging Economies*. Cheltenham, UK: Edward Elgar.

Mishkin, Frederic. 1996. "The channels of monetary transmission: lessons for monetary policy," *Working Paper*. Cambridge, MA: National Bureau of Economic Research, February.

Saxegaard, Magnus. 2006. "Excess liquidity and the effectiveness of monetary policy: Evidence from SSA," *Working Paper*. Washington, D.C.: International Monetary Fund, no. 06/115, May.

Worrell, DeLisle. 1997a. "Role models for monetary policy in the Caribbean," in *Central Banking in Barbados: Reflections and Challenges*, edited by H. Codrington, R. Craigwell and C. Haynes. Barbados: Central Bank of Barbados.

Worrell, DeLisle. 1997b. "Bank behaviour and monetary policy in small open economies with reference to the Caribbean," *Social and Economic Studies*, Vol. 46, nos 2 & 3, October.

Worrell, DeLisle. 1997c. "Working hypotheses about short term interest rates," Central Bank of Barbados, *Working Paper*, March.

Worrell, DeLisle. 1985. "Monetary mechanisms for open economies," in *The Economics of the Caribbean Basin*, edited by John McDermott and Michael Connolly. New York: Praeger Publishers.

Worrell, DeLisle, Michelle Doyle-Lowe, AntonBelgrave, Darrin Downes and Kester Guy. 2012. "A framework for interest rate policy in Barbados," *Working Paper*. Central Bank of Barbados, July.

10 Finance, Development and Stability in the Small Open Economy

The central thesis of this book is that economic performance should be judged by results in terms of the well-being of the population of the economy. In line with this focus, this chapter explores the relationship between the financial sector and development that improves scores on the indices that measure the quality of human lives. The first part of the chapter deals with the financing of investment, the efficiency of banking services and other credit mechanisms and the functions of capital markets, issues that directly affect employment, income spending and well-being. The second part of the chapter, on issues of financial stability, evaluates risks and mitigation strategies in terms of their potential to impair the material well-being of the population. The novel aspect of our assessment of financial stability in the SOE is to take the analysis through to a conclusion about the probable impact on level and quality of life in the affected population.

It comes as a surprise that the quality of life in Greece, Cyprus, Ireland, Iceland and other European countries appears not to have been affected in any perceptible way by the financial crisis which commanded global attention for almost a decade in those countries. In spite of the images broadcast across the world of the plight of pensioners in desperate circumstances and the extravagant estimates of the cost of financial rescue operations, these countries remain in the highest of the four categories of human development in the UNDP *Human Development Report*. The presumed massive economic cost of financial crises is also not evident in other instances of which I am aware. It has been estimated that the Jamaican financial crisis of the late 1990s cost the equivalent of about 40 per cent of GDP; however, there was no decline in consumption, investment, imports or any other expenditure of anything like this magnitude.

This apparent paradox disappears when we put the focus on development, and the impact of financial instability on our ultimate objective, which is the material well-being of the population. That is the unique contribution of this chapter. We begin with an assessment of the efficiency and effectiveness of financial services in channelling finance to fund investment, in affording household access to durable consumption goods and housing, in protecting the value of savings over time, and in widening access, reducing costs and

DOI: 10.4324/9781003247609-12

ensuring speedier national and international payments. Our overarching concern, in assessing financial stability, is to minimise the effects of instability on investment, the value of financial assets and payments. Financial failures should be managed in such a way that investment incentives are sustained, asset values are protected and payments systems are not compromised.

The financing of investment

We have established that investment is the source of growth, creating additional capacity in competitive industry and increasing productivity. In this section we discuss how investment is financed. Table 10.1 shows the breakdown of financing of capital formation in Barbados in 1981, the peak year for investment in a cycle that lasted from 1975 to 1985. It is derived from Worrell (1990, p. 14). The largest contribution evidently came from retained earnings and private sources, which were the source for 40 per cent of finance, with foreign debt contributing 32 per cent (Government sourced 18 per cent of the total, and private sector borrowing 14 per cent, all of it from long-term foreign currency loans from commercial banks). Finance from the banking system for investment other than mortgages was ten per cent. This is a typical pattern of investment in emerging market and developing countries. The bulk of investment in SOEs is undertaken by well-established local conglomerates and international firms which have their own networks of finance, including access to foreign finance. This allows them to secure funding for capital projects without resort to the local financial system. That is fortuitous, because the local institutions specialising in investment finance are few, and in the Caribbean they are all subsidiaries of international banks. Their purpose is expressly to secure funding for the commercial bank's corporate clients, mainly in foreign currency, because that is what is needed for the materials, equipment and other imports for any investment project. The investment financing needs of firms in activities whose international competitiveness is well established is fully taken care of, without much resort to the local financial system. Such companies use commercial banks only to fund working capital.

Table 10.1 Barbados: financing capital formation, % of total, 1981

Government, savings and domestic borrowing	9
Government foreign borrowing	18
Domestic financing	12
Of which, banks	*10*
Mortgages	8
Private foreign capital	14
Retained earnings, residual	40
TOTAL	100
Memo item: long term loans	16

Source: Worrell (1990, p. 14).

Mortgages are the commercial banks' main contribution to fixed capital formation. They are a low-risk and remunerative way to deploy the permanent core of the banking system's deposit liabilities, deposits that will only be called in the event of total bank failure. The risk in mortgage lending is low because there is tangible collateral, the processes are familiar and the transaction is covered by life insurance. In case of difficulty, some form of modification of the terms of the credit will usually serve to restore the mortgage to good standing. Outright default is usually problematic because real estate markets, like other asset markets in SOEs, are thin and illiquid, but defaults are rare.

The main lacunae in the funding available for investment are for financing of new products and services, and for small and medium enterprises. In both cases there is need for state participation, because the risks of failure are too high for this lending to be commercially viable for deposit-and-lending institutions. What is more, in the case of the development of new activities or markets, the initial investment or other parameters may be beyond the resources of even the largest private investors. Two successful Caribbean examples of state-led new development of sufficient magnitude to affect the overall development of the economy are the development of the tourist industry in Aruba and the establishment of the Cancun tourist resort in Mexico. A more controversial example, which I believe should also be considered a success, is the investment by the Trinidad and Tobago Government in the Point Lisas industrial complex, which provided the country with the basis for vertical integration of the oil industry (Chapter 4).

These examples, which are considered anomalous by most Caribbean opinion, might in fact be seen as challenges to Caribbean countries and other SOEs to develop a capacity for state entrepreneurship, so as to emulate their success. In Chapter 8 we offered some observations on the institutional frameworks through which the entrepreneurial state might provide funding, directly or indirectly, for innovation, increased productivity, adoption and adaptation of new technology, exploration of new products and markets, quality enhancements and other investment aimed to maintain and strengthen international competitiveness.

Small and medium enterprises play a vital role in creating employment and realising the multiplier benefits to the economy from the leading foreign exchange sectors of SOEs: in the tourism sector, the income from hotels and restaurants gets amplified through sports, entertainment, cultural activities and personal services such as spas and hairdressers. Manufacturing industries will support an industry to do repairs and servicing, provide spare parts, manage logistics, provide accountancy and design services, etc. All activities can stimulate demand for supporting waste management services, security services and similar enterprise.

The finance of the small and medium enterprises which provide most of these services is always problematic, because turnover is usually high, both of enterprises and their employees, and quality control in the sector is problematic.

Well-crafted training programmes, incorporating local knowledge and with an emphasis on learning by doing and mentorship, can do much to improve performance in the sector, but finance for small business remains too risky for commercial banks unless government absorbs some of the risk through some form of credit insurance.

Community banks and credit unions have reported more promising experiences in the financing of small businesses in the US, the Caribbean and elsewhere (International Monetary Fund, 2013).[1] Because of local knowledge, in the case of community banks, and the collective sanction of the mutual structure of credit unions, these institutions are better able to screen loan applications and recognise those applicants who are not credit-worthy. The critical expertise which any credit institution provides its depositors is identifying borrowers who can be depended upon to service their loans in full and on time (Zephirin, 1990). There is no better way to know who they are than by establishing a lasting relationship and by personal acquaintance over time; these are the sources of comparative advantage of community-based and mutual lenders like community banks and credit unions.

The early promise of non-governmental financial institutions, popularised by the Grameen Bank in Bangladesh in the 1980s (the bank was founded in 1983) has not been fulfilled. The model was refined and used in an attempt to replace informal financial systems with more efficient and safer credit arrangements in developing countries across the world. Examples of lasting success are hard to find: financial NGOs founded in the Eastern Caribbean and Barbados in the 1980s (Fairbairn and Worrell, 1996, p. 70) have largely disappeared; in the Comoros, where two financial NGOs were the only financial institutions available to the majority of the population, both were close to insolvency in 2006; in larger economies (Sri Lanka, Haiti, Pakistan, Tanzania, Ghana) financial NGOs' contribution to the financial system was too small to register in total financial system assets, and the majority of SME activity remained dependent on informal financial arrangements.[2]

State-owned development institutions have been successful in East and South Asia, providing financial and technical support for the development of new industries and for economic diversification. In the case of Singapore, that success laid the foundation for the development bank's transformation into an international commercial bank which is now a leading financial institution in the region. The Asian success is the exception; elsewhere, inefficiency, political capture and malfeasance has led to the closure of development banks or a reduction of their scope and activity. The only national development bank that still has a significant local presence in the Caribbean is the Development Bank of Jamaica. Development banks were wound up because of insolvency in The Bahamas, Barbados, Trinidad and Tobago and elsewhere; the surviving national development banks in the region are of no importance, in terms of their contribution to the supply of domestic finance.

Summing up the discussion on financing capital formation: the essential framework is an efficient, entrepreneurial state, formulating a carefully designed, well informed and documented development strategy, in close cooperation with local and interested international private entrepreneurs, and with a few central, widely-shared, clearly achievable objectives for improvements in the main indicators of material well-being. Government needs to identify the gaps in the institutional structure for financial capital formation for the execution of the development strategy. They are likely to reside in two areas: firstly, funding for new foreign exchange earning activities, and in the use of domestic sources of renewable energy (the only area of substantial import substitution in SOEs), where international financial markets are unaware of the competitive returns available in these activities; and secondly, finance for small and medium enterprises. On the basis of experience, the first of these funding gaps is best addressed by a combination of tax and cash incentives to raise the apparent rates of return on the desired investments to competitive levels, given the ruling international prices at which tradable products and services are sold. With respect to the financing of small and medium enterprises, the recommended strategy, again drawing on experience, is to provide guarantees to commercial banks and other lending institutions, and to foster the growth of well-run community banks and credit unions.

What should commercial banks do?

Commercial banks have evolved very rapidly in the last half century in ways that have not been acknowledged in most discussion and analysis. Banks evolved gradually from their earliest obscure beginnings as financiers of sovereigns, merchants and trading companies, to become the fulcrum of domestic and international payments and the principal vehicle for household deposits, both cash for transactions and for savings, in addition to providing working capital for companies. From the 1950s through to the 1980s commercial banks in Western countries were broadening their customer network, bringing banking services down to the community level. Banks had a sound, profitable and low-risk business model, with a stable deposit base providing funding for credit to businesses with whom the bank had established a long-standing relationship, as well as households well-known to the branch manager in their community. Banks exist to identify credit-worthy borrowers with whom they can employ the excess over consumption needs which savers place with the bank (Crockett, 1997). The saver pays the bank a margin on the return on the loan as payment for this service of filtering out from the list of loan applicants those who are unlikely to service their borrowings. By the 1950s this model of branch expansion provided banks with a cost-effective credit-worthiness system, through relationships and local knowledge at the community level. International banks came to dominate most markets, because they had found a way to match community and savings banks in terms of local knowledge, thereby offering services at comparable costs, while leveraging their far greater and more diverse sources of deposits.

This model began to fracture in the 1980s when commercial banks, led by the Americans, began to fund substantial proportions of their overall portfolios with funds borrowed on very short-term markets – the cheapest available sources – in efforts to increase profitability and franchise value. That began a new era of intense competition among major international banks, in the course of which they began to centralise credit administration in head offices far away from the countries and communities where borrowers were located. In so doing, international banks unwittingly gave away the basis of their comparative advantage over mutual banks, savings-and-loans and credit unions.

The banks' short-term funding strategy imploded when the short-term liquidity market failed in 2007. The proximate cause was the fact that the credit instruments used in this market were tainted by the inclusion of notes backed by sub-prime mortgages in the US, which had been aggressively marketed to unsuitable customers by unregulated, mostly nonfinancial institutions. The reaction to the ensuing global financial crisis, which came to a head with the failure of Lehman Brothers in September 2008, reflected a misunderstanding of the roots of the crisis on the part of the international banking regulatory body, the Basle Committee on Banking Supervision, administered by the Bank for International Settlements. The new regulations which the Committee has established for the operations of international banks have completed the process of rendering these banks uncompetitive in community and relationship banking. Predictably, international commercial banks have retreated *en masse* from the retail banking space.

The banking systems in many countries are in a state of transition: commercial banks still dominate the credit markets, both in servicing large corporate clients, where they retain a comparative advantage, and in offering deposit, loan and payments functions for small and medium enterprises and households, market segments for which they have lost their comparative advantage to community based banks, credit unions and similar mutual savings-and-loans, venture capital firms, nonbank credit (supplier's credit, leasing, etc), informal credit arrangements and crowdfunding and other new technologies. Small businesses and households have begun to migrate from banks to these substitutes, in a process that will undoubtedly accelerate, as knowledge of the alternatives spreads through credit markets. The switch away from banks is also being propelled by the oppressive bureaucratisation of commercial bank procedures, under pressure from international regulators, which has limited relevance to payments, credit and banking services for small nations, poor countries and informal activities. The compliance costs have also driven up the costs of all banking services, resulting in general dissatisfaction with high banking fees, and wide interest margins between deposits and credit.

Banks' provision of mortgage credit in the past half-century has made a major contribution to the quality of life in many countries, through a marked improvement in the quality of housing. This fact has gone largely unrecognised in economic discussions, perhaps because economists do not evaluate performance in terms of improvement in the quality of life. The benefits of home ownership cannot be overstated: besides the material comfort that good, uncrowded housing provides, accessible housing finance is a strong motivation for individual productivity, educational aspiration and achievement, and purposeful living. Secure home ownership is empowering .and a source of wealth that maintains its value in all circumstances other than armed conflict. (As an aside, failure to appreciate the contribution of good housing to human development in this wider sense has led many governments to remove tax and other incentives for home ownership in the past three decades.)

The provision of instalment credit and leasing arrangements are other financial services which have contributed directly and importantly to human development. The spread of banking services brought mortgages, instalment credit and leasing to households and small businesses, to the great benefit of all countries that now boast nation-wide coverage of banking services. The instalment lending space has always been shared with retailers and other non-banks, and banks may lose market share to these competitors over time because of the factors mentioned earlier.

Commercial banks offer the important service of maturity transformation, which they are able to do by virtue of aggregating a large number of individual and company deposits. In the absence of banks, people with surplus funds available for lending would not only have the burden of finding creditworthy borrowers, they would have to determine how much of their surplus they would have to retain, in case they had an unforeseen need to purchase anything. With the availability of banks, the entire surplus could be committed to the bank to earn a return, secure in the knowledge that the bank can always provide them with liquidity on demand, albeit with some loss in returns. The bank will be able to meet the liquidity demands of individual customers out of the liquid reserves it holds with the central bank. If for any reason reserve holdings are insufficient, the central bank offers short-term loans to enable banks to meet their obligations. This benefit of maturity transformation is difficult to quantify, but it is clear that it yields a material benefit to both deposit holders (by providing them a better and more secure return on surplus funds) and to borrowers, by affording them access to fixed term credit that would otherwise have been withheld from the market.

In contrast to these evident benefits, there are bank services and practices which have made the savings-and-loans process less efficient and sometimes harmful, leading the unwary into avoidable financial difficulty. One such practice is the over-use of collateral, which can lead to a relaxation in standards for credit evaluation and lead to unsound business decisions. As a general rule, loans should be collateralised only up the expected risk of failure, but not beyond that point. Banks aim to lend only to borrowers they expect to service their loans in full; in case of unforeseen difficulty, such as the onset of the COVID-19 pandemic, they expect to be able to negotiate a workout which avoids any delinquency. Collateral will be called only if the bank fails in the main service it exists to provide, that is, the identification of creditworthy borrowers. The bank should not presume that it will fail, which is what it does, in effect, when it demands excessive collateral.

It has to be acknowledged, however, that application of this principle is a matter of judgment. The risk of failure may be calculated from historical data, but the selection of data (by activity, country, size of enterprise, or other criteria), the time period that is pertinent for the analysis, and an evaluation of changes in the environment and the relevance of new technologies are all judgmental factors that must be taken into account. The nature of the collateral and its probable value under conditions of a forced sale are also factors that are material to a decision on the appropriate level of collateral.

The management of credit card debt is another problematic area, where on balance, credit-worthy borrowers are made worse off by using this instead of other borrowing, while borrowers who are not credit-worthy may be driven into insolvency. These disabilities are the result of excessively high interest rates, criteria for access which are far too low and minimum monthly repayment amounts that extend the life of credit to the point where cumulative interest exceeds the amount borrowed. Correcting these faults would destroy the viability of the credit card business, which would be a benefit to consumers.

The standard bank practice of imposing interest penalties on impaired debt is problematic; its universal application is puzzling. If the borrower is unable or unwilling to pay the agreed interest, it is not logical to expect them to pay an interest penalty in addition. The only circumstance in which the interest penalty will serve to bring the credit back on schedule is one where there was an oversight, in which case the customer-friendly action would be to issue a reminder. In other cases, the inescapable implication is that the interest penalty is an openly-sanctioned device to acquire assets owned by the borrower, over and above the value of the credit amount. That is a procedure which cannot meet any acceptable standard of fairness.

Banking systems in SOEs

Banking systems in SOEs are inevitably oligopolistic, and, increasingly, foreign-owned. This fact is dictated by the positive returns to scale in banking, which have been exaggerated by an unproductive overburden of international regulation in the aftermath of the global financial crisis of 2007/8. The Barbados experience is typical of trends in SOE banking system in the past 50 years. In 1970 the banking system consisted of just four international banks, three Canadian and one British. In pursuit of greater competition and diversification of ownership, three American banks were encouraged to establish branches on the island, and Government converted the Post Office savings bank into a state-owned commercial bank over the course of the 1970s.

By 1980 the American banks had departed after failing to make any headway with a strategy based on loan rate competition. Their willingness to enter the market in the first place was prompted by the observation that loan-deposit interest spreads were multiples of comparable spreads in the US, a fact that seemed to offer the prospect of luring business away from existing banks with competitive pricing. The strategy was a failure; the newcomers failed to capture market share from the established banks; their loan portfolios never increased to projected levels, and they contained an unacceptably high proportion of poor quality loans. The established banks had relationships of long standing with all the best available credits, and they tailored lending to their specific needs, reflecting the competitive value of local knowledge. The American banks came up against another feature of the local credit market: volumes of transaction were so low that it was necessary to maintain a wide margin between the cost and return on credits on each transaction to obtain a competitive return on assets. It turned out that there was no scope for narrowing margins, either to attract deposits with higher rates or good credits with more attractive loan rates.

The Barbados National Bank began life with a large portfolio of deposits, inherited from the Barbados Savings Bank, the Post Office bank. It immediately ran into the problem of attracting good credits, just like the other newcomers. The BNB was saddled with the additional disability that it was expected to have a bias in favour of "productive sectors", which most people seemed to understand as agriculture, manufacturing and tourism. However, the bank's ventures in those fields did not turn out well; as in all other production, the good credits in these areas were all fully taken care of by the established commercial banks, leaving only iffy propositions for the BNB to compete for. In the end, the bank's credit profile resembled that of the established banks, with a profitable core of mortgages, and most of the remainder of the well-performing portfolio shared between loans to consumers and retailers.

The combination of the small transaction volumes and the oligopolistic structure of the banking system characterises almost all SOEs. It explains two phenomena which are commonly observed in these economies: high levels of liquid funds held with the central bank, well in excess of stipulations and often with no remuneration (in local currency, if the exchange rate is predictable); and spreads between loan and deposit rates which seem excessive to observers in advanced countries.

Worrell (1997) explores the structure of the banking system in SOEs and the implications for monetary policy based on Caribbean experience. The study finds high levels of concentration in the banking sector, evidently reflecting economies of scale in banking. Even though the dominant banks in the English-speaking Caribbean boasted regional networks, the single available study of financial mobility within CARICOM up to that date uncovered variations in the degree of mobility, suggesting that individual countries were treated as separate markets. No firm conclusions could be reached about Caribbean banking efficiency; the usual arguments cited, such as high margins, were more likely to be a reflection of low transactions volumes and rigidities in the loan and deposit responses to interest rate changes. The study found that interest rates were adjusted infrequently and discretely rather than continuously in daily trading, even in liberalised systems. Financial liberalisation was found to have led to higher concentration, not lesser, as was anticipated. The implications for monetary policy were unclear: if there were indeed increasing returns to scale, banks might widen spreads in response to an increase in the policy rate, or their prime may remain unchanged, with higher premiums for less preferred customers; if interest rate functions were actually discontinuous, some interest rate changes would provoke no response. As a result, some increases in base money end up in excess reserves, because there is no demand response to the fall in loan rates. The banking system was plagued with information deficiencies, and reactions to policy changes in interest rates tended to be unpredictable; the financial institutions themselves did not appear to have had a clearly defined response to any policy change.

Stock exchanges in the English-speaking Caribbean

The Caribbean experience is typical of small economies worldwide, in that they have failed to realise expectations that securities markets would make a significant contribution to the financing of capital formation in any country. Securities exchanges were set up in Jamaica, Trinidad and Tobago, Barbados and the ECCU in the 1970s and 1980s, building on the informal trading arrangements between banks, trust companies, insurance companies and other non-bank financial institutions that previously existed. Governments actively supported the exchanges; in Barbados the Central Bank is a major shareholder in the exchange, having underwritten most of its setup costs. In all the countries where exchanges were established, governments provided tax exemptions and other inducements to encourage wide participation.

From the outset, trading on the exchanges was inhibited by the fact that the firms that attracted most interest were well-established conglomerates which seldom if ever had a need to secure finance from the open market. All their capital project financing needs could be met through retained earnings within the group and from their international networks of finance. Most did list some shares on the local securities exchanges as a way to support the development of the local market. Naturally these were the stocks that attracted most buyers to the neglect of smaller and newer firms which were in search of public subscriptions. As a result, new public offerings of shares were infrequent and there was little active trading. Holders typically held on to the stocks they purchased and waited for their value to appreciate.

Enthusiasm for involvement in securities markets was further eroded by the failure of what seemed to be promising investments, such as the Almond Resorts in Barbados. The group's flagship hotel was established with the assistance of international expertise and the support of the International Finance Corporation, a subsidiary of the World Bank, at a time of expansion in resort tourism in the Caribbean and elsewhere. The intention was to build a specialised brand of all-inclusive hotel that could imitate the pioneering success of the Jamaican all-inclusive chains. Almond chose to focus on the market for families with small children which was perceived to be under-served.

However the company ran into financial problems after a promising start and an enthusiastic reception on the Barbados securities exchange, and it was wound up after little more than a decade of operation.

The securities exchanges in Barbados and the ECCU have now essentially collapsed. The ECCU exchange never really got off the ground, with just a handful of listings and no active trading. Thanks to forceful backing by the Central Bank of Barbados, the Barbados exchange got off to what appeared to be a promising start, with many of the largest domestic companies listed, and ideas for attracting a second tier of smaller firms as well as providing a platform for trading of international securities. However, the exchange was never used as a source of funding for investment projects of any significance, trading remained very thin, with most buyers sticking to familiar names, and the initiatives to find new business for the exchange all came to nought. Over time, most of the attractive stocks have withdrawn from the exchange; some have shifted headquarters and funding sources abroad, others have been demotivated by erratic pricing, a result of the fact that, with only occasional trading and small lots, price discovery was problematic. This problem came to a head on every occasion when there was a bid for a majority shareholding in a large company. "Experts" always emerged to argue that the offer price was too low, when in fact there was no other offer on the market. In every such circumstance, the offer price becomes the new market price as soon as a sufficient number of holders accept it. This reality of market price determination contributed to growing disillusionment about securities market involvement. The exchanges in Jamaica and Trinidad and Tobago remain active, but only in Jamaica are the volumes of daily transactions sufficient for price discovery.

Securities exchanges in the Caribbean have failed to contribute meaningfully to the finance of investment for reasons that will be familiar to those active in the financial markets of other SOEs: the firms that are short of equity financing for projects are deemed to be too risky by buyers, and the companies people want to invest in have access to all their capital needs from other sources, which they prefer for many reasons, including avoiding the possibility of capricious price changes affecting their franchise value. The lacunae in the supply of finance for capital formation are with innovation, new ventures and small and medium enterprises. These are investments for which the state must cover the excess risk arising from the fact that agents on the securities market have no history available to them on which they can make an informed decision about the risk-return proposition. The conventional notion that market-based mechanisms can be made to address the capital formation needs of emerging market and developing countries is without foundation.

In the final analysis, the underdevelopment of domestic capital markets is of little consequence because of the need to secure funding in foreign currency to cover the imported inputs for investment projects. As we have shown, capital formation in the SOE is as import-intensive as is consumption, if not more so. What is important is access to international credit markets, which leads us back to the central role of credible fiscal policy and a sustainable external balance.

Financial crises and the increasing concern with financial stability

Issues of financial stability came to the forefront of international policy-making in the early 1970s in the aftermath of "serious disturbances in international currency and banking markets (notably the failure of Bankhaus Herstatt in West Germany)" (Bank for International Settlements, *bis.org*). These concerns intensified as a result of a succession of financial crises in various regions of the world: the Latin American debt crisis of the 1980s, the widespread failures of savings and loan banks in the US in the 1980s and 1990s, the Asian financial crisis of the 1990s, and the Mexican debt crisis of 1994. In 2007/2008 came the granddaddy of them all, the global financial crisis.

In the Caribbean, thanks to the dominance of Canadian and British banks, there was no major bank failure, a circumstance that was typical of SOEs with predominantly foreign-owned banks. There were a number of failures of small non-bank savings institutions and finance companies which left commercial banks without any competition in the loan market in some countries. Three episodes are noteworthy: one due to the collapse of an international bank that had a small presence in the Caribbean, the second a major collapse of asset values in Jamaica and the third being the failure of a Trinidadian insurance company with a regional presence. I make some observations on each of these episodes.

In the afternoon of Thursday July 4, 1991, I received a call to my office as Deputy Governor of the Central Bank of Barbados, from Desiree Cherebin, the Bank's Director of Banking Supervision, to the effect that a telex message had been received from the Bank of England that the Bank of Credit and Commerce International (BCCI), which had a single branch in Barbados, would be put into liquidation on the following day. The notice was a surprise, because we knew, through our inspection and financial reporting systems, that the local branch was liquid and solvent, so long as we could secure the full value of its assets at home and abroad. Desiree, her Deputy Ian Carrington and the staff of the Bank Supervision Department swung into action, contacting all other banks on the island, as well as insurance companies and other financial institutions, and coordinating with the Bank of England and supervisors throughout the Caribbean where BCCI had branches. The Central Bank was able to broker a sale of the local branch, separating it cleanly from the international bank, and making it whole with time-bound assistance from the Central Bank. There was no loss to depositors.

Jamaica is the only Caribbean country to have experienced a full-blown crisis. It arose, not in the banking sector, but among mutual funds, financial companies, financial brokerages and other non-banks. Non-banks had proliferated in Jamaica in the aftermath of the liberation of the exchange rate and the removal of restrictions on exchanges of all kinds in 1991. A sharp depreciation of the exchange rate, by about twice the 18 per cent devaluation that had been expected, generated high inflation and drove up interest rates, including lending rates. The combination of loss in real income because of double-digit inflation and loan interest rates which were also in double figures dried up the loan market, and with it the commercial banks' business model. Funds were diverted to non-banks, which offered returns that the banks could not match, sparking a boom in the non-bank market which drove up the prices of financial assets and real estate. By the middle of the 1990s the non-bank financial sector was as large as the banking sector. A market correction was inevitable, and when efforts to bring inflation under control began to take effect in 1995, a collapse in property values snowballed into a full-blown crisis, which is estimated by some to have wiped out financial asset values equivalent to 40 per cent of GDP, a figure which is probably exaggerated. The financial system was stabilised decisively with the establishment of a state-owned rescue and recovery institution, the Financial Sector Adjustment Company, FINSAC. The losses in asset value evidently reversed the earlier asset price inflation, and there was no noticeable impact on the real economy or on the balance of external payments.

The third instance of financial failure was as a result of the liquidity crunch experienced by a Trinidadian financial conglomerate in 2009. The firm, whose main business was insurance, made a large investment in a new upstream facility to produce by-products of the energy industry in Trinidad. The investment appeared to be in line with the country's competitive advantage, leveraging expertise gained in the petroleum industry to add value to the export of energy products. However, the company used short-term credits to augment its own resources for funding the project; in the event, a combination of an unexpected fall in output prices and a drastic reduction in the supply of short-term liquidity on the international market led to a run on the company's liabilities and to its eventual demise. The failure of this Trinidad venture led to loss of confidence and precipitated withdrawals in the company's network throughout the Caribbean, and the eventual winding-up of the company. However, the overall impact of this failure was not of major significance in any country in which the financial conglomerate operated.

There is evidence to be found as well in SOEs beyond the Caribbean to suggest that the impact of financial instability on the well-being of society is not of lasting significance. The banking sector in Iceland was a major casualty of the global financial crisis (Chapter 3). Three Iceland banks had made bold moves to establish themselves as financiers of investment projects worldwide in the early 2000s. The liquidity crunch in 2007/2008 left them over-exposed and they were forced into liquidation, the largest financial collapse, as a proportion of the size of the economy, ever recorded. The immediate impact was an economic slump which lasted until 2010, that reduced the real GDP by a cumulative ten per cent. However, Iceland's score on the Human Development Index was unaffected, improving by four per cent between 2000 and 2010. What is more, there was no lasting impact of the deep financial crisis, and the index rose a further five per cent to 2018. In that year Iceland was sixth in the world ranking of the HDI.

In response to rising concern about financial stability issues, in 1974 the Group of Ten of the world's most influential nations set up a Committee on Banking Supervision under the auspices of the Bank for International Settlements in Basel, Switzerland; because of that, the body has come to be known as the Basel Committee. With rapid expansion in the establishment and upgrading of financial oversight across countries, the Committee's membership expanded, and its guidelines for banking supervision are now applied across the globe.

In the 1990s the International Monetary Fund expanded its mandate to include financial stability issues, along with its surveillance of monetary, fiscal and exchange rate policies of member countries. I had the good fortune to join the Fund staff just about the time that this mandate was undertaken, and I spent a decade working in the department of the IMF that had responsibility for monetary, exchange rate and the newly established financial stability matters. The experience of working with the teams that designed the comprehensive Financial Sector Assessment Programme (FSAP), an in-depth evaluation of the entire financial sector of every country, proved invaluable.

The FSAP programme ran from around the turn of the century, with large teams of IMF Staff and consultants in insurance and other fields in which the Fund lacked expertise spending four to six weeks in interviews and data collection and analysis in every country. For Emerging Market and Developing countries the FSAP was a joint effort with the World Bank, to reflect a greater concern with development issues in these countries. By 2008, on the eve of the Lehman Brothers collapse in September, FSAPs had been undertaken in every country except for the USA, a fact which led to a degree of reassurance about the health of the international financial system which proved to be unwarranted.

Unfortunately, in ignorance of this comprehensive financial sector oversight, a narrative has grown to be established in the public mind that the global financial crisis might have been avoided, but for lax international financial supervision. That this should be so is difficult to understand, because the FSAP process was anything but a secret, and news media worldwide had reported numerous stories of discussions and frequent disagreements between assessors and country authorities about the details of the evaluations. Several countries had been assessed twice since the inception of the programme, and schedules were in place to visit every member country every five years. Only a few of us thought that the delay in scheduling the US FSAP was a potentially fatal fracture in the global architecture, and even among those of us who privately expressed concerns about financial soundness in the US, no-one saw the short-term liquidity market as a possible trigger. The main problem with an assessment of the US financial system is the complexity and variety of financial markets and agents, and the many overlapping layers of oversight.

The global financial crisis was triggered by a set of interlocking relationships, incomplete information and poorly-coordinated decisions (Geithner, 2014) in circumstances which were unprecedented. This event could therefore not have been anticipated, however intrusive financial scrutiny might have been. All inferences about future events and their probability have of necessity to be based on experience; beyond that is the realm of speculative fiction. Events that are without precedent cannot be anticipated, and will always be a surprise. Systems of financial sight, like all other policy, do best if they develop inventive and flexible operational methodologies, which enable them to deal with surprises, making up the responses on the fly.

Instead of a response to the global financial crisis using the well-established FSAP framework, the Group of Twenty most influential nations in the world chose to invent an entirely new body, the Financial Stability Board (FSB), a response that is as unhelpful as it was inevitable. The premise of the FSB is that tighter oversight is needed, and in pursuit of that goal it has embarked on an effort to put in place upgrades that have arguably made the rules governing the international financial system more obscure and inequitable.

The risk of bank failure

The poor selection and management of credits remains the main source of risk to the viability of banks in SOEs. The state of the art in the evaluation of credit risk is a combination of the analysis of historical experience and judgment based on the health of the economy, cyclical factors and knowledge of the strengths and vulnerabilities of the institutions in the financial sector and their interconnections within the country and abroad.

Econometric analysis of the historical experience of banking soundness uses logit, probit or discriminant analysis models of the form:

$$DtD = f_1(NPL,\ CAR,\ RoA,\ LIQ,\ FXE,\ other\ FSI) \tag{10.1}$$

The distance to default, *DtD*, is tested against financial soundness indicators, *FSI*, including nonperforming loans, *NPL*, the ratio of the bank's capital to assets, *CAR*, the return on assets, *RoA*, the ratio of liquid assets to deposits, *LIQ*, the net foreign asset position, *FXE*. Where the number of observations permit, macroeconomic variables such as GDP and inflation are also included in the equation.

Craigwell and Polius (1997) use a logit model of the probability of bank failure and of the time to central bank intervention on pooled data from banks in selected English-speaking Caribbean countries. The arguments in the test included variables to reflect the size of the bank, the distribution of its loan portfolio and macroeconomic variables such as the GDP, the interest rate and the exchange rate as well as the financial soundness variables. The size of the bank, the return on assets and macroeconomic variables were the influential factors that contributed to commercial bank distress in their sample; credit quality differences were not significant. These results indicate that smaller banks and less profitable banks were unable to withstand stresses from a weakening in the economy. In contrast, nonperforming loans provided the main warning signal of a bank in difficulty in Worrell, Cherebin and Polius-Mounsey (2001), a test of the probability of central bank intervention in an individual bank, using discriminant analysis for banks in the ECCU, Barbados, Belize, Trinidad and Tobago, Guyana and Jamaica.

Maechler, Mitra and Worrell (2010) tested for the vulnerability of a pooled sample of banks in 18 countries in Eastern Europe, using a measure of the distance to default as the dependent variable and including indicators of the strength of the regulatory framework along with macroeconomic variables and financial soundness indicators as explanatory variables. Their conclusion was that the acceleration of credit, rather than its rate of growth was the clearest signal of the risk of failure. The distance to default, the probability of equity depletion, was measured as the capital-asset ratio less the return on assets, as a proportion to the variance of the return on assets.

The econometric results are the first layer of the assessment of bank risk. They can be improved upon by exploring the variables in greater depth, including the nonperforming loans. The Basel Committee has established guidelines for placing nonperforming loans in three categories of risk: those that are substandard, but can probably be brought back to perform as intended; loans that are judged to be doubtful of recovery to acceptable performance; and loans that must be written off as losses. An analysis of the loan migration matrix, which shows the proportion of loans that migrate upward and downward in the substandard and doubtful categories adds to the analysis of credit risk, and it can be used to adjust the boundaries between categories and the extent of provisioning for the top two categories. Worrell, Grosvenor and Hurley (2011) undertook a detailed look at credit classification (substandard/doubtful/loss) for individual banks and the Barbados banking system, 1996–2010, taking account of macroeconomic developments, the distribution of loans across main categories, personal, mortgages, tourism and construction. They concluded that a recent increase in nonperforming loans was a discrete event, and that 85 per cent of loans were expected to return to an acceptable standard.

These examples illustrate the disparate circumstances that might contribute to bank failure. In the first instance, a macroeconomic downturn that is sufficient to impair the balance sheet of small banks and those that are less profitable leaves larger and more profitable banks in no difficulty. The second sample uncovers the more common case where the bank failure is due to the weakness in loan selection and administration. In the third case, failures were triggered by a credit boom, signalled by the onset of exponential growth in lending.

Stress tests: stressing to breaking point

Stress tests are a further layer of tools that may be used to build up the picture of the areas of vulnerability in financial institutions and the system as a whole. The stress test tools are often misused; the results of the tests are presented apart from the context of economic and financial assumptions and structures, and the tests themselves are based on arbitrarily chosen scenarios that are "possible but improbable or unlikely" or something to that effect. The results of these tests, reflected in headlines announcing that banks have passed with flying colours, offer reassurances that are unwarranted. As was the case in 2007/08, the next threat to global financial stability will come from a direction which is not anticipated in any of the "possible but improbable or unlikely" scenarios. Worrell (2008) proposes a more useful approach, which borrows from medical and scientific practice: stressing to breaking point. The paper illustrates how stress tests of banking systems may be designed to evaluate banks' reaction to shocks of increasing intensity up to the point where regulatory norms are breached or banks become insolvent. Scenarios are presented to show how capital adequacy depreciates for each of three (hypothetical) banks, and for the banking system comprising these banks, in response to a variety of stresses, as the pressure increases. The scenarios show how capital adequacy weakens with increasing losses on mortgages; with cumulative losses on mortgages, loans to exporters and personal loans; with different NPL migration patterns; with increasing exchange rate depreciation, including indirect effects via impact of exchange rate changes on non-performing loans; with increasing interest rates; with various rates of credit growth and migration patterns; and with capital inflow and reversal. By comparing the rates at which capital adequacy deteriorates under different stresses, the analysis illuminates the areas of greatest vulnerability for individual banks, and for the system as a whole. Using this approach, supervisors are primed to respond with special alacrity when there is a warning signal in the vulnerable areas.

Cooperative financial institutions, community banks and other household financing arrangements

After a long interval in which commercial banking spread widely across populations in cities and readily accessible rural populations in emerging markets and advanced countries, we are beginning to see a reversion towards credit unions, community banks, finance companies, peer-to-peer lending and informal pooling as major forms of supplying credit to households and small enterprises. Intimate knowledge of the local community provides institutions offering these types of services with a superior tool for assessing the creditworthiness of applicants and with powerful social sanctions on non-performance. That makes them very efficient, and this is reflected in the fact that their interest spreads are typically much lower than for commercial banks. Additionally, administrative requirements for the simplest cooperative forms are so low that they do not need to charge interest.

Not enough attention has been paid to the development of an appropriate regulatory framework for this segment, one which preserves its comparative advantage and efficiency while protecting consumers and small businesses from exploitative financial service providers. Clearly, all providers of finance should be licensed, supervised and regulated, but the guidelines for their operation must be designed with regard to their small scale and to avoid imposing costly administrative burdens. That suggests simple prudential requirements and reporting systems.

Institutions in this category need to be equipped with online banking systems, access to systems for domestic and foreign payments and debit cards and other mobile payments facilities in line with modern technologies. While remaining simple, the regulatory framework needs to provide adequate protection of these transactions. In addition, there is the troubling issue of setting outer limits to the institutions and activities that should be officially sanctioned. There is general agreement to discourage Ponzi schemes of all kinds, but most societies seem tolerant of payday lending and other arrangements that carry interest rates that are so high that they actually reduce the amount of income the customer has to spend in the short term, within the year. By any measure of financial services to increase well-being, such interest rates should not be allowed for any licensed financial institution.

This segment of the financial services sector does not contribute a large percentage of financial assets in any system where there are commercial banks. For that reason, it has received little attention in financial stability analysis. This situation needs to be addressed in view of the essential role these institutions have come to play in the financing of households and small businesses. Tailored guidelines are needed to ensure that the competitive advantages of these institutions are preserved, particularly invaluable relationships and local knowledge. The case for state-supported deposit insurance for credit unions, community banks and other deposit takers is a strong one: because they are small, these institutions are not guaranteed of the support that banks that are too big to fail are assured of.

Financial system vulnerability

Worrell (2004) outlines a framework for evaluating vulnerabilities and risks in the financial sector as a whole, taking account of macroeconomic effects and the structure of the financial system. The process involves a set of interdependent tests which together give an exhaustive picture of the health of the financial sector; a macroeconomic forecast; a forecast of the main aggregates of the financial sector derived from the macroeconomic forecast; and progressive stress tests of financial institutions, using the financial forecast as reference. For completeness, the analysis should be extended to evaluate risks of interbank contagion, and secondary effects from changes in household and corporate balance sheets. The health of the financial sector is evaluated using financial sector indicators and quantitative tests, to identify vulnerabilities in the financial system and to devise strategies to address them. The financial forecast will reveal what risks and challenges the system is expected to face over the forecast period. Stress tests can then be employed to provide a profile of the system's vulnerability under alternative scenarios that are in effect variants of the financial sector forecast. This framework, which has not been fully implemented in any country, provides benchmarks for the earliest detection of financial difficulty. An illustration of how the framework might be applied appears in Worrell, Chase, Greenidge and Moore (2006).

Global financial practice, as reflected in the IMF's Global Financial Stability Report and in the national reports of individual countries, still falls far short of what might be required to give confidence in the stability of the international financial system and its capacity to deal with a future crisis. This is mainly because the understanding of the links between the macroeconomy and the financial sector remains an area of insufficient research. The nature of relationships between economic expansion, inflation, interest rate and exchange rate changes have not been established. As a result many rules of thumb which are of long-standing but which have no theoretical or empirical foundation continue in common use, with little or no modification. Examples include single digit targets for nonperforming loans, levels of loan provisioning, the capital adequacy target minimum of eight per cent of assets, and external debt service maximum of 15 per cent of foreign earnings. Other norms have either not been established (overall ratios of public and private indebtedness in relation to GDP) or events have put the established norms in doubt, as is the case for the ratio of external debt to GDP, where the upper limit has been variously said to be 30, 60, 100 per cent of GDP, or even higher.

The unresolved technical challenges of financial stability analysis are many, and they are fundamental. They include the underdeveloped nature of stress testing methodologies: single factor tests are common, whereas many factors will in practice be impacting on the financial system simultaneously; network effects and feedback effects are not typically considered and progressive application of stresses is uncommon. Treatment of financial conglomerates is unsatisfactory, particularly for international banks and financial institutions. The small size of subsidiaries in SOEs means that their financial systems derive their stability mainly from the capital adequacy of head offices, in countries where foreign banks account for almost the entire total of banking assets. Arguably, financial stability in such cases (the smallest SOEs) should be treated in the context of the home countries of the foreign banks, but this consideration almost never gets the prominence it deserves in their financial stability reports. Analysis of network effects between and across financial institutions and between countries is in its infancy, and has as yet yielded few insights that are helpful in formulating financial stability policy. The treatment of credit quality is crude: there is typically no analysis of loan migration, and not much work to modify provisioning guidelines to reflect individual country experience. There is a dearth of robustness tests of any of the commonly used methodologies.

That does not represent the full extent of the remaining conceptual and empirical challenges. Much of the recommended insurance and risk mitigation for increasing financial system stability is based on capital adequacy. In general the analysis neglects the fact that the value of capital is determined in the financial market. This creates a circular problem in thinking of systems with built-in insurance, such as the elusive notion of loss-absorbing capital. Bank capital is the difference between the value of assets and the value of liabilities, both determined in the market. In times of financial crisis markets often fail and prices fall precipitately. It will not usually be the case that the price changes affect both sides of any bank's balance sheet equally. If the fall in the price of assets reduces their overall value sufficiently relative to its liabilities, the bank faces insolvency, no matter how large its stock of capital might be. Much of the scenario analysis on which guidelines for financial soundness have been built uses unwarranted assumptions about the stability of financial market values in very stressful times.

The divided international institutional framework for the assessment and surveillance of financial soundness and for the development and implementation of regulations is a major defect of the international system. The IMF should be at the centre of this system: its Board is fully representative, if in need of reform, to reflect the economic and financial weight of members, and it has a large and talented staff devoted to the analysis and surveillance of the international monetary, financial and exchange system. However, instead of reacting to the global financial crisis through empowering the IMF, the world's most influential nations chose to set up a new body, the Financial Stability Board (FSB), which has no analytical capacity, to take the lead on international financial reform. The FSB has had to rely on other institutions to do the analytical work that underpins its guidance, including the IMF and the Bank for International Settlements, itself a peculiar institution and one which is not fully representative. The FSB also attempts to coordinate guidance on insurance from the International Association of Insurance Supervisors (IAIS), on anti-money laundering from the Financial Action Task Force (FATF), the Global Forum on taxation, and other bodies. Unfortunately, the FSB lacks the capacity to ensure consistency between the often contradictory recommendations of these disparate bodies.

The international surveillance of financial institutions suffers from over-reliance on elaborate lists of judgmental "standards and codes" for banking supervision, anti-money laundering, tax compliance and financial conduct, evaluated by complicated and largely defective methodologies. These guidelines are administered by different bodies at different times, using widely different criteria. The resources of skills, finance and time devoted to reviews of standards and codes, peer reviews of tax regimes and evaluations of measures to combat money laundering and human trafficking, are enormous, both on the part of national and international regulators and the financial institution respondents. The benefits from this overburden of surveillance have not been systematically evaluated, but ongoing concerns about bank efficiency, financial inclusion, money laundering and international tax inequity suggest that the returns do not justify the costs. Rather than intensify the overburden of unproductive international regulation, the international financial community would be better advised to fortify the IMF and the other fully representational international institutions to develop improved tools, based on data and analysis.

This disorganised, uncoordinated and poorly informed surveillance system is further complicated by political considerations. What is required is an agreed oversight mechanism, administered by an international body whose legitimacy is assured by universal membership; the obvious candidate institution is a repurposed International Monetary Fund. Instead what we have is a confused and confusing welter of financial stability reports issued by the IMF and most nations, stress tests of international banks undertaken by US and European regulators, peer reviews produced by the Global Forum on Transparency and Exchange Information for Tax Purposes and reports of the Financial Action Task Force. In the absence of any internationally agreed legal framework, sanctions are imposed by black lists, issued capriciously by the OECD, the European Commission, individual advanced countries and some of the reporting institutions themselves. In addition, courts in New York and elsewhere are empowered to sanction international financial institutions.

As if this were not chaos enough, there is the influence of modern telecommunications, which have undermined due process in ways that preclude the possibility of equity and the rule of law in international finance. This fact is dramatically illustrated by the sanctions that have been imposed on international banks for interest rate manipulation and other wrongdoing. The evidence of presumed wrongdoing, such as it is, has not met what would normally be considered the minimum standard acceptable in a court of law, and in the overwhelming majority of cases the accused institutions have denied any wrongdoing. They have invariably paid the fines and other penalties, however. The reason is that the announcement of the accusation is enough to do permanent damage to the bank's reputation and, often, its franchise value, and any defence it might attempt to mount would be costly and time-consuming and would not repair the damage.

Further confusion and inequity has been introduced by the sensational releases of confidential records by whistle-blowers, in a succession which has brought us the Pandora Papers, the Panama Papers and, most recently, the Paradise Papers. These releases all serve to undermine the international rule of law. The transactions uncovered by the revelations are mostly completely legal by national and international law, according to the International Consortium of Investigative Journalists, which released the documents. However, the public perception is at variance with this reality; most readers conclude that whistle-blowers have uncovered fraudulent behaviour which fuels notions of widespread corruption. The consequences of this chaos of inconsistent, poorly informed and largely politically driven guidelines, assessments and sanctions is an international financial system that is arguably more fragile and less able to detect and react swiftly to crises than it was in 2007/08, one that is noticeably less efficient, less equitable and less inclusive.

The international financial system may be less primed for swift and effective response to a financial crisis than it was in 2008, mainly because markets in East and South Asia have grown in importance. Joint action by the New York Federal Reserve Bank and the Bank of England averted international financial collapse in September. The response to the next crisis may have to be coordinated with Asian financial markets. The international financial system has not equipped itself with an effective decision mechanism for quick action which includes all the likely players. The obvious place to situate that capacity would be with the Executive Board of the IMF, which has a global tracking mechanism to provide the information that would be needed for effective responses. However, the IMF Board has not been offered much of a role in international financial system oversight. The FSB, which is probably the body to which everyone would appeal, lacks the required information base.

The international financial system is now less efficient than it was before the global financial crisis, and is less inclusive. The massive overburden of regulatory compliance continues to expand, with no pause to reflect on whether it is fit for purpose. Shot through with poor information, inconsistencies and nationalist political considerations, the system has increased the cost of banking services everywhere, and it has slowed cross-border payments and settlement. Some previously profitable banking services, most noticeably correspondent banking services, are no longer viable, given reputational risks and possible losses of franchise value, brought on by new regulations (Brei, Cato and Worrell, 2020). International banks have withdrawn from many small markets and developing countries as a result. Because of poorly designed, obscure and inconsistently applied anti-money laundering regulations, innovators in digital technologies and other forward-looking activities have difficulty in obtaining banking services. Inequities in the design and regulation have resulted in discrimination against small financial centres which provide services which contribute in various ways to the efficiency of international transactions by virtue of geography, language, accumulated expertise, international networks or historical linkages. Small international financial centres are penalised for practices which US states and major financial centres are able to undertake without sanction (Ottolenghi, 2021). Some US states openly offer services and concessions for which small financial centres are blacklisted by the OECD, the Global Forum and the FATF (Zagaris, 2016).

Financial technologies and the efficiency and security of payments

A variety of new financial technologies have transformed the ways in which payments are made over recent decades, providing solutions to many of the inefficiencies and alleviating some of the risks that have plagued transfers of value over centuries. Up until the end of the twentieth century, payments with anything other than cash were slow, subject to risks that the instrument of payment might prove not to be valid, or that the payee might not be who they purported to be. In addition, all instruments of payment, including cash, might have lost some of their value between the time they were exchanged and the time they were presented for value. This section provides a taxonomy of payments processes to expand on the ways of making payments, and the ways in which electronics has provided solutions to many of these challenges.

Until the use of cheques gained currency in the Western World, payments were made in cash, a simple process where the buyer proffers notes and coins from their wallet to the vendor. The risks and problems associated with cash payments are well known: a wallet with large amounts of cash is a magnet for thieves, the currency has to be protected from counterfeiters and providing adequate currency supplies to rural locations and remote places is costly and difficult. In the Caribbean colonies of the British Empire in the seventeenth, eighteenth and nineteenth centuries there was an acute shortage of coins, leading to the use of Spanish pesos, often divided into eight "bits" (pieces of eight).[3] When I visited Bosnia-Herzegovina in the immediate aftermath of the civil war in the former Yugoslavia, as head of an IMF team advising on the payments system, a major headache was the limited availability of armoured cars to deliver currency across the country. Throughout the developing world, in countries where the banking system has not penetrated, populations have no access to payments systems because of a shortage of cash.

There are now digital cash alternatives which can overcome problems of risk and access, with the use of a cell phone or other digital wallet. In many markets they have allowed emerging market and developing countries to leapfrog advanced countries' systems directly into modern cashless, secure payments. The earliest digital wallets in common use were issued for use on public transport in Hong Kong, London, Washington and elsewhere. Commuters purchase electronically coded cards to which they can add value, redeemable for use on public transport through automatic entry turnstiles. A more readily usable digital wallet is the *Mpesa*, developed by a mobile phone provider in Kenya. The *Mpesa* is a logical extension of prepayment for cell-phone access, commonly referred to as "putting money on your phone". The phone company provided the service of allowing users to authorise access that value, in a secure way.

In the twentieth century, bank-based payments became established worldwide; they remain the predominant means of payment. In these systems the buyer writes an instruction to their bank, to make a payment to the account of the seller in the seller's bank. In the case of most retail transactions, the instruction is in the form of a cheque written by the buyer in favour of the vendor, which the latter deposits with their bank. In order to complete the transfer as per the instruction, the vendor's bank (Bank B) takes the cheque to the central bank's next cheque clearing, where it submits the cheque to the representative of the buyer's bank (Bank A), and the value is transferred electronically from Bank A's account at the central bank to the account of Bank B. The latter is now able to credit the amount of the cheque to the vendor. The vendor is not allowed access to the funds, however, until Bank A has verified the cheque against the buyer's account, and confirmed that there are sufficient funds in the account. Only then can the seller get access to the sale proceeds. The process is lengthy; in countries where there is only one cheque clearing session daily, a delay of two to three days is common.

Digital payments have provided ways to eliminate this wait time. Starting with wholesale transactions, instructions could be issued by the buyer directly to Bank A by way of a secure message to make the payment directly into the vendor's account at Bank B. The facility has been extended to retail payments through a variety of mechanisms, including credit and debit cards, standing orders, online banking and mobile apps. These all offer ways to combine the finality of cash transactions with the security of the bank-based payments systems.

Countries at all levels of development now have several alternative quick and secure payments alternatives, so long as they invest in universal digital access. These forms of payment all use familiar and convenient tools, and we have seen their usage expand rapidly in countries around the world, once they are introduced. Credit and debit cards came earliest and spread rapidly in all countries where there was an extensive branch network. In the Far East and in East Africa countries, which until recently were largely cash-based, have adopted mobile payments systems with remarkable speed. The availability of this range of payments options opens the way for market access to rural communities and over great distance. Payments should no longer be a limiting factor in human development. However, in order to take advantage of the opportunities that digital technologies have provided, other facilities and services must also be provided, most importantly reliable and affordable sources of power. The digital world runs on electricity.

International payments

International payments introduce an additional complication of currency conversion. The instruction to pay reaches the vendor's account via a foreign correspondent bank which makes the conversion to foreign currency (almost always US dollars) in the foreign seller's account. For international payments the only tools that remain fully functional for swift, secure payments are debit and credit cards issued by internationally recognised networks, of which there are only a handful. In most countries these cards can be used for international payments with the same facility as for domestic payments.

The same cannot be said of other means of payment. The traditional way of making secure foreign payments was by way of a draft issued by the payer's bank; that is still possible, but the verification process can take several weeks to be completed and allow the payee to have access to the funds. As a result a variety of mechanisms have emerged, in response to the very diverse needs of large and small companies and households in different circumstances.

The most consequential international payments challenge is providing affordable, secure mechanisms for the transfer of remittances, which are a substantial source of foreign exchange in many SOEs. A number of recognised international companies specialise in this service, but the number of smaller and informal companies offering remittance services is much larger. This situation is far from optimal, imposing high transactions costs and high risks on those who can least afford it.

Effective remittance transfers through the banking system has become very difficult. Offering correspondent banking services was a profitable, low risk business for international banks until the early years of this century. However, reporting and compliance requirements introduced by national and international regulators in the wake of the global financial crisis have undermined the business case for correspondent banking services (Worrell et al., 2016). As a result, the number of banks offering the service has shrunk dramatically. Even where the service is available, it is subject to uncertainty and risk of failure for any household transfer.

Efficient, affordable and safe facilities to transfer money between households across currencies remain a gaping hole in the international payments structure. The solution is obvious: an international protocol for correspondent banking services which frees banks of the requirement of acting as surrogates for tax authorities and financial police. It is a course of action that the countries of the Group of Twenty are unwilling to contemplate.

The initiatives aimed at addressing this problem through the use of crypto-currencies seem unsuitable: the costs of mining crypto-currencies are immense, and they have become a speculative asset class, with prices that are high and fluctuate wildly.

Instead, initiatives should be directed to setting up a network of the central banks of the world's reserve currencies (those that are included in the SDR basket) to devise a secure international form of digital cash that could be downloaded to an electronic device, and that would be acceptable in all countries for real time payments, anywhere in the world. A digital SDR along these lines would be a twenty-first century equivalent to cash. It would be better than the US dollar, the closest the world has to a universal currency. It would be electronic and instantaneous, so there would be no issue of the rate of exchange; the rate would be whatever the local currency equivalent of the SDR is in the currencies of payer and payee, at the instant of the transaction, just like withdrawing foreign cash on the other side of the globe, using your debit card.

How has the financial system contributed to the improvement in material well-being?

Perhaps the clearest and most widespread benefit of the broadening and deepening of the reach of banks and other deposit and pooled liquidity institutions has been in improving the access of households to durable consumption goods. The availability of mortgages and credit for the purchase of items of lasting value has lifted the average quality of life everywhere these facilities have been made available.

The banking system broadly defined has provided a vital lubricant to trade, domestic and international, at wholesale and retail levels through the provision of trade credit and working capital to producers, traders, distributors and the providers of transport, freight and a myriad of other supporting services.

Household needs are still mainly satisfied by commercial banks in most countries, but there are signs, in the US, the Caribbean and elsewhere, that co-operative financial institutions are out-competing international commercial banks in providing financial services to individuals.

Financial failures do not appear to have inflicted any lasting damage on the well-being of countries, even in those cases where there have been well-publicised systemic failures. This is what we should expect when the financial authorities intervene in a decisive way to preserve the value of financial assets. Even when they do not, there is no loss to the nation, so long as the financial failures are all denominated in domestic currency. In this case there may be consequences for the domestic distribution of income which may be undesirable, however. It is always preferable that financial authorities exercise their responsibility for taking appropriate action when market failure that will result in distress prices seems imminent.

The examples of external debt crises which we have discussed all eventually were resolved without permanent declines in well-being, even though there was usually a fall in real national income for a year or more. In the SOE, for reasons we have expanded on in earlier chapters, adverse shocks have to be accommodated to by a temporary loss in real income. The authorities should develop a strategy to secure an increased inflow of foreign exchange in the future to bring the economy back on trend, through policies to secure and enhance the country's competitive strengths.

A reputation for prudence in the management of the finances of the public sector attracts incoming investment, and it can therefore be a source of competitive advantage. To burnish their reputation the financial authorities should intervene when necessary in ways that are understood and acceptable to private agents in financial markets.

The efforts of small international financial centres to develop a competitive position in international financial markets through compliance with international guidance are doomed to failure, so long as the international regulatory landscape remains fragmented, inequitable and driven by political considerations in advanced countries. Fiscal prudence, together with a simple regulatory framework that is efficiently implemented, with timely publication of data and reports on financial stability indicators, credible information on the incidence of financial fraud and reports on taxation, are the best assurances of achieving a competitive position in the international financial market.

Beyond that, the public sector should aim to address the provision of equity for small and medium enterprises and for new ventures. Possible mechanisms for consideration are guarantees intended to share the risk inherent in this market, performance-based subsidies, tax incentives, and other initiatives, all guided by the principle that there is a sound business case, as assessed by knowledgeable and experienced practitioners. There needs to be a long-term financial development strategy within the national development strategy, with performance goals for sectors and enterprises and efficient monitoring to ensure that only well-performing beneficiaries continue to be supported.

Notes

1 Technical Notes, Barbados Financial System Assessment Program, unpublished.
2 International Monetary Fund Technical Reports: Comoros (2006), Sri Lanka (2002), Haiti (2005), Pakistan (1999), Tanzania (2008) and Ghana (2007), all unpublished.
3 Worrell, 2021.

References

Brei, Michael, Lauren Cato and DeLisle Worrell. 2020. "Credibility, reputation and de-risking in global banking: evidence from a theoretical model," *Journal of Globalization and Development*, February 19.

Craigwell, Roland and Tracy Polius. 1997. "Bank fragility in the Caribbean," *Central Bank of Barbados Collected Working Papers*, Vol. 1, pp. 239–250.

Crockett, Andrew. 1997. "The theory and practice of financial stability," *Essays in International Finance*. Princeton, NJ: Princeton University, April.

Fairbairn, Te'o and DeLisle Worrell. 1996. *South Pacific and Caribbean Economies: A Comparative Study*. Brisbane: The Foundation for Development Cooperation.

Geithner, Timothy F. 2014. *Stress Test: Reflections on Financial Crises*. New York: Crown Publishers.

IMF. Biannually. "Global Financial Stability Report," Washington, DC: International Monetary Fund.

Maechler, Andrea M., Srobona Mitra and DeLisle Worrell. 2010. "Decomposing financial risks and vulnerabilities in emerging Europe," *IMF Staff Papers*, Vol. 57, no. 1, pp. 25–60.

Ottolenghi, Emanuele. 2021. "For the United States, corruption eradication must begin at home," *World Politics Review*, November 30.

Worrell, DeLisle. 2021, "The time has come to permanently retire all our Caribbean currencies," *Studies in Applied Economics*, No. 179, April.

Worrell, DeLisle. 2008. "Stressing to breaking point: interpreting stress test results," *Working Paper*. Washington, D.C.: International Monetary Fund, no. 148, June.

Worrell, DeLisle, Karen Chase, Kevin Greenidge and Winston Moore. 2006. "Quantitative assessment of the financial system – the Barbados case," *Social and Economic Studies*, Vol. 55, no. 3, September.

Worrell, DeLisle. 2004. "Quantitative assessment of the financial sector: An integrated approach," *Working Paper*. Washington, DC: International Monetary Fund, no. 04/153, August.

Worrell, DeLisle. 1997. "Bank behaviour and monetary policy in small open economies with reference to the Caribbean." *Social and Economic Studies*, Vol. 46, nos 2 & 3, October.

Worrell, DeLisle. 1990. "Finance and investment in Barbados," *Central Bank of Barbados Economic Review*, Vol. XVIII, no. 2, September.

Worrell, DeLisle, Desiree Cherebin and Tracy Polius-Mounsey. 2001. "Financial system soundness in the Caribbean: An initial assessment," *Working Paper*. Washington, DC: International Monetary Fund, no. 01/123, September.

Worrell, DeLisle, Tiffany Grosvenor and Tamara Hurley. 2011. "Credit quality and economic fluctuations," *Central Bank of Barbados Economic Review*, Vol. *XXXVII*, no. *4*, December.

Worrell, DeLisle, Michael Brei, Lauren Cato, Sadie Dixon, Bradley Kellman and Shamika Walrond. 2016. "De-risking in the Caribbean: the unintended consequences of international financial reform," *Working Paper*. Central Bank of Barbados, October.

Zagaris, Bruce. 2016. "Why the US is becoming the largest offshore financial center," KYN360.com, April 13.

Zephirin, Mary. 1990. "Imperfect information and financial liberalisation in LDCs," *PhD thesis*, University of Warwick, unpublished.

11 Currency Unions and Dollarization

The Obsolescence of the Currencies of SOEs

The central reason for the existence of currency is to facilitate the transfer of value. Currencies may act as stores of value and units of account in addition to their function as the medium of exchange, but these secondary attributes depend on the ability of the currency to be used in transactions to assure all parties to the transaction that the values after the completion of the transaction are identical to those before the transaction were made. We have shown that the transactions which are material for well-being in SOEs are with the rest of the world: it is the foreign currencies which the country earns and borrows which provide it with a means of payment that is acceptable to those from whom it must buy the imports on which the economy runs. This has always been the reality of small societies, from the time that currencies first began to replace barter as the medium of exchange. Local tokens might from time to time be needed for exchanges within the society, but they literally had no currency for acquiring goods and services other than the local produce of the subsistence economy.

With the emergence of organised states the medium of exchange became whatever portable commodity was considered most valuable. The medium of exchange officially sanctioned within the borders of the state was stipulated as the weight of an ounce of gold or silver or the weight or fineness of some other valuable item, often of jewellery. The coins used for payment in most of recorded history were, until the twentieth century, specific weights of the commodity sanctioned for use in exchanging value, stamped and certified by the authority of the state. Paper notes, first used it is thought in China, bills of exchange and other forms of payment were legal certification of access to a specified value in terms of gold or silver.

The rise of international trade in the modern era was a chaotic business, with a welter of materials and standards for payments in countries which now wished to trade with others using different means of payment. Gold and silver came to displace other means of payment, though never completely, but that did not end the chaos and uncertainty, with major trading nations all having their own systems of coinage, of different weights and fineness of the two precious metals.

The history of currency is a long and fascinating story which need not detain us; our concern is the problem that emerged in small societies in the

DOI: 10.4324/9781003247609-13

international trading system. Their own currencies, if they had them, were of no relevance in international trade. They were therefore obliged to use the currencies of the European trading nations, with whom they exchanged products (and enslaved people) for industrial goods. The unique problem they faced was the shortage locally of currency in general circulation, in sufficient quantity and in denominations that were suitable for small transactions. (SOEs also faced the problem of uncertainty in the exchange rates between Sterling, the Spanish peso, the dollar and other trading currencies, as well as widespread counterfeiting and currency debasement, problems common to all trading currencies.) This was the problem that motivated the issuing of local currencies in many SOEs.

The currencies issued in colonies of European countries in the Caribbean and elsewhere were never intended as independent means of payment. They were meant to supply the proceeds of exports to the society in a form of money that facilitated commerce, particularly at the retail level. The total value of the local currency issued for circulation therefore was equal to the value of the sterling, pesos or dollars received by exporters. The bills of exchange written by commercial banks came in time to be accepted as the certified local currency. It was a short step for official currency boards to be set up in the colonies to provide an even more assured surrogate for international currencies. The monetary authority improved the efficiency of currency distribution by acting as a central hub for the interbank market in foreign currencies. For some time after currency boards were established in many SOEs, notes issued by commercial banks continued to circulate alongside notes and coins issued by the currency board. However, in most former colonies, the monetary authority was the sole issuer of currency at the time of Independence. The central banks which were set up in the aftermath of formal nationhood everywhere were all converted from currency boards with no essential change in the role or function of the institutions.

The monies issued by the currency boards of SOEs were assured of their value in terms of all other international currencies, in addition to the anchor currency, in the international system of fixed exchange rates which prevailed from the time of their establishment up until 1971. Reflecting the lessons learnt during a period of competitive devaluations in the interwar years that led to an unproductive race to the bottom, the designers of the post-war financial system set up the International Monetary Fund to issue a reference currency to anchor the international exchange values of sterling, the US dollar, the French franc and other international trading currencies. The proposal for a new money was never adopted, but the IMF was equipped with lending facilities designed to alleviate stresses on international exchange markets. These so-called "standby" lending facilities served to underpin a system anchored on the US Federal Reserve's stocks of gold, which the Fed undertook to sell to central banks on demand at a price of US$35 per ounce.

The above is a conceptual, rather than a chronological, history of currency issues in SOEs, intended to show that these monies were never intended as currencies with intrinsic value. In fact, the intention was exactly the opposite, to displace locally circulating tokens, debased and fraudulent coins and notes and barter arrangements, which local communities had resorted to for want of money that could be used in international transactions. (For those who may be interested in the actual history, the quick overview of the history of money that is found on Wikipedia is as good as any.)

The credibility of the US commitment came into question with expansion in the supply of US dollars in the 1960s. Increasingly the international media headlined concerns about the "dollar overhang", with the value of US dollar liabilities worldwide exceeding the value of the Federal Reserve's gold holding by a factor of four to one at the US$35 price. Matters came to a head in 1971, with President Richard Nixon under pressure to devalue the US dollar to give industry a shot in the arm in advance of the 1972 election. In an absorbing and informative account, Garten (2021) provides an insider's view of what then transpired. Determined to avoid the competitive devaluations of the interwar years, the US reneged on its commitment to maintain the gold price at US$35 per ounce. This was intended to signal to the US's allies the need for a realignment of the US currency relative to their own, with the objective of preserving the dollar exchange system at a new gold price which better reflected the Federal Reserve's gold stock. Although there were already liberal-minded economists arguing for the abandonment of the fixed exchange rate system, the prevailing sentiment, consistent with market expectations, was in favour of maintaining the par value system, with a one-time devaluation of the dollar.

It can be argued that the objective of revaluing the US dollar as the anchor of an international system of fixed exchange rates was in fact the best option, and that the international finance and payments systems would have evolved in a much more stable and efficient manner, had that objective been attained. The preferred course of action would have been through the agency of the IMF, which was, after all, the institution set up to bring stability to the international monetary system. An agreement brokered through the IMF would have had greater chance of success, because it might have been the result of mutual accord. Instead, the decision to unilaterally abandon the repeated commitment to the gold price was designed as an instrument of coercion, intended to demonstrate to the UK and Europe the necessity to accommodate to a new, higher gold price. An agreement brokered through the IMF might also have been fortified by mutual agreements to borrow to stabilise the new exchange rate regime. In the event, the US action set off a destabilising exchange rate chaos, whose consequences have plagued international exchange markets ever since.

With the end of the fixed exchange international system, the currencies of SOEs lost their universality. In almost every case, countries tried to maintain their parities with the anchor currency, but with very few exceptions they were unable to do so. The depreciations, unwanted and inflationary, were usually much larger than anticipated, larger even than the informal market rates that presaged them in many cases. The fall in US dollar values of local currencies around the world has made exchange rate depreciation a symbol of economic policy failure. In what follows we trace the history of the currencies of the English-speaking Caribbean as a parable of the management of the currencies of SOEs.

Caribbean responses to the 1968 sterling devaluation

Currency boards were established by the British colonial Government in Trinidad to issue local currency for the Eastern Caribbean, from St Kitts in the north to British Guyana in the south; in Jamaica, also covering the Cayman Islands; in the Bahamas and in Belize. Except for The Bahamas, they issued local currency at the same fixed value to sterling. Although most of the foreign currency inflows in all the countries were in sterling, their imports were all priced mainly in dollars. In the fixed rate system, this was not an issue: the value of sterling receipts in terms of their purchasing power in dollars was assured. However, a devaluation of sterling on November 18, 1968, from US$2.80 to US$2.40 created a dilemma for the region's monetary authorities. By then the monetary authorities in Jamaica and Trinidad had been converted to central banks, and a new central bank had been established in Guyana. In these early years of their existence they still operated by currency board guidelines, with respect to the issue of local currency. The seat of the Eastern Caribbean Currency, with Trinidad and Tobago and Guyana no longer members, had shifted to Barbados, and Cayman Islands had set up its own currency board, using its share of the foreign reserves held by the Bank of Jamaica.

The choice facing the Caribbean currency authorities was between maintaining the old parity with the US dollar and suffering a decline in the purchasing power of their exports when they came to buy imports, devaluing to the full extent of the sterling devaluation, and suffer 12 per cent inflation in import prices, possibly magnified by distribution mark-up or devaluing, but by somewhat less than the full depreciation of sterling. In the event, the currencies were all devalued by the full amount, and transactions returned to the usual pattern after an interval of adjustment.

The future of Caribbean currencies from this point onward would have been very different had the West Indies Federation not collapsed six years earlier. In January 1958 the British island colonies in the Caribbean, with the exception of a handful of the smallest islands, formed a federation which was intended to provide a vehicle for the members to gain independence as a single unit. The Federation fell apart in 1962 when the most populous country, Jamaica, held a popular referendum which was lost by the pro-Federation faction. (A major theme of those who opposed Federation was that the resource-poor countries of the Lesser Antilles – very much smaller islands north of Trinidad in the eastern Caribbean – would be a drain on the Jamaican economy, which boasted a thriving bauxite industry, along with agricultural exports and tourism. Ironically, the Lesser Antilles now all rank above Jamaica in the Human Development Index.)

The collapse of the West Indies Federation left the English-speaking countries of the region with as many as eight different currencies. They all maintained fixed pegs to sterling after the 1968 devaluation, up to the time when the US abandoned its commitment to an unchanged price of gold. By 1971 the case for switching to a US dollar peg was stronger in every country than it had been in the previous decade. With the emergence of tourism, data processing, offshore call centres and exports of clothing, all sold to the US, the dollar had become the main trading currency for exports as well as imports. The Caribbean currencies all maintained their pegs, and they were all switched to the US dollar, but at different times and at different rates, resulting in a plethora of currencies in the region. The intra-regional payments situation was further complicated by the failure of the largest economies to secure their pegs to the dollar, a story which is chronicled in Worrell (1987). The consequence was that, in contrast to the situation which had prevailed for decades, the regions' currencies could not be used even for trading within the region. The demand for US dollars was greater than it was during the era of fixed exchange rates; in addition to needing dollars for transactions with the rest of the region, dollars had to be bought for travel and trade with neighbours within the Caribbean.

An ingenious mutual credit arrangement, the CARICOM Multilateral Clearing Facility (CMCF), was devised by the region's central banks, to alleviate the demand for US dollars in regional transactions. Members of the CMCF opened accounts with the Trinidad and Tobago Central Bank, the designated agent for the facility, where they could place regional currencies that they had received from exports within the region, transfers from other countries and other sources. They made payments for imports using these balances, and there was provision that they could borrow regional currencies up to a specified limit from a common pool, should the available balance be insufficient. All outstanding credits were settled quarterly.

The CMCF, which began operations in 1977, was dissolved in 1983 after its Board of Directors, the Governors of the Central Banks of the participating countries, violated the guidelines they had themselves set up with respect to country credit limits. The problem was the chronic balance of payments in Guyana, as a result of which the country breached its credit limit to Trinidad and Tobago, which supplied fuel for power and electricity. Rather than terminate Guyana's access to maintain the viability of the CMCF, the Board allowed the institution to drift into bankruptcy, a decision which remains inexplicable. The collapse of the CMCF meant that the US dollar was by default the currency of transactions between the tiny economies of the Caribbean, further shrinking the reach of each of the local monies.

The futile search for a common currency for the Caribbean

The multiplication of currencies was a major set-back for efforts to attain the elusive goal of Caribbean regional integration. In the wake of the Federation's collapse, economists, political theorists, politicians and public intellectuals in the Caribbean concluded, not unrealistically, that a major weakness of the union was the region's lack of a strongly integrated economy. The effort to establish an economic foundation for regional integration was initiated by Antigua and Barbuda, Barbados and Guyana, the founding members of the Caribbean Free Trade Area, CARIFTA. CARIFTA soon grew to include 12 English-speaking countries, including two which were not part of the failed Federation who signed on to the Caribbean Free Trade Area in 1968. Even though the undertakings and structures for perfecting the free trade area were as yet to be given effect, the member countries in 1973 signed the Treaty of Chaguaramas to transition (on paper) to a Caribbean Economic Community with more far-reaching commitments. The timing could hardly have been more unfortunate: in the middle of a transitional period during the last half of the 1970s, when the Caribbean currencies switched from sterling to dollar pegs, with no coordination between them as to timing or with respect to their exchange rates to the dollar (see Chapter 5).

The resulting dysfunctional regional payments arrangements fuelled a search for a common currency for the region. The debate on the most feasible approach raged for most of the 1980s, coming to a head with recommendations made by the West Indian Commission, which was assembled in 1990 to travel around the region, collecting oral and written opinion on all aspects of Caribbean regional integration arrangements. The Commission contracted, among others, a study with recommendations on the establishment of a common currency (Worrell, 1992). The recommendations of that study were accompanied by a comprehensive set of studies analysing the implications of currency unification for government financing, debt and labour markets. The background studies also included a survey of options for monetary integration in the Caribbean and insights from the European Union and other regional integration arrangements (see Farrell and Worrell, 1994).

The 1992 decision on monetary union

The volume I edited with Terrence Farrell in 1994 tells the story of the initiatives taken by CARICOM Heads of Government in response to the influential West Indian Commission report, *Time for Action* (West Indian Commission, 1992). Our book documents the analysis and discussion surrounding proposals for monetary union, leading up to a decision by the CARICOM Heads of Government on July 2, 1992 for a staged approach to monetary union. The criteria set for membership of the currency union were as follows: the member country had to have maintained foreign reserves equivalent to three months of import cover, sustained for 12 consecutive months; they should have a record of a stable exchange rate (defined as variation of no more than two per cent in either direction), sustained for 36 consecutive months; and external debt service should have been kept below 15 per cent of foreign currency receipts, also for 36 months. Target dates were set for the establishment of a Caribbean Monetary Authority and countries were to join as they became eligible. The study on which the agreement was founded also recommended that the monetary authority should not finance any government deficit with new money.

The recommendations on currency union were supported by background studies that covered the expected implications for the balance of payments and fiscal and monetary policy, as well as the benefits that might be expected from the single currency. Among the findings was the fact that, with the establishment of central banks, the foreign exchange needed to insure local currencies against unpredictable devaluation set off by rumour and speculation had turned out to be almost 100 per cent of currency liabilities, so that the central banks had been obliged to observe the currency board rule. Furthermore, the quest for monetary policy autonomy had returned the English-speaking Caribbean to its historical condition of unsound money, with the currencies of the largest economies subject to capricious devaluation. The benefits to be expected from a common currency were accelerated investment in tradables, reduced incentives for capital flight and reduced costs of external transactions. It was recommended that the Caribbean dollar should be pegged to the US dollar, in recognition of an inherent trend towards Caribbean convergence on the US as the centre of economic integration for the region. The proposal was not without its critics: Courtney Blackman faulted it in a perceptive critique (Farrell and Worrell, 1994, p. 251), arguing that the central banks should promote development, engage in counter cyclical policy and act as lender of last resort. He also suggested, less convincingly, that the currency should start with a free float. In the same volume, Karl Theodore pointed to the need for rules to prevent fiscal imbalances from spilling over from one country to others, and for a stabilisation fund to take care of asymmetries in the impact of external economic factors on government revenues and spending.

It was envisaged that the initial core group of the monetary union would have included Trinidad and Tobago, along with Barbados and the ECCU. In 1992 they all had currencies which qualified as stable, as well as having met the other criteria. However, within the year, Trinidad and Tobago, which would have accounted for more than half of the group's GDP and foreign reserves, abandoned any commitment to intervene in support of a target exchange rate, leaving its value, ostensibly, to be determined by the foreign exchange market. Worrell (1993) inferred from the Jamaica and Guyana experience that the float was not the objective, but a way to find a sustainable rate on which to settle: "If by floating the TT dollar the Central Bank of Trinidad and Tobago is able to accumulate foreign reserves… the float brings the monetary union closer to hand" (Worrell, 1993, p. 8). This article also makes the point that countries with floating rates have a special need for currency union to restore the credibility for monetary policy which their central banks have lost. In the event, the Trinidad and Tobago currency soon settled at a new unchanged rate, a circumstance which should have been anticipated, because of the fact that Trinidad and Tobago has an oil-based economy. Foreign earnings come mainly from taxation of the energy sector, and the foreign exchange which this provides is paid directly into the Government's accounts at the Central Bank. The exchange rate therefore depends on the rate at which the Central Bank disburses foreign currency from these accounts. The exchange rate settled down to a new, unchanged level once new patterns of disbursement became established.

The debate on currency unification has continued in the Caribbean ever since, with no progress in the direction of implementation of the 1992 agreement. Worrell (2003a) is a comprehensive reassessment of the need for and practicalities of the currency union. I began by explaining that the conditions for an exchange rate to affect real output did not obtain: relative prices are sensitive to a change in the nominal exchange rate only if the change in exchange rate does not affect the fiscal outcome, if there is no interest response to the change, and if there are no wealth effects. In the Caribbean there are always wealth effects because of capital flight, and there are usually consequences for interest rates and fiscal balances as well. Furthermore, it was pointed out that the real effective exchange rate, the measure of relative prices used by the IMF and others, is not an acceptable proxy for the change in relative prices of nontradables, for reasons which are explored in Marsh and Tokarick (1994) and Masters and Ianchovichina (1998). Furthermore, an expected change in the nominal exchange rate has no real effect because it will be offset by changes in interest rates; an unexpected change has perverse effects because it is taken as a signal of policy failure. In summary, the Caribbean has a preference for an exchange rate fixed to the US dollar because there are no significant expenditure switching effects, the relationship between the nominal and real exchange rate is dubious and unpredictable, the financial market neutralises expected exchange rate effects and the Caribbean sits in the US currency area. The risk of an exchange rate crisis is the only cost of the peg; it can be minimised by adopting currency board rules. The paper argued for a Caribbean currency committed to currency board rules in preference to full dollarisation for one reason only: the maintenance of a secure peg lends credibility to economic (especially fiscal) policy. It was admitted that seignorage revenue is probably less than currency conversion costs, an argument made by Anthony and Hughes-Hallett (1999). The currency union provides a single investment space, offering gains from economies of scale, technical transfer and learning by doing.

Worrell (2003b) reprised the argument for a common currency operated by a currency board, and made a firm proposal for countries in the Eastern Caribbean to form a currency union without delay to remedy the uncertainty of the US dollar value of local currency. The case was made that the central banks of the Eastern Caribbean, Barbados and most recently Trinidad and Tobago, had shown the will to manage the value of their currencies, and a currency board provided them the means to do so convincingly. Active monetary policy in the English-speaking Caribbean had eroded credibility without lowering the costs of adjusting to external shocks. It was better to borrow credibility from the US Federal Reserve rather than engage in futile efforts to manage domestic liquidity. Seignorage revenue was in fact negative, because of the need to lend scarce foreign finance to the US government, at the expense of potential capacity-enhancing investment. Although a currency board cannot be a lender of last resort, the alternative of a supervised bank resolution is available. It was admitted that Trinidad and Tobago might be reluctant to relinquish the possibility of devaluation because it is a quick fix to excessive fiscal deficits in a country where government gets the bulk of revenue from exports of petroleum and related products. However, devaluation is second best policy for the country because it undermines the credibility of government policy. The paper reprised that currency union eliminates currency conversion costs, and improves the climate for foreign investment; coordination of differing regimes for overseeing capital flows was deemed unnecessary so long as there are effective barriers to speculation.

Subsequent papers advocating the common currency included Worrell (2005), pointing out that foreign currency markets perceive exchange rate variation as "evidence that actual or intended fiscal policy is looser than economic circumstances warrant". A single regional money would facilitate factor mobility among member countries of the union, and would increase its international competitiveness. The Caribbean Monetary Union should be introduced "in such a way that joining the union does not involve a change in the exchange rate regime for any country. Countries should be admitted only when they had demonstrated commitment to a US dollar peg" (Worrell, 2005, p. 75). Worrell (2016) argued that the benefits of exchange rate pegs outweigh the drawbacks. ". central banks in open economies have lost control of the money supply." ". the effect of the exchange rate on competitiveness is yet lower [than in larger economies, where its effectiveness is dubious]". "Where currencies have a credible track record… the local currency stands as a testament to sound economics" (Worrell, 2016, p. 21).

The argument for dollarisation is now compelling

The combination of a growing disillusionment with the lack of implementation of CARICOM agreements, and my experience with the Barbados economic adjustment policies during my tenure as Governor of the Central Bank of Barbados have now disabused me of the illusion that a currency peg is sufficient inducement for fiscal discipline, the last remaining argument for having an own currency. Almost 30 years after the CARICOM Heads of Government signed the agreement on monetary union, that agreement has been all but forgotten. The US dollar has become the currency of regional transactions, as it is for transactions with the rest of world, and regional economies have adjusted to that reality. Whereas thirty years ago a few local currencies were accepted in selected countries outside the country of issue (or region, in the case of the ECCU), that is now no longer the case.

In Barbados, in contrast to the experience in 1991, when decisive action was taken to correct a fiscal imbalance which threatened to exhaust foreign reserves and endanger the peg, in 2013 the Government back-tracked on the adjustment measures announced in the two budgets of that year, measures which, had they been implemented in full would have stabilised the external accounts and restored confidence in fiscal policy. The Government had in place a framework for economic management which had calibrated the size of fiscal cuts to be sufficient to close the balance of payments gap, and there was a coordinated monitoring system in place between the Central Bank, the Treasury, the Barbados Revenue Authority and the Ministry of Finance to ensure the programme stayed on track. The framework existed for quarterly meetings to keep social partners (trades unions, employers' representatives, non-governmental organisations and interest groups) abreast of the implementation of the programme (see Chapter 12). In spite of what appeared to be a robust framework for appropriate and sufficient adjustment, the adjustment was incomplete, and the commitment to fiscal prudence was not sustained. The result, five years later, was a rushed and poorly designed fiscal policy which destroyed real wealth amounting to perhaps 25 per cent of annual GDP. The programme, under which the incoming Mottley administration secured financial assistance from international financial institutions led by the IMF, has failed to address public sector inefficiencies and the declining quality of public services which impair the international competitiveness and reduce the potential growth of the Barbados economy.

Worrell (2021) contends that the time has now come to retire all of the inconsequential currencies of the Caribbean. Currencies fulfilled an essential need for means of payment until the 1960s, but local currencies have now become a nuisance in small open economies – the local resources to which they give access are meagre; citizens and companies with access to US dollars are privileged over those who have only local currency; local currencies are subject to risk of major loss of international purchasing power; a local currency gives government access to finance for wasteful spending; and local currency is a disincentive to investment if its exchange rate is unstable. The supposed benefits of an own currency are illusory: devaluation does not improve competitiveness, and inflation is an exogenous variable, determined by foreign inflation and the exchange rate. The only remaining usefulness of local currency is to lend credibility to fiscal policy through the readily visible evidence of a secure peg to the US dollar or other international currency; when that fails it is time to fully dollarise.

The study offers three examples of full dollarisation from Latin America: Panama, which has always used the US dollar as the local currency; Ecuador, which abandoned its inflation-ridden domestic currency in 2000; and El Salvador, which replaced its own currency gradually, starting in 2002. As may be seen from Figure 11.1, over the almost three decades to 2016, real GDP in Panama increased four-fold, compared with an increase of 73 per cent for Latin America and the Caribbean as a whole. The growth of GDP in the

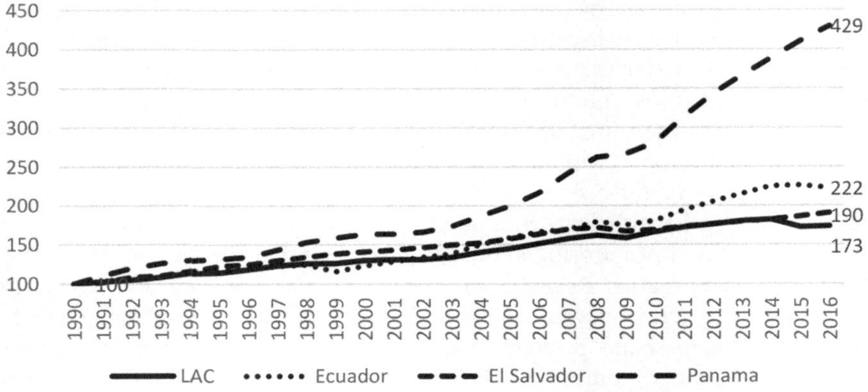

Figure 11.1 Dollarised countries: growth comparison
Source: Worrell, 2021.

other two dollarising economies also bettered the region as a whole, more than double the 1990 figure in Ecuador, and up 90 per cent in El Salvador. This evidence does not suggest that dollarisation puts a small economy at any competitive disadvantage or impair growth prospects in any way, rather the contrary.

References

Anthony, Myrvin and Andrew Hughes Hallett. 1999. "Is the case for economic and monetary union in the Caribbean realistic?" London: University of Strathclyde and the Centre for Economic Policy Research, January.

Farrell, Terrence and DeLisle Worrell (eds). 1994. *Caribbean Monetary Integration*. Port-of-Spain, Trinidad: Caribbean Information Systems & Services.

Garten, Jeffrey. 2021. *Three Days at Camp David: How a Secret Meeting in 1971 Transformed the Global Economy*. New York: HarperCollins.

Marsh, Ian and S. Tokarick. 1994. "Competitiveness indicators: A theoretical and empirical assessment," *Working Paper*. Washington, D.C.: International Monetary Fund, March.

Masters, William and Elena Ianchovichina. 1998. "Measuring exchange rate misalignment: Inflation differentials and domestic relative prices." *World Development*, Vol. 26, no. 3, March, pp. 465–477.

Theodore, Karl. 1994. "Fiscal issues in Caribbean monetary integration," in Terrence Farrell and DeLisle Worrell (eds), *Caribbean Monetary Integration*. Port-of-Spain, Trinidad: Caribbean Information Systems & Services.

West Indian Commission, The. 1992. *Time for Action: The Report of the Commission*. Black Rock, Barbados: The Commission.

Worrell, DeLisle. 2021. "The time has come to permanently retire all our Caribbean currencies," *Studies in Applied Economics*, no. 179, April.

Worrell, DeLisle. 2016. "Pros and cons of dollarisation: Benefits of exchange rate pegs outweigh drawbacks ," *Official Monetary and Financial Institutions Forum Bulletin*, December.

Worrell, DeLisle. 2005. "Exchange rate strategy for CARICOM: The way forward," *The Integrationist*, Caribbean Community Secretariat, Vol. 3, no. 1, June.

Worrell, DeLisle. 2003a. "A currency union for the Caribbean." *Working Paper*. Washington, D.C.: International Monetary Fund, no. 03/35, February.

Worrell, DeLisle. 2003b. "The monetary and financial authority of the Eastern Caribbean: A modest proposal," Nineteenth Adlith Brown Memorial Lecture, November 24. St Augustine, Trinidad and Tobago: Caribbean Centre for Monetary Studies.

Worrell, DeLisle. 1993. "The Trinidad and Tobago float: Implications for monetary union," *Canabusiness*: The Business and Financial Newsletter of the Caribbean News Agency, May, p. 8.

Worrell, DeLisle. 1992. "A common currency for the Caribbean," *Occasional Paper*. St Michael, Barbados: The West Indian Commission Secretariat, no. 4.

Worrell, DeLisle. 1987. *Small Island Economies: Structure and Performance in the English-speaking Caribbean Since 1970*. New York: Praeger.

Section C

Tools and Practical Considerations for the Economic Policy Maker

There are three chapters in this section. Chapter 12 outlines a forecasting model and framework for policy making in SOEs, based on models and systems developed at the Central Bank of Barbados in the 1980s which have been in use at the Bank ever since with refinements, extensions and modifications. The model follows the logic of Chapter 6, to ensure that the inferences drawn and the forecasts made are what one should expect of a small open economy. In this chapter we flesh out that skeleton to make the model directly useable to set economic targets, notably the level of foreign reserves at the central bank, and the impact on reserves of policy instruments such as central bank intervention in the foreign exchange and domestic treasury bill markets, changes in tax rates, government borrowing at home and abroad and other policy tools. The actions of the treasury, the government budget office and the central bank have to be calibrated and coordinated, both as to timing and magnitude, taking account of bank liquidity, the overall fiscal stance, seasonalities, the impact of global economic cycles and other relevant factors. The chapter describes the Barbados framework for coordination of all these aspects to devise and implement ongoing macroeconomic policies for development and stability, and to communicate those policies to the public whose response to changes in incentives will determine the success or failure of the policies.

Chapter 13 expands on economic characteristics of SOEs which policy makers should bear in mind in setting targets and devising policies for these economies. It offers a new perspective on many accepted economic nostrums that are the unstated assumptions of common news and analysis. In addition, we question the empirical basis of often-repeated claims about the weaknesses and limits on the potential of SOEs.

Chapter 14 is devoted to admonitions to economists and policy makers about the limitations and misuse of the tools that our discipline provides us. The tools available to economic policy makers are very crude and inadequate for the purposes for which they are employed. Economists are obliged to use measures of concepts which cannot be accurately measured, such as Gross Domestic Product, to proffer explanations which can never be definitively

DOI: 10.4324/9781003247609-14

tested, to provide explanations of behaviour so complex that no definitive statement can ever be found, to follow rules of thumb which are inconsistent with the logic of economic theory and to anticipate reactions to policy initiatives from a public that is fickle and poorly informed. In such circumstances, is it possible to devise and implement economic policies that will secure desired outcomes in any economy, large or small? The answer is that it is entirely possible, using a pragmatic approach, provided that policy makers always remain fully aware of the limitations of the tools being employed, and with sensitivity to the reactions observed in response to any policy initiative.

12 A Model and Framework for Economic Policy Design and Implementation in SOEs

This chapter may be considered something of a practical manual for economic policy makers in small open economies. The essential modules within the economic policy framework are:

- A model of long-term investment, competitiveness and growth, which serves to provide a benchmark for the growth of competitive production capacity in the economy;
- Structural forecasting models of sectoral growth, the balance of payments, public sector revenue/current expenditure/capital expenditure/financing, and the monetary accounts. Two models with similar structure are needed, a quarterly model with a rolling 18-month horizon and an annual model with a rolling five-year horizon;
- Quarterly and annual financial control frameworks for the public sector accounts, structured to provide data that is incorporated into the forecasting framework;
- A weekly forecast for domestic and foreign currency liquidity, which is used to manage the public sector's cash requirements, consistent with the foreign reserve targets.

This chapter will also speak to the options for managing this system, based mainly on decades of experience with the development of the framework used at the Central Bank of Barbados.

A forecast of the economy's long-term competitiveness and potential production capacity

It is helpful to frame economic policy against a background of current and prospective investment, the sources of the country's competitive advantage, the international investment climate, the impact of new technologies and emerging trends and what that might all mean in terms of incentives for foreign direct investment, particularly in building productive capacity for the export of goods and services. Such analysis, looking back over decades of economic performance and combining quantitative tests of the factors that

DOI: 10.4324/9781003247609-15

determine investment, as well as qualitative assessment of infrastructure, public utilities, the efficiency of government services and other factors, provides policy makers with a perspective of the economy's potential under alternative scenarios. Such a perspective is very helpful for strategic forward planning, and is essential for realistic goal setting beyond a five-year horizon.

$$i = f_1(\text{-}xcap_t(\text{-}1),\ a^*,\ p_t,\ ulc,\ r_f,\ emp,\ GCI) \qquad (6.1)$$

Equation 6.1 in Chapter 6 summarises the main economic factors that are expected to affect investment trends in the small open economy. Because investment projects have a life cycle which does not correspond to annual observations, it is not useful to try to estimate this equation as a single econometric model, using annual data. Instead, one must evaluate investment against each element on the right hand side of the equation over discrete periods of past experience, before pulling all the inferences together, putting them in the context of the country's political economy – such as evidence of an electoral cycle in government expenditure and fiscal deficits – to make forecasts of future investment trends under various conditions.

The device commonly employed when analysis of annual series is not appropriate is to examine economic behaviour in phases of the economic cycle, comparing relationships during periods of expansion with what has happened during downturns. Using this approach, we would measure how quickly output in the main foreign-earning activities reached capacity during upturns, and whether and how soon was there an investment response. Conversely, how severe was the excess capacity crunch during the downturn, and was there a pause in investment in response?

The expenditure variable, a^*, presents a challenge with which empirical economists are familiar. Looking back we can never measure how much people expected to spend, and much less what producers expected them to spend, which is the variable we're interested in. We are obliged to infer what firms expected people to spend from what was actually spent, which is the result of consumers' income, which might have been more or less than they expected, as well as how much producers offered and at what prices. Various approaches to addressing this conundrum are available, but none is really useful to a policy maker. As a result, the most common practice is to use the trend as the closest that one can get to a sense of what expectations would have been. Since we now know that money-financed fiscal expansion can add to the aggregate expenditure, it is helpful to add that to the analysis. People might reasonably have planned to spend more than they otherwise might if they expected a windfall from the government in the form of tax relief or unemployment relief of one kind or another.

International price inflation, unit labour costs, benchmark international interest rates are all standard economic variables, and the exchange market pressure variable is a combination of readily available variables: the exchange rate of the currency, the domestic interest rate premium and the change in foreign reserves.

Table 12.1 Information for the evaluation of expected investment

Variable	*Information needed*
Full capacity	Tourism: occupancy rates Unemployment level and trend
Expected expenditure	Expenditure trend Anticipated money creation
International price inflation	Commodity price forecasts US inflation forecasts
International interest rates	US interest rate forecasts
Exchange market pressure	$\sigma_{\Delta FXR}(\Delta FXR) + \sigma_{\Delta r}\Delta r + \sigma_{\Delta ER}\Delta ER$, $\Delta FXR < 0$, $\Delta r > 0$, $\Delta ER > 0$
Competitiveness	Global Competitiveness Index score Market share compared with relative prices

Notes: σ: Standard deviation; Δ: Change in the variable; *FXR*: Foreign reserves; *r*: Interest rate; *ER*: Exchange rate.

The final element in the analysis of the motives for investment is a measure of the economy's competitiveness. The available indices are the Global Competitive Index, published annually by the World Economic Forum, along with similar methodologies and an evaluation based on comparing relative price changes with changes in market share, as demonstrated in Chapter 8. The data that might be used to inform the investment forecast are summarised in Table 12.1.

Additional information that can be brought to bear to amplify a five-year forecast of annual investment might include surveys of major companies' investment intentions, surveys of bank and other funding agencies, surveys of builders associations, reports of real estate companies, information on major projects and schedules for implementation, the public sector investment programme (taking care to include only those projects which are already underway and those which are fully-funded and shovel-ready) and other qualitative information.

Choice of modelling technique

I learned by years of experience that sophisticated econometric models are of limited help in practical policy making. An economic team under my leadership developed the forecasting model used by the Central Bank of Barbados in the early 1980s, using an interrelated system of annual and quarterly accounts for GDP, the balance of payments, the public sector accounts and balances for the financial sector and the central bank. The system was modelled on forecasting systems developed by the Wharton School of the University of Pennsylvania, and the School provided training and advice on their methodology. Following Wharton practice, the main accounts were supported by a variety of supplementary accounts, to inform assumptions about capacity and investment, tax rates and performance, prices, interest rates and exchange rates, details of market performance for tourism, exports, and other production, labour market performance and other factors as necessary. The system also allows for modifications to the parameters based on qualitative information.

The accounts for Barbados were structured to reflect the peculiarities of the small open economy as described in Chapter 6, and as the Central Bank forecasting model was developed and expanded in the 1980s, I worked with a skeleton version to develop a robust simultaneous equation model forecast, an effort which reached its fullest articulation in Worrell (1992, see Appendix I, p. 97). The exercise, extended over more than a decade of research (versions of the model were tested in Holder and Worrell, 1985, Worrell, 1987 and Worrell, 1991), revealed the weaknesses of theory, data and economic implications which limit the usefulness of econometric models in application to policy prescription. The problems are numerous and fundamental, and even in Chapter 14, where I expand on them, we can only examine the portion of the iceberg that appears above the surface. Here I will recount the problem with which I began, and the implication which, after years of effort, convinced me that policy makers cannot improve on relatively simple methods, allied with a battery of simulation tools and monitoring, feedback and adjustment mechanisms. That problem is serial correlation (Worrell, 1973).

Correlation between the elements of two series which are being compared with a view to establishing a relationship between them is a fundamental challenge for statisticians. Statistical theory allows us to make inferences about random observations, that is, where the first observation bears no discernible relation to the second, or any other observation in the sample that is being tested; and so on, for every observation in the series. The token numbers that must be retrieved to gain access to some secure websites are an example of random numbers. Unfortunately, the observations of annual series of GDP, inflation, employment and other variables that economic policy makers are interested in are anything but random; except for countries which experience natural or man-made disasters or those newly exploiting a valuable natural resource, this year's GDP will not be much different from last year's. Testing with serially correlated variables such as GDP, inflation and employment will lead you to make inferences which are probably not warranted. If policy makers act on the basis of such inferences, they will be disappointed in the results.

In Chapter 14 we delve further into this and other challenges to expand on the reasons for my conclusion that the prevailing trends in model-building, including dynamic computable general equilibrium (DGCE) models and vector autoregressive models (VARs), are impractical for use as inputs for the calibration of economic policies. For the purposes of this chapter, I mention one factor which led me to conclude that simple methods are the most practical. It has to do with the margin of error in the forecast which economic policy makers produce to provide themselves with a benchmark against which to measure the impact of any policy. Nobody knows the future and, as every punter knows, most forecasts are off the mark. What the economist is trained to do is very similar to what the experienced punter does, that is, assemble knowledge and use their experience to narrow the odds against, for every forecast made. In both cases the savvy practitioner brings to bear the best available data, the most sophisticated analytical tools and their own experience. Unfortunately for the economist, the econometric tools available for our use throw up odds that are worse than what an experienced practitioner would have offered, by wide margins. What this means in practice is that an econometric model will typically throw up a one-year ahead GDP growth forecast of a figure that ranges, with a five per cent margin of error, between say two and eight per cent. That result is invariably presented as five per cent, but there is absolutely no justification for choosing the mid-point in preference to any other figure within the range. They all have equal probability. Furthermore, there remains a five per cent chance that growth will turn out to be less than two or more than eight percent; as every punter knows, the dark horse occasionally wins. The use of sophisticated methods does not narrow the odds, and simpler methods are easier to interpret and to modify in the light of experience and intuition.

Building the growth forecast up from the prospects for the foreign earning sectors

The foreign earning sectors are the drivers of the small open economy, so it makes sense to start with their economic prospects. From Equation 6.2 we know that the factors to be taken into consideration are the changes in the world prices of the product, domestic labour costs per unit of output and domestic interest rates. For the five-year forecast we also need the amount of spare capacity in foreign earning activities and the anticipated investment in new capacity. Detailed information on market strategies, the development of new markets and activities and other information should be brought to bear to make the forecast as robust as possible. Supporting models may be helpful, for example tourism models that are broken down by source markets and by quality of accommodation.

$$q_t = f_2(pt, ulc, r) \tag{6.2}$$

Extra care in the development of the foreign earnings forecast will be rewarded with a more dependable forecast overall, because the foreign earnings sectors are the base on which the forecasts for nontradable activity are built. The amount of additional nontradable production that can be expected depends on expected expenditure (Equation 6.3), which in turn is the sum of tradable output (the proceeds of exports and tourism and other traded services), nontradable output itself and money creation that adds spending power, over and above what is generated by output. Once we have a forecast for tradables we may derive a baseline forecast for nontradables, in a scenario where the central bank takes action to prevent any increase in the monetary base. Any such increase is a policy action whose consequences may be evaluated against this baseline.

$$q_n = f_3(a^*, q_n(-1)) \qquad (6.3)$$

In practice it is helpful to establish separate relationships between the foreign earning sectors and different activities, such as wholesale and retail, construction, the provision of public utility services, transport services, etc. In addition, forecasts of domestic inflation can be derived from Equation 6.4, using information about investment in additional production capacity of nontradables (new electricity generation, for example), domestic unit labour cost expectations, and forecasts of international prices and interest rates. In the absence of dependable five-year forecasts of the international variables – the usual case – the domestic price forecasts can be prepared under alternative scenarios.

$$p_n = f_4(q_n, p_t, ulc, r) \qquad (6.4)$$

An example of a forecast produced in this way appears as Table 12.2.

The GDP forecast is central to the completion of all other accounts. Proceeding to the balance of payments, we have already completed the forecasts of foreign earnings, which are equal to the value of tradable output with minor adjustments. Private foreign investment inflows are also already available, being the largest element in the total of all investment in the small open

Table 12.2 Example of a GDP forecast, $m

	2017	*2018*	*2019*	*2020*	*2021*
Sugar	28	19	10	2	1
Other agriculture	316	321	325	329	333
Manufacturing	317	301	284	268	252
Tourism	1,175	1,218	1,220	1,220	1,220
Mining	50	50	50	50	50
Public utilities	364	367	369	372	374
Construction	511	511	511	511	511
Distribution	2,023	2,032	2,032	2,032	2,032
Government	1,475	1,475	1,475	1,475	1,475
Transport, etc	1,018	1,032	1,045	1,059	1,073
Other services	2,013	2,041	2,042	2,042	2,042
Total	9,289	9,364	9,363	9,359	9,363
Tradables	1,836	1,858	1,839	1,819	1,806
Nontradables	7,453	7,506	7,524	7,540	7,557

Source: Author's calculations.

economy, as shown in Chapter 8. The remaining foreign inflows are for remittances, income from abroad and government foreign borrowing. The last should be treated as a policy variable.

The main factor behind the growth in the value of remittances in countries where they make a major contribution to incoming foreign currency is a large or growing discrepancy in per capita incomes between the sending country and richer neighbouring countries (often, but not always much larger), countries with which there have been strong historical ties or with which agreements permitting labour migration have been negotiated. Levels of education may also be a supplementary factor in some instances, because access to receiving countries is typically freer for those with higher levels of skill, such as medical workers and teachers. Projections for remittances can be made based on expectations for these underlying factors.

The largest element in foreign income in most small open economies is income from pensioners who have spent their working lives abroad. It tends to be of importance in small countries with characteristics similar to those where remittances are important, except that their per capita incomes are much closer to those of advanced economies, and the health, recreational and cultural activities of importance to seniors are well developed. Often these are countries where remittances were formerly of some importance, when discrepancies of lifestyles with the receiving countries were much wider.

As far as foreign outflows go, the items of importance are imports of goods and services, and outflows for the servicing of debt. Like nontradables, the import forecast is based on expected aggregate expenditure in the economy, as explained earlier. The debt service projection can be inferred from information on the terms of outstanding borrowings. Altogether, this produces a balance of payments forecast along the lines shown in Table 12.3, which is for a country where income has replaced remittances as a major source of foreign currency.

Our next step is the preparation of the forecast of the public sector accounts. Government's revenue will depend on the level of national income, as shown in Equation 6.6, but the relationship will vary with each specific tax measure, so in practice the forecaster will estimate separately the responsiveness of income taxes, consumption taxes, border taxes and property taxes, the main categories employed in most countries. The example shown in Table 12.4 includes taxes on personal and corporate income, and a value added tax of sorts (this is mainly a service economy, and the calculations of the taxable added value are something of a mystery).

$$Rev = f(Y, tx_i) \qquad (6.6)$$

The main expenditure items it is important to distinguish are wages, expenditure on the purchase of goods and services, grants to households for social welfare, grants to state-owned corporations, and expenditure on infrastructure, buildings, equipment and other capital expenditures. This breakdown is a

Table 12.3 Example of a Balance of Payments forecast, $m

	2017	*2018*	*2019*	*2020*	*2021*
Travel	2,213	2,358	2,364	2,364	2,364
Other services	1,122	1,136	1,149	1,163	1,176
Exports	543	551	559	568	576
Income	578	604	630	655	681
Transfers	108	92	77	61	46
Other inflows	650	650	650	650	650
Current Inflows	5,214	5,391	5,429	5,461	5,494
Fuel imports	517	498	498	499	498
Other imports	2,591	2,600	2,600	2,599	2,600
Other outflows	2,213	2,278	2,342	2,407	2,472
Current outflows	5,321	5,376	5,440	5,506	5,570
Gov't borrowing	0	0	0	0	0
Private capital	257	236	215	195	174
Net financial	257	236	215	195	174
Overall balance	149	251	204	150	98

Source: Author's calculations.

Table 12.4 Example of a public sector forecast, $m

	2017	*2018*	*2019*	*2020*	*2021*
Personal	390	395	394	394	394
Corporate	235	242	241	241	241
Property	190	191	191	191	191
VAT	1,011	1,026	1,025	1,024	1,025
Imports	243	243	243	243	243
Other	440	440	440	440	440
Revenue	2,510	2,537	2,535	2,534	2,534
Wages	822	841	861	880	901
Purchases	454	465	476	486	498
Interest	749	796	859	930	1,011
Grants to individuals	340	348	356	364	373
State companies	724	741	758	776	794
Other current	120	120	120	120	120
Current expenditure	3,209	3,312	3,430	3,557	3,696
Capital expenditure	181	185	190	194	198
Total Expenditure	3,390	3,497	3,620	3,751	3,894
Current balance	-699	-775	-895	-1,024	-1,162
Overall balance	-880	-960	-1,085	-1,218	-1,360

Source: Author's calculations.

convenient summary of the many options available for adjusting public sector activity and the sector's borrowing requirements in line with what is required to balance the external accounts, and to maintain that balance at a sustainable level, that is to say, a level that avoids foreign reserve depletion that threatens the US dollar (or euro) value of the currency at all times. No government with this range of options can avoid full responsibility for a balance of payments crisis, if it has the benefit of an appropriate economic management framework.

The final table that policy makers need for aggregate demand management is for the financing of the public sector deficit, as illustrated in Table 12.5. This example was prepared at a time when the economy was in crisis, indicated by the fact that banks no longer had confidence in government's credit worthiness, and there was no appetite for government bonds, domestically or in US dollar financial markets. (The forecasts were prepared for Barbados in mid-2017.) The entire burden of financing of a burgeoning public sector deficit was expected to fall on the central bank, a factor that heralded an impending balance of payments crisis. The forecasts were accompanied by a suite of recommendations for a three-year programme of adjustment measures, centred on public sector reform to raise low levels of public sector productivity, a challenge which remains unattended five years later, as of this writing (see Worrell, 2017).

Table 12.5 represents a crisis situation in which the usual sources of government finance have dried up. In more normal circumstances, the forecast would include some financing from banks, as well as by way of the issue of domestic and foreign currency bonds and other foreign financing. Explaining the net credit to the public sector by way of working capital balances to government departments, state corporations and agencies, and purchase of treasury bills with maturities less than one year, is problematic for policy makers in small open economies, because of the universal observance of unremunerated cash holdings and balances held with central banks. Monetary authorities typically require banks under their supervision to retain a small percentage of their deposit liabilities with the public in accounts with the authority. Interbank balances are settled over these accounts, and every

Table 12.5 Example of government financing, $m

	2017	*2018*	*2019*	*2020*	*2021*
Central bank	693	773	898	1,031	1,173
Banks	0	0	0	0	0
National Insurance	150	150	150	150	150
Private non-bank	37	37	37	37	37
Other Domestic	0	0	0	0	0
Capital markets	0	0	0	0	0
Total financing	880	960	1,085	1,218	1,360

Source: Author's calculations.

bank's holding is closely monitored by the central bank, because a persistent inability to reach the minimum reserve limit is the first sign of a bank in difficulty. However, banks in small open economies typically have balances well in excess of the stipulated minimum amount. These balances should be available for financing public sector deficits, provided a sufficiently attractive interest rate is offered. Therefore it should be possible to target public sector borrowing from banks, based on estimated surplus liquidity, and hit the bank financing target by offering a suitable interest rate. As explained in Chapter 9, this turns out to be feasible within narrow limits, set by the fact that the premium of domestic interest rates over a US dollar benchmark is a signal of government's credit-worthiness.

The limits to government bond issuance on domestic and foreign markets are usually set by rules of thumb with respect to the total interest burden as a proportion of government tax revenue, and the proportion of foreign debt service to foreign earnings. In recent times less attention has been given to the uses of debt finance, which is a more important concern. Government debt that finances infrastructure, particularly ports, airports, access roads for farm produce, public utilities, communications and other projects that have potential to open new economic opportunities for large populations and make permanent inroads on poverty, should be prioritised, because they add productive capacity and increase productivity. Such investment increases national competitiveness, attracts investment and boosts foreign earnings, so that the country can afford even higher levels of foreign debt in a virtuous cycle which plays out over the long term. It is short-sighted and development-inhibiting to set arbitrary maximum limits to such borrowing.

On the other hand, borrowing to fund current account spending should be avoided, even at low overall debt levels. The target should be to maintain a small surplus on government's current operational and interest expenditures, including all grants and transfers, to contribute for depreciation and partial funding for public sector projects. The counter that education and health improve human capital and that salaries of teachers and health workers should not be treated with other current expenditures is inadmissible, because borrowing to pay salaries and to meet current expenses is a policy that obviously cannot be sustained, whatever the purpose of the spending.

By much the same logic that deficits on the current account of the balance of payments may be sustained indefinitely provided they are financed by capital formation, governments may borrow without limit provided the purpose is investment in projects and facilities that make the country more attractive to investors at home and abroad, and that provide the infrastructure to enable people to use their initiative to improve the quality of their lives. As Nobel Prize winners Abhijit Banerjee and Esther Duflo (2011) argue, the poor are industrious, entrepreneurial and inventive, but they have no steady income and no safety net, so the slightest mistake can undo all their efforts to lift themselves up permanently. It is by facilitating this enterprise and inventiveness by providing rural access roads, rural electrification, health clinics and primary schools and similar facilities that the poor are empowered to better their lives.

Taking all these considerations together, it is possible to set out a five-year forecast for the public sector borrowing strategy. The exercise must start with a commitment to maintain a surplus on the current account, in the absence of which no borrowing strategy will be feasible. While it may happen that a current account deficit appears for a year or two because of unforeseen circumstances, a forecast should never contemplate a current account deficit, except in the context of a multi-year adjustment strategy to recover a fiscal surplus. The requirement for commercial bank finance will be related to working capital needs and depreciation expenses, and this should be compared with the projected liquidity of commercial banks and the expected credit demand by the private sector, firms and households. Attempts by the public sector to compete away bank finance from the private sector (known to economists as "crowding out") will always fail; for credit-worthy governments the better interest offered by the public sector will attract funds from abroad to enable banks to satisfy both private and public demand, while for other governments, their higher interest offer will be seen as a sign of desperation, likely to aggravate the flight of capital. However, the central bank will be in a position to access liquidity that is in excess of private sector credit needs by suitable interest rate offers, a matter to which we will shortly turn our attention.

The strategy for the issuance of new debt should be tied to the government's capital works programme, with a strong bias toward financing directed to specific projects. The larger proportion of borrowing needs to be in foreign currency, to provide for the high import content of all fixed investment. The issue of domestic debt instruments is mainly to provide low-risk financial domestic currency alternatives for savers rather than to fund additional investment, because any local currency funds that are surplus to the domestic costs of capital projects can be put to use only after conversion to foreign currency. The problem for many countries wishing to issue local currency bonds is that devaluation of the local currency and restructuring of local currency debt means that government debt, hitherto the only available low-risk financial asset, is now too risky to hold.

Personal experience has taught me that small open economies should be wary of bond issues on international markets that are not tied to specific projects. The main exceptions are for countries which are able to secure an investment grade credit rating. In such countries, a US bond issue may be a useful way to roll over existing debt, or to consolidate several loans into a single instrument that attracts better terms. So long as they stick to this conservative strategy they will attract the interest of insurance companies and other investors who are happy to purchase investment-grade offerings with a modest interest rate, and hold them to maturity. Such investors have no interest in the ongoing changes in the market value of these credits, so long as the issuer maintains their investment grade. Should the credit fall below investment grade they promptly sell, no questions asked.

Countries that do not attract an investment grade rating are well advised to stay away from international capital markets for bond issues that are not specifically for a single project. Small size is a distinct disadvantage in international capital markets, where the typical bidder wants only a small portion of any issue. A small share of a small issue (anything under US$1,000 million) is not worth the attention of most; they have limited research staff to monitor all their credits, and they have no spare resources to keep track of small investments. Because of this, some agencies maintain indices of various categories of market credit, to provide guidance and benchmarks for the performance of that type of credit. However, there is a minimum size of credit for eligibility for inclusion in the Emerging Market Index, the category in which small open economies sit, and this minimum may be well above what is prudent for the economic circumstances and needs of the SOE.

Tables 12.1 to 12.5 provide the essential framework for economic management of the small open economy. They contain the targets of economic management for growth the GDP, foreign earnings, investment, domestic prices – and for stability – the foreign reserves, the public sector balances. We also have the tools that policy makers will need to employ to secure their objectives: the tax rates, government expenditures, government capital works, the borrowing strategy, interest rates; and we have specified the relationships between the tools and objectives so that they reflect the behaviour of economic agents in the economy in question over a period long enough for us to conclude that the parameters we are using for the forecast are typical of that economy.

This core framework can be elaborated on in supplementary models, using a variety of methodologies. Structural models of the kind used in Worrell (1992) can help to tease out inconsistencies between the forecasting model setup and the structural assumptions that define the small open economy. Supplementary models for labour markets should be used to explore the interrelationships between wages, prices and productivity, and the ways in which they may be affected by migration of labour from agriculture to manufacturing, tourism and other services. Models to inform the reform of tax structures are also very helpful, as are models of the financial sector, through which issues of monetary policy and financial stability can be explored.

Coordination of public sector treasury management and central bank policy

We understand that, because of extreme openness to international trade and finance, economic stability in the small economy implies that a balance is achieved between outflows and inflows of foreign currency. We explained, in Chapter 7, how fiscal policy is used to manage aggregate demand to achieve this balance under all circumstances, and in Chapter 9 we showed that monetary policy needs to play a supplementary but essential role in the process. The second element in the framework for economic policy management therefore is the financial control mechanism for the public sector, operated by the government treasury and coordinated with the monetary authority. Best government financial management practice calls for a three-year rolling budgetary framework; in the system being outlined here the budget projection for these three years would be based on the five-year economic forecast described in the previous sector. For the purpose of maintaining economic stability, however, our focus is on the quarterly forecast, in particular the quarterly breakdown of the approved public sector income and expenditure over the financial year.

In the Treasury management system with which I am familiar, expenditures approved by the Parliament are broken down by department and agency and a table along the lines of Table 12.6 is prepared for the annual amount budgeted. This table is replicated for the four quarters, based on the usual seasonal patterns of spending, and the quarterly allocations in turn are divided into monthly allocations. The first column of Table 12.6 in each case is the amount approved by the Parliament. At the beginning of the fiscal year the Treasurer (the financial controller for the public sector; the title varies from country to country) of the public sector issues "warrants" to the financial controller of each department or agency, giving them authority to spend the allocated expenditure for the first three months of the year, not to exceed the total allocated for the quarter. The agency/department is required to report on the first month's spending within days of the month-end. Should the allotted amount for that month be exceeded, that agency's financial officer is warned that their allocations for the second and third months have been reduced to keep the quarterly total within budget. This process is repeated at the end of the quarter; should the first quarter's expenditure be exceeded, the agency's allotment for the remaining three quarters is reduced to keep the total within budget.

In the hands of a competent, professional public service, free of capricious political interference, this system can produce efficient public sector management

Table 12.6 Example of First Quarter Allocation, $m

	Allocation	*Actual*	*Difference**
State corporations	120	130	10
Health	69	75	6
Education	130	135	5
Law & order	35	35	0
Public works	21	15	-6
Foreign affairs	20	18	-2

Source: Allocations loosely based on Barbados Estimates of Revenue and Expenditure 2020/2021, actuals invented.

Note: *Excess of Actual over Allocation to be deducted from Q2-Q4 allocation.

that provides public services according to the priorities established by the cabinet (the committee of government ministers) and approved by the parliament, within the budget approved. What is required is a realistic budgetary process, which provides each public sector entity with resources sufficient to undertake all the responsibilities for which it is responsible.

The public sector budgets with expectations of tax and other revenues that will, if it is prudent, cover all its operational and interest expenses and grants and transfers, leaving a surplus amount to cover depreciation and a portion of capital spending. There will also be a plan for foreign and local borrowing to fund the bulk of capital spending. At the beginning of the fiscal year the central bank makes a financing plan for managing the public sector debt, to issue new government debt, to advise and assist in the financing of government projects, to service outstanding public sector debt, and to manage the public sector cash flow through the issue of treasury bills with maturities of less than one year.

In a well-functioning system of this kind, there would be no call for parliament to consider so-called "supplementary expenditures" for the conduct of the public sector business, except in unusual and unexpected circumstances. In such circumstances, major changes would be required, involving the re-ordering of priorities for government spending, or changes in tax or funding strategies. We shall discuss how these circumstances should be addressed later in this chapter. In contrast with the fiscal discipline which this system imposes, the parliaments of many countries are presented with frequent, unsystematic requests for supplementary expenditure for a variety of purposes, usually with no indication that supplementary revenue will be made available to cover the additional spending. The fault often lies with the process by which the budgeted expenditures are compiled, with cuts imposed on public sector entities which leave them with financing that is insufficient to fully undertake the tasks within their remit. In addition, the administration of financial controls is too often subverted by capricious political interference, so that public sector entities ignore the treasury manager's instruction to bring expenditure in line, on the instructions of the cabinet. The pervasive occurrence of these deficiencies renders meaningless the now-fashionable fiscal rules legislation, promoted by international financial institutions and put on the books by too many countries, there to remain a dead letter.

Apart from a reform of the public sector which frees it from arbitrary political interference, there is need for the establishment of a modern system of budgeting, where all public sector activities are fully provisioned for in the annual budget. All submissions by public sector entities should be realistic in terms of the services to be rendered and the cost of providing those services, and the submission should be accompanied by a report of current performance and expenditures, a report which should be made public within three months of the end of the financial year. Any cuts that are deemed necessary in the process of finalising the annual budget should be accompanied by a suitable reduction in personnel and services expected. The spending agency could then be held fully accountable for the provision of all services for which they are responsible, and they would be expected to report on their stewardship in an annual report that would be made publicly available.

Liquidity management and the public sector cash flow

The treasury bill auction is the main tool which the central bank uses to accommodate to the fact that, as with any economic activity, government revenues do not arrive at the same time as expenditures are to be made. For most small economies a weekly treasury bill auction is adequate. To inform the auction, the bank, working closely with the treasury, prepares a weekly table (to correspond to the auction period) as the basis for deciding what amount of bills should be offered for auction. The table lists the expenditures to be made each week, looking ahead for several weeks, the debt operations weekly (proceeds of foreign and domestic debt instruments with maturities of one year or more), and all tax and other revenues. The net amount is the additional liquidity in the Treasury account or government's cash needs, for each week.

The cash flow needs, whenever they occur, are compared with the amount of treasury bills that will mature each week. If there is a need for cash the central bank issues an amount of bills for that week that exceeds the value of the maturing bills. The actual amount of the excess does not necessarily match the public sector's cash requirement; it depends whether the interest rate achieved at the last Treasury bill auction was in line with the central bank's expectations. Only in that case would the auction amount match government's requirement. In other circumstances the bank might issue bills in excess of requirements in an effort to induce a reduction in the bill rate, or less than needed in an effort to raise the short-term rate.

Monetary policy in the small open economy, using the treasury bill auction

It is feasible to conduct monetary policy in small financial markets using the treasury bill auction, even when there is very little activity in open financial markets. The central bank can influence movements in the treasury bill rate through careful choice of the amount offered at auction, taking account of the government's cash needs, the state of bank liquidity and its own purchases at the auction and subsequently. The margins within which the central bank can act are defined by a narrow corridor around the US treasury bill rate (or other international rate which influences cross-border financial flows). The corridor is defined by the costs of exchanging local currency for US dollars, plus the current country market premium on the US rate, as perceived by commercial banks and the private sector. If local rates are pushed too low there are profits to be made by investing in risk-free US treasuries instead of buying domestic treasury bills. If rates are too high there may also be an outflow of finance, as a rate higher than the expected country risk premium may be seen as a warning sign that a potentially destabilising fiscal imbalance has emerged.

Within the corridor where monetary policy is possible, the central bank pushes rates up by intervening to create a scarcity of treasury bills available for purchase, relative to the banks' appetite for these bills, and continuing this policy at successive auctions until the desired rate is attained. To nudge the treasury bill rate downwards, the central bank intervenes in successive auctions at rates lower than the lowest bank bids, ensuring that the average auction rate falls, until it reaches the target rate. In the absence of an active market for the exchange of securities with longer maturities, the central bank can provide guidance for the market by issuing a notional yield curve, anchored on the treasury bill rate achieved at the auction, which would be used to set interest rates on government bonds with maturities over one year. In this way domestic interest rates for debt of longer maturities evolve in an orderly way over time, following the general trend of domestic short rates, which in turn follow the medium term evolution of the US treasury bill rate.

An illustration of fiscal dominance: Barbados monetary policy since 2013

In 2013 the Central Bank of Barbados adopted a fully market-based policy along the lines just described, finally abandoning the last vestiges of a regime of credit and interest controls which had long lost any relevance. This was the year in which there was the largest fiscal deficit since Barbados became an independent nation in 1966, and a year that witnessed an alarming fall in foreign reserves. Contractions in government expenditures, along with a handful of increases in tax rates, narrowed the fiscal deficit, but not to the extent required to eliminate a chronic shortfall in public sector revenues. As a result government borrowing requirements kept growing, and this was reflected in a continuous need to increase the treasury bill offer at virtually every weekly auction. The Central Bank was never in a position to exercise any discretion over the treasury bill rate, which kept rising well above comparable US rates. Eventually, as government's tentative and temporising efforts failed to close the fiscal gap decisively over the next four years, commercial banks dropped out of the market altogether, and the Central Bank was obliged to purchase ever larger amounts of treasury bills to cover wage payments and debt service, while other government payments went into arrears. The additional purchasing power created by the Central Bank's lending to Government was reflected in a continuous loss for foreign reserves every year, until a new party swept the polls in 2018 and imposed a punitive fiscal adjustment programme, including a coercive debt restructuring which has done lasting damage to the country's domestic and international credit-worthiness.

Coordinated fiscal and monetary policy for economic stability

The key economic policy actors are a top level committee of economic managers who have responsibility for keeping the economy on an even keel, and a smaller sub-committee comprising the treasury manager, the debt manager and the central bank's policy and operations managers, and their respective teams. During my tenure as Governor of the Central Bank of Barbados the top level committee was chaired by the Minister of Finance, with the Central Bank Governor, the Treasury manager, the head of the revenue authority, the debt manager, and other senior policy officials from the Bank and the Finance and Economic Ministries. Members of both committees were provided daily with updates of two charts, on the Central Bank's foreign reserves and on Central Bank's net credit to Government, both presented in the format of Figure 7.4 (Chapter 7). An unusually large fall in the foreign reserves is the first indicator of possible tightness in the foreign currency market, and a sharp and unexpected rise in net credit to government is an early warning of the possible source of the problem.

The top committee in Barbados met monthly, which is recommended, except in times of crisis when more frequent meetings may be needed. It has before it the forecast tables for output, the balance of payments and the government accounts for the next year to 18 months, at the highest frequencies available. At the first meeting of the year it will also deal with the five-year forecast, using annual data; we will come to that in the next Section. The committee's task, at the monthly meeting, is to evaluate the actual performance against targets for foreign reserves, government revenues, expenditures, deficits and financing, indices of production, employment, inflation and other economic indicators.

The main focus of the regular monthly meeting is to compare the foreign reserves outcome with what was expected, and to find explanations for the variance between expectations and the actual. That will determine when adjustments of policy are needed, and by how much. When foreign reserves are well above minimum levels a significant unexpected fall may warrant nothing more than close monitoring, whereas at more critical reserve levels a similar fall might warrant more immediate action, such as a decision of the committee to mount a detailed investigation and to meet weekly until it becomes clearer whether action in warranted. Equally, if there has been a recent episode of sustained money creation which has now begun to show up as a tightening of the foreign currency market, fiscal contraction is warranted, if it has not already been initiated. If in fact prompt corrective action had been taken, it might be best to wait to see whether the reserve loss persists, in which case stronger action might be needed.

The monthly meeting also pays special attention to the government revenues and spending, and remains vigilant in the detection of over-runs and evidence of a deficit that will put unwanted pressure on the credit market. The treasury manager's presentation, based on Table 12.6, stamps the committee's authority on his instructions to spending agencies with respect to living within their expenditure allocations at all times. This is key to keeping the overall budget within limits, and avoiding the danger of excessive borrowing and money creation.

At the monthly meeting the committee will also detect any challenges on the revenue side of the government accounts. The committee has the authority to make adjustments to expenditures if there appears to be room to do so, using budgetary savings which may result from such things as delays in project implementation. If there is room for additional borrowing while remaining within the limits of prudence, that decision too is within the committee's competence. In cases where the revenue loss is too large or is expected to persist, the committee will advise the cabinet of the alternatives for adjusting expenditures or increasing revenues or financing.

The system works well only when all the elements are in place: careful preparation of realistic public sector budgets, with a match for each spending unit between funds allocated and services to be provided, timely public accountability by way of published annual reports and accounts, a top-flight coordinating committee for monetary and fiscal policy with the requisite authority, a fully functional system of financial control along the lines of Table 12.6, and a cabinet which respects the realities of economics as well as politics.

Five year forecasts for the economic growth strategy

Before the start of each public sector financial year, the top economic management team meets in special session to review the forecast for investment and growth for the ensuing five years, and compares it with government's targets and strategies for maintaining and enhancing the economy's competitiveness and capacity to earn foreign exchange. The presentations to be prepared for these meetings will be based on analysis of the forecasts from the data and relationships summarised in Tables 12.1 to 12.5, covering investment, GDP, the balance of payments, the fiscal accounts and the financing of the public sector. The discussions will centre on an evaluation of the forecasts to secure agreement on the best-informed benchmark projections that may be offered for the ensuing five-year period. This discussion will highlight what priorities need to be rearranged in the forthcoming budget for the public sector, and what adjustments need to be made in the economic strategy to address any elements of the benchmark forecasts that are deemed to be unsatisfactory. Particular attention should be paid to the forecasts for the public sector and for the overall external balance to ensure that there are surpluses on the current account of the public sector and that foreign inflows and outflows remain in balance with an adequate reserve of foreign exchange. It may also be necessary to adjust long-term growth and investment targets, in timing or substance, in the light of recent events, as in the case of the COVID-19 pandemic.

These strategic review meetings are also the occasion to assess progress with renewable energy strategies, major infrastructural works, tax incentives and promotional strategies for private sector investment, reforms intended to increase public sector productivity, and other aspects of the overall development strategy. For these exercises a number of policy review papers would be prepared, with details of the implementation of each strategy, assessing whether, given what had been done so far, it appeared likely that the target for each activity for five years ahead – not the end-of-project target, which might well be further into the future – would be met. Where necessary, recommendations would be made to the cabinet of the country for actions to put matters back on track. Changes in the targets for these sectoral activities at the end of the five-year period will of necessity involve adjustments to the overall five-year growth targets.

These pre-budget discussions should be informed by in-depth sessions with representatives of private sector organisations representing workers, employers and important economic sectors. Their views are of crucial importance, because the actions they take in response to actual and proposed changes in public policy will ultimately determine the success or failure of the economic growth strategy.

The importance of the public information strategy

Economics is about the behaviour of individuals in the society, about what motivates them to produce and exchange goods and services. That behaviour will be guided by the public's ambitions and aspirations and their expectations with respect to official policies, among other things. Public policies will have their intended results to the extent that they understand and correctly represent economic behaviour in their models, and to the extent that policy makers communicate well the impact that their policies are expected to have on the goals desired by economic agents. Achieving this is more difficult than is usually appreciated.

The information communicated to the general public must be credible in the eyes of the recipients. In the modern information age, it is no longer sufficient that the information comes from an authoritative source; individuals have access to so many sources that everyone is obliged to make a choice of what to believe. To achieve credibility, information must contain easily verifiable data that is already common knowledge (because people do not have the time to check), and the implications that flow from that data should be readily apparent so that economic agents will wish to react in ways consistent with the policy maker's expectations immediately on receiving the information. This is an ideal seldom achieved by any public policy, but there are things that can be done to improve the chances of success. I conclude this chapter with personal observations about effective communications strategies for economic policy makers, the product of five decades of experience.

The founding Governor of the Central Bank of Barbados, the late Sir Courtney Blackman, had a passion for communicating economic information in ordinary English, a passion which I shared, as the Bank's founding Director of Research. Throughout the Bank's history, from its foundation in 1972, no communication intended for public consumption contained terms like "the terms of trade" or "real interest rates" which are understood (not always fully) by economists but not by a general audience. In press releases and other widely circulated material we always strove for intuitive explanations, and for language which conveyed the intended message in a form that was immediately apparent, conscious that the typical reader is not inclined to make their daily newspaper – or their twitter feed – an object of in-depth study. The use of familiar imagery is a helpful aid in getting the message across.

In this, as in other areas of economic policy, Sir Courtney and I spent our careers swimming against the tide, and the use of economic jargon remains commonplace. The implications are not inconsequential. An example is the persistent use of the term "printing of money" to describe government borrowing from the central bank to pay public sector wages and other current expenses when revenues are insufficient. If the problem really were the printing of currency which the banks and the public did not want, the simple solution would be to pass a law forbidding the practice. Policy makers know this does not address the problem; only a cut in public spending or an increase in tax rates will do that. The current fashion for fiscal rules is a form of hand waving; the existence of a rule does nothing to address the tax and expenditure changes that must be negotiated and agreed to balance the public accounts and return the fiscal strategy to sustainability.

The packaging of the presentation of economic messages is also consequential. There is no point to a carefully crafted message if it fails to attract the attention of the intended audience. There is a marked difference between the covers of the annual reports of the Central Bank of Barbados during the years I had responsibility for the report, and other years. I always insisted that the cover should attract attention, and cover and interior should be thematically related and reflective of some message that the Bank wished to convey. This was a departure from usual practice, that the Bank's report, like other official publications, should be a dour and slightly forbidding document, thereby ensuring that its preparation would be a pointless exercise, since it would not be widely read.

In the internet age, the emphasis is on online communications. As Governor of the Central Bank I introduced pre-recorded video of economic press releases, illustrated with video clips and charts. The bank's website was updated and systems established to maintain and refresh the site regularly. More video content was added and the design was updated, a process which should be repeated every few years. In addition, in an effort to provide public economic and financial education in an appealing format, a high-quality glossy magazine was introduced, in print and online, an initiative which has now been discontinued.

Innovations were made with respect to the content of the bank's press releases and other reports, continuously over the years. The bank's statistical output in the 1980s and 1990s was unparalleled in the Caribbean, in depth and sectoral and geographic range, and the *Annual Statistical Digest* of that period remains a valuable mine of economic and financial data for research on the recent history of the economies of Barbados and the English-speaking Caribbean. Paradoxically, with today's far more powerful computational and communications technologies, the Barbados central bank's statistical output is a small fraction of what was previously available.

The Central Bank pioneered the practice of appending a standard set of tables, similar to Tables 12.2 to 12.5, to every press release for the benefit of economists and anyone who cared to interpret the data for themselves. The practice continues to the present, even though the tables seem to attract less attention than the information they provide warrants.

The use of charts can be a powerful way to convey information, including economic information. Unfortunately, few economic policy makers have been schooled in the basics of graphical excellence: "Excellence in statistical graphics consists of complex ideas communicated with clarity, precision and efficiency" (Tufte, 2015). The best graphics tell a story at a glance, and they are exceptionally difficult to design and present. The effort always pays off whenever a measure of success is achieved, because the resulting image conveys a message which is not soon forgotten.

Finally, some words on the events at which communication takes place and the principal actors. For economic policy the principal actors are the minister responsible for the public sector finances and the governor of the Central Bank. It should be obvious that they need to speak with one voice; the notion of central bank independence, whatever merit it may have, cannot extend to public disagreement with the Minister of Finance on the direction and content of public policy. Public announcements should be made only when a consensus has been achieved among officials responsible for economic policy and strategy, taking full account of all available information, all policy options and after deliberating on the probable outcomes of every available option.

It is now very evident that impromptu media conferences are not a useful way to communicate policy. In a paper on central bank communications, a recognised expert in the field observed that it is difficult to ensure that the public receives reliable information from the press conference, and the quality of media participation and discussion tends to deteriorate over time (Bunemann, 2016). There are a variety of effective alternatives. In my experience, the most efficient way to communicate economic strategy is via carefully crafted documents of a length that the essential messages may be absorbed in a couple of minutes, and with the help of graphics whose import is self-evident. The documents are best discussed with the help of knowledgeable experts, including the authors of the document and others, and at events moderated by a communications expert who has in-depth knowledge of the subject. Major announcements should be pre-arranged and should be preceded and followed up with a wide range of informal discussions with interest groups, representatives of economic sectors and activities, thought leaders and others, conducted by all the members of the economic team.

References

Bunemann, Niels. 2016. "Searching for excellence in central bank communication," *Lombard Rates blog*, 7 June.

Banerjee, Abhijit and Esther Duflo. 2011. *Poor economics: A radical rethinking of the way to fight global poverty.* New York: PublicAffairs.

Holder, Carlos and DeLisle Worrell. 1985. "A model of price formation for small economies: Three Caribbean examples." *Journal of Development Economics*, Vol. 18, pp. 411–428.

Tufte, Edward R. 2015. *The Visual Display of Quantitative Information*, 2nd ed. Cheshire, Connecticut: Graphics Press.

Worrell, DeLisle. 1992. *Economic Policies in Small Open Economies: Prospects for the Caribbean*. London: Commonwealth Secretariat.

Worrell, DeLisle. 1991. "Fiscal and monetary policies in small economies," in *Increasing the International Competitiveness of Exports from Caribbean Countries*, edited by Yin-Kann Wen and Jayshree Sengupta. Washington, D.C.: The World Bank.

Worrell, DeLisle. 1987. *Small Island Economies: Structure and Performance in the English-speaking Caribbean Since 1970*. New York: Praeger.

Worrell, DeLisle. 1973. "Comments on three econometric models of the Jamaican economy." *Social and Economic Studies*, Vol. 22, no. 2, pp. 272–286.

13 Size Matters

Small Economies need Different Strategies for Stable Economic Development

It is now widely recognised that small countries are subject to vulnerabilities which can amplify the economic consequences of financial and economic crises, commodity price inflation and volatility, sea level rise and other physical, social and economic events when compared to the impact on large countries. Special attention to small economies is reflected in the establishment of specialised groups on the problems of small size in the World Bank, the IMF, the Commonwealth Secretariat and other international institutions, as well as some academic interest in the topic of small size, notably at the University of Malta.[1] Research has established that size is not an obstacle to growing prosperity if countries adopt strategies that build resilience to a variety of circumstances over which they have no control. In a comprehensive analysis of the vulnerability and resilience of small states (Briguglio, Cordina, Farrugia and Vella, 2006), the authors propose an index of resilience, which comprises sub-indices for macroeconomic stability, microeconomic market efficiency, governance and social development. They use this index to argue that, though the evidence confirms that small states are more vulnerable to events and circumstances beyond their control than larger counties, they may nonetheless ensure stable economic growth and keep on a path of development by taking steps to make their economies more resilient.

The countries with which this book is concerned have economies which are tiny by comparison with the countries where the majority of the world's population lives. The GDP of Cuba, the largest economy in our sample, is about the same size, in US dollars, as that of Brooklyn, one of the five boroughs that make up the city of New York. The smallest, Kiribati, has an economy no bigger than that of Amite County in the State of Mississippi in the US, one of the poorest in that nation. It is evident that economies of this size cannot employ the same strategies as even countries of modest size such as Canada and Australia (about 15 times Cuba's GDP), not to speak of leading industrial nations. The reality is that the fact of political autonomy does not, of itself, provide Ghana with options for policies with respect to taxation, government spending, monetary policies and interest rates that are not available to Rhode Island, a state of the US which has about the same GDP. With this perspective, it is possible to appreciate the argument for a

DOI: 10.4324/9781003247609-16

unique perspective on the tools to be used for stable, sustainable human development and how they should be employed in small open economies.

This more realistic perspective on economic management in small open economies has been largely absent from the policy debate in academia and in policy circles, both at national and international levels. In this chapter we shall show that this neglect is unwarranted, because over recent decades there has been a great deal of research which points to the need for a prescription for economic policies for small open economies that are different from the standard recipe. We also offer some observations on the very useful research done by the Commonwealth Secretariat, the Islands and Small States Institute and others who have explored the greater vulnerabilities of small states and the ways in which they can increase their resilience to natural and man-made shocks over which they have no control.

Our overall assessment of the possibilities that small nations have for economic strategies of their own making that secure the future human development of their populations is positive. We summarise the policy options that are suitable for small open economies, the opportunities their representation at the councils of international organisations affords them and ways these countries might adapt and evolve in a dynamic world economy.

What the literature says about monetary and exchange rate policies in small open economies

There is sufficient evidence from the existing literature to support the view that small states are different: they are more open, they are forced by their limited resources to be specialised in a few internationally competitive products and services, and they therefore do not have the option of adopting a closed economy strategy in pursuit of economic growth. Small states have outperformed large states, but only when they pursued strategies appropriate to their circumstances. The strategies for stabilisation and growth that work for large economies do not suit the circumstances of small economies, and if applied as in large countries, they invariably result in policy failure. In particular, the record shows that economic growth in the small open economy depends on increasing quality and productivity, and is unaffected by changes in relative prices. This section surveys the literature, concluding with insights it provides into monetary and exchange policies that are best for small economies.

Small states are very open, and therefore exceptionally vulnerable to the consequences of external shocks. Indices which measure these vulnerabilities have been developed by Briguglio (1995), Atkins, Mazzi and Easter (2000) and the UN Committee on Development Policy (2005); they all confirm the greater vulnerability of very small open economies. The sources of vulnerability identified in these studies include a high degree of economic openness, limited diversification possibilities, a narrow range of exports, limited applicability of domestic competition policy, an inability to influence international prices, high international transport costs, uncertainties of industrial supplies due to insularity and remoteness in some cases, a limited ability to exploit economies of scale in the private sector and in public administration, a paucity of natural resources in most cases and a high import content of expenditure, especially food and fuel. Other studies which support these findings include Frankel (2010), who identifies greater exposure to supply shocks and trade volatility in particular as among the characteristics of developing countries, as opposed to large industrial countries, and della Paolera and Taylor (2001), whose economic history of the Argentine currency board concludes that no monetary arrangement may insulate the small open economy from a severe global shock.

Small states produce a limited range of products at internationally competitive prices. Carter (1997) compares countries by size and export concentration (goods and services) and shows that micro states are all specialised in a few commodity exports. A corollary of this is that expenditure-switching policies are not available to the very small open economy because there are no domestic substitutes available at competitive prices for the range of import commodities (Worrell, 2012). Therefore if adjustment to (rather than financing of) shocks is the appropriate response, expenditure reduction is the only option.

The fact that expenditure switching is not possible means that economic growth is unaffected by changes in relative prices, including the real exchange rate (Worrell, 2012). In the standard monetary and exchange rate adjustment model a devaluation of the exchange rate shifts the external balance line outwards through a combination of expenditure switching (import substitution and lower domestic consumption of exportables) and greater profitability of exportable production, leading to increases in export capacity in the medium term (See, for example, Agénor, 2004). However, in the very small open economy there can be no expenditure switching because of the limited range of competitive domestic production of tradables, and the profitability of exportable production increases only when devaluation causes a loss of real income, which is reflected in a fall in real wages. This is because of the very high import content of consumption and production. In effect, the wage good is imported, and the only way to increase the profitability of exporting (other than increasing productivity) is to cut real wages (Worrell, 2013).

A consequence of the openness of the economy is that the stability of the nominal exchange rate becomes very important, as is now widely acknowledged. Ostry, Ghosh & Chamon (2012) recommend exchange rate targetting, alongside inflation targetting, for countries with a high pass-through of devaluation to inflation. Aizenman, Hutchison and Noy (2008) point out that inflation targetters follow a mixed strategy, with both inflation and the exchange rate as important determinants of policy interest rates. Aizenman, Chinn and Ito (2010) observe that open economies prefer to hold "massive" amounts of foreign exchange reserves to support exchange rate stability and maintain financial openness.[2] Blanchard, Dell'Ariccia and Mauro (2010) advise that small open economies should openly recognise that exchange rate stability is part of their objective function. Earlier Gali and Monacelli (2002) demonstrated that if a very open economy targets the consumer price index, it will end up with an exchange rate path that looks very much like a peg. Parrado and Velasco (2002) show that optimal exchange rate policy in a small open economy involves management of the exchange rate. In practice, as Parrado (2004) explains, the Monetary Authority of Singapore uses the exchange rate as an instrument to achieve its inflation target. Schaechter, Stone and Zelmer (2000) explain that the exchange rate is a possible channel through which monetary policy affects the inflation rate. The experience of countries which have given up their own currencies further illustrates the effects of a stable exchange rate: for Ecuador, Tas, Kamil and Togay (2011) report that inflation was lower after dollarisation, the GDP growth rate higher (all other things equal), and the variance of inflation was lower.

Both theory and empirical observation suggest that exchange volatility depresses potential investment in all economies, because it is a source of uncertainty (Pindyck, 1991). Pindyck and Solimano (1993) find, not unexpectedly, that the impact of volatility in the marginal profitability of capital on investment is greatest for developing countries, though it is only moderate for all countries tested. Tests for small open economies tend to confirm these results. For example, Schnabl (2007) reports a negative relationship between exchange rate volatility and growth for 41 small countries in the EU periphery. Boehm and Funke (2001) reported that firms react more cautiously to shocks if the exchange rate is managed, in a study which does not distinguish countries by size.

A successful exchange rate targetting regime lends credibility to stabilisation policies in small open economies. Berg, Jarvis, Stone and Zanello (2003) list hard pegs as apparently successful in countries that have experienced deep crises, though their bias is towards full-fledged inflation targeting and floating rates. They do not discriminate between large countries such as Brazil and small open economies such as Ecuador, however. Small economies in the periphery of reserve currency countries may borrow credibility from the reserve currency country (Buiter, Corsetti and Pesenti, 1998).

Up until the mid-1990s, exchange rate targets were used more frequently than monetary targets in the formulation of interest rate policy (Cottarelli and Giannini, 1997). The spectacular failure of the interest rate defense of the exchange rate in several countries at the time of the Asian crisis and in subsequent crises in Russia, Turkey and elsewhere, meant that this strategy for exchange rate management fell out of favour. More recently Asian countries (and others) have piled up massive stocks of foreign exchange reserves with which to maintain the stability of their exchange rates. In my own work I have emphasised that the maintenance of adequate foreign reserves lends credibility to aggregate demand management policies in small open economies. Because of the import dependence and financial openness of very small economies, the achievement of external balance to protect foreign reserves requires the appropriate management of aggregate domestic demand. As a result, a stable exchange rate which is protected by adequate foreign exchange reserves is interpreted by markets as evidence of sound economic policy (Worrell 1992, 2012). Views differ as to how the exchange rate target should be set. Dornbusch (1988) explored the merits of using crawling pegs and currency baskets to avoid overvaluation of the real exchange rate. In fact, a majority of small open economies still use a single currency reference rate, de facto or de jure, with or without discrete changes from time to time.

There are many studies of the relationship between real exchange rates and growth in very small countries, and some have purported to show that changes in the real exchange rate influence growth. Clearly, however, these are conceptually or methodologically flawed. There may indeed be a relationship between the real exchange rate and growth, but it cannot be that the exchange rate change is causing an acceleration (or deceleration) of growth, because, as we saw earlier, the expenditure-switching channels through which this would take place do not exist in small open economies. Therefore, the studies that find a relationship (for example, McIntyre, 1995, and Aslund, 2011a) are uncovering simultaneous effects caused by other factors, such as intersectoral changes in productivity, acceleration of wages or other domestic costs relative to international prices, or the discovery and exploitation of natural resources.[3] Moreover, it has been shown that in small open economies nominal exchange rate adjustment will probably not succeed if its objective is to affect the real exchange rate, because the mere existence of such a rule generates self-fulfilling revisions in expectations (Uribe, 2002).

Studies of exchange rate changes and price competitiveness are a subset of the literature on devaluation and growth, and suffer from similar conceptual problems. A fundamental tenet of microeconomic theory is that the atomistic producer has no influence on his selling price, and he cannot increase revenues by lowering his price. If he is more productive than his competitors, he will be rewarded with higher returns. It would make no sense to gift those productivity gains to his consumers, in the form of lower prices. However, that is precisely what is advocated by those who purport to find a positive relationship between devaluation and growth in the small open economy. Economic growth must be secured by increased productivity, as is widely recognised. It is of no benefit to gift productivity gains to foreigners, by way of an exchange rate devaluation.

Most studies of real exchange rate effects use a trade or transactions weighted combination of nominal exchange rates and domestic and foreign price indices as the measure of the real exchange rate, but this is known to be an inaccurate measure (Harberger, 2004; Marsh and Tokarick, 1994; Worrell, Greenidge and Lowe, 2013). These three studies are among those that suggest more appropriate measures of real exchange rates and price competitiveness which may be compiled from available data. However, the use of inaccurate trade-weighted indices remains commonplace.

We have evidence from the literature of the interconnectedness of monetary and exchange rate policies and the implications for monetary policy effectiveness.

Worrell (2000) argues that because of information asymmetries, uncertain expectations and changeable preferences, the central bank and the treasury must work together on the design, implementation, monitoring and, when necessary, the revision of macroeconomic policy and on providing the public with information on ongoing economic developments and interpretation of the macroeconomic strategy. That paper shows how the effectiveness of monetary policy in small open economies is limited because of capital flows, even when exchange rates are flexible, because of information asymmetries. International financial markets are slow to impose domestic fiscal discipline, and in the absence of such discipline, a lack of coordination with monetary policy often undermines the credibility of fiscal policy. As a result, monetary transmission channels are too uncertain to allow of credible monetary policy. What is more, central banks usually cannot be indifferent about growth or systemic bank failure, even if that means abandoning an inflation target. Finally, the central bank has privileged information, and with it, a responsibility in an oligopolistic market to guide private market agents, none of whom has the capacity to provide themselves an equally comprehensive macroeconomic overview. Worrell (1997) shows that the typical structure of banking systems in small open economies with high levels of bank concentration means that optimising behaviour on the part of the banks may lead to perverse interest rate movements from the point of view of intended monetary policy outcomes. Worrell, Craigwell and Mitchell (2008) confirm empirically that uncovered interest rate parity appears to hold in Barbados, an indicator of the openness of the financial market to international flows.

In a test for a small open economy (Norway) where interest rates and the exchange rate are both flexible, Bjørnland (2008) finds considerable interdependence between monetary policy and the exchange rate. Calvo and Vegh (1995) show that in an open economy with flexible exchange rates, efforts to fight inflation with high interest rates may be frustrated by exchange rate volatility, with an exchange rate that appreciates initially but then depreciates beyond its starting point, inducing even higher inflation than before the policy was implemented. Guender (2006) uses a "simple New Keynsian open economy model" to show that the conduct of monetary policy in an open economy differs considerably from the closed economy framework. If inflation is the target, monetary policy will fail to fully stabilise on the target because of exchange rate movement; if the consumer price index is the target, monetary policy is frustrated even if the exchange rate does not react to a demand shock. This link between monetary policy and the exchange rate may be used to advantage in the case of stabilisation efforts following a financial crisis, where monetary policy alone does not stabilise (Berg, Jarvis, Stone and Zanello, 2003).

The main tool in the small economy's armoury is fiscal policy. Worrell (2013) explains how fiscal policy may be employed to balance demand and supply in the foreign exchange market. Lindbeck, Arestis and Sawyer see

> limited scope for monetary policy given constraints on controlling money stock …and small open economy constraints on interest rate manipulation…

> they see very considerable potential for active fiscal policy...[in] ensuring an adequate level of aggregate demand over the medium term...
>
> (Lindbeck, Arestis and Sawyer, 1998, p. 166)

In their analysis of the Argentinian currency board between 1880 and 1935, della Paolera and Taylor (2001) conclude that monetary policy cannot completely insulate the open economy from severe external shocks, and no monetary arrangement can paper over fiscal profligacy. Leiderman (2003), Worrell (2000) and others stress the importance of coordination of the fiscal and policy stances. Leiderman points out that pressure from the treasury to make the central bank finance a large part of the budget can undermine the success of any monetary regime. One may also infer the importance of fiscal tools from Dornbusch's (2001) scepticism about monetary and exchange rate policy effectiveness in small open economies. He points out that interest parity constrains local rates; discretionary monetary and exchange rate policy cannot improve a bad fiscal situation; temporary shocks should be financed, not adjusted to; and exchange rate adjustment will not suffice to make an adequate response to permanent shocks. Farhi, Gopinath and Itskhoki (2011) recognise that fiscal policy may be used to achieve desirable resource reallocations, in circumstances where nominal exchange rate changes are not indicated.

The literature focusses on the impact of fiscal policy on the real exchange rate, see for example Aloy, Moreno-Dodson and Nancy (2008), Aslund (2011b, 2012), and Galstyan and Lane (2008). However, the aggregate expenditure effects of fiscal policy matter more for the small open economy, because, unlike for large economies which are not price takers, changes in the real exchange rate do not spur output increases in small states. The contractionary effects of devaluation are recognised as being "far more important for developing countries" and this is especially so when there is a currency mismatch (Frankel 2010). The slow adjustment of the price of nontradables in the wake of large devaluations, analysed in Burstein, Eichenbaum and Rebelo (2004) is equivalent to a worsening of the terms of trade, and a decline in real income in the small open economy.

The burden of this literature is that exchange rate targetting is highly recommended for small open economies: it promotes fixed investment and thereby enhances growth potential, it helps to contain inflation, and it lends credibility to the overall economic policy stance. There are no downsides to exchange rate targetting: it does not preclude adjustment of the rate, though exchange rate adjustment in search of competitive advantage is a futile strategy for small open economies; and the exchange rate target may be a peg, a crawling rate or a link to a basket of currencies.

If the value of an exchange rate target is so pellucid, why are so few countries willing to commit to an exchange rate anchor, or willing to admit that they do have an exchange rate target? The answer, I believe, is that country authorities fear that they may not be able to sustain an announced target. Up until the mid-1990s the popular view was that the targeting policy could be sustained by closing the capital and financial accounts, and there are still economists who believe that to be the case. However, the events of the past two decades should by now have put paid to the notion of a closed financial account (see Worrell, Craigwell and Mitchell, 2008), and all recent efforts to sustain the exchange rate by this route have failed, except in the very short run. The only effective way to equilibrate the external accounts of a small open economy is through the management of aggregate demand, using fiscal policy and (in the medium and longer term) the supply of foreign exchange through investment to increase productivity.

Revisiting the features of a macroeconomic model of small open economies

A fundamental misspecification of the neoclassical models in common use today, including most computerised general equilibrium models, is the use of a single good that is produced, consumed and traded, at home and abroad. For the analysis of the SOE we need at least three goods: an export good, which, to a useful approximation, is not consumed at home; an import good, which, to a useful approximation, is not produced at home; and a good that cannot be traded, a nontradeable. Petroleum is a prime example of the export good. A country like Norway consumes so little of the oil it produces that we may, without harm to the integrity of our analysis or its conclusions, neglect its own consumption altogether. Aircraft and heavy machinery are examples of import goods, using similar logic, while government services are unquestionably not a tradeable good. Our book uses a model with three goods to analyse the growth and stability of the SOE, and to explore the implications of fiscal, monetary, financial and exchange rate policies (Chapters 6, 7, 9 and 10).

The government of the SOE has no sovereignty over the prices at which it obtains the goods and services that provide for the material well-being of its population in exchange for the goods and services it obtains from abroad. The national sovereignty extends only to the wealth residing within the national borders; the value of that wealth is measured by the prices at which the products and services it produces are exchanged for needed imports. For a small country the achievement of national independence, and the opportunities it offers the new sovereign to re-order the distribution of wealth, production and consumption within the country, is inconsequentia, in the best of circumstances, because such reorganisation does not in and of itself affect the prices at which local products and services are exchanged with the rest of the world. On the contrary, all too often the internal redistribution of wealth on independence results in a decline in overall national productivity, resulting in a contraction in earnings from exports, tourism and other traded services. In these cases, the exercise of national sovereignty has worsened the material well-being of the population of the new nation.

In the small economy, the focus of the sovereign must be on the factors which can increase the volume of goods and services that can be produced for sale to foreigners, and which can improve the terms on which these foreign sales are exchanged for the imports needed to improve the well-being of the national population. These factors are national productivity, how competitive local producers are internationally, and the nation's voice in the formation of the rules, guidelines and practices which govern international trade and finance. The policies with regard to productivity and competitiveness explored in Chapter 8 are central to the exercise of national sovereignty by small states to the benefit of their populations. The issue of voice is not much discussed in relation to small states, but proves to be of crucial importance in its possible effect on the terms of international exchange as it affects them. This is especially the case for traded services and high-value exports.

Comparison of policies suitable for SOEs with conventional strategies

Table 13.1 summarises the differences between a conventional suite of fiscal, monetary and exchange rate policies, and similar policies as they should be

Table 13.1 Comparison between conventional and SOE strategies

Policy	*Conventional*	*SOE*
Exchange rate	Flexible, market determined	Managed, market determined (demand management)
Monetary		
Interest rate	Intervention in short term market	Intervention in short term market
	Target: inflation	Target: trend in US Treasury bill rate
Credit to gov't, banks	Use of marketable instruments	Use of marketable instruments
Fiscal		
Tax		Bias towards foreign currency sectors
Expenditure priorities	Health, education, infrastructure, public order	Health, education, infrastructure, public order
Current account	Modest savings	Modest savings
Overall balance	No more than can be financed from private markets	No more than can be financed from private markets
Gov't debt ceiling		Limited by expected impact on balance of payments, *EMP*

Source: author's compilation.

Note: *EMP*: excess pressure of demand for foreign exchange.

employed in small open economies. In contrast to the conventional preference for flexible, market-determined exchange rates, the small open economy needs to anchor fiscal and monetary policies on a predictable value of the local currency in terms of the US dollar, the euro or other international currency in which most external commerce is transacted.

The conventional approach is to use intervention in the market for short-term debt instruments, or, nowadays, announcements of the monetary policy intentions to influence interest rates, with a target of containing inflation at a target rate which is low and positive. The preferred approach for small open economies is also to use intervention in the short-term debt market, but with a view to keeping local rates on a trend that matches the expected trend of the US Treasury bill or any other international reference rate that is relevant, with allowance for a country premium and the cost of exchange.

With respect to public sector revenue and expenditure, the similarities are that the priorities for expenditure should always be public provision of health, education, law and order and other basics of a stable, productive society that promotes human potential. Tax revenues will depend on the social consensus on the balance of taxation and public provision of public services, which varies with the preferences of each society. The differences are that the tax system of the small open economy should be biased in favour of activities that earn foreign exchange, because the growth of foreign inflows is what increases the resources available for increasing the material well-being of the population. Performance-related support for innovative export-oriented enterprise is also indicated, for similar reasons. Importantly, governments must take account of the net effects of tax and government spending policies on aggregate expenditure in the economy.

Conventional practice does not emphasise the importance of maintaining a surplus on the current account of the public sector, but that remains the sensible strategy for countries large and small. Borrowing must always be directed to expenditure that increases the capacity to earn, otherwise the borrower is made worse off, because they have to divert earnings from other uses to service the new debt. While it can be argued that spending on health and education should increase national productivity, capacity and output, in practice it is impossible to measure that link in a way which enables us to account for how much additional capacity any additional current spending creates. Therefore practical policy makers are well advised to maintain savings on the current account of the balance of payments. The overall public sector deficit should be fully financed by borrowing from the private sector, avoiding deliberate or sustained money creation in all types of economy.

Finally, with respect to public sector borrowing, it is possible to define a limit to debt in the case of the small open economy, based on its impact on the flows of finance into and out of the economy, and the resulting impact on the foreign reserves stock that protects the value of domestic currency. If government tries to borrow too much, and the central bank intervenes to drive short-term interest rates well above the prevailing country premium in an attempt to attract sufficient finance, local financial institutions and the local private sector may become alarmed. Rather than take the bait, they are more likely to switch into US dollar debt instruments, leaving a shortfall in public sector finance which the central bank has to cover. The alternative, to allow the public sector to fall into arrears on current payments, will have consequences far more problematic.

It is much more difficult to find a limit for other countries, as is evident from the current debate in the US about so-called Modern Monetary Theory. While in a simple model of an economy with no growth and no technological change, one can make a back-of-the envelope calculation, comparing growth and interest rates in a closed economy, that calculation is too far removed from reality to serve as a practical guide for policy.

Risk mitigating strategies for small open economies

In contrast to macroeconomic policies, where a suite of policies suitable for all small open economies can be recommended, the risk mitigation strategies that suit individual countries will vary. In the case of hurricanes and tropical cyclones, for example, a high degree of resilience has already been built into structures and practices, which fortifies the economy against all but the most extreme events. Standards of building construction in the Caribbean are a case in point. In countries subject to hurricanes, homes are built mostly from steel-reinforced concrete, with steel ties to keep roofs in place, a practice that makes them resistant to very high winds. Well-managed utility companies engage in special maintenance drives in advance of each hurricane season, removing vegetation from the vicinity of power cables and renewing the distribution system where necessary.

An exemplary international warning system for hurricanes and cyclones also mitigates the risk, coupled with good disaster preparedness systems in most countries that lie within the latitudes where hurricanes and cyclones develop. Measures of preparedness, evacuation procedures and advisories minimise loss of life. Income levels that are sufficient to cover premiums for insurance equivalent to the replacement value is the best way to mitigate the risk of loss of property. Where insurance is adequate, a hurricane may cause little permanent loss of potential income and growth, thanks to the funding for reconstruction that flows in from foreign reinsurers.

An important implication of these factors is that, for any particular peril, such as a hurricane, the resilience of a country depends very much on the general standard of living. For more affluent countries, where structures are built to high standards with appropriate materials and features, and where most property is adequately insured, there may well be little lasting economic loss. In contrast, countries with poorly constructed buildings, where few can afford insurance premiums, may require substantial foreign assistance to restore their prospects after a disaster.

The extent to which resilience is built into the infrastructure requires judgement. Caribbean building standards are set to withstand hurricanes rated in the second highest of five categories. In recent years hurricanes of higher intensities have become more frequent, prompting demands in some quarters for even higher standards. However, the cost and practicality of retrofits of a substantial proportion of homes and buildings should be weighed against the probability of the incidence of a hurricane of that intensity. Moreover, having buildings intact may serve little purpose if, as in the case of calamities in Dominica and Tuvalu in recent times, all communications are cut, and it is impossible to supply power, fuel, water, food and medicines, because roads, ports, airports and other infrastructure are too badly damaged.

More attention needs to be given, and financial resources allocated, to the stockpiling of emergency recovery supplies and equipment in strategic locations across regions and within island archipelagos. The model has been provided by the US, which now maintains such strategic stockpiles in large centres across the nation, with all the road-building and earth-moving equipment needed to get them to the scene of any disaster in the continental US. It is a model that might be imitated at a regional level in the Caribbean and South Pacific, and across island archipelagos in more remote countries. Delivering supplies to the scene of the disaster would be a challenge, but not an insurmountable one.

The nature of the risk also influences what it is sensible and practical to do by way of risk mitigation. Insurance, where it is offered, is the only one of the strategies discussed so far that is of any relevance in the case of tsunamis, earthquakes and volcanic eruptions. Similarly intractable are the risks of sea level rise. In 1995 a volcanic eruption in Montserrat – among the smallest islands in the Caribbean – destroyed the capital, Plymouth, and rendered uninhabitable the entire south of the island, more than half the land area. Two-thirds of the population was forced to migrate. Such is the stark reality of some small countries.

Small open economies vary greatly in the nature and magnitude of exposure to natural disasters and in the impact on their economies. The options their populations have to secure their future well-being also vary very widely. Risk mitigation strategies must of necessity be tailored to the circumstances and the realistic options. In some circumstances, a majority of the population may choose, or be forced, to migrate, as in the case of Montserrat. The populations of atolls like Kiribati in the Pacific, a country with a tiny population living on two island archipelagos four thousand kilometres apart (the distance from New York to Los Angeles), young people are obliged to emigrate in search of the best education and prospects for enjoying the benefits of a modern lifestyle. We should not suppose that a majority will choose to return to a domestic lifestyle devoid of the benefits of modern technology. Over time a majority of the population may choose to forsake the islands, a movement that will be accelerated by sea level rise.

In contrast to the Pacific, the Caribbean features no populated atolls. Even a low-lying island like Barbados is less susceptible to adverse effects of storms than is the island of Manhattan (New York), as recent weather events have shown. In October 2012 Sandy, a Category 1 hurricane, caused widespread damage in New York City, shutting down transport and communications, and resulting in at least 43 deaths and an estimated US$19 billion in damage. In 2021 Elsa, a Category 1 hurricane, caused minor damage and no injuries in Barbados. The impact of sea level rise is not a clear and present danger to Caribbean nations, in marked contrast to island nations in the Pacific and Indian Oceans.

Remoteness is another factor which distinguishes the Caribbean from countries in the Pacific. The travel distance between Caribbean islands is very short, and the region is within easy reach of ports and airports from which recovery efforts can be launched. No Caribbean country finds itself in a situation similar to that of Tuvalu in the wake of the tsunami that struck in January 2022, cutting communications for more than two weeks.

The extent and nature of risk mitigation strategies against natural disasters for small open economies must be tailored to the nature of the peril, the country's average income level and the country's geography. There is a mix of avoidance, emigration, insurance, investment in strengthening infrastructure and recovery and rehabilitation that is available to suit the circumstances in every case.

Diversification strategies for small open economies

The fact that small open economies do not have the resources to produce a wide range of products at internationally competitive prices does not in fact deny them the possibility of diversifying sources of foreign exchange to reduce risk. Small size may actually make diversification easier with savvy investment strategies. Unpublished data on the tourism industry in Barbados shows a breakdown of the average per capita income of UK visitors by each major metropolitan area and region from which visitors came. The study provided guidance for a marketing strategy which placed proportionately more emphasis on London and the south-east, the most affluent areas, and therefore those that might prove most resilient in a recession. Barbados has three main sources of visitors, the UK, the US and Canada, which might make for greater resilience than tourist destinations that depend mainly on just one of the three. Then again, it might not. The US is so large, so rich and so diverse that destination countries can diversify within the US itself. In fact, the possibilities of diversifying the markets in which they sell internationally competitive goods are so many that there is a real danger of over-reach, if the exporters and tourism providers in small countries do not target strategically to optimise the use of available marketing resources.

Strategies that improve their share of international markets by adding value and variety to the product are an additional source of resilience to adverse market shocks. Worrell (2021) shows that Caribbean tourist destinations have maintained their share of international markets in large part because of such strategies. The market for premium spirits has opened new export revenue streams for Guatemala, Puerto Rico, Guyana, Jamaica, Barbados and several other countries of Central America and the Caribbean, through international marketing of premium rums. Mauritius has been even more successful in transforming its sugar industry, developing a wide range of output products for export to ensure the industry's continuing viability.

There are limited practical opportunities for small open economies to open entirely new sources of foreign exchange. For countries which have the advantage of geography, it may be possible to partner with international companies to develop large-scale transportation services by expansion or development of ports and airports. In Kingston, Jamaica, one of the world's finest natural harbours, a new trans-shipment hub has been developed to attract business from ships exiting the Panama Canal, now that the capacity of the Canal has increased. Already companies in the eastern Caribbean are paying a premium to secure supplies from Asia-Pacific via Kingston, in preference to slower deliveries via Miami.

Migrants' remittances have become an important source of foreign exchange for many emerging market economies, large and small. As we have argued in Chapter 5, emigration should be seen in a positive light, so long as it is not motivated by social and political upheaval or personal insecurity in sending countries. Unfortunately, the failure of industrialised countries to devise and implement policies to address the redistributional consequences of technological change has led to widespread animosity and an unwillingness to welcome the low-skilled immigrants these countries need for agriculture and construction. However, small countries might consider the example of the Philippines, for example, and raise standards of education and skill in the population, with a relaxed attitude towards the emigration of skilled people, who gain acceptance more readily in the industrialised world.

When all the possibilities for diversification within activities in which they are internationally competitive are taken into account, the small open economy has possibilities sufficiently rich to provide it with capacity to weather shocks as well as larger economies. The concluding remarks of so many economic policy reports, that small economies should venture into entirely new activities where they would need to go up against established players, would seem to be unnecessary and a recipe for failure. One does not find any success stories among the countries in our sample of countries to lend confidence to this suggestion.

The preoccupation with debt relief and concessional lending to small open economies is misplaced

As we have argued elsewhere, there is never a shortage of international finance for projects in small open economies, provided they offer a competitive rate of return. Nor is there a shortfall in the supply of finance for infrastructure and public capital works for governments with good credit ratings. Such lending, efficiently employed, increases productive capacity and the competitiveness of the economy, providing the resources for servicing the debt. It follows that an unsustainable level of debt, one where servicing the debt fully would deplete the foreign reserve stock, is evidence of inefficiency in the deployment of borrowed funds. It is always preferable to solve the efficiency problem, maintain government's international credit-worthiness and service the debt fully in these circumstances. If the debt service has grown too large, it may be necessary to negotiate a restructuring plan, once concrete steps have been taken to initiate the necessary reform of the public sector. What is fatal, in this circumstance, is to restructure the debt without addressing the problem of public sector inefficiency, because the restructured debt will again prove excessive after an interval of a few years.

The argument for concessional lending hangs on a country's level of development, not on its size. Very poor countries do need an extra injection, by way of grants, lending at low interest rates and other support, to help eliminate absolute poverty and to provide sound primary education, universal preventative and curative health care, housing, water and sanitation and basic law and order, with security for all of society. Countries where these basics are already in place have no basis for insisting on special assistance. Requests for special consideration on the basis of size are egregious, especially when made by countries that are chronically unable to implement projects for which they already have funding.

Assuring small nations of fair treatment in international markets

It has proven very difficult to give voice to the circumstances, interests and perceptions of small countries in the counsels of the International Monetary Fund, the World Bank, the World Trade Organisation, the Organisation for Economic Cooperation and Development, the Bank for International Settlements, the Financial Stability Board and other institutions governing international commerce and finance. This failure results all too often in regulations and guidelines which are unfair, disadvantaging small economies and blocking pathways to their engagement in international commerce in ways that reflect their competitive advantage. It has also been a barrier to agreement between the International Monetary Fund and member countries over exchange rate policy and other aspects of macroeconomic policy. The recent recognition by economists at the IMF of the implications of the universal practice of pricing in US dollars is a case in point. For economists working on the management of small economies the fact of US dollar pricing of exports, traded services and international finance has always been taken for granted, and it has always been a feature of our economic modelling. The only surprise is that it has taken so long to realise this, on the part of the leadership of a key international organisation of which countries discussed in this book have been members for half a century.

Overcoming this blindness to the perspectives of small economies has proved more difficult than anyone expected. The first challenge was to gain recognition that the challenges of small economies warranted special attention, in the face of some scepticism in academic circles (for example, Rose, 2005). That challenge was overcome in the late 1990s and early 2000s with the establishment of working groups at the IMF and World Bank on small countries. These working groups did succeed in creating greater awareness of the importance of predictable exchange rates for avoiding financial instability, but they failed to highlight the centrality of fiscal policy, and policy prescriptions influenced by the work of these groups continued to follow the orthodoxy of exchange rate flexibility and active monetary policy to target inflation. What is more, participants in these working groups, including from small countries, shared some of the misapprehensions about supposed vulnerabilities and risk-mitigating strategies we discussed earlier in this chapter.

The more fundamental problem that emerges is the lack of independent thinking, relevant perspectives and a systematically developed research agenda, centred on the economic development of small states. Universities have been established everywhere except in the poorest and most remote countries, but only one, the University of Malta, has an institute devoted to the economies of small states. A promising early economic research programme at The University of the West Indies, in collaboration with McGill University (Montreal, Canada) produced a minor classic in Beckford (1972), but it faded from the scene in the late 1970s. A long-running research collaboration between the same university and the central banks of Caribbean Community members in which I was involved produced important insights which were summarised in Worrell and Bourne (1989). That survey of research, done under the aegis of the Caribbean Regional Programme of Monetary Studies, identified the distinguishing features of Caribbean economies, including the fact that tradables and nontradables react differently to economic stimuli. The research pointed to the balance of payments as the most vital indicator of the impact of external economic changes in small open economies. The central importance of government expenditure and its allocation and the design of the revenue system were recognised: macroeconomic equilibrium is achieved when the fiscal deficit is compatible with the excess supply of finance in the private sector, and the financial sector adjusts to the public sector borrowing requirement and the demand and supply of foreign exchange. Already it was clear that the money supply is endogenous in Caribbean economies; that imported prices were the dominant source of inflation; that sustained growth was always export-led; that imports were elastic to income but inelastic to relative prices; and that devaluation is inflationary in small open economies. Sadly, this research programme no longer exists.

The need for an influential programme of economic research on economic development and macroeconomic policy in the small open economy is essential if these countries are to make use of the opportunities that they have and can create in order to make their case in the deliberations of international institutions.

The only opportunity that small nations have to expose the inequities which they face in international markets is by way of thoroughly-researched, data-driven studies which will command attention in the deliberations of the international institutions of which they are members. Cleverly crafted speeches will gain attention, but only so long as they are parroting the ruling orthodoxy; that is unhelpful when the orthodoxy challenges your own interests. Small open economies may command attention for effective policy strategies for their sustainable development only by the content of their message, when they have the opportunity to represent their interests at international fora. Economic research programmes which equip policy makers with data-driven analysis that faithfully reflects their economic structures, circumstances and interests is essential to equip the policy maker with persuasive presentations of what matters for their countries' development.

Notes

1 Islands & Small States Institute: L-Università ta' Malta (um.edu.mt).
2 From a theoretical point of view, the optimal level of foreign reserves is that level which equates the capital formation forgone by holding reserves, with the cost of income volatility from exchange market pressure (Worrell 1976). By this criterion, most countries hold excessive reserves.
3 Most studies are also flawed empirically, because they employ a trade weighted combination of consumer prices and exchange rates, which does not measure the true relationship between the relative prices of domestic and foreign production.

References

Agénor, Pierre-Richard. 2004. *Economics of Adjustment and Growth*. Cambridge, MA: Harvard University Press.

Aizenman, Joshua, Menzie Chinn and Hiro Ito. 2010. "The financial crisis, rethinking of the global financial architecture, and the trilemma." *Working Paper*. Asia Development Bank Institute. no. 213, 19 April.

Aizenman, Joshua, Michael Hutchison and Ilan Noy. 2008. "Inflation targeting and real exchange rates in emerging markets." *Working Paper*. National Bureau of Economic Research, no. w14561, December.

Aloy, Marcel, Blanca Moreno-Dodson and Gilles Nancy. 2008. "Intertemporal adjustment and fiscal policy under a fixed exchange rate regime." *Policy Research Working Paper*. Washington, DC: The World Bank, April.

Aslund, Anders. 2012. "Southern Europe ignores the lessons from Latvia at its peril." *Policy Brief*. Washington, DC: Peterson Institute for International Economics, no. 17, April.

Aslund, Anders. 2011a. "Post crisis – what Europe can learn from the Baltic states." *Policy Brief*. Washington, DC: Peterson Institute for International Economics, no. 6, 16 FEbruary.

Aslund, Anders. 2011b. "Lessons from the East European financial crisis, 2008–10." *Policy Brief*. Washington, DC: Peterson Institute for International Economics, 22 June.

Atlins, J., S. Mazzi and C Easter. 2000. "Commonwealth vulnerability index for developing countries: the position of small states." *Economic Paper*, no. 40. London: Commonwealth Secretariat.

Beckford, George L. 1972. *Persistent Poverty: Underdevelopment in Plantation Economies of the Third World.* Oxford, UK: Oxford University Press.
Berg, Andrew, Christopher Jarvis, Mark Stone and Alessandro Zanello. 2003. "Re-establishing credible nominal anchors after a financial crisis: a review of recent literature." *Working Paper.* International Monetary Fund, no. 03/76, April.
Bjørnland, Hilde C. 2008. "Monetary policy and exchange rate interactions in a small open economy." *Scandanavian Journal of Economics,* Vol. 110, no. 1, pp. 197–221.
Blanchard, Olivier, G. Della'Arricia and Paolo Mauro. 2010. "Rethinking macroeconomic policy." *Staff Position Note.* International Monetary Fund, 10 February.
Boehm, Hjalmamr and Michael Funke. 2001. "Does the nominal exchange rate regime matter for investment?" *Working Paper Series.* Center for Economic Studies and Ifo Institute for Economic Research, no. 578, October.
Briguglio, Lino. 1995. "Small island developing states and their vulnerabilities." *World Development,* Vol. 2, no. r 9, pp. 1615–1632.
Briguglio, Lino, Gordon Cordina, Nadia Farrugia and Stephanie Vella. 2006. "Conceptualising and measuring economic resilience," in *Building the Economic Resilience of Small States,* edited by Briguglio, Lino, Gordon Cordina and Eliawony J. Kisanga. Malta and London: University of Malta and Commonwealth Secretariat.
Buiter, Willem, Giancarlo Corsetti and Paolo Pesenti. 1998. "Interpreting the ERM crisis: country-specific and systemic issues." *Princeton Study in International Finance,* March.
Burstein, Ariel, Martin Eichenbaum and Sergio Rebelo. 2004. "Large devaluation and the real exchange rate." *Festschrift in honor of Guillermo Calvo,* International Monetary Fund, April 15–16.
Calvo, G. and C. Vegh. 1995. "Fighting inflation with high interest rates: The Small open economy case under flexible prices." *Journal of Money Credit and Banking,* Vol. 27, no. 1, February.
Carter, Adrian. 1997. "Economic size, openness and export diversification: a statistical analysis ." *Economic Review.* Central Bank of Barbados, December.
Cottarelli, Carlo and Curzio Giannini. 1997. *Credibility without Rules? Monetary Frameworks in the Post-Bretton Woods Era.* Washington, DC: International Monetary Fund.
della Paolera, Gerardo and Alan Taylor. 2001. *Straining at the Anchor: The Argentine Currency Board and the Search for Macroeconomic Stability, 1880–1935.* Chicago: University of Chicago Press.
Dornbusch, Rudiger. 2001. "Fewer monies, better monies." *American Economic Review,* Vol.91, no. 2, pp. 238–242.
Dornbusch, Rudiger. 1988. "Overvaluation and trade balance," in *The Open Economy: Tools for Policy Makers in Developing Countries,* edited by Dornbusch, Rudiger and Leslie Helmers. Oxford: Oxford University Press for the World Bank.
Farhi, Emmanuel, Gita Gopinath and Oleg Itskhoki. 2011. "Fiscal devaluations." *Working Paper Series.* National Bureau of Economic Research, no. w17662, December.
Frankel, Jeffrey A. 2010. "Monetary policy in emerging markets: A survey." *Working Paper Series.* National Bureau of Economic Research, Vol. w16125.
Gali, Jordi and Tommaso Monacelli. 2002. "Monetary policy and exchange rate volatility in a small open economy." *Working Paper Series.* National Bureau of Economic Research, no. w8905, April.

Galstyan, Vahagn and Lane, Philip R. 2008. "The composition of government spending and the real exchange rate." *Discussion Paper*. Centre for Economic Policy Research, no. DP6903, July.

Guender, Alfred. 2006. "Stabilising properties of discretionary monetary policy in a small open economy." *The Economic Journal*, Vol. 116, no. 508, January.

Harberger, Arnold. 2004. "The real exchange rate: issues of concept and measurement." International Monetary Fund Conference in Honour of Michael Mussa, 4–5 June.

Leiderman, Leonardo. 2003. "Inflation targeting: lessons from experience." *International Monetary Fund Survey*, Vol. 32, no. 2, February.

Lindbeck, A., P. Arestis and M. Sawyer. 1998. "Policy forum: New Keynsian economic policies." *Economic Journal*, Vol. 108, no. 446, January.

Marsh, Ian and S. Tokarick. 1994. "Competitiveness indicators: A theoretical and empirical assessment." *Working Paper*. International Monetary Fund, March.

McIntyre, Arnold. 1995. *Trade and Economic Development in Small Open Economies: The Case of the Caribbean Countries*. New York: Praeger.

Ostry, Jonathan, Atish Ghosh and Marcos Chamon. 2012. "Two targets, two instruments: Monetary and exchange market policies in emerging market countries." *Policy Paper*. International Monetary Fund, February.

Parrado, Eric. 2004. "Singapore's unique monetary policy: How does it work?" *Working Paper*. International Monetary Fund, no. 10, January.

Parrado, Eric and Andres Velasco. 2002. "Optimal interest rate policy in a small open economy." *Working Paper*. National Bureau of Economic Research, no. w8721, January.

Pindyck, Robert. 1991. "Irreversibility, uncertainty, and investment." *Journal of Economic Literature*, Vol. XXIX, no. 3, September.

Pindyck, Robert and Andrés Solimano. 1993. "Economic instability and aggregate investment." *Working Paper*. National Bureau of Economic Research, no. 4380, June.

Rose, Andrew. 2005. "Size really doesn't matter: In search of a national scale effect." *Discussion Paper Centre for Economic Policy Research*, no. 5350, November.

Schaechter, Andrea, Mark Stone and Mark Zelmer. 2000. "A practical guide to the adoption of inflation targeting by emerging market countries." *Occasional Paper*. International Monetary Fund, no. 202.

Schnabl, Gunther. 2007. "Exchange rate volatility and growth in emerging Europe and East Asia." *Working Paper Series*. Center for Economic Studies and Ifo Institute for Economic Research, no. 2023, June.

Tas, Bedri KamilOnur and Togay Selahattin. 2011. Effect of Official Dollarization on a Small Open Economy: Ecuador. https://papers.ssrn.com/sol3/papers.cfm?abstract_id=1955949.

United Nations Committee on Development Policy. 2005. Report on the Seventh Session, March 14–18. New York: United Nations.

Uribe, Martin. 2002. "Real exchange rate targeting and macroeconomic instability." *Working Paper*. National Bureau of Economic Research, no w9294, October.

Worrell, DeLisle. 2021. "The Caribbean holds its own in global tourism competition." in *Handbook of Caribbean Economies*, edited by Robert Looney. Abingdon: Routledge.

Worrell, DeLisle. 2013. "Exchange rate targetting through aggregate demand management." *Working Paper*. Central Bank of Barbados, February.

Worrell, DeLisle. 2012. "Policies for stabilisation and growth in small very open economies." *Occasional Paper*. Group of 30, no. 85.

Worrell, DeLisle. 2000. "Monetary and fiscal coordination in small open economies." *Working Paper*. International Monetary Fund, no. 56, March.

Worrell, DeLisle. 1997. "Bank behaviour and monetary policy in small open economies with reference to the Caribbean." *Social and Economic Studies*, Vol. 46, nos. 2&3, October.

Worrell, DeLisle. 1992. *Economic Policies in Small Open Economies: Prospects for the Caribbean*. London: Commonwealth Secretariat.

Worrell, DeLisle. 1976. "The theory of optimal foreign exchange reserves in a developing country." *Social and Economic Studies*, Vol. 25, no. 3, pp. 259–279.

Worrell, DeLisle and Compton Bourne (eds). 1989. *Economic Adjustment Policies for Small Nations: Theory and Experience in the English-speaking Caribbean*. New York: Praeger Publishers.

Worrell, DeLisle, Roland Craigwell and Travis Mitchell. 2008. "A small foreign exchange market with a long-term peg – Barbados," *Applied Financial Economics*, Vol. 18, no. 8, pp. 673–682.

Worrell, DeLisle, Kevin Greenidge and Shane Lowe. 2013. "Competitiveness in the Caribbean and Central America." *Working Paper*. Central Bank of Barbados.

14 What's Wrong with Economics? The Limits of Economic Theory and Practice

Economic policy makers have the difficult task of designing policies that will improve the material well-being of the population, using very approximate and incomplete measures of well-being and how it is distributed, weak or questionable data on many crucial aspects of the economy, such as the GDP, inflation and the balance of external payments, and a variety of interests and opinion about the workings of the economy. Moreover, the tools at their disposal are limited in number and slow to reach their maximum impact. The links between policy initiatives and outcomes are often of uncertain scope and magnitude. Our book makes the case that successful strategies for sustainable development of the SOE are always accessible (except in countries where there is armed conflict or widespread insecurity), provided policy makers are fully informed about the limits of the discipline of economics and the limitations of the tools at their disposal, and provided they employ a suitable model and policy framework. This chapter covers the difficulties of measuring GDP, inflation, unemployment and the many other variables which are commonplace in economic discussion; the nature of causality and the basis for forecasting; why economic propositions are not "scientific" as that term is commonly understood; the archaic and unhelpful grounding of economics in equilibrium physics; the fact that few if any of the usual guidelines for economic policy have any foundation in theory; and the fact that the outcomes of any and all policies depend on the largely unpredictable responses of everyone who is affected by the policy. The key to successful policy making under these circumstances is to be fully aware of all the limitations of theory, measurement, causality and impact, and to design economic strategy accordingly.

False concreteness in economics: measurement, causality, forecasts

Failure to recognise the flaws in measurement of economic quantities and variables lends a damaging sense of concreteness to economic analysis. Variables used in economic analysis are usually simplified or aggregated approximations of the "true" variables; also, economic variables are time-bound, and observations are never independent or randomly selected. For example,

DOI: 10.4324/9781003247609-17

this year's income is always related to last year's, and the time period over which the income is measured matters for the analysis: monthly, quarterly and annual income show different levels and behaviour, and financial and calendar years may differ. Furthermore, for economic development which shows up over the long period, multi-year periods should be used for the analysis.

GDP is a made-up concept

Gross Domestic Product (GDP) is the measure that is used to describe the total value of the goods and services produced in the economy, and is perhaps the most widely quoted statistic in economics. It will therefore come as a shock to be informed that "GDP is a made-up entity ... an abstract statistic derived in extremely complicated ways, yet one that has tremendous importance" (Coyle, 2014, p. 5), and that

> The community of national statisticians with a command of all this detail is small. In other words, very few people indeed truly understand how the regularly published GDP figures are constructed – this includes many of the economists who comment on GDP.
>
> (Coyle, 2014, p. 25)

What is more, the GDP is not a very good measure of what it purports to describe: "It is a measure designed for the twentieth century economy of physical mass production, not for the modern economy of rapid innovation and intangible, increasingly digital, services" (Coyle, 2014, p. 6). In this short, readable and often entertaining book, Dr Diane Coyle, Visiting Research Fellow at Oxford University and an authority on the subject, explains that GDP is a relatively recent concept, which dates from the post-WWII period. Richard Stone and Professor James Meade published the first modern GDP in 1941, for the UK. The first UN System of National Accounts dates from 1953, and as recently as 1985 there were only 60 countries in the world for which GDP estimates were regularly published.

Dr Coyle explains why GDP is such an elusive concept. The GDP purports to be a measure of the value of all goods and services produced in the economy, less the value of all intermediate goods and services used in the production of this final output. A difficulty immediately arises with the valuation of services. In Adam Smith's view, services were a cost to the economy, and added no value. Under the system of social accounts used by the USSR up until the breakup of the Soviet Union, services were not counted as "productive output". Even under the UN system which is now almost universally employed, there are services which are added to the total of output which are arguably inputs to production and should therefore be subtracted from the total, such as the provision of sanitation services. The logic is that the provision of sanitation services does not provide a benefit in and of itself, but is among the inputs which facilitate the provision of useful goods and services.

An intractable problem with services in GDP is the measurement of a unit of service, as opposed the price of that unit. In the case of physical goods, we can measure the actual number of shirts or cans of soup produced; for services measures of actual output are harder to come by. This is especially true of financial services and government services, though the problem arises with all services. For services such as education and health, there are measures such as scholastic achievement and health indicators, but they are all complex and it is difficult to attribute outcomes to the delivery of particular services. What is more, the data requirements for applying these measures to all transactions are so demanding that few countries actually employ them. The measurement of the value of financial transactions is even more problematic: in principle financial institutions add value by managing risk, but what best measures that value added is a matter of debate. Dr Coyle believes that the value of financial services in the national accounts may be overstated by as much as a quarter, based on the current definitions of the UN System of National Accounts.

In order to arrive at a measure of changes in the real value of goods and services produced, market values have to be adjusted for inflation. Inflation adjustment is complicated and there are many ways of doing it, all producing different results. Among the complications are the weights attributed to various items in the basket of expenditures used to compute inflation. The computation of a good weighting system involves carefully designed census and survey data collection, informed choices of a base year, allowances for technology changes and new products, and other analytical challenges. A poorly informed weighting system can lead to very large errors: Ghana's GDP increased overnight by 60 per cent when it updated the weights used in the price deflator between November 5 and 6, 2010. Developed countries mostly use chain-weighted deflators that change month by month, but then the expenditure components don't add up to the total. The UK secured an IMF loan in 1976, but much later (in the 1980s) when the GDP and borrowing data were revised, it was discovered that there had been no crisis in 1976 after all!

The GDP excludes goods and services which are produced and consumed within the household, and goods and services which are traded on informal markets, both of which are known to be substantial. The problem with this procedure is often illustrated by the hypothetical case of the widower who marries his housekeeper and ceases to pay her a wage, thereby *reducing* the GDP. Household production is excluded because of the impracticality of collecting the data. Informal markets create a similar problem of access to data for reliable estimates. Estimates of the size of the informal economy vary widely across countries: Dr Coyle cites estimates of seven per cent for the US, eight per cent for Switzerland, 20 per cent for Italy and 25 per cent for Greece, all in 2012. What is more, formal production and government production are measured differently. In his Nobel Memorial Lecture on 8 December 1984, Sir Richard Stone, one of the originators of the GDP measure commented "This treatment, whereby commercial products are valued at market price, government services are valued at cost and unpaid household activities are simply ignored, is not a matter of principle but of practical convenience" (quoted in Coyle, 2014, p. 105).

The comparison of GDP across countries gives rise to another set of complications, which have recently surfaced in international media, in the discussion as to whether China is about to become the largest economy in the world. If we measure GDP in all the national currencies of the world and convert them at current exchange rates for the US dollar, as is often done, you reach the conclusion that GDP declines by the amount of any local currency devaluation, even if the actual amount of domestic production and the prices in local currency remain unchanged. That is obviously misleading. To get around the problem, statisticians have devised measures of the purchasing power of local currencies, based on global surveys of what the local money will buy. The GDP values in US dollars are adjusted to reflect these differences in purchasing power. For example, in 2012 Trinidad and Tobago's per capita GDP of US$17,500 was only just ahead of Barbados' US$15,000, but because the TT dollar goes so much further in Trinidad, their per capita income in terms of purchasing power parity (PPP) was much higher, at US $29,000, compared to Barbados' PPP of US$15,000, according to the Human Development Report. The PPP calculations are complex and highly controversial, however. The government of China refuses to accept the validity of the UN's most recent estimates because they indicate that China is already the world's largest economy.

There is a host of other complexities and compromises in the compilation of GDP: how do we establish the real value of services which are not bought and sold on open markets? How should we value those that are sold on markets where prices are dictated by a few dominant producers? How can we take account of and measure productivity changes? How do we distinguish between changes in value which reflect changes in quality, rather than price inflation? Is it acceptable to ignore public goods which are not marketed, and public "bads" such as environmental degradation? How should we treat complementary products and services, such as the organisational changes needed to realise the potential productivity gains from the use of new technology? How should technological change be accounted for?

Dr Coyle concludes that at present we have no alternative to the GDP that is generally available for comparison among countries globally. Because of its deficiencies, wherever possible we should use supplementary measures or alternatives: the Human Development Index, "dashboards" of composite measures, and measures of household value added and the informal economy. No good measure of environmental sustainability is available, and conclusions drawn from GDP and supplementary measures need to be evaluated with this in mind. The collection of statistics needs to be modernised to take advantage of real time data; the periodic surveys on which the GDP estimates are now based cannot keep up with the changes in economic structure. Dr Coyle argues that GDP definitions have become too convoluted, complicated and their "accuracy is spurious" (Coyle, 2014, p. 139). A radical rethinking of what is meant by "the economy" is needed: today's economy is largely intangible, and quality, choice and variety are the essence of value added. In addition, we need to account for voluntary value creation, such as the creation of the online encyclopedia Wikipedia and the open systems software Linux. Dr Coyle observes that the gap between GDP and social welfare is larger than ever. The evidence is the marked difference between reported success of adjustment programmes in many countries, and the sentiment of the affected populations, who see no improvement in their livelihoods or prospects.

Causality in economics is an elusive concept, difficult to model and measure

The notion that a policy action or a change in economic variables have more or less predictable results is the basis of all modelling and the unstated assumption of all policy. On closer examination, however, it proves very challenging to establish and measure cause and effect in econometric practice. The essence of the challenge is to devise a model that explains how an action – an interest rate increase, let us say – will affect the level of credit in the economy, and then finding a way to test whether our model is a sufficiently reliable representation, and if so, what is the magnitude of the credit adjustment that results from any interest rate change. Our test will use recent historical data. Over that time factors other than interest rates will have affected credit: the growth of the economy, the extent of competition in the banking industry, the existence of other credit sources, the importance of informal channels of credit, inflation, changes in the property market, foreign investment, and a multitude of other factors. How do we distinguish the impact of credit changes from these other factors, and how do we decide which factors are not really that important and can be omitted? How can we be sure that we have thought of all the possible influences? Assuming that our test does throw up an apparent association between the interest rate and the level of credit, how can we be sure that this is not the result of some other fact that is influencing both variables, and how do we know which is cause and which is effect?

There is no settled consensus among econometricians about how to proceed under these circumstances. The only thing that seems to be agreed is that there is no guiding precept: there are no laws in economics in the sense of scientific laws that cannot be broken, and economists do not interpret or use "laws" in that way. There is merit in alternative approaches to modelling, and the case has been made that historical narrative should be given equal weight to econometric tests in explaining economic processes. Morck and Yeung (2011) observe that economics and history both strive to understand causation, economics using instrumental variables and history by weighing the plausibility of alternative narratives. Instrumental variables can lose value with repeated use; each successful use of an instrument may create a bias for all other uses of that instrument – past and future. Economists should therefore consider historians' approach to inferring causality from detailed context, and they should assess the plausibility of alternative narratives, and its consistency with the economic context beyond the issue being investigated. We need also to bear in mind that free will makes human decisions intrinsically exogenous. Others propose a notion of causal structure that goes beyond the probabilistic association which is the foundation of econometric testing. Pearl (2000) observes that a causal machinery underlies and propels our understanding of the world, even for things about we have a limited understanding; he is a leader in the graph theoretical approach to causal analysis.

Prominent among econometricians Hendry has proposed an influential approach that attempts to find the model that yields the best explanation of cause and effect by starting with the most general specification and using an automated process to reduce it to the so-called "specific" model that gives the most plausible results (see Campos, Ericsson and Hendry, 2005; Clements and Hendry, 2003, 2005; Doornik and Hendry, 2007; and Hendry, 1995). Hendry explains that model selection theory poses great difficulties: all statistics for selecting models and evaluating their specifications have distributions, usually interdependent, and possibly altered by every modelling decision. General-to-specific (*Gets*) modelling mimics reduction by simplifying a congruent general unrestricted model (GUM) to a dominant minimal representation. Computer automation of selection algorithms have revealed high success rates, and allows operational studies of alternative strategies. Hendry's *Autometrics* allows performance across different states of nature (unknown to the empirical investigator) to be considered. The consistency of its selection procedure, and the extent to which model selection is non-distortionary at relevant sample sizes can be examined, as well as collinear data problems, simultaneous systems modelling, and tests for, and modelling of, non-linearity and invariance.

Hoover (2001) argues for the "structural approach" to causality, based on a notion that cause can be established by a block-recursive ordering of equations, where a variable estimated in the first equation is used, along with other variables, to estimate a second variable, which in turn helps to estimate a third variable, and so on. He argues that while no economic model can be used to build a realistic economic system, parts of a model may mimic parts of real systems vaguely and qualitatively. He suggests building empirical models using intuition and interpreting results by analogy.

Official targets for public sector finance and foreign reserves serve different purposes than forecasts of economic outcomes[1]

Government announcements of targets for levels of foreign reserves, the public sector deficit and government-financed projects reassure individuals and companies about government's ability to manage the exchange rate and ensure that domestic inflation remains in line with international inflation. Announcement of a growth target which is in line with the expectations of the private sector and consistent with the country's international competitiveness may also reassure the private sector about the consistency of public policy with the production plans of businesses and the expenditure plans of households. In contrast, economic forecasts are useful only to policy makers in the public sector and in business, and for academic and policy research purposes. The targets are earnest of government's intentions to keep the economy stable and to maintain a fiscal programme which is compatible with, and consistent with private sector intentions and expectations. The forecasts, on the other hand, are the baselines that the public sector and private firms use to plan their budgets and expenditures, and which they review monthly and quarterly to guide policy changes that need to be made in order to stay on target. Anything that the public sector announces as a target must be something that is within government's competence to attain, otherwise government loses credibility. Persistent failure to reach targets undermines the effectiveness of all government policy because the private sector cannot base its plans and expectations on the announced targets. It is for this reason that most governments do themselves no favours by announcing targets for growth and inflation; few governments have the ability to ensure they hit the announced target, irrespective of the expected level of aggregate spending, foreign direct investment, the value of domestic currency, international commodity prices and a host of other factors. Instead, it makes sense to write alternative scenarios under different assumptions for internal policy use. The policy maker, whether in the private or public sector, then uses these scenarios to evaluate where they are in relation to announced targets and budgets for revenue and spending.

Developing the forecasts on which scenarios may be constructed is a mind-numbingly complex business with which even experienced specialists struggle. The complexities include challenges of model selection, model specification (whether to use values, changes, logarithms, second and higher derivatives), model structure (individual relationships or combinations, incorporating feedback effects), completeness and excluded variables (no model can include all the possible influences, so we need a method of determining which are most necessary), data selection (finding series that are as close as possible to what is needed), periodicity (hourly, daily, quarterly, annual or even longer intervals), statistical inference (how well does the actual data fit what our model led us to expect) and what weight should be placed on intuition and experience. We can do no more than give a flavour of what continues to be a rapidly evolving field: "Practices used to address economic forecasting problems have undergone substantial changes over recent years" (Elliott and Timmermann, 2016), and access to "big data" (instantaneous statistics generated by internet activity) opens new opportunities and poses new challenges.

> Forecasting involves an underlying conceptualization of probability. It is this that gives sense to the notion of precision in number that makes us think of economic forecasting as more than simply complicated guesswork. We think of it as well-founded statement, a science and not an art of numbers. However, this understanding is at odds with the nature of social reality and the attributes of the forecaster. We should think differently about how we both anticipate and make the future and what this means. Foresight is perhaps a more appropriate term.
>
> (Morgan, 2012)

Morgan adds a necessary caution:

> Forecasting tends to forget that it is conjecture and what that really means. Its scientism overburdens how it is articulated and how it is perceived. We tend to think of forecasting as degrees of precision in prediction and of successful prediction as successful description of phenomena at some future point.

Clements and Hendry (1998) is a tour de force on the forecasting of economic times series, treating with the sources of "error" (the difference between the actual values of the variable and the value thrown up by the estimating model) in forecasting. They include non-constancy (the possibility that the nature of the relationship changes over time); misspecification (including variables for which there is no justification, excluding essential variables), parameter uncertainty (the estimate does not serve to pin down the nature of the relationship); and measurement error (economic variables can seldom be precisely defined). The book is devoted to providing suggestions for narrowing the range within which the forecast should lie with a reasonable degree of confidence. It provides a theoretical foundation for modifying the forecast values to incorporate discrete changes that are known to have occurred, or can be detected from the data. The authors warn that including these "structural breaks" may come at the cost of a wider range within which the forecast can be confidently expected to lie.

A bewildering range of approaches and models is available; my preference, reflected in the model described in Chapter 12, is for an approach which is rich in data, and flexible enough to incorporate informed experience, qualitative information, intuition and inputs from sub-models, but which avoids statistical sophistication in favour of simple intuitive relationships between variables. Examples of alternatives that might be used to complement this approach would include Christoffel, Phillip, Coenen and Warne (2008), who show how a model using Bayesian inference (an approach which makes inferences from a theoretical model) is used to do forecasting and policy analysis for the euro area. Bardsen, Jonasson, Nymoen, and den Reijer (2011) describe an aggregate econometric model for Sweden, estimated on quarterly data, and intended for short-term forecasting and policy simulations. The range of approaches and models discussed in Diebold (1998) includes stochastic forecasts (those based on estimates derived from relationships between economic variables) of various kinds, as well as models which are calibrated, that is, the values of relationships between variables are supplied to the model.

Worrell and Craigwell (1997) provided a survey of the state of the art in the Caribbean towards the end of the last century:

> Inevitably, the papers [in this compendium] offer no more than a glimpse of the economic processes at work and their policy implications. Even the most modern of econometric techniques gives definitive results only in limited circumstances. For example, cointegration procedures, which offer reliable results from serially correlated variables in certain cases, have been developed only for single equation models. A promising effort in this volume to address non-stationarity in multi-equation models shows clearly the difficulties that remain and the compromises that have to be made.
>
> Further, even with single equations the conceptual foundations of best practice are controversial. Indeed economists are today increasingly suggesting that the popular "causality" test attributed to Granger is based on a notion of causality which is rejected by many philosophers. Because of this uncertainty economists are extremely cautious about using the results of these tests as a guide for policy, especially when the results violate our priors.
>
> The picture is further clouded by the extent of aggregation used in empirical work, the simplification of economic processes to reduce the analysis to a manageable number of variables, the difficulty of finding close proxies for many variables and the weakness of some data.
>
> (Worrell and Craigwell, 1997, pp 1, 2)

The definition and measurement of economic variables is a process fraught with difficulty

The variables used in economic analysis are abstract entities, and it is challenging to find actual data that correspond to them. The problems are many. You have to choose the time when you measure, and the period which each observation in the series should cover: should it be daily, weekly, monthly, annually or even longer, and should you use data for a particular day (month-end) or the total for the month? Why does the cut-off point for an observation need to correspond to a calendar period? It is never self-evident what data is to be collected, and how it is to be aggregated. Which prices should we choose to measure the world price of oil, for example, a number which is quoted in the news every day? How can we be sure that the number being quoted is the "correct" one? What do we mean by a "market", an "economy" or an "industry"? We also need to know who collects the data, what data they collect and how often, and what they report to us of what they do collect. Do they collect all the data from everyone, as in a census, or do they survey a sample of the population to make inferences about the entire population? How is the data aggregated? How should we add apples and oranges? Which is the best method of averaging, linear or exponential, and should we use means, medians or the mode? How should we define the relationship between variables such as wealth, of which there is a certain amount at any point in time, and variables such as income, which accrues over time, resembling a flow rather than a stock at any particular moment? How should relationships between variables be most usefully represented – in levels, changes or in logarithms?

The time period over which each observation of each variable is measured matters

A basic problem of all empirical work in the social sciences is that we deal with processes that evolve continuously over time, whereas our analysis is based on a series of individual observations, each relating to a discrete period of time. There is an ongoing stream of goods and services being produced in the economy every working day in waves which rise and fall with seasonal patterns, major festivities and sales events and a variety of market influences. The things that interrupt this pattern do not happen on 31 December each year, or at any other fixed time, hourly, daily, monthly, quarterly of annually. Imposing arbitrary segmentation methods on this continuous stream has been necessary for our understanding of economic processes, at least until the advent of "Big Data", about which we will make a brief comment later, and it is still the case for all that we do in the realm of economic policy making. The periodicity we choose for the analysis is dependent on the questions we are trying to answer, as we have shown in Chapter 12. For the five-year forecast of GDP we will want to use annual data, while for the purposes of fiscal, monetary and exchange rate policy we need to use quarterly data. We must then use ad hoc techniques to ensure that the quarterly forecast sits within parameters that correspond to the five-year forecast. Also in Chapter 12 we touched on the need to incorporate into the five-year forecast the limits to productive capacity resulting from investment, a variable for which we need periods of observation that are more than one year.

Careful econometricians understand and respect the need to use appropriate observation periods that suit the purposes of the investigation. Sadly, however, the general practice in policy making circles too often falls short in this regard, and we all need to be on guard for five-year forecasts derived from quarterly or monthly models, of claims that twelve years of quarterly observations represents a larger data set than 12 years of annual observations of the same variable, and of carelessness about the consistency between estimates and forecasts of the same variable at different periodicities. We also need to pay careful attention to how well the estimates fit the actual observations, and the margins within which we can be reasonably confident about the forecasts.

It is never self-evident what data is to be collected and aggregated

This issue is best understood by way of illustration. What data should be used to report on the international price of petroleum? The price often quoted is the Brent Crude Oil Continuous Contract price, the name given to a light crude oil made from a blend from 19 fields in the North Sea, but there are two other main benchmarks, the West Texas Intermediate from North America and Dubai Crude Oil from the Persian Gulf. These prices are only loosely connected to the price any electricity producer or other user actually pays for oil on any given day, however. The quoted oil prices fluctuate with the purchases and sales of oil contracts by speculators betting on future price moves, and hedge funds who are taking bets, up to certain limits, that the speculators have got it wrong. This continuous trading activity accounts for the rapid response of oil prices to news of disruptions, decisions of the Organisation of Petroleum Exporting Countries, and other events. However, most users buy oil on term contracts, and they may also have insurance against price increases above a certain percentage for the term of the contract, so the prices actually paid by individual users will vary from the quoted international price. It may still be useful to use one of the three available "international" prices in many contexts, but care must be taken to ensure that this is in fact a good proxy for the price each estimation requires.

Problems of a different sort arise in the compilation and use of an index of consumer prices. Individual households buy different goods and services. Not everyone earns enough to buy a motor car, so cars may not be included in the list of things (what economists call a "basket") used to compile the index. However, everyone needs to travel, so bus fares or some other means of transport used by households of average income is preferred. In this context, the best "average" to use is the mode (the group that contains the largest number of persons) rather than the mean (the income of each group weighted by the number of people in each group), because rich people's incomes are so high that the mean always turns out to be higher than what most households earn. We still have more careful choices to make; within the most numerous group are households with widely differing tastes and preferences which influence what items they purchase (and therefore which items go into the index) as well as whether they buy better quality items at higher prices or are satisfied with lesser quality at lower prices. There is also the problem of new goods and services being introduced to the market, such as computers and internet services. Prices, to be useful, should be compiled quite frequently, which has meant, until very recently, it would not have been possible to collect price information on every item sold in the economy on any date; the usual practice is to conduct a monthly survey of carefully selected items which have been found by comprehensive investigation to be most typical of the consumption of the modal purchasing group, and to compare the prices with an identical list of items over time. There are several levels of aggregation, from the price of X brand of sardines to the price of tinned foods, to the sub-index for food, to the consumer price index. The resulting change in the consumer price index will not usually match the change in the amount any particular household pays for the items they buy monthly; the higher your income, the greater will be the discrepancy. At the other end of the spectrum, there is also a discrepancy between the consumer price index and the price increases any household experiences; the discrepancy will not usually be as large as for the more affluent, because the populations in the groups with the lowest incomes are far larger than the populations in the higher regions of the income distribution. With the advent of Big Data it is now possible to compile data on the prices of every transaction as soon as settlement for the payment is made. However, this poses a new problem of developing algorithms to process and compile the data in continuous time, and present it in a usable summary that looks something like the consumer price index.

An issue of a subtler kind arises in relation to what seems to be a more straightforward variable: the foreign reserves, the net of the public sector's holdings of liquid foreign assets and liquid foreign liabilities. These are mostly held by central banks, and may be read directly from the central bank's balance sheet. But what about liquid foreign assets public sector entities hold with commercial banks? Should they not be included as well? And what about Singapore, Hong Kong, Panama and other countries where there is no central bank and the foreign holdings are all with commercial banks? Logically it would seem that all public sector liquid balances (net of short liabilities) ought to be included. But in that case why take account of the liquid net foreign assets of the public sector, rather than the total net liquidity of the entire banking sector? We would argue that so long as timely action is taken to ensure that fiscal policy remains credible, the entire foreign liquidity position is available as a temporary stop-gap, until aggregate demand management cures the underlying cause of any drain on the foreign reserves. Surely it gives greater confidence to nervous financial managers in troubling circumstances to know that the determined efforts of their government are likely to be successful because of the availability of this additional pool of reserves.

The question of the definition of what is to be measured may be a consequential one, which can lead to error if it is not fully appreciated. I am confident there are many economists more knowledgeable about tax policy than myself who are, like me, puzzled by the sudden decision by a majority of nations in the international system to impose a uniform tax on corporate income, everywhere in the world. Such uniformity would imply that there could be an international understanding of what constitutes corporate net income, how that quantity, however it is defined, should be measured, how it is affected by prices, how to account for differential pricing, interest rates, exchange rates, and how would such a system be policed. There are also issues related to levels of government. In the US, individual states have autonomy with respect to exemptions and special conditions which provide loopholes which are routinely used to evade strictures with respect to money laundering, subsidies, and stipulations about company domicile, all of which are strictly enforced on small nations. We may expect that these loopholes will be used by states and provinces of large nations to avoid the universal corporate tax, in similar fashion, in the unlikely event that a way can be found to make such a tax operational.

Considerations of practicality and cost determine who collects what data and how often they do so

Frequently published data, such as monthly consumer prices and quarterly unemployment rates, are computed from surveys of small samples composed of individuals chosen more or less at random from among the population. Each sample should be sufficiently large that it includes an adequate number of individuals with every feature of the larger population to which the estimate is to be applied, in roughly the same proportions of the total population. These ideals are almost always beyond reach, and even when they are not, the experiences of the individuals in the sample may differ from the total of individuals in the total population because of personal reasons or factors affecting individual communities or regions (floods, power outages and such). Even the most carefully constructed surveys will throw up occasional anomalies in such circumstances. It is acceptable practice in these cases to use other available evidence to make a modification to the published data in order to avoid evident misinformation. This practice is often not followed. The unhelpful consequence of publishing data which is evidently incorrect may be illustrated by an incident that occurred during my tenure at the Central Bank of Barbados, when the Barbados Statistical Service in 2011 issued an estimate for employment which indicated that the public sector had shed about ten per cent of its workforce in a single quarter, at a time when there was no announced retrenchment activity. The sudden mysterious loss of 3,000 jobs became an instant nine days wonder, but there was little notice when those jobs were "reinstated" in the following quarter's report.

The best that most countries can afford with respect to collection of data for GDP is to conduct a completed census once every five years, or thereabouts. This may be accomplished by taking a census of a different sector (or several at a time) each year, in rotation. In between censuses annual and more frequent data is collected by use of surveys based on lists of operating companies which should be kept up to date.

The raw data must be aggregated in the way most suitable for the purpose to which it is being put

The individual items of data have to be combined to produce series of observations that are aggregated in ways that make them useable. We saw this in our discussion of the consumer price index, and it applies to all other economic variables. If we are using an average to represent the individual items of any series, we have to choose between the mean (the weighted average), the median (the observation which sits at the mid-point of the distribution) and the mode (the most numerous category, as we saw in the case of the consumer price index). If we are using means we must decide whether we would get better results from using arithmetic weights (each observation multiplied by the proportion of the sample that shared that particular value, all summed up), geometric weights (where the weighted observations are multiplied together instead of being added, and the total divided by the *n-th* root of the total number of observations) or some other basis.

There are other aggregation problems. In our discussion of the GDP we mentioned the need to ensure that inputs which are included in the final value of any product are not separately added in to the accounts. A similar caution applies to balances that one bank has with another and other interlinkages within the system, in computing the financial accounts. There is an "apples and oranges" adding up problem in computing the "real" GDP, the total of all goods and services in the economy, discounting any increases in prices. The standard practice is to use the actual dollar values and apply a discount factor, known as a deflator, equivalent to the price increase. But what price index should we use as our deflator? There are a number of approaches that may have to be used to find proxies for deflator, in the absence of producer price indices of other direct measures of real output.

The nation state is not the most useful way to define an economy

The economic relationships between communities are constrained by geographical, cultural and historical links, not by national boundaries. All other things being equal, communities that are separated by language, a history of open conflict, high mountain ranges and oceans or other large bodies of water will usually have less commerce between them than communities where such barriers do not exist. Equally, communities which are contiguous or which are linked by navigable rivers will enjoy greater commerce. Advancing technologies have opened new possibilities of overcoming these barriers to commerce internationally, but they have modified, rather than erased, the dominant influences previously mentioned. It remains the case that commerce across contiguous land borders is commonplace everywhere in the world in defiance of national boundaries, so long as there is no armed conflict that impedes it. Countries in the global south trade overwhelming with countries in the global north, thanks to transport and communications systems which have been developed over centuries. There is virtually no commerce between Spanish, French, Dutch and English-speaking islands in the Caribbean despite the fact that the islands are all within a short flight of each other.

Economic policy makers need to take these realities into consideration. To illustrate: the fortunes of the Barbadian economy are heavily affected by those of the country's larger neighbour, Trinidad and Tobago (see Chapter 3). Nationalistic concerns by some Barbadians about an influx of investment from oil-rich Trinidad and Tobago are misplaced; what matters is that the investment is for projects that increase the country's capacity for producing internationally competitive goods and services. On a somewhat larger scale, the Caribbean sits in the US currency area, by virtue of its geography, and the US dollar has been the international transactions currency and store of value for well over a century.

Recognition of the economic power of geography, language, cultural heritage and the investment in transport and communication infrastructure over many decades opens opportunities for future development and gives a clearer perspective on where new possibilities for competitive advantage might lie. The following examples serve to illustrate.

My late mother was an avid florist, and over 20 years ago I accompanied her and a team from Barbados to an international conference of floral arrangers in Wellington, New Zealand. In a tour of the North and South Islands of that nation, we discovered that they had developed a substantial new market for their tourist attractions by providing a comprehensive infrastructure of Japanese-language facilities and services, in hotels, on tour buses and at major attractions.

The Kingston harbour expansion, mentioned in Chapter 5, is a second illustration of an initiative which geography provides. The Panama Canal was built in the first decade of the twentieth century to provide a sea route between the east and west coasts of the US. In the decades since it has become one of only two funnels for swift bulk transit between Asia and the major industrial nations of the north Atlantic. The widening of the Canal to allow transit of much larger modern cargo ships was a major investment in enlarging its role in this commerce. The newly-enhanced Kingston port enables the Caribbean to open a small tap into this massive trade flow, to siphon off what is needed to satisfy the region's needs, more swiftly than is possible through Miami, the southernmost US port and the main redistribution for the Caribbean region and much of Latin America.

Another illustration of the possibilities offered by geography was mentioned in Chapter 13, when we discussed diversification strategies for the tourism industry, showing the potential which small countries have to reduce the risk of downturns in tourism activity by increasing their appeal to the wealthiest counties, communities and municipalities within the nations from which visitors come, without the cost and risk of investing in marketing to new destinations.

"Big Data" is a promise for the future, rather than a useful policy tool

All the current examples of the use of "Big Data" in economics remain curiosities, of little practical analytical or policy use. The power of the new technologies is that they permit us to observe and record economic production and economic transactions in continuous time, but we have no analytical tools to calibrate continuous data in a fashion similar to the way we do with discrete data. In order to frame the record in a way that allows us to retrieve it for economic analysis we need to record it as a series of discrete observations. With the tools now available we are able to extract very little information from the masses of data produced, that we can use to gain confirmation of any intuition we may want to test. The word puzzles that result from processing texts to highlight words used most frequently, and the record of internet "hits" are examples of outputs that tell us nothing other than the obvious.

Economics does not offer an objective theory of value

In a path-breaking book on the theory of value Mazzucato (2018) raises issues that are fundamental to all economic analysis. The discipline of economics purports to explain how value is exchanged in society. If I choose to sell my property, I expect to receive its fair value in exchange. If I go to work as a barista, a teacher or an office manager, I expect to be paid wages in exchange for the value of the work I do. If I am a nail technician, an attorney or an economic consultant, I charge fees in exchange for the services I provide. Economics is about what motivates these exchanges and what value results. *The Value of Everything*, the title of Professor Mazzucato's book, therefore lies at the heart of all economics.

Unlike meteorology, where there are independent, invariable measures of temperature, or physics, where there are invariable measures of length, economics has no independent, invariant measure of value. Instead, economics derives value from prices. The value of the land I sell is the price at which I sell it; the value of the services the barista, teacher or office manager provides is their wages; and the value of the services of the nail technician, attorney or economic consultant is the fee charged for their services.

This is clearly problematic. What price I obtain for my property depends on the conditions of the sale: am I in urgent need of funds, or can I wait for the best offer? Is the property market in a boom or slump? Is the property in a desirable neighbourhood? Similarly, economic and non-economic factors will decide what wages I can expect for my services or what fees I may charge for them. There are other problems: how are we to compare the services of the barista with the services of the teacher or the economic consultant? How do we take into account the varying quality of goods and services offered for sale? Why are the prices of identical goods and services so different in different countries and in different regions of the same country?

Using price as the measure of value has an even more consequential defect: it implies that anything which does not have a price is of no value. That cannot be true, because it would mean that many things we value highly, such literacy, essential health services, security of person and property, garbage collection, law and order and all unpaid household work, are of no value.

This is by no means the extent of the problem. We have not yet taken account of new technologies, new products and services, the impact of marketing, monopoly powers and many other factors that result in prices that do not seem fair.

Professor Mazzucato challenges the economics profession to rethink what has become the accepted theory of value. In the early days of economics, the founders of the discipline sought to derive value from labour, inputs and organisation. The time taken in production and the quality of labour were taken into consideration. This approach was replaced in the mid-nineteenth century with a theory which essentially says that value is in the eye of the beholder. We are reminded that Adam Smith, whose *Wealth of Nations* is a classic of economics, proposed a theory where value depends on time spent by workers in production. Following Smith, free trade proponents of that period argued that value was created in production, and wealth was accumulated value. For Karl Marx, exchange is the activity that crystallises the value inherent in commodities. That value is created by labour power, defined as the capacity to work. However, because of power disparities, capitalist societies do not reward workers with the full value that their labour power creates. They should resort to class struggle to recover their fair share.

Adam Smith was Professor of Moral Philosophy; the emergence of economics as a distinct discipline only becomes apparent with the contributions of Alfred Marshall, whose *Principles of Economics* was published in 1890. This marks the introduction of the theory that price determines value, rather than vice versa. This school of thought, still taught in economics departments, is labelled "marginal utility theory". According to this theory, the price of any commodity is determined at the point where the cost of producing one extra unit (the marginal unit) of that commodity exactly matches how useful it is (its utility) to the most "recent" customer (the marginal customer). "Prices, then, reflect the utility that buyers get from things. The scarcer they are - the higher their marginal utility - the more consumers will be willing to pay for them" (Mazzucato, 2018, p. 64).

Marginal utility theory was appealing because it seems to explain "how prices were arrived at and how much of a particular thing was produced" (Mazzucato, 2018, p. 65). The value of every commodity is determined by this price. However, in practice there is no independent way of knowing what the utility of any commodity is to everyone who might think of buying it, and the same item will usually appeal more to one individual than to another. Moreover, how are we to identify the "marginal" customer, and how does it happen that everyone who is shopping gets to know when the bargain is struck between the producer of the marginal unit and the marginal consumer? There is a long list of other unresolved questions in translating this marginal utility theory of prices into something that can be used in practice to record actual prices.

Professor Mazzucato gives examples of the practical difficulties which arise from the fact that we cannot in practice identify the marginal price. They include pervasive pollution problems, when producers are not made to account for pollutants that they dump as waste and do not pay the cost of cleaning up the environment. Very powerful companies which achieve domination of the market can also force consumers to pay more than an item is really worth to them if they need to have it. In these circumstances profit is no longer a reward for the investment the producers have made; instead they extract extra value, in excess of "normal" profit, by virtue of their monopoly.

The marginal utility approach also ignores the social context: whether an individual lends out capital or works for wages depends on their inherited wealth, whether they live in a rich country, their access to advanced education, whether they live in a city, their parents' social and economic circumstances, and a large number of other factors. The marginal utility approach is also applied to the determination of wages: workers are supposed to work as many hours as they need to balance their need for income with their desire to relax and entertain themselves. Obviously, this theory does not resemble actual practice in any way.

A chapter of the book is devoted to the disconnect between financial markets and the funding of investment projects, which has been a defining feature of the last 50 years. It used to be that the prices of equities reflected the returns that were expected on the underlying investment, and price to equity ratios stabilised around a market norm. The values of financial instruments were a fair measure of the value created by the investment. However, with the burgeoning of financial markets in New York and London, and more recently in the Far East, financial market values no longer reflect real investment returns. This disconnect is at the root of controversies over executive pay and under-investment in long-term projects.

Professor Mazzucato shows how price-determined value, in circumstances where there is strong patent protection, inhibits innovation and encourages unproductive rent-seeking (i.e capturing a share of the value created by others, to which you have contributed nothing).

> [T]he most modern form of rent-seeking in the twenty-first-century knowledge economy is through the way in which risks in the innovation economy are socialized, while the rewards are privatized.
>
> (Mazzucato, 2018, p. 191)

This chapter of Mazzucato's book concludes with recommendations for "confident and capable government" with the ability to "explore, experiment and strategically deliberate inside the public sector" (Mazzucato, 2018, pp. 226, 227). Also needed are new types of contracts between private and public actors.

Her final chapter, "The Economics of Hope", offers some suggestions for the direction in which economists should seek a new, adequate measure of value. Professor Mazzucato favours a mutualistic ecosystem, involving different actors in the economy, including government. They should together "fashion markets in ways that produce desirable outcomes such as 'green growth' or a more 'caring' society" (Mazzucato, 2018, p. 275). Within such markets there would be systems of arriving at agreed measures of value which reflect an acceptable social consensus. The prices of things that are bought and sold would be accepted as fair if they accorded by and large with the mutually agreed consensus on their value. However, any price that appeared to be seriously out of line with accepted values would trigger agreed market mechanisms to bring it back into line.

In a lecture in Barbados in 2014, I offered three examples of the subjective nature of value. The first, my favourite, is from a short story by the late Jamaican novelist Anthony Winkler, entitled "The man who knew the price of all fish":

> Baba was a black man with no past. …
>
> … He had no future; he had no wife; he had no children; he had nothing, except a small black hulled canoe, and some wire fishpots and mangrove-stained lines he used to catch fish with.
>
> Every night he rowed out in his canoe and set his fishpots and threw down his lines, and every morning he rowed into Giddy Beach with a canoeful of dead fish and sold the dead fish to women as poor as himself, who would higgle him furiously, insult his fish, call him a jinal, meaning that he was intent on robbing them, paw over the corpses of the fish, hold him up to cynical comparison with more successful fishermen, accuse him of having a white mother, call him a Rastafarian, then walk away clutching contemptuously at the dead fish wrapped in newspaper for which they had paid Baba's price. For it was impossible to higgle him down, because he had no past and could not be either insulted or deprecated.
>
> It did not matter what they called his mother, because he had no mother. He had no wife they could say cuckolded him; he had no children who got poor marks at school; he had no grandfather who bubbled over his senility on street corners; he had no cousins who were cat-o'nined for stealing; he had no aunts who painted their faces for tourist men at nights; he had no attachments which made him vulnerable to abuse; he had no one to be called into shame over.
>
> And so no one had ever higgled him down on the price of his fish. If he said that the green-skinned, beak-teeth parrot-fish were a shilling each, it was impossible to shake him. The woman could call the fish gangrened, she could say it had slimy skin, she could say it was not a fish, she could say anything, it would not matter. She could higgle until her black face was greener than the parrot-fish, it would not matter. For once Baba had decided that a fish was worth a shilling, God could not alter its price. The fish was always sold for a shilling.
>
> (Winkler, 2004)

My second example involved the purchase by a Canadian company of shares of the Barbados Light and Power Company on the notoriously inactive Barbados Securities Exchange in 2011. Some opinion in local financial circles was that the price being offered was too low, and that, based on the company's earnings or some other criteria, the shares were worth much more. I argued that from an economic point of view the offer turned out to be the fair market price, because a majority of shareholders, myself included, were happy to sell at that price.

My third case study was the London Inter-bank Offered Rate (Libor) scandal. A problem emerged in 2007 when the major banks in the London market stopped borrowing from each other at short term. Until then banks did borrow from each other when they were temporarily short of cash. Every day each bank reported to the Bankers' Association the rate at which it had borrowed, the Association computed the average, and the whole world used that as their reference. Round about 2005 British banks were sourcing as much as one-third of their funding by borrowing on financial markets at short term, rather than through customers' deposits. Confidence in the value of the short-term instruments used in the financial markets began to evaporate in 2005, with the large-scale failure of sub-prime mortgages in the US. By 2007 short-term international funding had all but dried up, including the sourcing of funds on the London interbank market. Libor had ceased to exist, and the most important reference rate for international financial transactions had disappeared. The market had no solution to this problem; in market economics there is no price if there is no transaction. Since 2007 there have been no transactions of substance between the major banks in the London market, and therefore no short-term London interbank interest rate.

The crucial word is "offered"; the banks continued to make token offers to buy and sell liquid funds, but those offers were deliberately set at unrealistic levels, for reasons that are obvious. I like old cars, and in 2014 I owned a version of the original Mini, built by the British Leyland Company. I had no intention of selling, so if anyone had offered to buy, I might have quoted an outlandish price rather than saying an outright no. In similar fashion, banks on the London market had a motive to quote unrealistic rates, since they did not wish to borrow.

The difficulty arose because the calculation was based on *offered* rates, rather than actual realised rates. I presume that while the market was active the offered and realised rates were not materially different so the difference was of no importance. That changed when the realised rate disappeared in 2007. Offered rates remained, as many of them as there were banks, and none of them realistic, because nobody wanted to lend or borrow. The realised rate at which transactions are agreed no longer existed.

These three examples illustrate some of the conundrums economists face in their search for an objective way to determine what is a fair trade. Can a trade be fair if the seller adopts a take it or leave it attitude? Can we say that a trade is unfair if both buyers and sellers are happy with the price, even though others not party to the trade say it is unfair, whether or not they had an opportunity to participate? What is the fair price, in circumstances where no transaction actually takes place?

One approach adopted by economics to answer this question is to imagine that everything in the world is traded by open auction, and that the final auction price is the fair price. The seller hopes for top dollar, the buyer is looking for a bargain, and the auctioneer achieves a price that is within an acceptable range for both parties. Except when he doesn't. It often happens that an auction item fails to reach the reserve price, so this is not a complete answer to the question of the fair value. The auction is also not objective. The result depends on who attends, where and when it is held, the skill of the auctioneer and many other factors. Similar items may fetch widely different prices at different auctions.

An alternative economic approach to determining fair value is to establish the cost of the item to be traded, and a fair profit for the trader. This approach is of limited applicability in practice, because the cost of bringing items to market is information which is seldom available to all parties at the time of the trade, and the notion of a fair or "normal" profit is completely arbitrary. In practice there are so many discretionary factors which go into the pricing decision that there is no single unambiguous cost of producing anything. The problem is especially intractable when we're talking about services, such as airline transportation, hotel accommodation, legal services, banking and educational services, to cite just a few random examples.

Economics has made many attempts to make either of these two basic approaches – cost plus and the equilibrium of demand and supply – a better match with our everyday transactions in the real world. This is not the occasion to go into detail, but it is fair to summarise by saying that no convincing model has emerged that would adequately provide a fair value in the circumstances of the examples with which we began, or in many other instances that might be cited.

The ruling prices that we observe in daily commerce cannot be explained by established economic theory, even though theory may be employed to rationalise them after the fact. That becomes clear whenever there are abrupt changes in the prices at which trades take place, in circumstances where nothing fundamental has been altered. The markets for property and financial assets provide the most striking examples. With no extraordinary change in demand or supply, and with little increase in cost, market prices from time to time spiral upwards, only to come crashing down eventually. That was the case with the housing boom in the US and Europe in the mid-2000s. The rapid upward spiral in prices from around 2003 cannot be explained with reference to changes in the demand and supply of housing; prices developed a momentum of their own. Naturally, the price spiral did come to have an effect on demand and supply; more and more property developers vied to construct new homes, which in turn spurred frenetic activity in building supplies, furnishings, transport and related services. At the same time, as the price of housing soared beyond the reach of ordinary folk, many over-reached themselves, and many more were pushed out of the home buyers' market. With supply going up and demand falling, the twain could never meet, and the famous intersection point with which is the enduring symbol of market economics became unattainable. In these circumstances, the market can never find the fair price.

The evidence is all around us of our failure to understand what drives prices and our inability to determine when a transaction is fairly valued. The increase in the demand for gold from wealthy Asians, and from others seeking a safe haven for their investments, is admittedly large, but it is nowhere near enough to explain the enormous spiral in gold prices. Violence and political instability have clearly been an element driving an upward spiral in oil prices, but actual supplies and new sources and technologies have not produced the expected correction. The relative values of the dollar, the yen and the euro owe much to traders' guesses about what markets will do next, and little to the fundamental weaknesses or strengths in policy or economic performance of the countries concerned. Airline pricing is a complicated mystery to us all, involving so many factors that have to be projected years into the future, that an objective measure of operating cost, which takes replacement costs fully into account, is beyond practical reach.

Craigwell, Moore and Worrell (2012) analyse price changes in Barbados, Curacao, St Lucia and Trinidad and Tobago, using data from the consumer price surveys conducted every month for the compilation of the Consumer Price Index. We found that in Barbados between 50 and 80 per cent of consumer prices were changed every month, by as little as three per cent for some items, and by as much as 29 per cent for others. Moreover, very few prices moved in tandem with the prices of substitutes or similar items, and prices jumped around, rising rapidly one month and barely increasing or even falling in the following month, a phenomenon economists refer to as "low inflation persistence". These features are not at all what might have been expected from either of the two approaches that economists use to determine value. The demand for consumer items hardly fluctuates from month to month, nor does the supply, which, in the short term, will be taken from inventories which have already been priced.

Is there no way of determining what is a fair trade? The answer to that question is nuanced.

In cases where today's offer price is not much different from the price I paid the last time I bought a similar item, the markets work perfectly well. Everyone accepts that the price is fair if it accords with their expectations, and our expectations are formed on the basis of previous experience. The market does work, for known products with which everyone is familiar, and for modest price variation.

The market cannot provide a fair estimate of value when the product is unknown, and when prices vary sharply over time. For new or unfamiliar products there is no reference price to use as a point of departure. Typically such a price appears in due course, after a small number of dominant firms arrive at an understanding among themselves on the range of values at which the product will be offered. Other problematic cases occur when there is an abrupt change in the value at which the market makes a trade, and in circumstances when a fair value is needed, but there is no trade. The value may be needed for accounting and reporting purposes, as for example when assets have to be booked at market value, or it may be needed as a reference price for other transactions, as was the case with Libor. Unless there is official intervention at this point, or unless a market leader emerges with sufficient power to impose their will, no settled price may emerge. In the latter case, when a price is imposed through market dominance, traded values may not be considered fair. It is possible to arrive at a fair price, but only with official intervention. These circumstances warrant aggressive and credible official intervention, sufficient to establish a benchmark for values, determined on a basis which is fully explained, and which is consistent with market understanding of the fundamentals that drive that particular market, as well as being sensitive to production costs and market demand for the product.

Official intervention has gotten a bad rap in recent policy discussions, often because the policy has not been fully understood, is not in line with market sentiment or is based on economic assumptions that are unrealistic. However, official intervention which is in line with economic fundamentals, which is fully explained, and which takes full account of the intentions, motives and resources of market participants, may be the only way of attaining a fair value in trade in circumstances where there is no established norm for prices, or where there has been a large departure from the norm.

In the case of Libor, my view remains that the Bank of England needs to set a benchmark rate on the basis of a full analysis and documentation of the underlying market liquidity situation, and invite banks to use that as their reference rate for international transactions, should they choose to do so. No unofficial financial institution in London has the wealth of data and analytical resources to take an informed view of the real costs of liquidity, comparable to what the Bank of England may deploy. The Bankers' Association would be free to circulate offer rates, and should be encouraged to do so, but the only rate that may logically be averaged for the guidance of the market should be the Interbank Realised Rate, the rate at which money was actually borrowed and lent.

The management of asset price bubbles, including surges in property prices, also justifies aggressive intervention by official institutions. The nature of the intervention will be determined by individual circumstance, but it must be large enough and must be pursued with determination and persistence, until the steam goes out of the inflationary surge. Sound data, convincing analysis and effective communication are the key to success.

Economics is more art than science: the problems of discreteness, replicability and homogeneity have proved intractable

Although physical and social sciences often employ similar statistical techniques, they are obliged to use them in very different ways. The physical scientist is able to carry out experiments; the social scientist cannot. Both physical and social scientists start with a theory, which may be based on previous research and writing, their own reasoning, experience and intuition, or other source. This theory always abstracts from reality, which is an impossibly complicated web of facts, ideas, impressions and influences, in order to single out some item or interrelationship of interest. It's what they do next that differentiates the physical and social scientist: the biologist takes his or her theory to the laboratory, where all other items and influences are excluded, and performs many experiments in the effort to disprove the theory. Only when all these attempts fail, and the best attempts of sceptical colleagues also fail, is the thesis accepted.

The economist, on the other hand, has to resort to statistics about the past behaviour of the economic variables which provide the evidence to support her or his theory. There are intractable problems in defining and measuring the variables, and ensuring that each individual "observation" is unrelated to previous or subsequent observations. Moreover, uncountable other factors are at play over the period of the statistical test, and it may be difficult to definitively exclude the possibility of their influence. As if that were not sufficiently disturbing, economists seldom have the large numbers of observations needed to make reliable statistical inferences.

Although these problems of empirical research in economics have been of concern to applied economists for many decades, common practice, even in leading journals in the profession, has gotten progressively worse since the 1980s. In a collection edited by Colander and Brenner (1992), the authors of the essays included complained that the practice in empirical work too often reported results with a degree of confidence that was unwarranted given the obvious tentativeness and ambiguity of measurement of economic phenomena. All too often economic analysis is blind to the historical and institutional context, and no account is taken of sociological, political and cultural considerations. Data is used with little regard to, or discussion of, its provenance or accuracy, or how closely it mirrors the concept that the theory requires. The inevitable result is predictions that are way off the mark, and policies that are poorly guided.

In a searching exploration of empirical papers published in the *American Economic Review,* perhaps the most widely read journal in the field, McCloskey and Ziliak (1996) analyse how economists draw inferences from their statistical tests. Their conclusion: "We would not assert that every economist misunderstands statistical significance, only that most do, and these some of the best economic scientists." Furthermore, "no one believes a finding of statistical significance or insignificance" (McCloskey and Ziliak,

1996, p. 111). They observe "Massed observations, clever common sense, elegant theorems, new policies, sagacious economic reasoning, historical perspective, relevant accounting: these have all led to scientific success. Statistical significance has not." Instead of reifying the notion of statistical significance McCloskey and Ziliak suggested that economists pay "serious attention to the scientific question" (McCloskey and Ziliak, 1996, p. 112).

However, matters have only gotten worse. In a special edition of the *Cambridge Journal of Economics* edited by Kitson (2005) on "Economics for the future" we are told that

> The inspiration for this Special Issue and the conference that preceded it was the pluralism and usefulness that characterised economics at Cambridge. But recent changes at Cambridge suggest a retreat from relevance and a tightening of the neoclassical noose. The Faculty of Economics and Politics has become the Faculty of Economics with the "Politics" discarded as unwanted cumbersome appendage. And the Department of Applied Economics (DAE), the source of some of the best of Cambridge economics no longer exists.

Highlights from this volume include a paper by Luigi Pasinetti that identifies eight building blocks for a viable alternative to the neoclassical school. These include a focus on reality rather than on abstract rationality; a stress on non-ergodic[2] rather than timeless systems; recognising that instability, not equilibrium, is the normal state of affairs; and taking account of the importance of economic growth and social concern.

In the same volume the effectiveness of mathematics in economics is considered by Vela Velupillai, who argues that interactions in economics are too complex to be captured by a reliance on maximisation axioms.[3] In particular, he argues that political economy cannot be value-free and that if heterodox economics is to dislodge neoclassical economics it must engage directly with politics, culture and values.

David Colander identifies the process which has led to economics becoming more technical by its focus on the "holy trinity" of rationality, greed and equilibrium. But Colander takes an optimistic view of the future of economics, as he believes that modern orthodox economics is beginning to build broader and more useful foundations based on "purposeful behaviour, enlightened self-interest and sustainability". He goes on to argue that the discipline of economics will shift from "the study of infinitely bright agents in information rich environments" to "the study of reasonably bright individuals in information-poor environments" – thus returning to Marshall's notion of sensible people doing the best they can in an uncertain environment.

David Colander has been a leader in recent efforts to improve on economic paradigms and economic practice. In a paper entitled "Complexity and the history of economic thought" Colander he notes that "Formal models do not develop in a void. The beginnings of science in all areas involve developing informal insights" (Colander, 2008, p. 3). Science may be thought to be successful where the formal model does not lose the informal insights. The advocates of what is referred to as the "complexity approach" – one which admits of qualitative, historical, social, cultural and intuitive "evidence" – argue that even though structural simplicity cannot be achieved, science still has something to say in the formulation of economic theory, achieving simplification through an iterative processes, rather than by imposing a structure. The scientific foundation of this approach is that it is known that patterns develop when nonlinear processes are repeated for long periods of time. The search for patterns can be done with the help of the mathematics of nonlinear dynamics, using open models with no deterministic solution and where many solutions are possible, depending on the initial conditions and the path followed. The research can explore how different patterns develop with one or other dynamic relationships, as well as how sudden change can occur. Complexity economics avoids the need, as in traditional economics, to pre-judge which simplification process is preferable, an ongoing matter of contention. The complexity approach leads to use of Monte Carlo and bootstrap methods of statistical testing, and it "demotes theory to a lower level and replaces it with conjectures and patterns that temporarily fit" (Colander, 2008, p. 6). This approach unearths things that structural approaches miss or downplay, such as path dependency (where different sequencing of identical measures produces different outcomes), increasing returns (for example, by spreading costs over a larger volume of sales), multiple equilibria (for example, where inflation settles at a relatively high level where a lower level should have been achievable), the impact of technology, and changes in institutional structure.

Economic heterodoxy and the search for better explanations of economic outcomes

The book *New Horizons in Economic Thought* (Samuels, 1992) is a revealing selection of insights from the work of 13 economists who have challenges to the mainstream of the discipline. In his introduction Samuels notes that diversity and controversy have always been characteristic of economics. Although neo-classicism has triumphed for the moment, there is no agreement as to what constitutes the neo-classical paradigm, and critiques of neo-classical modes of analysis abound.

Among the issues raised in the volume are: how to deal with uncertainty, the relationship between rationality and human psychology, the effects of psychology on decision-making, the formation and operation of institutions, the effects of information, the philosophical assumptions of economic methodology and the importance of power relationships. Samuels notes that mainstream economics has a way of absorbing and sanitising history. He cites the example of the Chamberlain-Robinson imperfect competition "revolution" (Robinson, 1969) which has been absorbed into conventional thinking in ways that have defused it's critical implications for the conventional wisdom. A similar fate has befallen notions of price inflexibility introduced by Hicks and Gardiner Means (Hicks, 1963).

George Akerlof's contributions to micro-economics include the observation that reputation, conformity, belief and personal tastes all enter into utility functions along with consumption of goods and services. Furthermore, loyalty and beliefs may change with experience. Akerlof introduces the notion of "near rational behaviour": if the rewards of achieving an optimum are small and the costs are not trivial, inertia may prevail. If a sufficiently large percentage of the population engages in near rational behaviour, results indicated by classical microeconomic theory do not obtain.

William Baumol made a wide variety of path-breaking contributions to the understanding of economic processes. He argues that the differential productivities of labour in industry and services will depress prices and labour absorption in industry if wages rise at the same rate in both sectors, an issue of great moment which the US, Europe and other industrialised nations have found no way to address. Baumol also noted that period-by-period profit maximisation may not be optimal for businesses over the long term; instead, an optimal profit stream my require a large flow of output or a high growth of output over time. Among many other insights, Baumol pointed out that sunk costs (the capital that established companies have invested in buildings, machinery, marketing networks, etc.) may be their strongest weapon in defending against potential new competitors in their field.

Jon Elster's philosophical and methodological concerns have to do with how economists think about what motivates behaviour. For example a person who practices deception will behave in ways very different from what rationality would lead us to expect. Outcomes are always determined by interactions between social decision processes and individual preferences, which makes it very challenging to make generalisations.

Nicholas Georgescu-Roegen raised unresolved considerations at the foundations of stochastic theory – the idea that we can infer something about the effect of airfares on tourist travel by doing a test on a selection of actual fares and passengers, selected at random, for example. The test is conducted with the airfare as the known quantity (the x-factor, because that is the variable that is usually measured on the horizontal axis). Georgescu-Roegen points out that there are a very large number of ways the test may be set up; in technical terms, the observations on airfares and passengers may have been generated by many different stochastic structures, and the choice to put the fares on the hoizontal axis is described as "a bit of hand-waving" (Samuels, 1992, p. 91). The pretence that any set of observations is a sample from some larger population is "a sham". Georgescu-Roegen also worries about the neglect of qualitative factors and preferences: "Neo-classical models of preferences and expectations .... misrepresent and obscure the importance of quality in human life".

Albert Hirschman's contributions to development economics included the interaction of "loyalty" to a product or service, which can sustain demand in the face of cost or other pressures for the provider to "exit" an industry, and "voice", access to the decision process that decides on the fate of the company. Economists also need to take account of passions and interests, including hostility to new sources of wealth, infatuation, addiction, benevolence and public spiritedness. Economists should seek to observe and support processes of change that lead in the direction of hope, rather than try to control change.

Janos Kornai explores the concept of equilibrium. Factors influencing demand, apart from prices, include imitation, fashion, novelty and status; supply may be influenced by stock market reports, direct information from buyers and expectations. Equilibrium should always be discussed in the context of the control mechanisms and social regularities that make it possible. Kornai envisages equilibrium, not as a settled state, but a tendency towards which the market is pulled from two opposing directions, buyers seeking best value (which Kornai terms "suction") and sellers cutting buyers (which he calls "pressure").

Edward Leamer points out that there are so many potential explanatory variables that might qualify for inclusion in any equation that every researcher is obliged to narrow the field to a manageable number. Either explicitly (seldom) or implicitly (usually) economists assume *a priori* that the coefficients (that measure the impact on the *y*-variable) of all excluded variables are zero, and that the variables that we choose to include have significant impact, though we don't know just how significant that impact that is. How can we know that these variables may be excluded, if we don't know how significant they are? Leamer provides suggestions for more logical and systematic ways of searching for a suitable model specification.

Harvey Leibenstein points out that the nature of human decision-making vitiates conclusions drawn from a simple logical system. Reasoning is a process "costly in many dimensions" (Samuels, 1992, p. 186) and many decisions necessarily have to be made by instinct, convention, and so on, if individuals and institutions are to function at all. Leibenstein is best known for the concept of "X-efficiency", the effect of relationships, obligations, responsibilities, coordination and firm efficiency.

Charles Lindblom describes macroeconomic decision-making as the unplanned outcome of a "complex interplay of partisan opportunism, accommodation and consent despite the cognitive limitations of the participants" (Samuels, 1992, p. 204). Policy making operates by small deviations from what actually obtains, limiting the range of possibilities to make the problem manageable. "The spontaneous mutual adjustment continuously produces new values, new problems and new agreements. toward. outcomes no-one could possibly have predicted" (Samuels, 1992, p. 213).

Douglass North points out that US economic growth in the nineteenth and twentieth centuries was due in large measure to the assignment and enforcement of property rights, improvements in transportation and education, the development of commercial law and the introduction of mechanisms for income distribution. He observes that "The process of institutional change is so complex that the emergence of institutions which support economic growth cannot be taken for granted" (Samuels, 1992, p. 244).

John Roemer is a neo-Marxist economist who developed a theory of trade between groups with different initial endowments which leads to the exploitation of the partner with the smaller initial endowment. This deserves greater attention in addressing African underdevelopment and the uncertain prospects for closing the gap with the rest of the world.

Tibor Scitovsky focussed on the sources of economic power and human satisfaction. A sample of his many insights: rationing may be preferable to price adjustment in some circumstances because the price structure reflects an established distribution of wealth and income that may be very inequitable. Quality matters in trade: opening markets to trade may lead to imports of higher quality; conversely, barriers to entry may be helpful where they are designed to raise the quality of local products. Also, price is an indicator of quality, so a higher price will often not result in a loss of custom.

Samuels discusses just three of Amartya Sen's contributions. In anticipating economic behaviour we must take account of such things as people's sense of duty and commitment. Tax systems work because of that sense of obligation; in its absence, evasion is so endemic that collections are minimal, no matter the severity of the penalties. Capability is a better measure of the achievement of a good life than are surveys of people's sense of happiness or contentment, because people in unsatisfactory or less-desirable circumstances often resign themselves to their lot. Sen also treats with the difficult question of the extent to which individual liberties should be allowed to infringe on the rights of others, an issue of the moment in respect of mandates for vaccinations against COVID-19.

New developments in heterodoxy

In the new century, growing disillusionment with the results of policies informed by conventional economic approaches have spawned a new international society, the World Economics Association (WEA). The association published a collection of papers on "Irrelevance and ideology" (Guerrien, 2004) in which it was argued that

> Even in the simplest model – bargaining – it is supposed (as a minimal requirement) that people don't use force (that trade is voluntary). But bargaining results depend on a lot of factors, such as bargainers' psychology, resources, impatience, etc. To obtain a determinate result (or prediction), more "social structure" is needed. Consider the neoclassical benchmark model, perfect competition. It supposes a very special and strange "social structure": households and firms are *obliged* to "take" prices, given by an auctioneer, and to inform him of their supplies and demands at these prices; they *are not allowed* to bargain and trade directly among each other, even if the auctioneer has found equilibrium prices.
>
> (Guerrien, 2004, p.10)

A contribution by Jack Vromen pointed out that

> Economic theory is only committed to the belief that economic agents behave as if they actually went through these deliberations and calculations. For example, business men need not actually base their decisions on a comparison of marginal costs and revenues, as is assumed in neoclassical theory of the firm. As long as their actual behaviour is consistent with this assumption, the theory is applicable. At this juncture one might rightly wonder what then are the actually operating underlying mechanisms that make economic agents behave the way they do, if they are not the deliberations and calculations ascribed to them that make them do so.
> (Vromen, 2004, p.1)

In his contribution Tony Lawson urges economists to model real underlying mechanisms explicitly, whereas many mainstream economists seem to think that this is not necessary. Lawson wants to assign greater weight to other theoretical virtues such as truth, realism (or realisticness), credibility and plausibility. Elegance, simplicity, parsimony and the like cannot compensate for the deficiency of theories lacking in these respects. Theories and models that have greater plausibility in identifying real and important underlying mechanisms should be preferred over theories and models having less credibility in this respect, even if that would go at the expense of parsimony and tractability. Social rules and social positions are allotted a prominent place in Lawson's economic analysis.

How economists explain: the use of nineteenth-century physics, the death of markets and the need for a new paradigm

It has been pointed out that the conceptual tools used in economics are based on long-outdated models borrowed from the physics of the nineteenth century. The concept of equilibrium as employed in economics is a prime example. Over a century ago theories of relativity overtook the notion that there is an equilibrium which represents a desirable objective or a state of nature to which systems will revert if left to their own devices. Yet notions of market equilibrium, fair market prices, the natural rate of interest and other static concepts remain at the heart of economic thinking.

The Origin of Wealth: the Radical Remaking of Economics and What it Means for Business and Society

In 2010 I read a book with the above title (Beinhocker, 2006) which profoundly influenced my thinking about economics. The preface of the book begins:

> As I write this, the field of economics is going through its most profound change in over a hundred years. I believe that this change represents a major shift in the intellectual currents of the world that will have

> substantial effects on our lives and the lives of generations to come. … just as biology became a true science in the twentieth century, so too will economics come into its own as a science in the twenty first century.
> (Beinhocker, 2006, p. ix)

The book makes a first stab at establishing the scientific foundation of economics, arguing that economies evolve by the same laws as those that govern biological evolution.

Early in the book Beinhocker describes a cross-disciplinary workshop on economics, arranged by Citicorp's CEO John Reed, that brought together ten leading economists (including Nobel Laureate Kenneth Arrow) and ten physicists, biologists and computer scientists. The physical scientists were "really shocked" to find that "economics was a throwback to another era" (Beinhocker, 2006, p. 47). Economists' mathematics [seemed] "like a blast from the past", and physical scientists were surprised by economists' assumptions, objecting particularly to the assumption of perfect rationality. Physical scientists craft their assumptions to ensure that they do not contradict reality, though they are designed to simplify it. The assumption of perfect rationality contradicts reality, and economists know that, but they still use the assumption, however modified.

Beinhocker argues that what he calls Traditional Economics (TE) remains trapped in a time warp defined by the concepts that Leon Walras borrowed from the physics he knew at the time of the development of the marginalist theory of market economics which underpins the classical, Keynsian, neoclassical and New Keynsian views of the world. At that time only the first law of thermodynamics – the conservation of energy – was known. The notion of equilibrium is a form of expression of the first law. Physics subsequently discovered the second law – that entropy (disorder or randomness) is always increasing. The implication of the second law is that if the system were ever to reach equilibrium it would be dead. In effect, TE classifies economy as a closed equilibrium system which violates the laws of physics as they are now known to exist.

Beinhocker proposes an alternative to TE, "complex economics", CE. The complex economy evolves according to the same laws as biological evolution. Evolution is an algorithm for finding "fit" designs in enormous design spaces. It has been described as "creating design without a designer". Three elements feature in the evolutionary process: *variation* within the population, *selection* of the fittest, and *replication* of the successful design. The economy will evolve, at what is literally a glacial pace, driven by this evolutionary process, without any deliberate design on the part of economic agents. But economic agents can improve the success rate in selecting fit designs, by using processes of induction and scientific deduction. In Beinhocker's schema, business plans are the selection process by which the fittest physical technologies (PTs) and the fittest social technologies (STs) are selected and replicated.

PTs are methods and designs for transforming matter, energy and information from one state into another in pursuit of a goal or goals. In the case of the economy, business goals are to be profitable and to have the resources to grow and cope with change. The evolution of PTs combines induction (learning from experience) with deduction (drawing inference from theory and observation). Technology evolution is the result of humans' deductive tinkering search through the near infinite possibilities of PT space. The invention of science, which derives laws from theories which are tested repeatedly under controlled conditions, dramatically increased the hit rate of deductive insights.

STs are methods and designs for organising people in pursuit of a goal or goals. They may include institutions, structures, roles, processes and cultural norms. Fit ST designs are those which enable people to play non-zero-sum games, and to capture the gains. Such designs require that there be the potential for non-zero-sum games; that payoff schemes provide incentives to play the games; and that techniques are in place for sanctioning anyone who thinks of defecting.

The third process contributing to economic evolution is the *business plan*. A business is defined as a person or group who transforms matter, energy or information from one state to another with the goal of making a profit. Businesses make plans to improve their profitability and chances of survival. These plans are envisaged as comprised of what are termed "modules". A module is a component of a business plan that has provided or could provide a basis for differential selection among businesses in a competitive environment. Business plan selection is more tinkering than deduction, but it is deliberate, not a blind process like biological evolution. The alternative schemes by which business plan selection is made are either by the decision of a "Big Man", or by competition within markets. The economy evolves as agents use deductive tinkering to find fit business plans, and successful modules are rewarded by access to greater resources. "Business designs evolve over time through a process of differentiation, selection, and amplification, with the market as the ultimate arbiter of fitness" (Beinhocker, 2006, p. 16). The coevolution of PTs, STs and business designs accounts for the patterns of change and growth we characterise as wealth creation.

In developing his argument, Beinhocker makes a number of observations which resonated with me, among them a refutation of Milton Friedman's thesis that forecast accuracy is all that matters. He supposes that someone were to proffer the theory that the sky is blue because a giant paints it that colour overnight, every night. Preposterous though this theory may be, it will forecast accurately every time. Science, Beinhocker reminds us, is about explaining, not forecasting.

Beinhocker notes that theories are like maps: they provide a simplified representation of the landscape, but they must agree both in distant and in detail views, and both distant and detailed views must agree with observations of the underlying reality. The theories of traditional economics fail to meet this test. For example, real people do not pursue their self interest in "fantastically complex and calculating ways" (Beinhocker, 2006, p. 51); instead they depend on recognising patterns, interpreting ambiguous information and learning. Beinhocker is an entertaining writer, and his description of the rational consumer of traditional economics deciding to buy tomatoes is hilarious. He says:

> Imagine you walk into your local grocery store and see some tomatoes. You have well-defined preferences for tomatoes compared with everything thing else you could possibly buy in the world, including bread, milk, and a vacation in Spain. Furthermore, you have well-defined preferences for everything you could possibly buy at any point in the future, and since the future is uncertain, you have assigned probabilities to those potential purchases. For example, I believe that there is a 23 per cent chance that in two years, the shelf in my kitchen will come loose and I will need to pay $1.20 to buy some bolts to fix it. The discounted value of that $1.20 today is about $1.00, multiplied by a 23 per cent probability, equals an expected value of 23 cents for possible future repairs, which I must trade off with my potential purchase of tomatoes today, along with all my other potential purchases in my lifetime.
>
> (Beinhocker, 2006, pp. 116, 117)

This is by no means the end of the story. Beinhocker goes on for another half a page to describe the calculations a perfectly rational consumer would make to buy tomatoes. In contrast, Complexity Economics proposes an "inductively rational" consumer whose decision process is described thus: "Hmmm … tomatoes. They look nice and fresh. I kinda feel like salad tonight. Price looks OK" (Beinhocker, 2006, p. 117).

Equilibrium makes no sense as a way of thinking about the real world, because you cannot create models that combine equilibrium with complex dynamics *and real world timescales*; the settling down time after a single disturbance using the fastest computer is estimated at 4.5 quintillion years (4.5×10^{18}) but earth is only 1.2×10^{10} years old. "Even if we were as rational as possible and had all the information we could want, the computational complexity of the economy is such that the future would happen before we would have had time to predict it" (Beinhocker, 2006, p. 323). In the complex economy prices move dynamically around an "attractor" (Beinhocker, 2006, p. 92). They are not the result of an equilibrating process.

Adam Smith gave "nuanced" view of human nature in *The Theory of Moral Sentiments*, his other seminal work, which is discounted by traditional economics. Humans are "conditional cooperators" who reward cooperation and punish free riders. The human mind works by induction, with "occasional forays" into deduction, " almost the exact reverse of TE" (Beinhocker, 2006, p. 129). A human model is one where there is an *agent* who has *goals* which he/she addresses using *rules of thumb*, modified by *feedback and learning*.

Networking can act as a catalyst for this process. Networks act as computers for society, providing the feedback for learning. Even so, the potential outcomes of a complex networked system are so outrageously numerous that they cannot be practically calculated. Still, large networks offer far more *potential for novelty*, which increases exponentially as the network expands.

Beinhocker recognised the following competing TE theories of economic oscillations at the turn of the twenty-first century:

- Micro based real business cycle theories stating that fluctuations are caused by exogenous shocks such as technical change; or
- Macro based neo-Keynesianism, the theory that fluctuations are due to market imperfections, time delays and similar phenomena.

In contrast, CE views cycles, growth, inflation as endogenous, emerging from interactions within the economic system. Inherent volatility is characteristic of the stock market, the one market where transactions are thought to come closest to resembling the TE model. He gives a factual illustration from the London Stock Exchange, on a day when a 1.4 per cent price change on a trade worth $28,000 added $658 million to AstraZeneca's market value. What economists refer to as "news" does affect stock prices, but much volatility is simply the result of market interaction. It is persistent; it is not random noise.

We will continue to frustrate ourselves if we continue to pursue prices and institutional mechanisms that will bring markets into equilibrium, which is the guiding principle of traditional economics. Instead Beinhocker offers thoughts on how business plans may be designed to be "fit", to have the greatest change of survival and therefore the greatest chance of being replicated. As a result of evolution, we are naturally inclined to cooperate, but we are sensitive to cheating, and we are inclined to reciprocity in ways that are culturally determined. As a result, high cooperation, high-trust cultures in companies tend to lead to better economic performance. In the process of economic evolution, agents use deductive tinkering to find fit business plans, and successful modules are rewarded with access to greater resources.

Beinhocker offers some suggestions for managing periods of change, such as were being experienced by the global economy in the first decade of the current century. A shift in perspective requires major redesign of strategic planning, involving in-depth discussion and debate among principal decision makers in small fora. The discussions should be informed by facts and analysis, and strategising must be divorced from near-team decision making and budgeting. The adaptive mindset emphasises learning and adapting over predicting and planning; plans and forecasts provide some guidance for the start of the journey, but they must be continuously evaluated against the goals of the organisation, and changed as needed to keep on track to achieve those goals.

Beinhocker concedes that we will often misinterpret the results of our designs, because the economic environment does not change in a smooth linear fashion.

> If the environment is biased toward one type of strategy, people who follow that strategy will be more likely to rise to the top … But when the environment changes, the organization is stuck with people who can't change with it.
>
> (Beinhocker, 2006, p. 363)

Often the environment changes in clusters, rather than randomly, so that it will favour one kind of strategy for a time. When this happens, what were thought to have been successful strategies begin to fail spectacularly.

Beinhocker has something to say about the culture of organisations. If individual performance norms are deeply embedded, you can get good performance without a strong hierarchical structure. However, in low-trust, low-cooperation environments, interactions must be spelled out in great detail, with lots of rules and little flexibility. In times of change, norms are needed to push individuals to take risks and to protect those that do take risks. Beinhocker recognises that the inherent tensions between performance-oriented meritocracy and the need for team work need to be managed by strong leadership of organisations.

Beinhocker has ideas about productive styles of organisation: they value both execution and innovation, they feature a carefully engineered induction process, and senior management behaviour and communications "play an enormous role" (Beinhocker, 2006, p. 376) in their success. In managing change he notes that stories, analogies and patterns help people to get the message, and that intense repetition is essential. There needs to be an interactive process for managing change, because learning is interactive. He also notes that experiments prove that people care about outcomes, but they also care about whether processes are fair.

Economists use terms that imply something different from what they really mean

In a lecture delivered to the Barbados Economics Society in June 2010 which was heavily influenced by Beinhocker's ideas, I commented on ways in which the concepts used by economists misrepresent reality in ways which impair an understanding of the behaviour of economic agents and the consequences of that behavior. The lecture offered two examples, with respect to exchange rates and markets.

The exchange rate is not a price of anything

Economists cannot understand how the exchange rate of small, resource-poor countries like Barbados, Cayman Islands, The Bahamas and the Eastern Caribbean Currency Union can remain unchanged in terms of their numeraire (the US dollar) indefinitely, because the exchange rate is thought of as a price. Economists believe that prices are arrived at by demand and supply in a market, and since the demand and supply will change over time, then the price has to change as well, otherwise the market will not clear. Economists feel obliged to ascribe the durability of long-term pegs to the use of exchange controls, an argument which has lacked plausibility for four decades or more.

In fact the mistake is to believe that the exchange rate is the price of foreign exchange. You can't eat, drink or smoke foreign exchange; foreign exchange is not a commodity. Rather, the exchange rate is a statement about the relation between one measure of value and another. The value of the shirt I bought at Havana Nines in Miami airport for US$50 is worth twice that amount in Barbados dollars, because the exchange rate of the US dollar to the Barbados dollar is 1:2 in exactly the same way that a ten-mile walk is equivalent to a walk of 16 kilometres, because the "exchange rate" of miles to kilometres is 1:1.6. It makes exactly as much sense to keep changing the exchange rates between currencies as it would to keep changing the value of a mile in terms of a kilometre.

Prices have not been set in markets since the end of the agrarian economy

A second example of economists' misrepresentation of the world is the notion that prices are determined by an equilibrium of supply and demand in a market. This notion is so fundamental to economics that it is accepted without question, and not only by economists. A visitor from Mars would find this quite strange, because when he looked around him he would be hard pressed to find anything resembling a market in which buyers and sellers negotiate the price of things bought and sold. In real life retail prices are nearly always predetermined by the seller, and wholesale, producer and other prices are determined by contract.

This was not always the case. Economic history is not my specialty, but my understanding is that in the agrarian economy economic transactions typically took place via markets. The farmer would till his fields and raise his livestock five days a week, and on the sixth day he would load his produce on some form of transportation and take it to the nearest market town, where he would trade it with artisans, fishermen and other farmers who had products that he needed and that his household did not produce. In many African societies, I am told, the marketing is done by women. The seventh day was often the day of rest and recuperation, at least in the Western societies from whom we draw our traditions. In this economy, sellers will adjust their prices over the course of the market day to ensure that they dispose of the entire supply that they have brought to market.

This was the world in which the early economists like Adam Smith would have grown up, and these were the arrangements which they reflected in their models of the economy. It was a quite literal description of the behaviour they experienced every day. The overwhelming proportion of the populations of the day lived in villages in the countryside, their daily activity for most of the week was production and consumption. Trading, that is, economic exchange, took place only on a single day, in a discrete space, for a specified time. It made sense to think of economics as the business of trading in markets.

Unfortunately for our subsequent understanding of our discipline, economics was born at the sunset of the agrarian age, and at the birth of an industrial age in which the nature of economic transactions was completely transformed. The founding fathers of our discipline invented theories for a world which was about to vanish from history. In the industrial society, the overwhelming proportion of the population lives in conurbations, where people live, work, produce, consume and conduct economic exchange in the same space, and contemporaneously. In the agrarian economy the worker tends his farm during the week, and goes to market on market day; in the industrial economy the hotel worker travels from home to workplace every day, and he or she may go supermarket shopping any day. In the agrarian economy the farmer takes his produce to market on market day, in the industrial economy he sells it on contract to the supermarket. In the agrarian economy goods and services are exchanged in the market on market day; in the industrial economy shops and businesses are open every day. In the agrarian economy each market is clearly defined in time and space; in the industrial economy there is no special restriction – commodities are exchanged right across the world – and there is no single defined period over which all transactions must be completed. Buyers and sellers make contracts for whatever period is mutually agreeable. I have come to believe that economists have built a discipline for a world which has largely vanished, and that is one reason why we stumble so badly in understanding and explaining the challenges that face the world economy today.

Diedre McCloskey's 40-year-old plea for polite, sensible, reasoned arguments among economists

In what many economists of my generation expected would be a path-breaking article in the prestigious *Journal of Economic Literature*, now largely forgotten, Donald (now Diedre) McCloskey (McCloskey (1983) made a plea for a new approach to the search for new economic knowledge, one that dethrones mathematical "logic" and statistical "rigour" in favour of a reasoned discourse to finding new insight and deeper understanding, using all the cognitive tools at our disposal, including intuition, logic, logical deduction, and a variety of ways of viewing and interpreting information, and bringing to bear institutional, historical, social, political, psychological and other factors, where they served to enrich our understanding. She argued that such an approach was a potentially fruitful rhetoric, the art of discovering warrantable beliefs and improving those beliefs in shared discourse. The words "logic" and "rigour" are in inverted commas because, as McCloskey explains, mathematical logic is not absolute and, as we have shown at some length, statistical rigour is not achievable.

This approach does not privilege the "scientific method" or quantification over other kinds of knowledge. The standard approach to econometric inference, based on falsification (a test by which the economist establishes that she cannot reject her theory) is not really practical, because we can never be sure that we have tested for all the other theories that might explain the data we observe. Even if we take the time to test for all the known theories, we cannot test for those theories that haven't been discovered yet. We have of necessity to exclude a very large number of relationships and variables that may be discovered to have relevance. The argument is not that we should not test; simply that the test have no greater authority or credence than experience, logic, experience and intuition, contrary to common attitudes. We have shown that prediction is impossible in economics, on the basis of the data we have and the methodologies we use.

McCloskey demonstrates that knowledge can never be free from doubt, metaphysics, morals and personal convictions. All too often theories become firmly established, not because of the weight of evidence, but for reasons that have to do with style and form rather than substance. McCloskey argues that the thing that won the day for monetarism was the size and weight of the Friedman-Schwartz book (Friedman and Schwartz, 1963) and the richness and intelligence of its arguments, not the empirical evidence presented.

Quantitative studies are best seen as searches for numbers with which to make specific a theory which is already believed on other grounds. Mark Blaug's (1992) claim, that standard falsification procedures may reliably be used to determine which research programmes should be discarded, affords the standard statistical techniques an unwarranted claim to stand as evidence. The actual practice ignores the precept of respecting the empirical evidence when we reject solid results such as the impact of oil prices on inflation and focus instead on the supply of money, because of our prior belief that the central bank controls the rate of inflation. The "scandal"[4] of economic practice is in the failure to articulate reasons why one may need to ignore the empirical results, in cases where it makes sense to do so.

McCloskey points out that "The abuse of the word 'significant' in connection with statistical arguments in economics is universal" (McCloskey, 1983, p.497). In practice we would need to know what are the costs – not just the economic costs, but social, environmental, etc. – of admitting a chance of one in ten, in preference to one in 20, or any other level of risk of being wrong. This is almost never attempted, no doubt because it proves so difficult an exercise to compute a plausible loss function for all probabilities.

McCloskey points out that we all use rhetorical devices in economics, including the use of humour or ridicule to dismiss opposing arguments. She offers other examples, drawn from the introductory economic textbook by Paul Samuelson, in common use at the time the article was written. The devices include demonstrating mastery of mathematics for no other purpose than establishing the author's erudition (at a time when most economists had little mathematical training), appeals to recognised authority, such as Keynes,

Hicks and Friedman, using "toy economies" with one or two sectors, and the use of analogy.

McCloskey shows that economics is heavily metaphorical, using analysis of "models", "supply", "demand" and "markets", all images abstracted from experience. We also speak of "human capital", "lemons.", "putty-clay models", "turnpikes", "auctions", "the invisible hand", "stability" and "equilibrium". Indeed, mathematical reasoning is itself metaphorical: the "production function" is an abstraction, which aggregates a large number of disparate activities, within a single metaphor, for example.

McCloskey's invitation to rhetoric is a call to move to the rationality of "arguing like human beings". It is an appeal for clearer writing, better teaching, making common cause with the humanities, more humility about the fragility of empirics, and more politeness in economic discourse.

Notes

1 This section is about official forecasts. A survey of business forecasts in the Caribbean that may be of interest is Craigwell, Downes, Odle, Peter and Worrell (1998). That paper describes existing practices and what forecasts are used for. Simple techniques predominated: a percentage increase or decrease on the previous year's value, the subjective views of management and linear trends. The forecasts were used for strategic planning, cash flow management and product development. The variables forecast most frequently were sales, demand, cost and cash flow. Forecast were usually for less than two years.

2 The time series commonly used in economics are assumed to be "ergodic", meaning that it doesn't matter for the economic significance of the variable, say inflation, whether you have data for the 1970s or the 2000s. The economic implications are assumed to be the same irrespective of the time of observations.

3 A common example is the assumption that firms maximise profits.

4 McCloskey's term.

References

Bardsen, Gunnar, Patrik Jonasson, Ragnar Nymoen, and Ard Den Reijer. 2011. "Moses: Model of Swedish economic studies." *Working Paper Series*. Sveriges Riksbank, no. 249, January.

Beinhocker, Eric. 2006. *The origin of wealth*. Cambridge, Massachusetts: Harvard Business School Press.

Blaug, Mark. 1992. *The Methodology of Economics: Or how Economists Explain*, 2nd ed. Cambridge, UK: Cambridge University Press.

Campos, Julia, Neil R. Ericsson, and David F.Hendry. 2005. "Introduction," in *General-to-Specific Modelling*. Cheltenham, UK: Edward Elgar Publishing.

Christoffel, Kai Philipp, Guenter Coenen and Anders Warne. 2008. "The new area-wide model of the Euro area: A micro-founded open-economy model for forecasting and policy analysis." *Working Paper*. European Central Bank, no. 944, October.

Clements, Michael P. and David F. Hendry. 2005. "Guest Editors' Introduction: Information and model transformations in economic forecasting," *Oxford Bulletin of Economics and Statistics*, Vol. 67, Supplement.

Clements, Michael P. and David F. Hendry. 2003. "An overview of economic forecasting," in *Companion to Economic Forecasting*, edited by Clements, Michael P. and David F. Hendry. Oxford: Blackwell Publishing.

Clements, Michael P. and David F. Hendry. 1998, *Forecasting Economic Time Series*, Cambridge UK: Cambridge University Press.

Colander, David. 2008. "Complexity and the history of economic thought." *Economics Discussion Paper*. Middlebury, VT: Middlebury College, March.

Colander, D. and R. Brenner (eds) 1992. *Educating Economists*. Ann Arbor, Michigan: University of Michigan Press.

Coyle, Diane. 2014. *GDP: A Brief but Affectionate History*. Princeton, NJ: Princeton University Press.

Craigwell, Roland, Winston Moore and DeLisle Worrell. 2012. *Price formation and inflation dynamics in the Caribbean*. St Augustine, Trinidad: Caribbean Centre for Money and Finance.

Craigwell, Roland, A. Downes, C. Odle, S, Peter and DeLisle Worrell. 1998. "Business forecasting in the Caribbean." *Economic Review*. Central Bank of Barbados, June.

Diebold, Francis. 1998. "The past, present and future of macroeconomic forecasting." *Journal of Economic Perspectives*, Vol. 12, no. 2, pp. 175–192.

Doornik, Jurgen A. and David F.Hendry. 2007. *Empirical Econometric Modelling Using PcGive 12*, Volume I. London: Timberlake Consultants Press.

Elliott, Graham and Allan G. Timmermann. 2016. "Forecasting in economics and finance." *Discussion Paper*. Centre for Economic Policy Research no. DP11354, June.

Friedman, M. and A. J. Schwartz. 1963. *A Monetary History of the United States, 1867–1960*. Princeton, NJ: Princeton University Press.

Guerrien, Bernard. 2004. "Irrelevance and ideology," *Post-Autistic Economics Review*, Vol. 29, December.

Hendry, David F. 1995. "The theory of reduction," in *Dynamic Econometrics*. Oxford: Oxford University Press.

Hicks, SirJohn. 1963. *The Theory of Wages*, 2nd ed. London: Macmillan.

Hoover, Kevin D. 2001. *The methodology of empirical macroeconomics*. Cambridge and New York: Cambridge University Press.

Kitson, Michael. 2005, "Economics for the future." *Cambridge Journal of Economics*, Vol. 29, no. 6, pp. 827–835.

Marshall, Alfred. 1890. *Principles of Economics*. The Online Library of Liberty A Project Of Liberty Fund, Inc.

Mazzucato, Mariana. 2018. *The Value of Everything: Making and Taking in the Global Economy*. New York: PublicAffairs.

McCloskey, Donald N. 1983. "The rhetoric of economics." *Journal of Economic Literature*, Vol. 21, no. 2, June, pp. 481–517.

McCloskey, Deirdre and S Ziliak. 1996. "The standard error of regressions." *Journal of Economic Literature*, Vol. 34, no. 1, pp. 72–95.

Morck, Randall and Yeung, Bernard Yin. 2011. "Economics, history, and causation." *Working Paper Series*. National Bureau of Economic Research, Vol. w16678, January.

Morgan, Jamie. 2012. "Forecasting, prediction and precision: A commentary," *Economic Thought*, Vol. 1, no. 2.

Pearl. Judea. 2000. *Causality: Models, Reasoning, and Inference*. Cambridge, UK: Cambridge University Press.

Robinson, Joan. 1969. *The Economics of Imperfect Competition*, 2nd ed. London: Palgrave Macmillan.

Samuels, Warren (ed). 1992. *New Horizons in Economic Thought: Appraisals of Leading Economists.* Cheltenham, UK: Edwin Elgar.

Vromen, Jack. 2004. "Conjectural revisionary ontology," *Post-Autistic Economics Review*, Vol. *29*, December.

Winkler, Anthony C. 2004. *The Annihilation of Fish and Other Stories.* Oxford, UK: Macmillan Caribbean.

Worrell, DeLisle and Roland Craigwell. 1997. *Macroeconomics and Finance in the Caribbean: Quantitative Analyses.* St Augustine, Trinidad: Caribbean Centre for Monetary Studies.

Section D

Political Economy and Institutions

The chapters in this section treat with a selection of issues that have been in the background of everything that has been discussed up to this point. The chosen topics are matters on which I offer a perspective which differs from economic orthodoxy and popular perceptions in ways that are crucial for the success of macroeconomic policy. The chapters in this section cover the role of central banks in small open economies; factors that affect the degrees of freedom of policy makers, including history, geography and technology; the rationale for the use of the Human Development Index as the measure of well-being in this book, with an explanation of how the Index is computed; and some observations on anti-globalisation sentiments.

DOI: 10.4324/9781003247609-18

15 The Small Open Economy

Central Banking for the Real World

This chapter makes an argument for a wide scope of responsibility for the central bank, including growth promoting activities and providing input into the central economic decision-making apparatus of the country, in addition to the more common focus on monetary policy and financial oversight. The rationale is that economic growth and development are the principal targets of policy in most SOEs, and there are crucial growth-promoting measures which the monetary authority is best placed to provide. Furthermore, a central thesis of the approach to policy making advanced in this book is the benefits of coordinated action by the treasury and the central bank in the formulation, monitoring and revision of policies in order to keep the economy on track. The assignment of tasks between the institutions should be fluid and focused on achievement of the objectives of policy. The organisational arrangements for the research, formulation, design, implementation, monitoring and modification of policies, and for accounting for performance and adjusting targets, are all of crucial importance. Facile generalisations about central bank independence and fiscal rules are unhelpful; we must get behind the façade to uncover effective and practical arrangements that make for effective economic policy which has the best chance of securing economic outcomes which further the interests of the society.

The topics covered in this chapter include:

- What should a central bank do? Promoting effective financial arrangements for growth-promoting investment must be a major focus, including financial structures and arrangements for innovation and upscaling of production by small enterprises which are judged to have competitive or innovative potential. The conventional view that central banks should limit their investment-promotion activities to the development of capital markets will be challenged.
- The governance of central banks must take account of political institutions and political realities. This is a prime example of the practical policy maker's need to take off the *cateris paribus* blinkers. A case is made for the governance arrangements put in place in Canada after the infamous Coyne Affair as being a practical model, in contrast to the

DOI: 10.4324/9781003247609-19

notion of central bank independence. The point will be illustrated by the Barbados Central Bank experience.

- The notion of central bank independence, which gained wide acceptance until the circumstances of the US recession and the COVID-19 crisis brought it into question, needs to be carefully defined. The central bank should be free of political influence in its staffing, processes and analysis, but the results of the bank's economic analysis, undertaken jointly with the treasury and others, must be fed into a process which is political in order to produce policies with which the representatives of the people are satisfied.
- Effective fiscal-monetary coordination mechanisms are a minimal framework for successful policy making. The coordination should cover all aspects of fiscal, monetary, financial and exchange rate policy, including taxation policy, the level and allocation of public sector expenditure, the financing of government operations, interest and exchange rate policy, financial stability, forecasting, monitoring and course correction as needed, and public information. The notion that those responsible for monetary policy should be required to maintain a public distance from those responsible for government finance is a recipe for market uncertainty and policy failure.
- While it is not possible to be definitive about the arrangements that will work best in any specific country, we can offer some suggestions about the nature of the information and analysis which makes for policies with a good chance of success, and those which are unlikely to do well.

The central bank in any emerging market or developing country should have the financing of investment as a priority

In a memorable conversation over lunch with Agustín Carstens, then Governor of the Bank of Mexico, he recounted to me the story of the Mexican central bank's financing of the infrastructure, from virgin territory, of the resort at Cancún, which overnight created one of the largest and most competitive tourist destinations in the Caribbean. By any accounting, Cancún has to be among the most successful investments in Mexico's recent history, in terms of its lasting contribution to the economy, as well as the spinoffs in terms of living standards in the State of Quintana Roo, where the resort is situated. However, Carstens was adamant that such investment by the Bank of Mexico would not be countenanced nowadays, because the Cancún investment was made on the instructions of the then President of Mexico, something which is now prohibited by law.

The concern which animates the fashion for laws mandating so-called "central bank independence" is real, and one which I share. I have been described by economists who know me well as the most extreme of fiscal conservatives, a reflection of my conviction of the overwhelming power of fiscal policy as the essential tool of adjustment in the open economy. When fiscal deficits exceed the private sector's willingness to finance them, the central bank is the agency that steps into the breach, to provide new money to fund the public sector's excessive spending. This is the circumstance, evidently, in which an independent central bank which is prohibited by law from creating money to fund the public sector, is supposed to force government to apply the brakes on spending. We will return to discuss what happens in practice in that situation in a moment. What concerns us here is the fact that a blanket prohibition of all direct financing from the central bank to the public sector may inhibit the seeding of potential growth-enhancing investment.

Our point of departure is the contrarian notion that the premier financial institution in an emerging market or developing economy must have a major focus on the finance of competitive, growth-enhancing investment. We marry this notion with that of the "entrepreneurial state", a perspective of the pivotal role that the state plays in economies exhibiting every modern system of government, a term coined by Mazzucato (see Chapter 8). Mazzucato argues that the entrepreneurial state makes big bets on new technologies and shapes the markets of the future, exactly along the lines of opening a new tourism resort with transformative potential, as in the case of Cancún and Aruba (Chapter 4). Mazzucato provides convincing evidence of entrepreneurial activity in capitalist economies like the US, in the roles played by the National Science Foundation and the National Institutes of Health. Although Mazzucato's work offers the most all-encompassing argument for the important growth-enhancing benefits that successful state entrepreneurship provides, the idea is not new. The importance of public policy in the rise of East Asian economies in the past four decades was evaluated in a study by the Page (1993) of eight countries in that region. While acknowledging "the complexity of public policy strategies" among them, the study concludes that "policies contribute to the attainment of three central functions: accumulation, allocation and productivity growth" (Page, 1993, p. 102). On the distaff side, there is a mountain of literature on the squandering of economic resources and loss of competitiveness and economic potential due to poorly conceived and inefficiently applied public policies for development financing. What follows are thoughts, based on my experience in the Caribbean, for the role that an operationally-independent central bank – a notion we shall elaborate on later in this chapter – may undertake in the provision of efficient, innovative, performance-oriented development finance.

Central banks and the financing of development – exploiting the opportunities and avoiding the pitfalls

Caribbean economies cannot contemplate quantitative easing (QE) of the sort engaged in by advanced economies because the resulting pressures on the balance of payments and international reserves would be unsupportable in the absence of growth in exports, tourism and other services. However, there is a need for investment in infrastructure, systems for business facilitation and external marketing and branding to increase productive capacity and competitiveness in the foreign exchange earning sectors. In addition, there is a chronic shortage of funding for new ventures and innovation. This section looks into the possibility of a form of QE specifically designed to address these niches. By increasing competitiveness this funding will produce a future stream of foreign currency which assures the sustainability of the credit over the medium term. We also review critically other ways in which Caribbean central banks have attempted to address the issue of finance for development.

The insufficiency of finance is among the most frequently cited obstacles in the path of growth and development in the Caribbean.[1] Since these countries have a chronic surplus of bank liquidity, the problem cannot lie with the overall supply of finance in the economy. Moreover, the shortage of finance is not evident at large and multinational firms, which have no difficulty in financing any project which they find to be profitable. Rather, the shortage is felt most keenly by small and medium-sized firms, start-ups and firms that are trying to introduce new products and processes, or trying to enter new markets or market segments.

This is an issue at the forefront of the development of Caribbean economies which are in the process of introducing new sectors of economic activity, principally green energy production and the production and export of cultural products. In the embryonic stages of these sectors, as has been the case with all industrial advancement worldwide, firms will need strong official backing in various forms, including equity and concessional finance. That is because the early growth stages of any activity involve a steep learning curve, and an inherently risky process of learning by doing. Inevitably there will be early stumbles, and there must be mechanisms to provide these firms with second chances, otherwise there is little prospect that the sector will grow to a size that permits the synergies and economies of scope and scale that are essential for an economic take-off.

The development banks and other state-owned supporting institutions that were so successful in this role in Asia have been an almost universal failure in the Caribbean, where they have been subject to political capture and insolvency. (The Caribbean Development Bank, a regional institution, is a success story and the most significant exception to a very poor record for development banks in the region. Its success is undoubtedly due to its regional character, which has protected it from political pressure from individual borrowing countries.) The nongovernmental and small business services that have replaced our development banks have had modest success, but the scale of resources needed for the development of new economic activity that is of national significance is well beyond their capacity.

The burden of this section is that Caribbean central banks are in a position to step into this breach. The global movement for the independence of central banks over the past decades has spilled over into the Caribbean. Provisions for central bank independence are written into the central bank statute in many cases, and central banks now have greater autonomy almost everywhere within the region. That puts the central banks in a position where they may provide financing for innovation and diversification in ways that are insulated from political capture.

The provision of finance for development by central banks is not without precedent. Some central banks have provided funding directly for major projects. Others have supported financial institutions in the private sector with a view to increasing the efficiency of financial flows for development.

The central bank, in its role as overseer of the financial system and in making and implementing financial policy, has to embrace all aspects of financial development, not only stability and inflation. This is not a novel idea. The Central Bank of Barbados, and most central banks that were established from the 1960s onwards, have charters which include financial development as a central objective of the bank's mandate. In the conceptualisation and development of the Financial Sector Assessment Programme (FSAP), there was an explicit focus on financial development, and this is now reflected in the publication by the World Bank of an annual Global Financial Development Report, the first of which was issued in 2013.

There is an evident inefficiency in Caribbean financial markets which predates the financial crisis and which persists today: it is the widely observed scarcity of finance for investment, particularly in innovative activity, in environments where there is ample liquidity lying idle with commercial banks. My suggestion is that central banks should consider novel ways to re-channel some of that finance to activities that are national development priorities.

Our starting point is the importance of financial systems to development: financial development is about the efficient allocation of finance to enhance economic growth and the well-being of citizens. The focus on financial stability should be seen in this light: stability is a means to an end, namely the overall development of the economy and the improvement of the living standards of all citizens. Stability, which tends to get top billing in popular discussion, is one of four benchmarks suggested by the World Bank's Global Financial Development Report (GFDR) for assessing the level of financial development. The others are: financial depth, access to finance and the efficiency of the delivery of financial services.

The rationale for a central bank role in development is therefore twofold:

- The necessary role of the public sector in innovation and the development of new products, services and markets; and
- The independence of the central bank, which protects its activities from political capture.

Historically, the state has played the leading role in all major economic transformations in economies of every political stripe, including the US, Canada, modern Europe, Japan and South Korea, countries with liberal, market-oriented economies, as well as in countries and regions such as

Russia, China and Latin America which are reputed to have more interventionist traditions. The reasons why this is the case are well known: early movers entering new markets, using new technologies, developing new products and services, do not have a track record of performance by which their credit-worthiness may be judged. Potential financiers, whether lenders or equity partners, therefore lack what is the most dependable marker of a credit-worthy borrower, that is their track record of performance in areas pertinent to the intended financing. In the early days of any new activity, external economies such as widespread availability of relevant skills, supporting services and information such as marketing and quality control and many other ancillaries, are not widely available. A gestation period is invariably needed, when the enterprise is working out teething problems before production can be ramped up and secure marketing arrangements put in place to ensure a steady revenue stream. For all of these reasons, conventional market financing mechanisms such as term loans, equity participation and the issue of corporate bonds have failed to meet the financing needs of innovating firms and small and medium enterprises.

This much is not new. In the World Bank's Global Financial Development Report 2013 it states "there are sound economic reasons for the state to play an active role in financial systems". However, the report also cautions that "there are practical reasons to be wary of the state playing too active a role" (World Bank, 2013, p. 1). Caribbean experience bears testimony to both statements. Over the past half century, Caribbean nations have experimented with state owned commercial enterprise, directed commercial bank credit, specialised financing institutions for credit and insurance, development banks, credit guarantees and other credit support facilities, the promotion of stock and bond markets, tax incentives and direct subsidies. The extent of success has been very limited and as a result, governments have retreated from the most intrusive forms of intervention. That remains problematic, however, because it results in a situation where there is inadequate finance for innovation, even in the presence of excess funding in the financial system as a whole.

The Barbadian experience is instructive. Over the past 50 years the Barbados Government has owned or established specialised banks and financial institutions, all of which have now been liquidated or sold into the private sector. The Barbados Development Bank had to be liquidated when it became insolvent, weighed down by an excess of bad loans. It operated on a scale that turned out to be too small to make a decisive impact on the overall magnitude or direction of investment in the productive capacity of the economy. A number of other state-owned financial institutions, including the Barbados Savings Bank, the Barbados Mortgage Finance Corporation and the Agricultural Credit Fund, were consolidated to form the Barbados National Bank (BNB) in the late 1970s. The BNB was in direct competition with privately-owned commercial banks, and its portfolio and pricing came to resemble them in every way. Over time it became clear that the BNB could not address the perceived lacunae in the financial market, especially with respect to the financing of investment, and when the opportunity arose to earn foreign exchange by sale of the BNB, the Government sold its entire stake in the bank. Government established a successful general insurance company, which also operated much like its commercial competitors. It too was sold to private sector interests.

The Barbados Government has established several minor funds in support of small and medium enterprises, most in the last two decades. They have all been modestly funded and when initial funding has been exhausted the funds have become dormant for want of adequate reflows or new funding. The aggregate impact of these funds on investment and growth has been very little.

The Central Bank of Barbados has always had financial development as part of its mandate, and it has used both interventionist measures and support for financial market development in pursuit of this objective. In the 1970s credit directives were seen as an important tool in the Bank's armoury, mainly in an attempt to bias commercial bank lending away from consumer durable purchases. By the mid-1980s it was evident that these directives were ineffective: there was no change in the allocation of bank credit away from consumer purchases. What is more, the Central Bank stipulations, which applied only to commercial banks, had the unintended effect of diverting business from commercial banks to credit unions and other financial institutions which were not regulated by the Central Bank. The credit stipulations were quietly laid to rest in the late 1980s.

A second and more successful thrust for financial development by the Central Bank was by way of its schemes in support of lending by banks and other financial institutions. The Central Bank acted as conduit for funding from official foreign sources to the financial system. However, the demand for additional finance by commercial banks was always very weak, because the banks suffer from a chronic surplus of finance over the amount that creditworthy borrowers need. There has been somewhat greater interest in the Bank's credit guarantee schemes, which insure some part of banks' credit risk, for a small premium. These schemes have had some beneficial effects on the finance of small and medium enterprises, but have not made much of a contribution at an aggregate level.

The Central Bank's most aggressive and sustained effort to stimulate financial development was in the establishment and support for the securities market. In terms of its impact on the allocation of finance for development the Bank's efforts in this direction cannot be considered a success. The Barbados Securities Exchange, of which the Central Bank was a promoter, founding member and part financier, has been a stilted infant. There have been very infrequent new issues, and none has been for a major investment project. The largest have been associated with mergers and acquisitions, and the firms that have attracted buyers' greatest interest are those large and established businesses who have no difficulty in funding investment from their own or borrowed resources, including foreign sources. Their participation was a patriotic gesture of support for the exchange, and most have since withdrawn. On an annual basis the average contribution to fixed investment of the Barbados Securities Exchange over its life has been no more than one per cent.

Caribbean countries have an excess of short-term funds, represented by non-interest bearing balances at central banks, at the same time that innovators are unable to obtain financing on suitable terms. This is a situation that may be observed throughout the region, and one which characterises small emerging market economies worldwide. The reasons for this persistent mismatch would appear to lie with the institutional structure of small economies, in particular the observation that economic activity in these economies is dominated by a handful of conglomerate companies and companies with interlocking directorships. Companies of this size and range will always have external commercial and financial links, which give them access to global financial markets, and they are therefore never short of funding for viable projects. By the same token, they are not constrained by the availability of local savings. What is more, because of the high import content of investment in the small open economy, access to foreign exchange sets a limit: investment stalls when there is a shortage of foreign exchange, even in circumstances where domestic savings are readily available.

The strategy for accelerating investment in these circumstances must be twofold: 1) providing incentives for the dominant conglomerates with international market access to invest in innovation and emerging competitive activities, and 2) providing alternative financial instruments and channels for innovators to finance new processes, products and industries such as culture and green energy. This chapter speaks to the second element of that strategy.

We suggest that the most impactful contribution the central banks of small emerging market countries may make to promote financial development is to provide alternative channels and instruments for the finance of innovation. By doing so the central bank applies a remedy directly to the heart of the problem, which is not the availability of finance per se, but rather the supply of finance in a form that meets the requirements of an innovator.

The initiatives that the Central Bank of Barbados and other central banks in the region have taken have all failed to achieve anything like the intended impact. Securities markets have been a disappointment: issues of new securities have been few and far between, trading volumes have been low, trades are infrequent, prices are highly volatile, and price movements often do not reflect perceived fundamentals. Most relevant for our purposes, new issues were mostly motivated by mergers and acquisitions rather than to finance new projects, and innovators attracted no interest in a market dominated by conglomerates and mainstream establishments.

Barbados' experience with credit insurance and other forms of credit support is typical: the schemes are helpful, but their overall effects are too little to make a marked difference to the overall growth and development of their economies. This is the conclusion reached in the World Bank's Global Financial Development Report 2013 in relation to similar schemes worldwide.

There is, therefore, a strong argument for government intervention to provide appropriate financial services for this type of activity. However, the institutional mechanisms that have been tried in the Caribbean have failed in their intended purpose, largely because of political pressures. Central banks are protected from such pressure. Central bank independence is a central tenet of international financial theory and practice, and it is reflected in central bank laws throughout the Caribbean. In most cases central bank decisions may be overridden by ministers of finance only with the assent of parliament, and the independence of the central bank is one of the criteria by which the soundness of financial regulation is judged by the IMF and World Bank in periodic Financial Sector Assessment Programmes.

The independence of the central bank allows it to stand in for government in the provision of infant industry finance in appropriate forms and linked to demonstrated performance, measured against clearly stated objectives. The focus on financial development reflected in the World Bank's Global Financial Development Report is welcome, offering a perspective on global financial reform which properly reflects the priorities and circumstances of emerging market economies. For such economies, financial stability is the means to an end, that is, financial development.

We do not venture any suggestions as to the institutional form that the innovative financing should take; any of the traditional forms, such as development banks, export credit and guarantee banks, partnership with venture funds or similar arrangement are feasible. What distinguishes our recommendation is the governance of the funding institutions, so that they are free of political influence, and that they should be part of a reformed public sector where all agencies, including public financial institutions, publish annual reports in a timely fashion, to account for their performance against previously stated targets. The public sector-funding institutions, for their part, should disperse credit in instalments over time, conditional on the achievement of agreed targets. Oversight of credits should be flexible, allowing for teething troubles and second chances, but non-performance should be penalised and should result in disqualification for further funding. A second feature of our suggested central bank funding initiative is that it be substantial, of a magnitude sufficient to stimulate internationally competitive activity sufficient to add noticeably to foreign earnings over many years.

The case for operational independence of the central bank is strong

The extensive literature on central bank independence, the foundations of which are surveyed in Worrell and Belgrave (1997), focusses on inflation policy and the respective roles of the central bank and the treasury. This glosses over essential detail about how policy is formulated without which practical advice on best options is impossible. In this section we make the following points: 1) a high degree of independence in the staffing and operations both of the central bank and the treasury is absolutely essential to ensure that they are staffed by skilled professionals of great integrity, who can provide top policy makers with policy advice that is analytically sound and based on reliable data and information; 2) the policy documents prepared by the treasury and central bank should be fed into the top body responsible for the design, implementation, monitoring and modification of policies, as described in Chapter 12; and 3) the decision process must be designed to produce a single unified stance on policy, to be articulated jointly and severally by the central bank and all public sector agencies.

Independence of staffing and operations is essential for the efficiency of both the central bank and the Treasury

A major reason for the poor design of economic policies in very many countries is the infection of the public service by political influence, to the detriment of the quality of data compiled and analysis available to policy makers. It is obvious that good policy design makes for a greater success rate, which resounds to the benefit of the political faction that was credited for these policies, so the motive for politicians to maintain a hands-off position with respect to staffing and operations seems compelling. However, in my experience politicians are unable to resist the temptation to interfere in the staffing and operations of the public sector, and in some cases this has extended to the central bank.

In the Caribbean the decline in the quality of public services has been gradual over several decades. The efficiency of public services in the region in the late colonial period varied from tolerable in a few countries, such as Guyana and Barbados, to spotty, in much of the rest of the region. Over the decades since Independence levels of efficiency have fallen slowly and continuously almost everywhere in the independent Caribbean, in a downward spiral which often began when the political directorate believed that socially desirable policies were being frustrated by treasury officials' insistence on fiscal prudence. The measures taken to overcome that resistance in particular circumstances in the early years of independence have proved to be the fracture that has, over time, compromised financial control in the public sector as a whole.

Contrary to the usual assumption, the treasury and the central bank are almost always on the side of fiscal prudence in the design of fiscal and monetary policy. It is the spending ministries who are ranged on the other side, with a list of expenditures, always in excess of available finance, all of which are said to be of the highest priority. Whether a practical, implementable, performance-driven policy package emerges depends on the skills and abilities of the public servants, including the central bankers, who are at the table when the final decisions are made. What typically eventuates nowadays in all too many instances, is decisions on expenditure allocations based on political expediency, with arbitrary cuts in allocations. The public servants charged with implementation know the resulting funding allocations will be inadequate to deliver the quantity and quality of services for which they are responsible, and that they will inevitably fall short of the targets for implementation. This explains the widely reported "implementation deficit" and much of the widespread demoralisation of Caribbean public services.

The treasury and the central bank should present and explain the economic development strategy jointly

Worrell cautions:

> In the real world of information asymmetries, uncertain expectations and changeable preferences ... the central bank and the treasury must work together on the design, implementation, monitoring and, when necessary, the revision of macroeconomic policy, and on providing the public with information on ongoing economic developments and interpretation of monetary policy.
>
> (Worrell, 2000, abstract)

"Information asymmetries" is technical shorthand for what is in practice a typical situation, where opinions differ as to how large a fiscal deficit can be tolerated without causing an excessive drain on foreign reserves, how large an impact an oil price increase might have on the fiscal balance, the effect of world events on foreign earnings, or other developments that might depress economic activity and destabilise the exchange rate. Those economic agents who are most nervous may opt to switch financial assets into foreign currencies, postpone intended investment or take other decisions which bring on the very perils that caused their apprehension in the first place.

The top public sector decision makers can calm nerves and reassure the market by setting credible targets for foreign exchange holdings and making and realising commitments to take fiscal and monetary measures to hit those targets under every circumstance. The announcement of the targets will only have credibility if the entire official management team speaks from the same hymn sheet, in messages that are delivered in fora of all kinds over the entire life of the programme. Crucial to the credibility of the official strategy is the choice of target. It makes sense to target the exchange rate, because fiscal and monetary adjustment will always protect the essential war chest of foreign reserves by trimming aggregate expenditure to the inflow of foreign currency. The management of the exchange rate is within the government's control. On the other hand, committing to a target for inflation undermines the credibility of official policy, because in effect government thereby commits itself to contain the effects of a spike in the international prices of food and fuels over which it had no control. That will not prevent a clamour from the public for relief whenever foreign prices rise, but it is less damaging for the leadership to point to the obvious than to promise what they cannot deliver.

The governance of the central bank must be sensitive to political realities while not being susceptible to political pressure

The demand for public goods is infinitely large if we include poverty alleviation, environmental remediation and climate change mitigation in addition to things more normally considered as public goods, such as education, health services and law and order, when compared to the finances available from taxation, other revenue and prudent government borrowing. The world is currently in a period of great uncertainty about the governance arrangements which resolve these tensions between priorities and finances in ways that can produce practical, progressive policies. The governance of central banks is just one small part of the puzzle. As the government's banker the bank is charged with providing expert advice on the prudent limits to borrowing and the management of debt. A dilemma arises from the fact that the government's banker is owned by the government. How can the central bank be structured to ensure that it provides dispassionate, objective advice to its owners? And why should the government accept that advice in any circumstance which they believe threatens the ruling faction's hold on power?

The International Monetary Fund's answer to this question, that limits to the central bank's lending to government or to the size of government deficits be imposed by legislation, is naïve. In a crunch, the legislation will be amended or ignored, or some device will be found to get around it. This much should be obvious; on 19th Street in Washington DC they have apparently never heard the phrase *quis custodiet ipsos custodes* (from the *Satires* of the Roman poet Juvenal), known to every secondary school student of my generation.

The problem of political pressure on the central bank was uppermost in the minds of those who advised on the statute for the Central Bank of Barbados in 1972, just over a decade after the much-publicised "Coyne Affair" in Canada. James Coyne, the second Governor of the Bank of Canada, resigned in 1961, after a disagreement with Prime Minister John Diefenbaker and Finance Minister Donald Fleming over government's attempts to spur economic activity by borrowing, against the central bank's advice. Diefenbaker's Conservative Party majority in the House of Commons, the lower chamber of the Canadian Parliament, passed a motion to declare the Governorship of the Bank of Canada vacant, on the irrelevant grounds that the Governor had raised his pension. The motion was rejected by the upper chamber, the Senate, which was controlled by the opposition Liberal Party, but Coyne resigned anyway.

In the wake of the Coyne Affair the Canadian Parliament passed legislation, on which the law governing the Central Bank of Barbados was based, mandating that, in any situation where the central bank's advice on monetary policy was not accepted by the Minister of Finance, the Governor was to submit his advice in writing to the Minister of Finance, who was required by law to put the matter to a vote of Parliament for resolution. This is a practical arrangement which does not presume that technicians at the central bank have to power to frustrate the will of the people's elected representatives. What it does ensure, presumably, is that a fully informed debate takes place, in which the risks and possible consequences of ignoring the central bank's recommendations can be fully ventilated.

However, my own experience serves to demonstrate that even this arrangement is not fool-proof. In January 2017, as the Barbados government's top economic policy committee, chaired by Minister of Finance Chris Sinckler, convened to plan for the fiscal year beginning in April, the administration faced a dilemma. The government's term of office would come to an end in February of the following year, and the ruling party faced an almost certain prospect of defeat. In a last desperate effort to stave off the inevitable, they had begun gearing up to boost employment and spending by creating short-term programmes in the public sector. However, several years of over-spending and current account deficits had already created a crushing burden of debt service and foreign reserves were depleted. Under the circumstances the Board of the Central Bank of Barbados recommended to Minister Sinckler that the government reverse its previous opposition and seek a Standby Arrangement with the International Monetary Fund. However, in the event, Minister Sinckler was unable to convince his colleagues of the necessity of Fund support, because it would have put paid to their last-ditch attempts to boost employment through irresponsible spending.

I then invoked the provisions of the legislation, writing to Minister Sinckler advising the Government to begin discussions with the International Monetary Fund, setting out the reasons and outlining what terms the Government should seek to obtain. My letter was never laid in the Parliament as the law required. Instead the Minister sought to have me removed from office, against which I sought an emergency injunction. That injunction was rejected by the Barbados Court of Appeal, a result which I expected. My legal team was primed to take the appeal to the Caribbean Court of Justice on the next working day after the Court of Appeal gave its verdict (without providing a justification, which came only a week later). In order to forestall my appeal to the Caribbean court, an appeal which they were afraid would have been sustained, the Minister delivered a letter removing me from office at 11pm on the evening of the Barbados Court of Appeal hearing. This experience demonstrates both the fact that legislation *per se* does not compel the desirable action, and the fact that fiscal policies which do not respect the limits will inevitably fail. By the time the election was finally called, in May 2018, the foreign reserves were so low that the incoming administration was forced to accept a punitive debt restructuring programme and deep expenditure cuts, as the price for saving the currency from major devaluation under an IMF-supported programme.

Arguably, the legislation governing the Bank of Canada's operations, which is mirrored in the corresponding Barbados legislation, is still the best compromise between the will of the people and the limits of what the finance available to government will permit. Legislation can never compel action, and implementation always depends on the strength of the institutions and the depth of the analytical skills and knowledge of the leadership. One may conceive of circumstances where, both in the Canadian and Barbadian cases, fiscal discipline might have been imposed despite the removal of the Governor, but that would have required collective leadership responsible enough to have resisted policies which were bound to be detrimental to the economy.

Unified fiscal, monetary and exchange rate policies for development and stabilisation

We should resist the temptation to think of fiscal, monetary and exchange rate policies as separate programmes with distinct goals. Instead we need to consider all the elements of macroeconomic policy as being integral to an organic whole, which becomes dysfunctional in some sense, whenever any element is out of sync with all others. The central bank, the treasury and the revenue administration will have different operational responsibilities, for underlying economic and financial analysis, for forecasting, for debt management, for financial control, for banking and exchange operations, for clearing and settlement, for revenue collection, for the analysis of public projects, and all the other elements and arrangements concerning funding and cash management in the public sector. There are some functions that fall naturally to one or other agency, there are others that may be shared, and there are yet others where the location of responsibility varies from country to country. However, these functions should all be seen as feeding into a single command centre, with responsibility to process inputs from them all, in the formulation and execution of a strategy covering all elements of government's activity and economic influence, and with a view to continuous improvement in national well-being. It is the efficiency that is manifest at the decision-making centre, and the seamlessness of the internal links in the organisation, that matter for overall economic success.

As for any organism, there are several features that make for effective functioning. The information which is collected should be comprehensive, timely and well defined. Much needs to be done in most countries to improve the statistical reporting systems to provide the reliable data needed for macroeconomic decision-making. Data on the most essential series, such as GDP, employment, foreign earnings and spending, the national debt, and public sector revenue and spending are needed at monthly and quarterly frequencies. Often, what is available is of uneven quality: inflation statistics are available monthly, but the items included in the consumer basket may be very out of date; key data such as foreign reserves are available daily at the central bank, but they are seldom distributed to the entire economic management team every day in readily digestible form. It is vital that all members of the team receive the earliest alerts to possible balance of payments problems, and are primed for action if it becomes necessary to convene an emergency meeting to address the situation. Annual data on health outcomes, educational achievement and social conditions are often not available on a timely basis to allow for the preparation of performance-driven public sector budgets and public accountability, an often misused term. What is needed are timely reports that account for how budget allocations have been spent, explaining how much has been achieved of what the allocation was intended to finance. That provides the basis for an informed decision about the next year's allocation. Audit reports and the pursuit and prosecution of infelicities after the fact are necessary, but they are of no value for policy-making purposes. Macroeconomic decision-making may be improved in most Caribbean countries by devoting more resources and deploying higher-level skills in the collection of data.

A second feature of the well-functioning policy framework is the efficient processing of data. It is not helpful to present data to the top macroeconomic policy committee in raw form; reports must be prepared which interpret the data, put it in context and set a framework for any decisions that have to be made. The nature of such reports will vary: a report may be a single graphic, as for the Central Bank of Barbados' daily foreign reserves chart (Chapter 12); an analytical report, with an executive summary with conclusions and recommendations, as for Staff Reports to the Executive Directors of the IMF; or a carefully structured graphical report. The analytical reports reaching macroeconomic decision-makers in small open economies are mostly deficient in that they fail to recognise that foreign exchange and international competitiveness are essential for their economic growth, as a foundation for the analysis. We therefore often see such items as plans for domestic currency investment in housing, with no recognition of the need for foreign currency to meet the import needs for that investment.

The effectiveness of the framework depends on coordination, more difficult for governments to achieve than it should be because public sector departments and agencies so often operate in silos. During my tenure as Governor of the Central Bank of Barbados I had occasion to enquire why the Bank's Director of Banking Operations, who had made tenders for treasury bills for the Bank and government agencies, had tendered for one agency at a rate different from that agreed at the meeting of the joint committee responsible for executing monetary policy. The response was that no instruction had been received from the responsible officer at that agency, a typical example of bureaucratic mindlessness. The public services of many countries are riddled with spurious confidentiality stipulations, vertical ladders that require approval from heads of department for trivial exchanges of information, and poor or non-existent channels of collaboration.

Effective policy making arrangements also feature monitors at all levels of implementation and efficient feedback loops which allow for fast reaction to unexpected circumstances. In addition to the institutional arrangements for monitoring and response at the level of the top policy committee, high levels of sensitivity at all operational levels within the decision structure makes for a more alert and responsive economic management system. Such sensitivity comes of expertise and experience. The experienced taxman will immediately spot when revenue is not consistent with developments in the tax base, the persons or companies paying that particular tax. That intuition may be the first indication of an as yet undetected slowdown in business activity. Similarly, the knowledgeable debt manager will sense when conditions have become unfavourable for a particular debt issue, even though a weakening of investor sentiment may not yet be evident in the data.

Finally, effectiveness requires a single intention and purpose. An important reason for a joined-up decision process, involving all the agencies involved in implementation, is to secure buy-in from everyone, and a commitment to make the agreed strategy work, a commitment born of conviction thanks to their active involvement in the formulation of the strategy. The best chance of convincing everyone around the table about the strategy that is finally chosen is to present high quality analysis and to have full discussion of all the options, looking carefully into all the feasible ways forward. Provided the participants are persons of the right calibre, determined to take action sufficient to achieve the economic objective, the team will emerge with a sense of mission, committed to spreading the message and overcoming the inevitable obstacles that will be encountered on the way to achieving the agreed targets.

Note

1 For example, World Economic Forum, Global Competitiveness Report 2013–14, where this is cited as among the three most frequently cited challenges of doing business in Barbados.

References

Mazzucato, Mariana. 2013. *The Entrepreneurial State: Debunking Public vs. Private Sector Myths.* London: Anthem Press.

Page, John, 1993, *The East Asian Miracle: Economic Growth and Public Policy.* Oxford: Oxford University Press for the World Bank.

World Bank. Various years. "Global Financial Development Report," Washington, DC: The Bank. worldbank.org.

Worrell, DeLisle. 2000. "Monetary and Fiscal Coordination in Small Open Economies." *Working Paper.* International Monetary Fund, no. 00/56, March.

Worrell, DeLisle and Anton Belgrave. 1997. "The treasury and the central bank: Independence or consensus?" *Working Paper.* Central Bank of Barbados, August.

16 Sovereignty, History, Geography, Technology and the Degrees of Freedom for Economic Policy

In this chapter we offer comments on some non-economic factors which have to be taken into account in shaping economic policy in every country. The countries discussed in this book are sovereign and independent, with the exception of a few UK and US dependencies mentioned in Chapter 4. They all value their sovereignty, but we need to look more closely into the real value of the sovereignty of a very small independent nation. No country can free itself of the legacy of history, and there will be costs in attempting to undo the consequences of history if a society determines that is what must be done. Geography also affects the costs of different choices in obvious ways. The fourth factor discussed in this chapter has to do with technology and technological change.

Sovereignty and the economy

Sovereignty does not equip the small open economy with any additional economic tools, and may mislead leaders into adopting policies that impair the well-being of the society, or large sections of it. In a provocative essay entitled "The Free Colony" the Trinidadian poet and essayist Andre Bagoo says that the "conclusion that the colonised should follow nationalist independence policies in Africa, the South Sea Islands, Madagascar and the West Indies" in the aftermath of the second world war

> has to be questioned. What should have been the priority was equality, not independence. What was needed was integration that had human dignity at its heart. The empire should have been made to absorb, as the heart expands over time when exercised by the body's limbs. A deeper, more genuine union, premised on equal rights in all areas of life, should have been the centre of a multicultural ferment in a space where the intoxicating mixture of races and cultures could have enhanced world society.
>
> (Bagoo, 2020, p. 121)

The question of sovereignty keeps popping up wherever I lecture on the topic of dollarisation, in criticisms of foreign ownership of banks, ports, airports and natural resources, and in discussions about adding value to domestic production by

DOI: 10.4324/9781003247609-20

doing more local processing. On dollarisation, I always point to countries ranging from Cuba to Venezuela to Zimbabwe and Iran, whose difficulties are with accessing dollars, even though they have their own currencies. The counter-example usually proffered, that of the US arrest of former Panamanian President Manuel Noriega in 1988, was as a result of a military invasion of the country, and had nothing to do with the fact that Panama has never had a currency of its own.

Foreign banks are prominent in the financial systems of most small economies because they have the advantage over domestic banks of size and international networks. The testimony that these factors, not ownership, are what determine the costs and allocation of bank credit is the similarity in costs and credit distribution of successful local banks. Local banks who bias their activities towards small enterprise without the backing of the marketable collateral that foreign banks demand, or who lend with tighter interest margins soon discover, to their cost, that loan losses and credit administration costs threaten their viability. The fact that local banks need to secure foreign corresponding banks with access to markets that trade US dollars puts them at an additional disadvantage in competition with foreign-owned banks.

The advantage that international companies bring to the operation of ports and airports is a worldwide network of connections, marketing and services, and access to finance that can transform well-situated locations into important hubs in a global or regional network. No government boasts a comparable network with a similar range of specialised and marketing services. By insisting on local ownership, or worse, national ownership and operation, a government deprives the country of access to what could be transformative investment, financed by an international company on a lease or partnership basis, as part of their global expansion strategy.

There is little to distinguish locally-owned and foreign-owned producers of similar agricultural produce and manufactured goods in terms of the value they add to the product before sale. The critical determinants of their contribution to the local economy have to do with weight, volume, transport costs, shelf life of the product and size of the local demand for the product, and nothing to do with ownership. The one legitimate ownership concern, from an economic point of view, has to do with the ownership and exploitation of natural resources, an issue which is beyond our scope.

The value of national sovereignty also comes into question in a comparison of the Caribbean islands of Puerto Rico, the US Virgin Islands, Martinique, Guadeloupe, the Cayman Islands and the Turks and Caicos islands, which are all dependencies of or integrated into the US, the UK and France, with independent Caribbean nations of similar size. The population of Jamaica, almost three million, is about the same as that of Puerto Rico, and the islands are about the same size. Puerto Rico's GDP (US$103 billion in 2020), however, is seven times that of Jamaica (US$14 billion). Martinique, a neighbour of Barbados, about the same size and population, records a GDP of US$9 billion, twice as large as Barbados' US$4.4 billion. The Cayman Islands, with a quarter of Barbados' population, has a GDP which is almost 20 per cent larger.

We may also compare the life prospects of young Martinicans with those of young Barbadians. Some weeks ago my friend Professor Cardinal Ward of MIT, founder of the Caribbean Science Foundation, told me that he had been contacted by a young Martinican professor who teaches at an Irish university. The young man was excited by the announcement that Barbados had become a republic, a symbolic gesture, involving little more than a change of title for the head of state. I remarked ruefully to Cardinal that had the young man been born in Barbados, independent since 1966, he would probably not be teaching in an Irish university. Having been born in Martinique, with a French passport and free access to education in the metropole, he was able to apply for a post at any university in the European Union on graduation. This is a set of privileged circumstances which his Barbadian counterpart would die for, limited as he would be to the local educational system and the single university on the island, with an immigration barrier to any job beyond the country's 441 square kilometres.

Residents in the sovereign countries of the Caribbean are, with the exception of The Bahamas, chronically short of US dollars for foreign purchases and to secure the value of domestic savings. The residents of dependencies, associated states and territories integrated into the metropolis do not have that problem. Puerto Rico and the US Virgin Islands are part of the US Federal Reserve system and use the US dollar, and Martinique, Guadeloupe and Guyana are part of the euro area. The English-speaking dependencies are an interesting case study. Like The Bahamas they all have own currencies, but the US dollar is used alongside the local currency, and the proportion of US dollar deposits in the banking system is very high. The populations are nonchalant about the use of local currency because none of these countries has ever experienced a balance of payments crisis of the kind that have repeatedly destabilised currency markets elsewhere in the Caribbean, leading to exchange rate depreciation. This, in spite of the fact that the economies have been buffeted by similar forces, external and domestic, over the years. The most remarkable contrast is between the Jamaican and Caymanian dollar. Up until the establishment of the Bank of Jamaica in 1961, and for some time thereafter, the Cayman Islands used the Jamaican pound, as it then was, as the domestic currency. When Cayman Islands issued its own currency in 1972, its value was set equal to the value of the Jamaican currency at that time, US $1.13, that is 13 cents higher than the value of one US dollar, a rate which persists to this day. In the meanwhile the value of the Jamaican currency has fallen to about one half of one US cent (US$0.0065 as I write this).

Sovereignty limits the access to internationally competitive skills and may stifle career development

The corollary of the limitation of small size on the range of production (Chapter 6) is that the small economy is limited in the range of skills in which it can reach internationally competitive standards in numbers sufficient to form an economically competitive supply. Those whose talents lie elsewhere than in the country's specialties, and those wishing to pursue careers in other fields, have to overcome immigration barriers to fulfil their aspirations. What is more, within the career options on offer domestically, the room for advancement will inevitably be limited. The further up the career ladder you go, the fewer the domestic options. Every year a new batch of school-leavers arrives to compete for the available openings in competitive industries, and there are many aspirants for every good opportunity that opens up for advancement. These pressures animate policies to restrict immigration into the small economy, policies reflected in laws that require firms seeking to recruit skills internationally to demonstrate that they have been unable to source those skills domestically.

While understandable, policies restricting the admission of immigrant workers on the grounds of availability of local labour must be considered an abuse of national sovereignty for several reasons. In the first place, an ongoing influx of international expertise is the most effective way to maintain international competitiveness and to become aware of the possibilities offered by new technologies. Immigrant workers bring this expertise with them and employ it in the course of daily operations. They also help to set and maintain international standards of conduct, process and quality of product or service, all of which contribute to competitiveness. International workers can help the local workforce to establish international networks which can open new opportunities for jobs, products and technologies. These networks help to secure openings abroad for the local workforce, to accommodate aspirants seeking to advance their careers in the congested local space, with too few opportunities open to them. Overseas exposure for the local workforce is highly desirable, to accustom them to the standards, practices and expectations of the international market, and to enable them to build self-confidence. A lifetime career spent at home will seldom provide the environment, exposure, experiences and challenges that bring out the finest in an individual, and the international contacts and networks that foreign residence afford are hard to replicate from home base, if that is your starting point. On the other hand, the contacts made abroad can be invaluable on the worker's return to the home country after an extended period of foreign residence.

The challenge is to develop new policies for emigration and immigration that open up the advantages and avoid the often-ventilated pitfalls. They include the fear that saturation of the domestic labour market or the market for particular skills may drive down the local wage. One way to address that is via the Social Partnership, where government commits to fiscal policies that control the exchange rate to ensure that local inflation does not rise above international inflation, while workers' representatives undertake to limit wage demands to inflation plus a negotiated share of the returns to increased productivity. Cultural differences between migrants and the local population must also be managed, a circumstance which might warrant temporary quota limits or short-term contracts when signs of strain are becoming evident. Such arrangements should not be permanent or long-term, for fear that they will motivate a new economy of widespread evasion. There is also the issue of controlling for quality of work and level of skill, which can only be partially alleviated through standardisation. There is an ongoing difficulty in taking on board excellence in "soft skills" and such imponderables as company culture across markets, factors which may be important in maintaining the competitive advantage of particular products, services or brands. The bottom line is that it is not the exercise of sovereignty so much as the sensitivity with which migration policies are designed, that matters for international competitiveness.

Sovereignty yields economic benefits only when people and resources at the sovereign's command are put to an economic use

In February 2019, just before to onset of COVID-19 brought air travel to a halt, my wife Monica and I visited a bird sanctuary on the estate of the massive, derelict Petrotrin refinery in nearby Trinidad. The refinery, once the largest single export enterprise for Trinidad and Tobago, now lies rusting and abandoned, beyond hope of renewal, a blight on the landscape, of no benefit to its owners, the Government of Trinidad and Tobago. Less than 400 metres away from my home office as I write lies the abandoned shell of the Andrews sugar factory, which ground its last canes a couple decades ago, now useless to its owner, the Government of Barbados. Another useless asset is my late cousin Neville Stuart's home in the southwest of the island of Montserrat, in the part of the island now uninhabitable in the wake of the volcanic eruption in 1995.

Worrell (1987, pp. 98–101) recounts the story of the collapse of the Guyana bauxite industry in the 1970s, the victim of a precipitate nationalisation strategy which ultimately robbed the industry of essential skills and knowledge. The Barbados government's experiment with the establishment of a national bank in 1978 did not produce an institution with a credit profile any different from that of its foreign-owned competitors, and the bank has since been sold to a commercial bank headquartered in Trinidad and Tobago. In the late 1970s the government of Jamaica tried establishing a large agricultural cooperative on sugar lands acquired by the state. Ownership shares in the new cooperatives were distributed to the sugar workers, in the naïve expectation that a stake in the business would awaken new enthusiasm for the enterprise on the part of the workforce. Rather than the expected productivity increase, however, what transpired was a strike by the worker-owners, demanding an immediate wage increase.

The evidence is overwhelming: the assertion of national sovereignty by a small open economy does not increase the scope or effectiveness of public policies in any way that opens avenues for improving national well-being beyond what would be possible without assuming final responsibility for the society and the territory it occupies. Failure to recognise this reality, and to accept its implications, actually worsens outcomes for small sovereign states, in some cases very substantially. Independence is of benefit only when the sovereign makes better decisions with respect to the productivity and competitiveness of local production and the terms of exchange with the rest of the world, than were made prior to national independence.

In order to make better decisions the small independent nation must invest in developing more appropriate theory, and in creating independent centres of creative thought that expose the international intellectual community to the small society's view of the world. Independent think tanks and research institutes provide reports and analysis that may be used to make the case for non-standard policy approaches, such as is advocated in this book, in the councils of international institutions such as the IMF and World Bank. The qualities of leadership needed to make a success of the independence project are exceptional: the leadership must provide resources for the intellectual activity of the centres of creative thought and the development of the theory of small size, and it must ensure that commerce in ideas remains open, to share insights with thinkers who share a small country view of the world, and so that the theory of the small economy can be refined in the crucible of global intellectual ferment. The national powerhouses of knowledge and thinking should host and be hosted by the world's thought leaders, and there should always be a flavouring of participation in the small country centres from staff of international institutions and others who would not have lived the small country living experience, to enrich everyone's understanding with this perspective.

The national leadership needs to be visionary, able to imagine a new desirable future and a way to bring it to reality. In Lauren Groff's brilliant new novel *Matrix* (Groff, 2021), the shadowy historical figure of Marie de France, the earliest known French woman poet, is brought to life as the powerful head of the richest abbey in all of Angleterre. She builds the abbey from a wretched shell into a powerhouse of influence, with a network of spies throughout Christendom, on the basis of a series of transformative visions over the course of her long lifetime. After each vision she marshals her nuns and all the ever growing retinue of supporting staff and peasants on land the abbey owns, to design and build some new enterprise that everyone, including many of her own confidants and advisors, believes to be impossible. Matrix Marie is the best example that may be offered of what may be described as a practical vision, one that imagines a hitherto unknown future, together with a way to get from here to there.

The legacy of history

History has bequeathed mankind with patterns of wealth distribution, national boundaries, transportation systems and languages, all of them barriers to the advancement of well-being. In this section we offer brief comments on aspects of the world's historical legacy which stand in the way of economic activity that would serve to improve the quality of individual lives everywhere. These factors are of general import; in contrast to most of the rest of this book, the discussion in this section does not apply only to small open economies.

The distribution of wealth among societies is a permanent historical legacy which stands squarely in the path of the future of mankind. The clearest example of this is with respect to climate change. Although the American economist Larry Summers is the only person of influence I have heard say anything to that effect, it must be evident to all knowledgeable leaders, activists and observers that the magnitude of financial transfers that would have to be made to South American and African countries for there to be any chance of saving what remains of tropical rain forests is beyond anything that current international financial arrangements would permit. What is needed is a financial transfer from wealthy countries that is large enough to raise living standards in all the countries whose populations are encroaching on the rain forest in an irresistible tide, sufficient to alleviate that surge. It would involve imitating China's achievement in the elimination of absolute poverty for a start, and pathways to a better future for poor people, pathways that leave the rain forest pristine. No nation in Africa or South America has the finance and resources to do what China has done; China herself could not have done it, had she not built the world's manufacturing powerhouse over the course of four decades, on the foundation of the productivity of hundreds of millions of middle income jobs. This is not the place to elaborate on the ramifications of this problem, and in any case that is beyond my competence. My point is to contrast the magnitude of the financial transfers that would be required with the discussions about debt relief for emerging market and developing countries which have absorbed the attention of international lending institutions, amounts which are piddling by comparison. History has left our world with a global maldistribution of wealth so monstrously large that the world's leadership appears unwilling to admit its magnitude and implications for mankind's future, much less to do anything about it.

History has also left us national boundaries which set limits to the reach of policy. These boundaries form dense barriers to global commerce that benefits all mankind. National boundaries are always an artifact, even when they appear to follow natural geographical features. The natives of the island nation of Kiribati in the Pacific share a language and culture, even though the easterners live on an archipelago 4,000 kilometres away from the archipelago where the capital Tawara sits, with the only airline connection being via Hawaii, thousands of miles to the north. In the southwest of the US there are Spanish-speaking American-born citizens who are more culturally akin to their neighbours in Mexico than they are to New Englanders from the northeast. The absorbing Netflix series *Bordertown,* set in the Finnish town of Lappeenranta, offers a fascinating glimpse of the way a border community adapts to influences from a neighbouring metropolis in another country, in this case St Petersburg in Russia.

Whatever the rationale for national borders, they can seldom be justified from the point of view of economic production and exchange for the mutual benefit of producers and consumers. The benefit of exchange is the basis of economics and of the accumulation of wealth. Border tariffs and restrictions on the exchange of goods and services of whatever kind deprive both parties to every cross border transaction of potential economic gains. It is therefore difficult for economists to understand why borders are so jealously guarded, and why there is such fervour about buying local products. From an economist's viewpoint, local producers will have little difficulty in marketing their output domestically if they are perceived to offer better value for money than all others. Their problems have to do with matching their prices to the quality of their offerings and with their marketing skills; anything beyond that cannot be addressed by tariffs or any other economic remedy. The product is simply uncompetitive, not best value for money.

A third legacy of history that impairs strategies that would yield maximum benefits from international commerce is the north-south orientation of most international trade and transportation infrastructure, especially in the Americas, Europe and Africa. In order to travel to any major capital city in Latin America from the Caribbean island where I live, I must first fly three and a half hours north to Miami, ruefully referred to as the capital of Latin America, and take a flight south from there. A direct four-hour flight to Manaus in Brazil, which was available briefly in the 1990s, now involves an overnight stay in Miami. The failure of that direct flight illustrates the challenge of opening new channels of international commerce that do not flow along the long-established routes. The infrastructure and associated services and networks that have been established over decades and centuries funnel international exchange through channels that connect through major hubs in North America and Europe, benefitting financial and other service providers in the wealthy countries of the North. China has emerged as the only country in the Global South with the resources to invest in global infrastructure that has an east-west orientation. The fury and misrepresentation with which China's Belt and Road Initiative (BRI) has been greeted in the West is difficult to understand, until one sees a map of the major networks of the BRI. The Initiative is in fact a visionary conceptualisation of trends that were already emerging as Chinese construction and finance companies went in a competitive international search for new business opportunities to deploy the construction skills they developed so remarkably in the transformation of their own country's infrastructure.

Language is a fourth historical constraint that has consequences for international economic policy. English-speaking Barbados has strong economic ties with St Lucia and St Vincent and the Grenadines, about 200 kilometres to the west, both English-speaking, but very little commerce goes between Barbados and the larger and more prosperous Martinique, whose population speaks French. The archipelago known as the Lesser Antilles forms the eastern boundary of the Caribbean Sea, situated between North and South America. The western boundary is the Central American isthmus, with six Spanish-speaking and one bilingual country. Central America is an economic fulcrum between the Americas; the Lesser Antilles, English and French-speaking islands where few understand Spanish, has no part in commerce between North and South America. As a 13-year old high school student I was faced with a choice of French and Spanish as the foreign language in my programme of study. With geography as a favourite subject I chose Spanish, in the confident expectation that Barbados and the rest of the Caribbean had a bilingual destiny thanks to its geographical location, an expectation that has never materialised.

I do not believe that history determines a country's destiny, even for a country whose size limits its sovereign reach and how it may deploy what resources it has to its best economic advantage. However, to escape the curse of repeating history, the political, social, economic and intellectual leadership must distil the lessons of history and find ways around the constraints it imposes. Had the leadership of Caribbean countries taken effective, purposeful action towards bilingualism in the region, the economic opportunities available might today be much richer, with possibilities of trade, financial and commercial ties with Latin America. Countries of East Africa which have embraced infrastructure projects under the Belt and Road Initiative have been given an important lifeline towards an eastward-facing direction of commerce, to complement their existing northward-looking trading patterns. These are both examples of what I refer to as practical visions, one going abegging and the other with promise of realisation.

Geography, like size, is a characteristic that must be taken account of in the design of economic strategy

In the late 1960s I lived in Montreal, Canada, a city with cold, snowy winters, where every year a dirty grey blanket of snow covered the ground from early winter until the onset of spring. The city had invested in squadrons of mighty snowploughs and dump trucks that cleared all major thoroughfares as soon as practical after every snowfall, so that normal life continued in the face of all but the most extreme of winter storms. Snowfalls were so frequent that the city would have been dysfunctional during the winter otherwise.

Three decades later I lived much further south in Washington, DC, the US Capital. In Washington the Federal Government offices and all business comes to a halt whenever there is a major snowfall, of a kind that Montreal routinely shrugs off. Washington does have a fleet of snow removers, but nothing on the scale of Montreal's armada. It would hardly be cost-effective for the City of Washington to make an investment of that magnitude, only to have the vehicles lying idle for all but a handful of days in the year.

The contrasting strategies for treating snow removal in the two cities are an example of how policy choice, in this case risk management policy, must be adapted to geographical circumstance. An example of the need to bring cost considerations into the management of climate risk, one pertinent to small economies, was given in Chapter 13, in the discussion of hurricanes in the Caribbean.

In general, managing the risks and consequences of extreme weather and natural disasters requires a calculation of the relative costs and practicality of prevention, fortification to withstand the peril, insurance costs and costs of recovery and reconstruction. Early warning and prevention are impractical in the case of earthquakes, volcanic eruptions and tsunamis; early warning systems for hurricanes and storms are well developed. It will be cost effective to invest in securing economic assets against perils that occur frequently, such as snowfalls in Montreal, or Category II hurricanes, where all that is necessary is the enforcement of existing standards. The Japanese have developed building techniques adapted to their homeland, which is especially prone to earthquakes, and they continue to develop and refine those methods. No other industrial country has a sufficient exposure to earthquakes to justify a similar investment. The international insurance and reinsurance industry has matured into a network than can provide pay-outs calibrated to cover recovery from weather-related risks, because they appear with sufficient frequency to permit useable estimates of probable claims, on the basis of which premiums can be set. With every new experience the calculation is updated. In these cases, the desired strategy is one which maximises the growth of average incomes, such that all economic assets can be adequately insured. There is no preventive, early warning, mitigation or insurance option for addressing the risk of earthquake, volcanic eruptions, tsunamis or other infrequent catastrophes. In all of these cases the priority is to strengthen the institutions and networks of global cooperation that exist to respond to the disaster.

Thanks to their proximity to the mainland, major tourist destinations in the Caribbean all source their visitors from North America. In a short article (Worrell, 2022) I demonstrated how policies for diversifying the sources of demand for tourism services might take advantage of this proximity to do selective marketing within counties and metropolitan areas, rather than venture further afield in search of entirely new markets. Selected marketing within established markets is a strategy that should be uppermost in the minds of most exporters and tourism service providers in small economies, as the preferred option for marshalling their limited marketing resources to diversify and to secure new business.

Geography determines who your main trading, commercial and financial partners are. The irrationality of the UK's exit from the European Union lies in the assumption that the country can pursue an alternative strategy which strengthens its economic ties with the US and the rest of the world at the expense of its links to Europe. What has eventuated, inevitably, is that links with Europe persist, but have become less efficient. The notion of flexible exchange rates is another example of a failure to appreciate the realities of geography. The Canadian economist Robert Mundell (1961) introduced the notion of "optimal currency areas" which all these years later remains a more useful concept. The value of the Canadian dollar deviates from parity with the US dollar in line with changes in the price of petroleum, of which Canada is an important supplier to the US. The equivalence is not exact, but if you use that as a rule of thumb you will never be far wrong. The case is much stronger for the puny currencies of Caribbean countries. Thirty years ago I advocated for a common currency for the Caribbean that reflected the reality that the region is part of the US currency area (Worrell, 1994, p. 27). The failure to proceed with that project means that there is now no point to issuing independent currencies anywhere in the region, when all commerce between islands within the area is conducted in US dollars.

Twenty years ago I was assigned by the International Monetary Fund to assist the newly-established Central Bank of Bosnia and Herzegovina on currency and payments matters, in the aftermath of the civil war which ended with the breakup of the former Yugoslavia. There was no argument that the local currency had to be pegged to the deutschmark, if it were to have any chance of widespread acceptance. With the introduction of the euro, the aspiration has been to follow the path of other small eastern European countries to full membership of the EU and the euro area.

Another example that may be cited from eastern Europe is the Greek debt crisis that erupted in 2009. There were those in the economics fraternity who argued that it had been a mistake on Greece's part to have joined the euro area, because the country lost the option to devalue the domestic currency as part of the package of measures to alleviate the burden of the debt. That counterfactual cannot be tested, but it is implausible. The debt was denominated in euro, so local currency devaluation would not have inflated it away. The rest of the EU is Greece's largest trading and financial partner, and all transactions are priced in euro, so a local currency devaluation would have had no effect on the availability of the euro to service the debt. In the event, Greek membership of the euro is vindicated by the country's Human Development Index score, which remained unaffected by the protracted debt crisis.

The geographical evidence has to be carefully read, if we are to draw inferences that reflect reality. A comparison between the island economies of the Caribbean and the South Pacific reveals vital differences which are much to the Caribbean's advantage: there are no low-lying atolls in the Caribbean similar to Tuvalu and Kiribati in the Pacific. Caribbean islands are all similar to Vanuatu and Fiji, neither of which is any more susceptible to sea level rise than is any other land mass, and less so than those coastal areas of continents which are below sea level, for example the Netherlands.

In addition, the island nations of the Caribbean are all part of one archipelago that stretches northward from the mouth of the Orinoco River in South America to the eastern coast of Florida in the US, swinging west across the mouth of the Gulf of Mexico. The distance from Port-of-Spain in the southeast to Havana in the northwest, the two extremes of the entire chain, is 2,600 kilometres. That distance is only 500 kilometres more than the distance between Fiji, the closest access point by air, and Tuvalu, the capital of Kiribati, with nothing but empty sea in between. The island nations of the South

Pacific are incredibly remote from each other and from major countries and large land masses. This presents them with challenges of transport and communications, and access to financial, educational, health and other services of a magnitude which is unknown in the Caribbean.

Nor is it the case that all tropical countries are at risk of hurricanes and cyclones. In fact, in the Caribbean there is a zone close to the equator where the incidence of hurricanes is very infrequent. Barbados, which sits at 13 degrees north latitude, is on the edge of that zone. The island has not experienced a major hurricane, with loss of life and widespread destruction of property, since Hurricane Janet in 1955. When countries outside the hurricane belt do experience one, it tends to be especially destructive; Janet caused an estimated 1,000 deaths in the eastern Caribbean and in Mexico.

Small open economies need to become adept at recognising the economic opportunities which technological change opens up

History offers us many examples of the way new technologies lend economic worth to assets that were previously of no value. Small open economies will not have the human or financial resources to lead technical change, but they should ensure that they are plugged into international networks that afford them insight into new technologies that may be of economic benefit, and they should remain alert to ways in which they can turn new technology to their benefit. In this section I discuss examples from Caribbean experience, including past successes, current challenges and future possibilities.

The development of refrigerated marine transport in the late nineteenth century (Joseph, Illimootil and Kunjumon, 2022) made possible the export of fresh fruit from the Caribbean to markets in North America and Europe. In response many countries in the region diversified from the export of sugar, previously the mainstay of Caribbean export trade, to add bananas as a major export from the early years of the twentieth century. In the Caribbean and Central American region, Costa Rica, the Dominican Republic, Guatemala and Honduras remain significant banana exporters.

A more recent transformative technology was the introduction of commercial jet transport to the Caribbean region in the 1960s, which created the popular tropical resort tourism market. The Caribbean is the exemplar of that market because of its geography, making it the most accessible destination for North Americans, and its history, which bequeathed its markets in European countries with which the region had political and economic ties of long standing. Thanks to the higher wages available in tourism, the opportunities it offers for small business and its spread effects through the services required from other sectors of the economy, tourism has displaced agriculture almost entirely in the Lesser Antilles.

Computerisation has radicalised the production of alcoholic beverages, and is largely responsible for the flowering of fine spirits everywhere. The

Caribbean rum industry has been a major beneficiary, including a handful of independent producers. In Barbados a small local company has repurposed an old sugar-producing factory for the distillation and aging of fine rums for export, controlling the entire process remotely from a small office. In doing so, the company has created a visitor attraction to enrich the island's tourist appeal. Several Caribbean countries have taken an opportunity to add historical rum-producing tours and tastings to the list of tourist attractions. One may visit traditional wooden stills from the late eighteenth century in Guyana, an active mill for grinding canes that is 100 old in Barbados, and tour on a rail line once used to transport canes to a factory for milling in St Kitts, among many similar activities in Central America and the Caribbean.

Developments in communications technologies in the past five decades have created revolutionary possibilities for trade in services, changes which have brought economic policy makers, companies and labour markets into conflict. The possibilities for international trade in services are multifarious, from call centres and data processing, to legal, accounting and marketing services. However, an ongoing problem in realising the potential benefits of trade in services is the absence of an agreed international framework that sets the guidelines within which the exchange of values should be set. The current disarray in this area is the best illustration we have of the fact that markets are artifacts which are created by the rules agreed by the participants. When it comes to traded services, there is no agreement, and the main body which is tasked with negotiating an agreement is structured in a way that precludes the possibility of arriving at arrangements that are globally acceptable. In order to restore its capacity to reach agreements that powerful nations will respect, the World Trade Organisation would need to be restructured on some basis similar to the World Bank, where countries would be grouped into constituencies by some criteria that reflect their relative stake in global trade in goods and services.

In the absence of an agreed international framework small economies have little chance of establishing a foothold in the provision of international services if they do not already have a corner in some niche of the financial services market. Barbados' experience in this regard has been instructive. The island has an enviable reputation for financial regulation and international tax compliance, with regulations and practices modelled heavily on Canadian institutions. As an English-speaking Caribbean country offering health, educational, personal security services, communications and public utilities of a quality comparable to those on offer in New England, Ontario or Sussex, Barbados would appear to have excellent potential for development as an international centre of financial, trading, marketing, accounting, insurance and merchandising services. In the late 1970s the Barbados government decided to actively promote the island's potential, with some initial success. In its marketing, in which the Central Bank of Barbados, with responsibilities for banking supervision then within my purview, was involved, the Bank's role was to vet all activity in accordance with the guidelines of the Committee for

Banking Supervision of the Bank for International Settlements, known as the Basle Committee, the international regulator. Barbados has continued to fall in line as new guidelines were issued, and laws and regulations have been brought in line as new international institutions have been set up to address problems of money laundering and tax avoidance. In spite of resources expended on compliance over the decades, Barbados has been repeatedly sanctioned for non-cooperation, along with other countries in the Caribbean and Central America, all of whom are in active cooperation with the international regulatory bodies. As a result, much of the region's actual and potential business has been lost to the US, where companies regulated by State governments are not bound by international agreements entered into by the US Federal Government. In the absence of an international framework and oversight, the potential efficiency gains from trade in services will not be realised, and small economies will face repeated challenges to their offerings in this area.

New technologies open up sources of comparative advantage

The recent expansion of the Kingston port in Jamaica is a herald of the potential that may open up as a result of the confluence of geography and new technology. Over a century ago the development of construction technologies, combined with advances in medicine, were instrumental in making possible the construction of the Panama Canal, which linked the economies of the Atlantic and Pacific rims, and because of that, made the isthmus of Panama among the most valuable property on earth. But for medical advances in the identification and treating of malaria and yellow fever, the Panama Canal might not have been completed. The renowned French diplomat Ferdinand de Lesseps, who founded the enterprise which had successfully constructed the Suez Canal, opened in 1869, subsequently turned his attention to the Central American Isthmus. His attempt to build a canal across the isthmus was frustrated by the mountains that stood athwart the most direct route, and the endemic scourge of yellow fever and malaria in the rainforests of Panama. The efforts of his Panama Canal Company ended in failure, with millions of dollars' worth of equipment abandoned to rot in the forest in 1889, after seven years of effort.

The US took control of the abandoned project in 1904, and were able to successfully complete the project a decade later, thanks to a change of concept which involved the use of locks to raise the canal part-way over the mountain spine of the isthmus, using an artificial lake to re-charge the locks. This new concept proved to be technically feasible, though hauntingly expensive in lives and treasure. The project required an enormous labour force, which was recruited principally from the eastern Caribbean, over 2000 kilometres away. Attempts to recruit labour in Jamaica, just half that distance, were largely fruitless, because that island had been the main source of the labour for the failed French attempt, and that project's fearsome death rate from disease had entered into the folklore. The Americans owed their success to the discovery of the *Aedes aegypti* mosquito as the carrier of infectious diseases that had decimated the workforce of the French company, and the measures taken to suppress it.

Improvements in shipbuilding, propulsion, navigation and ship control resulted in the prevalence in the late twentieth century of vessels too large to transit the Panama Canal, and a nine-year long project enlarged the waterway to accommodate ships with twice the previous cargo capacity in 2016. This increased volume opened an opportunity for newly established or expanded ports to compete for a share of the trans-shipment business for cargo bound for the Caribbean and South America, business in which US ports, principally Miami, have had a near-monopoly. The recently expanded port of Kingston in Jamaica is well positioned to gain a substantial share of this market, with additional economic benefits from the associated services and industrial activity.

Technological advances have opened exciting new opportunities for productive investment

The twenty-first century has brought many technological advances which have great potential for development that benefits people at many income levels, because the investment needed is affordable by all but the very poor. We highlight three in this section: solar and wind power, electric mobility and electronic payments.

A combination of improvement in materials and technology, energised by the great weight of rapidly expanding Chinese production, has driven down the costs of solar photovoltaic power to levels that are within the reach of middle income households all over the world. This has the potential to reduce the energy deficit in many tropical countries substantially and endows them with an abundant power source that reduces their dependence on fossil fuels. What is more, the solar systems can be as large or as small as necessary, for individual households and for industrial plants and cities. This eases the challenge of financing, because so many homes and industries are able to finance their own power supplies.

Wind power requires a larger minimum investment to be worthwhile in most circumstances, but it has also fallen in price as a result of the combination of engineering developments and large scale Chinese production. It has become a significant income supplement to farmers in many parts of the world. A wind turbine has a very small footprint, and therefore no agricultural production has to be sacrificed to make way for it. A distinction has to be made between onshore wind turbines, whose output is, along with solar photovoltaic and hydro, by far the cheapest of any source of power, and offshore wind, which remains more expensive. Also, commercial offshore wind turbines are a proven resource only in near-shore locations on continental shelves. The few turbines in operation in deep near-shore waters on the west coast of the US are still in test mode as of early 2022.

A combination of abundant sunshine and location in the path of dependable Southeast Trade Winds, so-called because they supplied to power that drove commerce westwards across the Atlantic in the era of sailing ships, endows the island of Barbados with limitless power potential. Solar and wind technologies mean that Barbados should be wealthier than oil-rich neighbours like Venezuela, Trinidad and Guyana. No-one in Barbados has yet woken up to this reality. The country's government continues to encourage oil exploration in the territorial waters, with the attendant dangers to the tourism-based economy, offering the unconvincing argument that it needs revenues from oil which is yet to be discovered to finance the country's transition to renewable power, which is already underway.

A combination of hydro power, for many decades the cheapest of all sources, and solar and wind has enabled Costa Rica to reach a target of 100 per cent use of renewable power for electricity. Of the total, two-thirds comes from hydro. Hydro and naturally-occurring thermal power are the main sources for Iceland and Norway, two other countries that source all their electricity from renewables.

Recognition of the transformative potential of solar and wind power for small economies that depend for their growth on foreign exchange is not reflected in the policies of any country in the sample that we have chosen for review in this book. Those countries that have already reached the goal have done so on the basis of hydro and thermal power, both of which require very costly initial investments and construction that can stretch over a decade or more. With solar and onshore wind we have power sources which can be built up in small increments, which households and enterprises large and small can finance and install on their own, if provided with the right incentives to do so.

In order to realise a goal of supplying all electricity from solar, wind and other renewables, countries like Barbados which have no hydro or thermal resources, would need to put in place a strategy for the transition to renewables, with a target for completion that stipulates the percentage power supply of each resource, the sources of stable power, and the responsibility and financing for the distribution of electricity. Once the strategy is finalised, agreed by all parties and publicly articulated, implementation should be set in motion with the aid of a set of appropriate tax and other incentives, and a monitoring system to track progress and make adjustments to stay on course. Because of the many actors, possible conflicts of interest, lack of in-depth knowledge and coordination problems, anything less than this has little hope of success.

Exciting new possibilities are opening up in electric mobility

The vision and initiative of a small local company, Megapower Inc., has given Barbados a big head-start in electric mobility. The remarkable woman who founded the company, Jo Edghill, recognised that, with the introduction of the battery electric Nissan Leaf, a fully electric family car that a middle income family could afford, and that had a range that was ideal for Barbadian conditions, was finally available. The island is a triangle with axes 14 and 21 miles long, and the first Leaf had sufficient range to dispel any anxiety about the longest journeys. Moreover, home ownership is an aspiration shared by an overwhelming majority of Barbadians, so buyers would be charging their cars at home, overnight. To further prepare the market, Megapower's first imports were UK demonstration cars, used but unmolested, offered at discount to narrow the differential with internal combustion-engined cars. In addition, Megapower offered a comprehensive service from the outset, with installation of home power supplies as part of the overall package, a charge card for trouble-free charging at all public chargers, and troubleshooting. In spite of a lack of any tax incentive, Megapower established the credibility of electric vehicles in the eyes of a sceptical public. The company has since facilitated the purchase of 60 fully electric buses by the public transport company.

Thanks to Megapower and the affordability of solar photovoltaics, my wife Monica and I now own a Leaf, and supply most of our power from panels on the roof of our home. Over the past six years, since the publication of a study demonstrating possibilities for achieving 100 per cent renewable electric generation in Barbados (Hohmeyer, 2015). I have publicly advocated for a strategy for implementing such a strategy, something which has not yet materialised (Worrell, 2019).[1] Reaching a target of 100 per cent renewable generation of electricity, together with 100 per cent electric mobility would add the equivalent of an additional fifty per cent of GDP, at a conservative estimate. However, neither target can be attained within thirty years from where the country stands in 2022.

Digital payments technologies have now developed beyond our capabilities to employ them to best effect

Despite the universal interest in and enthusiasm for digital currencies, countries have had scant success in improving the speed and efficiency of international payments systems and broadening the access to those systems to people wherever they live and regardless of their income level. These are the most urgent defects of financial systems everywhere and, in theory, technologies already in use can be deployed to solve them both.

The international payments system retains the design developed in the analogue age. To complete any transaction the buyer must have money to the value of the item or service being purchased, that money must be in a form that is true and not counterfeit, there must be a transfer to the vendor, and the vendor must transfer that value of product or service in exchange. In the analogue world that is accomplished seamlessly, using notes and coins; the buyer hands over cash, and that's the end of it. However, very little value is exchanged that way nowadays, of the world's total of transactions on any given day. Most retail transactions have been settled digitally for many decades, via an instruction provided by the buyer to their bank to change the digital record of their deposit account, reducing its value by the agreed value of the purchase, and informing the vendor's bank to make a corresponding change in the digital record of the vendor's account, increasing the value by an equivalent amount. For many years this instruction was by way of the cheque, a standard form with security features, on which the buyer filled in the individual transaction details. To complete what was already a digital transfer of value via cheque involved a lengthy process of transport and verification, which saw the cheque deposited by the vendor, sent by their bank to the central bank, exchanged there with the buyer's bank with an equivalent transfer of value between the banks, before the value is finally deducted from the purchaser's account. In effect the value is a flow that is first identified at its destination, and is then traced backwards to its origin, where it is verified. If the payment is to a vendor overseas an additional step is needed, involving a transfer over an account with a correspondent bank abroad. This process accounts for the delay the seller encounters before they have access to the value of purchases made by cheque.

Telecommunications technology now permits the transfer of value in real time, with all instructions and verifications reaching the accounts of purchaser and seller at the time of the transaction, and this has now become the dominant form of payment. The actual tools and processes used are various: credit and debit cards, digital plastic wallets of the kind used by transportation systems, mobile phones and computers and tablets. However, payments systems are not yet seamless in any country, even for domestic payments, and little progress has been made in reducing settlement times and eliminating settlement risks for international payments. The fault lies not with the technologies, some of which – the blockchain is the prime example – are actually for more sophisticated than is needed. The problem is the failure to imagine a payments design that is fit for a world where value is exchanged via digital records, and to agree or engineer a global transition from the present analogue-based design.

The second challenge, to broaden and deepen access to payments systems, is easily addressed with existing tools and systems, as the Chinese have demonstrated. In the process of eliminating absolute poverty – communities with levels of living so deprived and life chances below an acceptable human minimum; the Chinese do not claim to have eliminated all poverty – the Chinese have ensured reliable power and communications in the remotest areas of that country, allowing rural farmers to market their produce in urban centres. Mobile phones are now ubiquitous, and payments systems such a Kenya's well-known *mpesa* and similar exchanges of value using digital wallets at cellular companies can be completed on simple phones. The remaining barriers are unreliable power sources and lack of communications links to more remote areas.

Note

1 The Barbados Government has published three separate reports, all referring to an officially announced target of 100 per cent renewables by 2030, but no practical measures have been taken in pursuit of that target. Government Ministers now openly acknowledge that it is beyond reach.

References

Bagoo, Andre. 2020. *The Undiscovered Country.* Leeds, England: Peepal Tree Press.

Groff, Lauren. 2021. *Matrix.* New York: Riverhead Books.

Hohmeyer, Olav. 2015. "A 100% renewable energy strategy for Barbados." *Working Paper.* Europa Universitat Flensburg, Center for Sustainable Energy, January.

Joseph, Jomol, Ashitha Illimootil and Meenu Kunjumon (downloaded 2022) "Refrigerated maritime transportation." *MBA paper,* (Indian Maritime University). Aca demia.edu.

Mundell, Robert. 1961. "A theory of optimum currency areas." *American Economic Review,* Vol. 51, pp. 509–517.

Worrell, DeLisle. 2022. "Increasing earnings from tourism." *Economic Letter,* April.

Worrell, DeLisle. 2019. "A practical, consistent strategy for renewables is urgently needed." Economic Letter. December. http://www.delisleworrell.com/A%20Practical%2C%20Consistent%20Strategy%20for%20Renewables%20is%20Urgently%20Needed.

Worrell, DeLisle. 1994. "A common currency for the Caribbean," in *Caribbean Monetary Integration,* edited by Terence Farrell and DeLisle Worrel. Port-of-Spain: Caribbean Information Systems and Services.

Worrell, DeLisle. 1987. *Small Island Economies: Structure and Performance in the English-speaking Caribbean Since 1970.* New York: Praeger.

17 Measuring Material Well-being

It has proved difficult to come up with a measure of the quality of life for comparisons among societies around the world. That is because the quality of one's life is largely subjective; researchers who have surveyed societies worldwide have found some dissonance between people's happiness, as reported in response to questionnaires, and commonly used measures of economic performance, such as GDP per capita. Happiness may, arguably, be what we all aspire to, but since everyone has a unique vision of happiness locked into their own consciousness, we are obliged to resort to less comprehensive measures that are more susceptible to measurement across societies worldwide.

The measure that is used universally, GDP per capita, has known flaws and limitations. Some of these relate to the concept itself, and have been discussed in an earlier chapter. Others relate to differences within and between countries in how income is distributed, the differing purchasing power of a given income in different countries, differences between countries in the availability of free public services and amenities, gender inequalities, environmental conditions and many other factors which help to determine the quality of life.

The usual excuse for using the GDP for international comparisons is that it is the only measure that is computed for countries around the world on a common methodology. However, this has not been the case since 1990, when the UNDP's Human Development Report first appeared. The Human Development Index (HDI), which has been published every year since, corrects for three major defects of the GDP per capita: differences in the purchasing power of incomes, and variations among countries in health facilities and educational opportunities. International comparative research has shown that, once income rises above a minimum subsistence level, health and education are even more reliable markers of the quality of life than is the level of per capita GDP. As a result we now have a far more faithful indicator of the quality of life in countries across the globe, and it is the HDI that is our preferred measure in the discussion throughout this book.

The HDI passes the intuitive test of international comparison as anyone who has lived in many countries can attest. The world's countries are listed in descending order by quartile in the Human Development Report. Invariably, one finds that, in countries in a given quartile, amenities, housing and

DOI: 10.4324/9781003247609-21

environmental quality, public utilities, habits of dress and other aspects of lifestyles are all comparable. Furthermore, anyone moving from a country in a lower quartile to a country in a higher quartile can expect to find better lifestyles on offer.

Why the Human Development Index?

The index is the indicator which most closely reflects observed conditions of living in all countries, and which is widely available. The use of the level and growth of GDP as the measure of economic success has always been inexcusable. Not only does it not correspond to common observation, it often motivates policies that are doomed to worsen material well-being. The discovery of new reserves of fossil fuels is an obvious example. As this is being written, there is a flurry of conferences being held, papers being written, experts being flown in, and general excitement in neighbouring Guyana, now the envy of all the Caribbean thanks to the start of production from newly-discovered reserves of petroleum. The GDP rose 44 per cent in 2020, the year oil production began. As always happens, expectations of improvement in the well-being of Guyanese are running high. These expectations are bound to be disappointed. The reason is that the changes in social and political organisation which are essential to ensure that the income from the oil revenues actually reaches the average Guyanese household involve health, educational and social services, infrastructure, communications and a variety of institutional and organisational changes that can only be productively accomplished over the medium term. What is more, the public sector must equip itself with new knowledge about all aspects of the evolving changes, with mechanisms of oversight, coordination, monitoring, guidance and regulation. In fact, experience suggests that the early exploitation of new fossil fuel discovery should be extremely modest, minimising the initial boost to GDP while at the same time building domestic capacity in all the areas just mentioned. This is just the opposite of what you would do, if you judge success by the rate of GDP growth. However, if your target is the HDI, a strong case for going more slowly can be made, since we have shown that improvements in the indicators for health and education have proportionately a much larger impact on the HDI than does the growth of GDP.

The inadequacies of GDP as a measure of economic success have long been recognised. In the 1970s and 1980s economic policy in what are now called emerging market and developing countries was focussed on economic development, the improvement of the "well-being and quality of life of a nation, region, local community or an individual" (Wikipedia definition). This was reflected in seminal works aimed at advancing knowledge and providing guidance on paths to achieve higher levels of development, such as Lewis (1954), Rostow (1960) and Meier (1989). These ideas fuelled a political economy approach to the design of economic policy, reflected in the research programmes of the once-influential "structuralist school" in Latin America, of which the leading exponents were Prebisch (1950) and Furtado (1964), and in the works of the lesser known "plantation school" in the Caribbean (Best and Levitt, 2009). However, the macroeconomic approach to development policy fell out of favour in the 1980s, and the sub-discipline of development economics has since focussed on microeconomic topics which have had no measurable impact on public policy at the national scale in any country. The reasons arguably lie with the divergence of sub-disciplines of economics and the fact that macroeconomics has become highly quantitative, to the neglect of recent insights such as those that are provided by the Nobel Prize winning economists Esther Duflo and Abhijit Banerjee (Banerjee and Duflo, 2019), insights which have had no effect on the design of macroeconomic policies.

Disaffection with the sterility of macroeconomics and economic policy has fuelled interest in alternative approaches to the measurement of well-being, the most well-known among them a methodology that uses surveys of levels of satisfaction with individual lives to produce an index of "happiness". The approach was popularised in an influential book by Layard (2005), from which the following quotes are taken:

> I am an economist – I love the subject and it has served me well. But economics equates changes in the happiness of a society with changes in its purchasing power – or roughly so. I have never accepted that view, and the history of the past fifty years has disproved it. Instead, the new psychology of happiness makes it possible to construct an alternative view, based on evidence of what lifestyles and what policies are sensible, drawing on the new psychology, as well as on economics, brain science, sociology and philosophy.
>
> (Layard, 2005, Preface, p. ix)

> So by happiness I mean feeling good – enjoying life and wanting the feeling to be maintained. By unhappiness I mean feeling bad and wishing things were different. There are countless sources of happiness, and countless sources of pain and misery.
>
> (Layard, 2005, p. 12)

> [Happiness] is supremely important because it is our overall motivational device. Without this drive we humans would have perished long ago.
>
> (Layard, 2005, p. 24)

> So there is an evaluative faculty in each of us that tells us how happy we are with our situation, and then directs us to approach what makes us happy and avoid what does not. From the various possibilities open to us, we choose whichever combination of activities will make us feel best. In doing this we are more than purely reactive.
>
> (Layard, 2005, p. 26)

The "big 7" factors Layard lists as affecting happiness are family relationships, one's financial situation, work, community and friends, health, personal freedom and personal values, in that order of importance. He borrows from the literature: "This is the principle of the Greatest Happiness: the right action is the one that produces the greatest overall happiness" (Layard, 2005, p. 112). The economics framework is described as "terrific" (Layard, 2005, p. 127), but it must be amended to include the following features of human nature: the fact that extra income matters more to poor people than to rich; the fact that other people affect us indirectly, and not only via exchange; that our norms and values change in response to external influences; that we hate loss more than we value gain; and that we behave inconsistently in many ways. Layard also notes that "Economists and politicians have tended to assume that when financial motives for performance are increased, other motives remain the same. In fact, these motives can change" (Layard, 2005, p. 158).

> A key element of most people's well-being is work. Indeed… unemployment is one of the worst things that can happen to anyone. In impact it is similar to marriage break-up – you cease to be needed. This psychic effect comes on top of the effect of reduced income.
>
> (Layard, 2005, p. 172)

Layard (2006) elaborates:

> I conclude that economics uses exactly the right framework for thinking about public policy. Policy instruments are set so as to maximise the sum of (cardinal) utilities, with additional weight being given to those whose utility is low. What is wrong is the account we use of what makes people happy. Broadly, economics says that utility increases with the opportunities for voluntary exchange. This overlooks the huge importance of involuntary interactions between people – of how others affect our norms, our aspirations, our feelings of what is important, and our experience of whether the world is friendly or threatening.
>
> One might wish to say that these things are the province of other social sciences. It would be convenient if life worked that way,. But it does not… take mobility policy… More mobility certainly increases income but it also affects the quality of relationships in the community and in families. Economists should not advocate more mobility without considering these effects also.
>
> (Layard, 2005, p. C24)

Attractive as it seems, the definition and measurement of happiness is fraught with problems. Melo (2011) points out circumstances in which individuals might not be the best judges of their own happiness (because of obvious bias or limited knowledge of the world) and difficulties in establishing happiness as a consistent normative concept across cultures. Offer (2006) cites empirical evidence that poverty, divorce, unemployment and other individual circumstances have a major negative impact on personal well-being. Oswald and Powdthavee's paper (2006) shows how one's happiness may adapt to circumstances, citing evidence that individuals who become disabled go on to exhibit recovery in mental well-being, although not in cases of severe disability.

Analysis using happiness or other survey-based data[1] as the measure of well-being will always fail to reach the minimum standard of objectivity needed for comparisons across countries and over time. That is the great advantage of the Human Development Index: it uses a known quantitative methodology which does meet minimum standards of objectivity and it is available for all countries, for thirty years in many cases.

The HDI meets minimum standards of objectivity and it has been available for all countries for two decades or more

The Human Development Index combines indices that reflect a long and healthy life, the acquisition of knowledge and a decent standard of living. The rationale for the choice of these elements is given in the first issue of the United Nations Development Programme's Human Development Report (United Nations Development Programme, 1990):

> Human development is a process of enlarging people's choices. The most critical of these wide-ranging choices are to live a long and healthy life, to be educated and to have access to resources needed for a decent standard of living.

The basic indicators chosen for each item are those which are available for all countries on the basis of comparable definitions. The indicator(s) for each index is (are) converted to an index with a value between zero and one, and the three indices are aggregated using the geometric mean: the HDI is equal to the cubed root of the product of the indices for health, education and income.

The indicator for health is the life expectancy at birth, the number of years a new-born infant is expected to live if current mortality rates persist. The range for life expectancy is from a minimum of 20 years (value zero) because no country has had a life expectancy of less than 20 years in the twentieth century, and a maximum of 85, because the highest recorded by any country is 84.9 years (Hong Kong).[2]

Years of schooling is the indicator now used to calculate the education index, replacing adult literacy rates, the variable originally used. Two indicators are used, each given equal weight: the mean years of schooling, the duration of schooling at each level and the expected years of schooling, a product of the number of children in school and the school age population. The minimum is zero for both indicators; the maximum for mean years is a projection for 2025, and the maximum for expected years is 18 years, equivalent to a master's degree in most countries.

The considerations that influenced the choice of the indicator for access to resources for a decent standard of living is fully articulated in the first issue of the Human Development Report:

> The third key component of human development – command over resources needed for a decent living – is perhaps the most difficult to measure simply. It requires data on access to land, credit, income and other resources. But given the scarce data on many of these variables, we must for the time being make the best use of an income indicator. The most readily available income indicator – per capita income – has wide national coverage. But the presence of nontradable goods and services and the distortions from exchange rate anomalies, tariffs and taxes make per capita income data in nominal prices not very useful for international comparisons. Such data can, however, be improved by using purchasing power-adjusted real GDP per capita figures, which provide better approximations of the relative power to buy commodities and to gain command over resources for a decent living standard.
>
> A further consideration is that the indicator should reflect the diminishing returns to transforming income into human capabilities. In other words, people do not need excessive financial resources to ensure a decent living. This aspect was taken into account by using the logarithm of real GDP per capita for the income indicator.
>
> (United Nations Development Programme, 1990, p. 12)

The minimum for the income indicator is US$100 per head (at international purchasing power parities), a reflection of the fact that much of the output of the poorest societies is the result of subsistence and informal activity which is not recorded in the national income. The fact that this level of purchasing power does not provide resources sufficient for an adequate level of human development is indicated by a score of zero for this level of income. The maximum is set at US$75,000 per head, a level beyond which research (cited in Technical note 1 of the Human Development Report) suggests there is no gain in well-being.

The countries included in the Human Development Index are divided into four groups, from the highest scores (Very High Human Development) to Low Human Development. The cut-off points for the groups are calculated by first dividing the distribution of values for each indicator (life expectancy, mean and expected schooling and gross national income at purchasing power parities) into four equal groups. The values of the indicator at each cut-off are aggregated in the usual manner, i.e. by taking a simple mean of the two education indicators, followed by the geometric mean of the values of health, the combined education indicator, and the income indicator. The resulting cut-off points, which have been kept constant since 2014 to provide a benchmark of improvements in human development, are, for Very High Human Development, 0.800 and above; High, 0.700 to 0.799; Medium, 0.550 to 0.699 and Low, below 0.550.

The HDI is flexible and extendable

The HDI is a flexible index that has been enlarged to incorporate a richer evaluation of human development for countries where data are available. The HDI is adjusted to account for inequality in the distribution of life expectancies, mean years of schooling and income per capita at purchasing power parity, for countries where the UNDP is able to source data. For each indicator, the values of the indicators for every country are modified by an index of inequality devised by Atkinson (1970). Each indicator is grouped into ranges: for life expectancy, ages zero to one, one to five, five to ten, etc, up to 100 years and over. For a country with life expectancy at birth of 75 years, for example, life expectancy of healthy adults at age 60 might be 20 years. The inequality index is computed by comparing the arithmetic and geometric averages of the resulting distribution, using the fact that the two calculations will yield the same value for a perfectly symmetrical distribution. Household incomes are grouped in similar fashion to produce the inequality adjuster for income, and the mean education is each income group is used to group and adjust the education indicator. The geometric mean of the adjusted indicators is the Inequality-adjusted HDI (IHDI), and the difference between this index and the HDI is the loss due to inequality, shown in the Human Development Report.

The strength of this procedure is that the implications of the adjustment are clear. The Technical Note for the 2020 Human Development Report offers the example of Barbados, where inequalities of health, education and income cause a loss of 17 per cent in average well-being, as measured by the HDI. In other words, if the distribution of groups for each indicator were to fall away from the average equally in both directions, Barbadians would be that much better off, with the actual levels of health, education and health. To illustrate, the lowest life expectancy is 20 years, and the highest 85 years; with a symmetrical distribution, if there was one per cent of the population with life expectancy of 20 to 25 years, there would also be one per cent with life expectancy of 80 to 85 years, and similarly for every matching group above and below the mean value. The fact that inequality loses the country 17 per cent of its HDI score means that Barbadian society could improve the average quality of life, with no increase in performance or resources, if only those resources were utilised in a way that distributed outcomes (life expectancy, education and purchasing power) more symmetrically across the population.

This is useful information, because it provides some guidance for policy. However, while the calculation provides information on the direction of policy, it says little about the design of policy which will move the society in the desired direction. As it happens, a major change is contemplated in the schooling system in Barbados, but because of poor diagnosis of the weaknesses of the system, it is unlikely to achieve the intended gains in equality of educational opportunity. As of 2022 Barbados has a common island-wide examination for transfer from primary to secondary schools. As often happens, there are a few schools for which places are highly coveted, because they have consistently achieved high rates of admission to tertiary education, especially to institutions in North America, the UK and elsewhere. The range of scores in the common secondary entrance examination is very wide, the average is unacceptably low and the worse performing students have not mastered the basics of mathematics and English that would equip them to benefit from secondary education. Herein lies a problem, the solution to which requires a thorough investigation and revamp of primary education, to ensure that all eleven year olds are equipped with the basics to enable them to benefit from secondary education. This problem is being ignored by everyone, including government and the educators, and instead a decision has been made to do away with the common examination, in favour of individual student assessments by primary school teachers, a measure which fails to address the problem.

Gender development and gender parity are also dimensions in which the HDI has been extended in the Human Development Report. The Gender Development Index is computed by separating the data for each element into series for males and females. Data on wages for males and females is used to split the average national income into two streams. Since females live longer than males in most societies, the zero and unit boundaries for life expectancy are adjusted accordingly. While the resulting index is useful for comparison among countries, the implications for policy are less clear at an aggregate level, except for education. Few would argue against equal provision of education for girls and boys. With respect to life expectancy, it seems that a gap between the sexes in favour of females is to be expected. Wages are the trickiest, because they are the result of inequality of pay within any occupation, and the choice of occupation by each gender. There is a clear case for equality of pay within each occupation, but the choice of occupation is the result of factors which are not so easily assessed. Added to which, there are ranges of pay, productivity and responsibility within each occupation, which are often where obstacles to fair treatment arise.

The Gender Inequality Index compares males and females with respect to labour force participation, the share of seats in parliament and the percentage with some secondary education, with the addition of two maternal health indicators, maternal mortality and the percentage of births by adolescents. The policy implications of the health and education indicators are clear, but the factors affecting labour force participation are more complex and nuanced by country, community and society.

The analysis of human development has been extended to assessments of poverty, the quality of development, details of women's life chances, women's empowerment and environmental and socioeconomic sustainability. These extensions are limited in scope because of the challenge of collecting and analysing reliable data, using uniform definitions and methods. The data for poverty assessment includes information on nutrition, child mortality, school attendance, access to electricity, sanitation, access to clean drinking water, housing, fuel used for cooking and household assets. Data for the quality of development include incidence of physicians, hospital beds, pupil-teacher ratios, teacher training, proficiencies and security of employment, in addition to some poverty data. Data for the gender gap include male-female comparisons with respect to births, school enrolment, youth and total unemployment, time spent in unpaid work and old age pensions. Gender empowerment looks at access by women in different income groups to health, educational, financial and other services, as well as the incidence of gender violence and female genital mutilation. Environmental sustainability data include fossil fuel consumption, carbon dioxide emissions, deaths from disasters, and information on land use, forested areas and agricultural practices. The data for the socioeconomic sustainability assessment include savings, debt service, gross capital formation, skills, production concentration, research and development, military expenditure, and the assessment of socioeconomic sustainability includes the inequality-adjusted HDI, the Gender Inequality Index and poverty data.

These extensions of the HDI show the way for countries and regions to develop improved benchmarks for the evaluation of economic performance and policy by collecting relevant data on the many dimensions of human development. The issue of comparability with data from other countries is not so important for the formulation of policies with respect to health, education, income inequality, gender inequality, and environmental and socio-political stability within any particular country. Testing economic policies and strategies against several aspects of human development can inform the design of policy to achieve the best trade-offs between alternative uses of the resources available to the society. Such an encompassing set of benchmarks, analysed and discussed together, can also be used to condition public expectations by highlighting obvious contradictions and programmes which exceed the available resources and capacity for implementation. The case of newly-exploited natural resources, such as the incipient oil exporting industry in Guyana, may serve to illustrate the point. The fact that there is a massive jump in GDP and foreign currency inflows obscures the fact that the capabilities and human resources needed to translate this into meaningful human development are not in place. The task of building and staffing the health and educational facilities, and ensuring their services are distributed across the country and available to the poorest communities will be the work of years and decades. Paying attention to the country's HDI score, which is below the Caribbean average, would help to temper expectations. Attention paid to issues of building quality in public services, education and health in any country will pay dividends in the design of policies which can gain public support for well thought-out programmes, spaced over realistic horizons, and monitored to ensure performance according to expectations.

The HDI gains credibility from the fact that country scores are in line with lived experience

Everyday experience in a variety of countries confirms the relative scores of countries in the HDI. Greece, Cyprus, Iceland and Ireland all remain in the highest category of human development as measured by the HDI, notwithstanding highly publicised financial crises which caused a fall in national income for some years. China has not yet joined these countries in the highest category, despite its remarkable achievements in lifting hundreds of millions of workers' incomes into the middle class, eliminating desperate poverty and growing domestic output to a level which rivals that of the US. The Chinese government is aware of, and focused on, problems of inequities, housing and infrastructure, which are vital for human development of the society as a whole. Further credibility for the HDI comes from the lived experience of people who have been residents of more than one country, among countries in the very highest category of human development. Despite large differences in per capita, those who have lived in The Bahamas or Barbados in the Caribbean, Costa Rica or Panama in Central America, Mauritius in the Indian Ocean or Malaysia in Southeast Asia, will attest to the fact that the lifestyles and quality of life in these countries are comparable with what is typical in North America and Europe. The countries mentioned are all listed in the top category of the HDI, as are the majority of European countries, the US and Canada. At the other end of the distribution, all the countries with low scores on the HDI are characterised by widespread inadequacies of public utilities, health and educational services, with poor housing, sanitation and amenities and a high incidence of poverty.

The use of the HDI as the measure of economic success would help to restore the credibility of policy makers and economists with the general public. Here is the IMF's assessment of a three-year programme of financial assistance to Jamaica:

> Jamaica has successfully concluded its economic reform program, which was supported by a US$1.66 billion Stand-By Arrangement from the IMF. The country's strong ownership, as well as the government's steadfast reform implementation have resulted in a stronger economy, an all-time low unemployment rate, and a significant reduction in public debt.
>
> (International Monetary Fund, 2019)

This positive report contrasts with the country's HDI score, which remained unchanged at 0.734 for the duration of the programme. It can be argued that the benefits of the programme would hardly appear within such a short time frame, but that is precisely the point. You will always lose credibility if you claim success before the gains everyone is expecting become apparent. It does not help your case if, as happened in this instance, a global pandemic depresses the economy immediately after you have declared victory.

A contrasting example may be drawn from the experience of Iceland during the period of its financial crisis, 2008–2014. As we saw in Chapter 3, Iceland suffered a period of severe economic contraction that lasted until 2010, with GDP recovering to 2008 levels only in 2014. However, the improvement in the country's HDI score continued its upward trend, uninterrupted. The 3.6 per cent gain between 2010 and 2014 was as large as had been achieved over the full decade to 2010. The fact that the economic downturn would not have impaired the institutional framework and delivery of health and educational services (and led to no permanent redistribution of income, though that is not reflected in the HDI score) meant that the material well-being of the population continued to improve during the period of the crisis. This would doubtless have contributed to public acceptance of the adjustment measures that restored economic prosperity.

The use of the HDI to improve the efficiency of policy design

The use of the HDI as the measure of economic success ought to lead to policies that are better focused and more efficiently designed. National economic policies and strategies that use the HDI for setting targets and evaluating progress would entail a focus on improving life expectancy, enlarging access to schooling and increasing resources available to the average household for securing their members a decent standard of living. With the collection of additional data, the targets could be enriched to include reduction of income inequality, inequality of gender, poverty reduction, improving the quality of public services and public amenities and environmental protection. Action plans and programmes would be evaluated and reported on in terms of the HDI targets.

The benefits would be seen in increased credibility and improved efficiency of macroeconomic strategies. The targets of the strategy would be articulated in terms of goals for the quality and comprehensiveness of health and educational services, reduction in poverty and unfairness of livelihoods and genders, as well as usage of renewables and recycling. Interim reports would track progress in every dimension so that responsible public sector officials and agencies could make course corrections as necessary to hit the targets. Periodic evaluations would also be the occasion to revise the targets in light of circumstances and to correct for errors in the design of the strategy. This is a framework which improves the credibility of policy by ensuring that the lived experience of the population changes in line with the indicators, because the HDI uses indicators which draw from that experience.

The HDI framework should also improve the efficiency of macroeconomic policy in important dimensions. All too often, public policy fails to respect funding constraints: the funds needed to improve the quality and accessibility of health and educational systems, and to attain other goals of public policy, exceed the public sector revenues and the level of borrowing that is available to government and within the limits of fiscal prudence. The HDI framework forces the public sector to make adjustments until there is a programme which sits within the envelope of the available finance. To the extent that programmes do not fit within that envelope, that fact will emerge at the periodic evaluations, as someone or other of the programme falls behind schedule for want of funds, or budget deficits balloon beyond what is sustainable. The corrective mechanisms that should be built into the evaluation procedures can be used to make adjustments as needed to ensure efficient use of the available financial and material resources through a process of trial and error over the life of the macroeconomic strategy. If the process works well, over time the efficiency in the public sector's use of resources will improve.

Using the HDI as the objective of macroeconomic policy might also aid in the design of public policy by influencing public perception of realities. The US trade war with China offers what may be the best illustration. The universal notion that the US can protect domestic employment to the benefit of the society at large is a fallacy that is obvious to anyone with economic training. In fact, the main benefit that Americans derive from trade with China is the access to affordable imports, a benefit that is shared throughout the society:

> What all this China-bashing leaves out is that cheap Chinese imports have drastically improved the quality of life of American workers, whose median income has stagnated for 40 years. According to the consultancy Oxford Economics, buying Chinese imports saves American families around $850 annually. Given that 63 per cent of American households do not have even $500 saved for emergencies, this is not an insignificant amount.
>
> (Mahbubani, 2018)

The reason that this benefit goes unrecognised is that there is no counterfactual. We do not have an alternative world without a hugely productive Chinese workforce against which to evaluate the price advantage that American consumers enjoy. The misperception problem might be less acute were public policy in the US to target the HDI, however, in the following circumstances.

Let us imagine a US government which set macroeconomic targets using a sophisticated version of the HDI, incorporating income equalities and quality indices of access to health and educational services, with an effective mechanism for monitoring and reporting on progress. Such a system would detect and address the income inequalities which are at the root of the disaffection with globalisation in general, a disaffection of which the trade war with China is only one manifestation. Arguably it is the fact that wages for low income earners have not kept pace with what is considered necessary for a decent standard of living, and their insufficient access to health care and a good education, that fuels the animosity to immigrants and the enthusiasm for things made in America in preference for seeking best value for money.

The US government has been unable to devise and implement policies to address these inequities, despite the widespread concerns that have been the subject of active debate in the country for much of the last two decades. A large part of the problem has to rest with public perceptions, which are focused on GDP growth, inflation and unemployment. In a growing economy, with inflation and unemployment at the lowest levels in several decades, there is a disconnect between what purports to be a prosperous economy and the lived experience of a majority of the population. Elevating an alternative metric which more nearly reflects lived experience would not solve this problem, but it would condition the discussion, creating fertile ground for constructive policies by closing the gap between perception and experience.

The use of the HDI as the measure of economic success might also motivate more effective policy-making at international organisations such as the World Bank and the IMF. Apart from the obvious implications for the credibility of their policy advice to member countries and the effectiveness of their financial assistance that would come with curing the dissonance between their analysis and the lived reality in member countries, such a focus would help to motivate more realistic policy objectives for the international economy, in order to make progress with sustainable development goals, renewable energy and the environment. The gap between the African countries, most of whom reside in the lowest category of human development, and the top-scoring countries of Europe and North America gives a realistic idea of the magnitude of the transfers to African countries of finance and capabilities that must be contemplated in order to achieve the global targets. At the same time, the HDI suggests that the magnitude of that transfer will be smaller than for countries with higher HDI scores, because a dollar goes farther at the bottom end of the scale. In addition, the HDI puts the spotlight on the effectiveness of finance and other transfers in securing real gains in health and educational outcomes, and on securing gains sufficient to make an impact on the macroeconomic level.

The HDI is the best generally available measure of economic success

The HDI is the best generally available measure of economic success, and it is therefore the metric of choice for the guidance of economic policy. Most readers will have no difficulty with the premise on which the calculation of the HDI is based, that every human ought to be able to enjoy a long and healthy life, access to the world's store of accumulated knowledge, and the means to provide themselves with a decent livelihood, irrespective of whether they were born in Arouca, Atlanta, Armenia or Antofagasta, Zanzibar or Zhejiang. We might argue, in addition, for happiness, fulfilment of potential or other desirables, but the three included in the HDI computation are the least common denominator. The variables chosen to measure each of these three qualities are credible and widely available on a comparable basis for all countries, and the computation produces an index which does not depart from the observed conditions of societies all around the world. The basic HDI may be enriched to capture inequities over various kinds, to provide a framework for judging the quality of services under each dimension of the index, and to highlight inconsistencies and resource limitations. There is no other measure of economic success that comes close to matching these attributes.

It follows that macroeconomic policies and strategies that use the HDI and extensions as the target they seek to attain, employing the HDI to monitor progress along the way and adjusting policies and targets where necessary, will have a greater chance of success than any other metric. What is more, because success would be achieved by securing increases in life expectancy at birth, in the mean and expected years of schooling, and in the purchasing power of average incomes, along with other desirable changes, the credibility and authority of economists and policy makers would be restored, over time, by the match between claims of success and the lived experience of the population.

These are powerful arguments in favour of giving primacy to the HDI over GDP, employment, inflation, happiness or any other metric as the measure of economic success. These and other metrics are useful, but if they cannot be incorporated into an enhanced HDI measure such as the income inequality-adjusted HDI, then they are best used to supplement the picture painted by the HDI.

Notes

1 See, for example, WVS Database (worldvaluessurvey.org).
2 See United Nations Development Programme, 2020, Technical note 1.

References

Atkinson, A. B. 1970. "On the measurement of inequality." *Journal of Economic Theory*, Vol. 2, no. 3, pp. 244–263.

Banerjee, Abhijit and Esther Duflo. 2019. *Good Economics for Hard Times*. New York: PublicAffairs.

Best, Lloyd and Kari Levitt. 2009. *Essays on the Plantation Economy*. Kingston, Jamaica: University of the West Indies Press.

Furtado, Celso. 1964. *Development and Underdevelopment*. Oakland, California: University of California Press.

International Monetary Fund. 2019. "Jamaica: On the path to higher economic growth," *Country Focus Note*, November.

Layard, Richard. 2006. "Happiness and public policy: A challenge to the profession," *The Economic Journal*, Vol. 116, no. 510, pp. C24–C33.

Layard, Richard. 2005. *Happiness: Lessons from a New Science*. Allen Lane, UK; New York: Penguin.

Lewis, W. Arthur. 1954. "Economic development with unlimited supplies of labour," *The Manchester School of Economic and Social Studies*, Vol. 22, no. 2, pp. 139–191.

Mahbubani, Kishore. 2018. "America's collision course with China." *Project Syndicate*, May 15. project-syndicate.org.

Meier, Gerard. 1989. *Leading issues in economic development*, 14th ed. Oxford: Oxford University Press.

Melo, Santiago. 2011. "Eudaimonia and the economics of happiness." *Documento CEDE no. 2011–2005*, February 1.

Offer, Avner. 2006. *Economic Growth and Wellbeing: A Behavioural Analysis.* Oxford: Oxford University Press.

Oswald, Andrew J. and Nattavudh Powdthavee. 2006. "Does happiness adapt? A longitudinal study of disability with implications for economists and judges." *IZA Discussion Paper no. 2208, ERN IZA Papers,* Vol. 6 no. 67, August 28.

Prebisch, Raul. 1950. *The Economic Development of Latin America and its Principal Problems.* New York: United Nations.

Rostow, W. W. 1960. *The Stages of Economic Growth: A Non-communist Manifesto.* Cambridge: Cambridge University Press.

United Nations Development Programme. 2020. "Human Development Report," New York: UNDP.

United Nations Development Programme. 1990. "Human Development Report," New York: UNDP.

18 Globalization is not a Choice; it is a Statement about our World

In the ongoing debate that rages about the causes and consequences of globalisation (Dollar, 2021; Economic Commission for Latin America and the Caribbean, 2020; Global Development Policy Center, Boston University, 2021; Moyo, 2017; Posen, 2021; Sachs, 2022; Slaughter, 2022) one can lose sight of the fact that there is now a consciousness on the part of humanity everywhere, except in the world's most remote areas, that we share the globe with hundreds of millions of other humans, whose existence and activities impinge on our own lives and prospects in some way. The ubiquity of radios, televisions, and now mobile phones and tablets, means that in towns and villages where, 50 years ago, people lived and died with little knowledge, awareness or concern beyond the borders of family and community, nowadays current events in distant lands are a daily concern. The choice therefore is not whether there should be more or less interconnection, whether actions and events in one part of the world will have greater or lesser impacts elsewhere; it is rather about whether these interactions will be to the benefit of all humanity, about what can be done to ameliorate the undesirable effects and to enhance the positive effects, about who bears the greatest burden of the costs of amelioration and suffers the greatest loss from adverse consequences, and about the fairness of the distribution of costs and benefits. The debate is not globalisation vs anti-globalisation; it is about costs, consequences and fairness.

The world is a single economic space

In the twenty-first century, more than ever before in our world, it is apparent that the world is a single economic space. It comes as no surprise that the 19-year old Swedish activist Greta Thunberg is a leader of the global campaign for action to ameliorate the worst consequences of climate change; the real surprise, as Thunberg herself says, is that there are so few people, especially of her age, who are as passionate:

> I think that in many ways, we autistics are the normal ones, and the rest of the people are pretty strange, especially when it comes to the

DOI: 10.4324/9781003247609-22

> sustainability crisis, where everyone keeps saying that climate change is an existential threat and the most important issue of all and yet they just carry on like before.
>
> (Thunberg, 2018)

The reality is that, as things now stand, the worst consequences of climate change seem inevitable during the expected lifetimes of everyone born in the twenty-first century. All the indicators are still moving in the wrong direction: global temperatures continue to rise, the use of fossil fuels continues to rise alongside the increasing use of renewables, rainforest loss continues apace, species extinction has not been appreciably slowed, the north polar ice cap is disappearing, permafrost is thawing, waste forms vast floating islands in mid-ocean. The actions of dedicated environmentalists and the earnest commitments of nations come up against realities of finance, the distribution of wealth, and the disparity of livelihoods, opportunities and life chances across the globe.

The media responses to the outcomes of the most recent international conference on climate change, the 2021 Conference of the Parties to the United Nations Framework Convention on Climate Change (COP26, 31 October–13 November), were summarised by Wikipedia in the following terms:

> Current targets for 2030 remain "totally inadequate". Coal and natural gas consumption are the main cause for the gap between pledges and policies. They assessed pledges by 40 countries that account for 85 per cent of pledged net-zero emissions cuts and found that only polities responsible for six per cent of global greenhouse gas emissions – EU, UK, Chile and Costa Rica – have pledged a set of targets that they rated to be "acceptable" for comprehensiveness and for having a published detailed official policy-plan that describes the steps and ways by which these targets could be realised.
>
> (Wikipedia, downloaded April 13, 2022)

The spread of the COVID-19 pandemic offers a potent current example of the reality of globalisation, and the world's inability to marshal resources to react appropriately to a global threat. From the earliest days it was clear that a truly global response to the pandemic was essential to ensure that the loss of life worldwide would be minimised. At a time when total cases of COVID-19 globally were just 100,000, the World Health Organisation was already urging all countries to act: "WHO calls on all countries to continue efforts that have been effective in limiting the number of cases and slowing the spread of the virus" (World Health Organisation, 2020c). Just over a week later, in a joint statement with the International Chambers of Commerce, the WHO repeated the call: "Governments should commit to making available all necessary resources to combat COVID-19 with the minimum of delay and to ensure that cross-border medical and other essential goods supply chains are able to function effectively and efficiently" (World Health Organisation, 2020c). A month later the WHO issued a more forthright statement:

> Humanity is collectively facing its most daunting challenge since the Second World War. COVID-19 knows no borders, spares no country or continent, and strikes indiscriminately. By all accounts, we are at least 12 months away from a vaccine.
>
> In this race against an invisible enemy, all countries must fight back, but not all begin from the same starting line. In countries where the world's most vulnerable need humanitarian aid and supplies to beat back the pandemic, cancelled flights and disrupted supply routes hit disproportionately hard. It is in everyone's interest to stop the virus from spreading unchecked, destroying lives and economies, and continuing to circle around the world.
>
> (World Health Organisation, 2020b)

Against this background, the shambolic national response allowed the pandemic to take a toll on lives, especially in the world's richest nations, large enough to cause a dip on life expectancy in the US and elsewhere. The failure to promote equitable responses across the globe, especially in developing Africa, has had the predictable result of creating fertile ground for the evolution of the deadly Delta variant and the super-contagious Omicron variants, which have aggravated the costs, economic and human, and extended the timeline for bringing the pandemic to an end. Once again, the inability to mobilise the world's resources for effective action to deal with a global challenge has been exposed.

The magnitude of the financing transfers from rich to poor countries that is required to effect the changes needed to address any of the existential challenges to civilised lifestyles globally is not generally recognised. With respect to the resources needed to address pandemic risk Okonjo-Iweala, Shanmugaratnam and Summers (2021) observe:

> we need a global funding mechanism to mobilize the much larger and sustained investments needed for pandemic prevention and preparedness. A new multilateral fund to mobilize at least $10 billion each year would provide a critical overlay on today's siloed and underfunded system of global health security.

Summers has been consistent in pointing out the insufficiency of financing for achieving global targets, including for environmental sustainability and reducing harmful emissions. In general, the linkages between the sustainable development goals and achievement of targets for climate change have not been acknowledged. For example, so long as there are deficits in the supply of clean fuels for cooking and scare opportunities for rural communities in the global South, forests will be consumed for fuel, exploited for mineral extraction, burned to make way for cash crops and poached for illicit trade. Environmental remediation is not only about financing alternative energy and recycling; it is also about creating good livelihoods for poor communities who have no way out, other than exploiting earth's resources in ways that threaten the health of the planet.

The development of communications and transport technologies has had profound effects on the interactions of populations around the world. New communications technologies have already altered the way much of the world works, and have fostered linkages of organisation and networking that span the globe; practices and systems that were already in use have become generalised thanks to the restrictions that came with the COVID-19 pandemic. Modern communications have contributed in major ways to the global wave of migration which continues unabated, through channels both legal and illegal. Images of life in major international metropolises and of educational and job opportunities now travel swiftly and through multiple channels, formal and informal. People are motivated to abandon circumstances of deprivation and limited opportunities for a chance to find a better life, even in the face of considerable risk. Their choice may be more rational than is usually admitted; the life expectancy in some violence-wracked and drought-stricken communities may be so low that the risks of not surviving passage to a better life are actually lower than staying put.

The power of modern communications is manifest in business, social life, exchange of ideas, and in personal relationships. The global reach of new technologies is also put to negative uses, not only in the spread of destructive ideas, misinformation and bias, but also by undermining the basic principles of justice. In today's social media, the accusation of wrong-doing makes one guilty on being charged. If in fact you are innocent, and are able to afford the legal costs of proving it in a court of law, not only will you not be able to recover those costs; you will also never erase the stain on your reputation. The point to be made is that transport and communications now bind us more closely than ever across the globe, in myriad ways, with apparently limitless potential for both good and evil.

The global financial crisis of 2008 was a wake-up call with respect to the depth and pervasiveness of interconnections within global financial systems. As Timothy Geithner's enlightening memoire reveals (Geithner, 2014) it was a failure of coordination between the Bank of England and the Federal Reserve Bank of New York, of which he was then President, which resulted in the closure of Lehman Brothers, the fallout of which immediately caused a roiling collapse of asset prices as financial markets opened across the world. Central banks of the world's financial centres reacted swiftly, intervening massively and collectively to provide liquidity and guarantees sufficient to stabilise markets, sensibly discarding their ideology and acting responsibly. (Strangely, instead of congratulating the central banks on a job well done, economists and policy makers castigate themselves for not having prevented the financial crisis, and continue to pursue the fantasy that they can create a self-correcting system that is immune from collapse.)

The digitisation of finance is now all but complete; except for trivial amounts of notes and coins, all finance is in the form of digital records maintained by banks and other financial institutions, and every transfer of value is an instruction to transfer value from one digital account to another. However the international legal framework and guidance for the maintenance of the digital records of value worldwide, and for the content and probity of instructions to transfer, are still as they were designed for an analogue world. This has left regulators with the impression that there are ways to control flows of finance in line with national priorities of whatever motivation. That is an illusion; as for the movement of people, transfers of value and other financial transactions are driven by global interconnections of economic activity. The concern of international regulators should be to ensure the efficiency of the international financial system through a redesign that uses new technology to secure real-time verification of international payments.

The development of air, sea and land transportation systems, networks and technologies have fuelled international migration at unprecedented levels in recent decades. The World Migration Report 2020 (International Organisation for Migration, 2020) reports the number of international migrants worldwide in 2019 at 272 million (3.5 per cent of the world's population), more than three times the number in 1970, when migrants were 2.3 per cent of total population. The surge in international migration in the twenty-first century (Figure 18.1) is the result of a complex combination of factors. The global reach of new communications technologies has widened perceptions of income disparities and fuelled aspirations of people in poor countries to imitate the lifestyles of affluent societies. The failure, over five decades, of

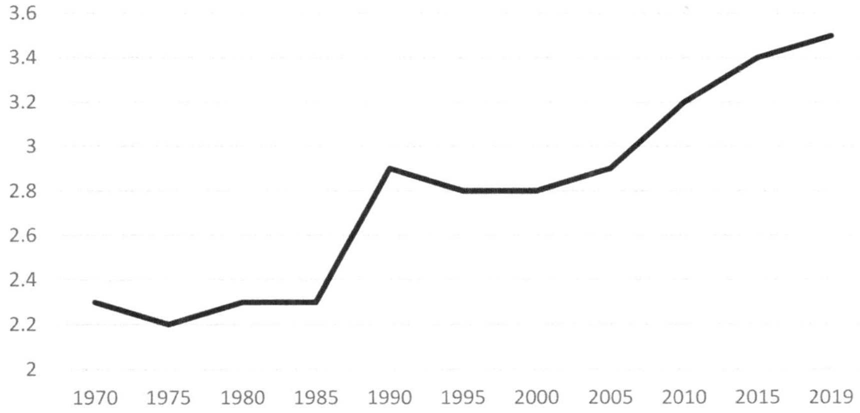

Figure 18.1 Migrants as a percentage of world population
Data source: International Organization for Migration (2020).

national and international economic development programmes which were intended to close the gap between the livelihoods of Europeans and North Americans on the one hand, and the populations of Africa, Asia and South and Central America, has resulted in irrepressible economic forces driving workers to Europe and North America: medical workers, technicians, and other skilled workers, as well as the unskilled, are drawn by the pull of better wages and working conditions in rich countries. This international migration has had effects on relative wages, labour productivity and the choice of labour-intensive technologies, which have proved problematic. Cross-border movements of people have been greatly complicated by social and political conflict, widespread insecurity of person and property in some countries, natural disasters, and outright wars. The almost universal response, of placing ever stronger barriers in the way of immigration, without addressing the factors that are driving people to leave their homes, will not substantially reduce the cross-border flow; it will, however, make it much more costly in terms of lives and treasure than it needs to be.

A global debate rages around the concept of globalisation, its effects and the policy implications

A selection from contemporary literature will serve to illustrate the main themes and issues that have arisen in debates on globalisation in international policy fora. The difficulty in achieving effective strategies for international cooperation that are sustained over the long run is highlighted by Moyo (2017):

> Essentially, the problem with globalization is a mismatch of the economic intergenerational aspects of economics versus the short-termism that we see in the political decision-making process. Put another way, politicians are basically very rationally courting and catering to their national electorates and will always very rationally want to protect their voters. But as a consequence, they can never have a global interest as the priority, because ultimately [issues] will be decided in terms of their political opportunities based on national agenda.
>
> Although there are many reasons to pursue globalization, and I, myself, love the idea of globalization, I do believe it can lift all boats. The problem is, the only way that you can have effective globalization is if you have global institutions who oversee the aspects of the key pillars of globalization – trade, capital flows, and immigration.

Much of the discussion, within countries and internationally, has been about the effects of globalisation on the distribution of income and life chances, nationally and between rich and poor nations. Slaughter (2022) takes the temperature of globalisation, discussing ways of tackling distributional challenges and ensuring that policies work for ordinary families. He also reflects on the evolving demands on leaders of corporations in the twenty-first century, positing that those who recognise their wider purpose in society tend to outperform on productivity growth and profits.

Dollar (2021) points out that globalisation is controversial because there are winners and losers, even though trade and international finance make all parties richer. He cites examples of winners in the US context, including farmers and high tech sectors, including Pfizer, the pharmaceutical company, and Apple. In the US losers include semi-skilled labour that is abundant in developing countries. As an example of the challenges this presents he mentions that Apple contracts mainly with a Taiwanese company based in China for its products; there is no benefit for US workers even though Apple is a US company. One result of these redistributional changes has been the emergence of distressed regions in the US, such as New England.

Ortiz-Ospina and Beltekian (2018) summarise:

> For some households, the net effect is positive. But for some households that's not the case. In particular, workers who lose their job can be affected for extended periods of time, so the positive effect via lower prices is not enough to compensate them for the reduction in earnings.
>
> On the whole, if we aggregate changes in welfare across households, the net effect is usually positive. But this is hardly a consolation for those who are worse off. This highlights a complex reality: There are aggregate gains from trade, but there are also real distributional concerns. Even if trade is not a major driver of income inequalities, it's important to keep in mind that public policies, such as unemployment benefits and other safety-net programs, can and should help redistribute the gains from trade.

Largely because of inadequate and unhelpful responses to distributional challenges and policies driven by short-term expediency, nationalism and populist isolationist policies have become a major roadblock on the way to solutions to global challenges. Sachs (2022) admits that the rising opposition to free trade means inward-looking populist movements have become more successful, most notably in the US and the United Kingdom. The COVID-19 pandemic has sped up the retreat from globalisation. Rodrik (2020) believes that what he terms "hyper-globalization" will remain on the defensive as nation-states reclaim policy space. Mueller (2021) argues that the visions of global economic governance developing in the United States and China today both mark a break with neoliberal interpretations of globalisation that expected the process to be market-driven, requiring official frameworks of regulation but little or no intervention on the part of the public sector.

On the issue of international migration, the World Migration Report 2020 reports that

> The long-term and growing body of evidence on migration and mobility shows that migration is in large part related to the broader global

> economic, social, political and technological transformations that are affecting a wide range of high-priority policy issues. As the processes of globalisation deepen, these transformations increasingly shape our lives – in our workplaces, in our homes, in our social and spiritual lives – as we go about our daily routines. Increasing numbers of people are able to access information, goods and services from around the world because of the ongoing expansion in distance-shrinking technologies. ....
>
> The overwhelming majority of people migrate internationally for reasons related to work, family and study – involving migration processes that largely occur without fundamentally challenging either migrants or the countries they enter. In contrast, other people leave their homes and countries for a range of compelling and sometimes tragic reasons, such as conflict, persecution and disaster. While those who have been displaced, such as refugees and internally displaced persons (IDPs), comprise a relatively small percentage of all migrants, they are often the most in need of assistance and support.
>
> (International Organization for Migration, 2020)

For small open economies, their relationship with the wider world has always been paramount

All the economies included in the analysis throughout this book have always been irretrievably linked into networks of commerce and migration that have endured over centuries. The indigenous cultures of the Caribbean have left us no written records, so our knowledge of Caribbean economies begins in the fifteenth century, with the arrival of Europeans, motivated by the need to extract precious metals and develop production of tropical crops, for export to Europe. A triangular trade soon formed the basis of the Caribbean economies, with armaments, cash and valuables shipped to the west coast of Africa, there to be used to buy slaves, transported across the Atlantic to be sold on to Caribbean plantation owners. On the third leg of the journey ships returned to Europe laden with sugar, precious metals and other tropical products, carried by the Gulf Stream, a current which skirts the east coast of the US to cross the Atlantic in its northern latitudes.

The cultures of Central America left few written records that have so far been discovered, and those few have not been deciphered. In their case, incorporation into the European-dominated commercial system came in the nineteenth century. The islands were more accessible for the cultivation of sugar cane, the main agricultural export until that time, and the Caribbean littoral of the Americas, South and Central, attracted attention mainly in the search for precious metals, with some logging and little else. The commercial introduction of refrigerated cargo and the development of techniques of fruit preservation were major factors in the development of the economies of Central America, which were based initially on the export of fruits and juices. In the twentieth century clothing, pharmaceuticals and other light manufacturing developed, all for export to North America and Europe. Until the opening of the Panama Canal in 1914, the Central American isthmus was a major barrier to east-west trade. The Canal immediately became an immensely valuable economic resource, creating a large international service economy in the Canal Zone.

The experience of Mauritius in the Indian ocean is not dissimilar to that of the Caribbean, except that the island's integration into the European-dominated global economy dates from the nineteenth century, and the labour force for their sugar industry was mainly indentured labour (on fixed-term contract, at the end of which most labourers settled, rather than returning to their homelands) from the Indian subcontinent. In the case of the Seychelles, the Maldives (also in the Indian Ocean), and of Fiji and Vanuatu in the Pacific, economic activity raised living conditions above subsistence levels only in recent decades, with the advent tourism as a major source of foreign currency. Other small islands subsist on remittances and the export of migrant labour to provide foreign currency for imports.

Bosnia-Herzegovina, Cyprus, Iceland, Latvia, Malta and Montenegro are all integral to the European economy, and their trading and financial networks are not materially different from provinces or districts of the countries with which their economies interact. The activities which they export and from which they earn the wherewithal to import are what would be expected, had they been fated by history not to be independent states.

While the sources of foreign exchange have differed among small open economies and for countries over time, the one constant for all has been the fact that consumption and investment needs are sourced abroad, for anything above primitive subsistence activity. Even basic agricultural and building tools and household equipment, furnishings and clothing, are all imported or fabricated using imported materials. The fact that external commerce is the mechanism of the open economy and that foreign currency is its fuel means that foreign currency, not domestic money, is the important standard of value. For all the economies with which we are concerned, this interest in the currencies of their main trading partners has always been an aspect of the global economy which is part of the background of daily life and commerce. The populations of all small open economies have struggled to make sense of the notion of international exchange rate flexibility. Up until 1971 gold was the international standard of value, proxied by the US dollar, thanks to the fact that the US Federal Reserve guaranteed to exchange the dollar at US$35 per ounce of gold. The practice of depending on the gold standard was so well established that the dollar has continued to be the standard of value worldwide. Despite all attempts to displace it, and in spite of the financial excesses of the US Government over several decades, the globalisation of money has persisted.

The outward-looking nature of commerce, finance and money is reflected in a heightened sense of their place in the world economy, on the part of the populations of small open economies. They, above all others, understand that globalisation is a way to describe their reality; they cannot decide to have more or less of it. As a result, people from small countries often find that they are more informed about the countries they visit or to which they migrate, than are natives of those countries. They do not have the leisure to ignore global economic events, secure in the knowledge that only a global pandemic or a surge in international petroleum prices will have effects large enough to have an impact on their lives. Their economic prospects are always conditional on economic circumstances in the countries from which they buy and sell and of all the factors that may affect finance, prices, trade, transport and communications, and they are obliged to adapt to changes in all these dimensions.

What has changed?

I grew up in a middle-income household just two miles from the centre of Bridgetown, the capital of Barbados, in the late 1940s and 1950s. Until age 11 I recall travelling to Broad Street, the town's main shopping centre, only once a year, to purchase shoes and supplies for the new school year. My family did not own a motor car, nor did our neighbours, teachers, policemen, tailors and nurses, all middle-income earners like my father, a trained jeweller who worked as a clerk. The best that households like ours could afford was a bicycle. Televisions were unknown, and news arrived via the daily newspaper. There was a single wired radio service, in effect a single speaker linked by wire to the broadcasting centre. We did not have Rediffusion, as it was called, so, like most Barbadians, we had virtually no notice of the arrival of Hurricane Janet in 1955. We secured telephone service in the late 1950s; anything beyond local calls was so expensive as to be out of the question. My first air travel at age 19 was to attend university across the Caribbean in Jamaica, a long trip north and then west by propeller-driven aircraft, with two stops on the way. The contrast with the transport and communications tools and technology available to middle-income households today illustrates the extent of the change in the quality of the relationship of Barbadian economy and society with the global economy.

The fundamental fact that the Barbadian economy is embedded in the international economy has not changed: tourism has replaced sugar as the main source of foreign earnings, but the country continues to earn most of its foreign exchange from the UK market, and imports are sourced mainly from American companies, as they have been for many decades. Barbadians are exceptionally well informed about our world, as they already were in the 1950s, when compared to rich countries. What has changed beyond recognition is the technology of transport and communications, the opportunities that have opened up to Barbadians as a result, and the challenges it poses for Barbadian society and culture.

The essential point is that though the nature and extent of global engagement by small open economies remains unchanged, the tools, systems and patterns of communications, travel and transport, and international financial systems, institutions and organisation have all changed in ways that policy makers have to take account of, if their actions are to be effective.

A notable result of emigration from small open economies over the past five decades or more is the existence of a large diaspora in Europe and North America of people born in these countries. Caribbean-born residents of the US are estimated at ten per cent of the population of the insular Caribbean. Other large concentrations of Caribbean-born residents are to be found in Europe and Canada. The diaspora extends the Caribbean economy in ways which are reflected in available statistics as well as in economic transactions which the data does not capture. Remittances from this diaspora make a major contribution to foreign currency inflows in many countries, as we have seen in Chapter 4. Not captured in this data are remittances in kind; people throughout the Caribbean are familiar with the "barrel trade", gifts of food and household items shipped by members of the diaspora to their friends and relatives at Christmastime and on other festive occasions. Other ways in which the diaspora contributes to the home economy are through providing an export market for foods and other items from the home country, visiting for holidays and festivals, building retirement homes and providing foreign exchange by way of retirement income, and extending the market in which musicians, bloggers, and other cultural entrepreneurs can sell their offerings.

Globalisation has implications for the concepts we use to think about economic activity and economic processes

The American novelist Lauren Groff, author of *Matrix*, the Albanian-born philosopher Lea Ypi, author of *Free* and the Barbadian graphic novelists Matthew Clarke and Nigel Lynch, authors of *Hardears*, share the ability to conjure into life worlds which are strange but somehow very familiar. It is this faculty which is needed to effect the transition from the world economy as it is, to realising the potential which new communications technologies open up to us. Not many of us have it. Instead we confront new technologies with old concepts, legacy systems and targets and expectations based on what we are used to. The dissonance between our thought patterns and the logic of new technologies inhibits our ability to benefit from these technologies. Some personal examples will serve to illustrate ways in which the dilemma manifests itself.

As a lifelong bibliophile, I mourn the disappearance of independent bookstores in all the places I have lived in recent years. I pride myself on staying on the cusp of productive technologies, and was making use of remote bibliographic services before there was a Worldwide Web. Before it became a reality the idea of remote access to everything published seemed a book lover's utopia. Of course it has proved to be anything but. My tastes are eclectic, so browsing bookstores is a delight, uncovering titles, authors and topics I never knew existed. Internet searches, by contrast, turn up endless lists of items like the one I've just read, titles in which I have not the slightest interest. Internet searches are like finding oneself alone in London's Trafalgar Square or New York's Times Square, with no knowledge of the city and no guide. The internet is of little help, unless you have a knowledgeable guide.

The obverse is the problem of finding customers online. The introduction of social media has given anyone virtually free access to the entire world market, in theory. However, every other aspirant also has that access, reducing the chances that you will attract the attention of your target audience in the midst of the maelstrom of billions of messages being issued daily. When I set up my website DeLisleWorrell.com in 2017, I opted to forego social media links in favour of an email list of known contacts to advertise new posts and publications, so that I could target the audience I wanted to reach.

The device on which I am writing this chapter is a BlackBerry Passport. The last cellphone produced by BlackBerry that used the company's proprietary operating system, it was a market failure, and proved almost the last gasp of the dying company. However, the Passport is the ideal road warrior's tablet, with a physical two-thumb keyboard that allows for rapid touch-typing on the fly, and with no need for a desk, table or any support whatsoever. Since I acquired this example six years ago I have used it for note-taking at meetings and conferences, as backup for speeches and speaking notes and for all my writing. The battery is now failing, so I will soon lose my productivity tool, with no replacement available, anywhere in the world. It is a tragedy born of failure by any tablet manufacturer to recognise the niche that technology has opened up for a highly efficient hand-held business tool.

I believe a similar failure of perception lies at the heart of the inability until now to deploy available communications technologies to dramatically improve the world's system of international payments. In redesigning the international payments system we bring to the table a baggage of currencies and exchange rates which is not necessary now that technology allows us to send instructions digitally across the globe in real time. If instead we were able to strip the payments problem down to its essence, that of transmitting verifiable instructions for the transfer of value from one digital record to another, it would not matter what currency that value was expressed in, so long as the rate of exchange between the currencies of the sender and receiver were known in the instant that communication takes place. Indeed there is no reason to use different measures of value at the beginning and end of the transfer. If people are shy of using the US dollar for nationalistic reasons, the IMF currency, the Special Drawing Right (SDR), is available as the world's common standard for the exchange of value. To my mind, all that stands in the way of a seamless international payments system that exchanges SDR-denominated value in real time is our failure to imagine a new and different world of payments.

Concepts that have become unhelpful in the twenty-first century

As we have shown in Chapters 5 and 14, the spaces within which economic exchanges and interactions are most intense do not correspond to the boundaries of nation states. In Chapter 5 we described the level of interaction within the Caribbean region, demonstrating how national boundaries have defined transactions in ways that defy economic logic and the interests of both the Caribbean and its economic partners. The dissonance of the concepts of nation and economy is generalised in Chapter 14. One way to demonstrate this dissonance is to compare transactions across national boundaries with transactions across provincial or other second-level administrative boundaries. The movements of people and goods between Detroit in the US and Windsor across the border in Canada is not dissimilar to that between New York and New Jersey, adjacent states within the US, in terms of intensity, relative to total movements and transactions. In the Caribbean, economic links between St Kitts, a member of the Caribbean Community, CARICOM, and the neighbouring US Virgin Islands, a US dependency, are far stronger than are St Kitts' economic ties with Barbados, a CARICOM member that is much further away.

Our conceptual frameworks determine the way in which information is collected and aggregated, resulting in gaps which lead to misperceptions and false conclusions. The challenge I set myself in Worrell (2021) was to estimate the benefit that Caribbean countries received from importing affordable products from China. That this benefit is considerable is evident: I am listening to a Chinese-made radio as I write this, sipping tea from a Chinese-made teapot, my Chinese-made computer open on the desk beside me. When I consulted the trade data, however, Caribbean imports from China are only a very small percentage of the total, thanks to the fact that most of the Chinese-made products are imported via the US, appearing as imports from that country. Also, there is a scarcity of reliable data on intra-company trade, an issue that has come front and centre in a world of global supply chains.

Conceptual issues arise in the valuation of international trade within global conglomerates, something which has become a defining characteristic of production in the twenty-first century. Economists do not seem to have internalised the subjective nature of value and pricing (Chapter 14) which makes it impossible to value internal transactions within a company, because no actual exchange of value at an agreed price takes place. All of the fictions to which officialdom usually resorts may be challenged: cross-border prices for intermediate goods by rival producers assume that independent producers have similar cost structures and similar efficiencies as internationally integrated companies, a policy which may squander efficiency gains from integrated production. Cost-plus pricing and other expediencies may have similar efficiency-suppressing effects. The challenge of pricing traded intra-company services is even more acute; in practice such pricing appears quite arbitrary.

Globalisation, technology and human development in small open economies

Technological developments in the past 60 years have opened world markets in ways that have already helped to transform the livelihoods of populations in small open economies. The most dramatic example is tourism. In Chapters 3 and 4 we have shown how the transition from export agriculture to tourism as the main source of foreign exchange has effected a significant increase in average incomes, employment opportunities, spinoffs to other sectors, improvements in amenities and better prospects for the populations of host countries in the Caribbean, the Indian Ocean and the Pacific. We also recorded the growing importance of workers' remittances as a source of foreign currency in a number of countries, a second phenomenon which was made possible by the improvements in technology and communications that have facilitated the surge in migration over the past five decades. A number of island states owe their high rankings in the Human Development Index to tourism and workers' remittances; they include The Bahamas, Barbados, Cuba, the Dominican Republic, Fiji, Iceland, Jamaica, the Maldives, the Seychelles and the member countries of the Eastern Caribbean Currency Union.

The globalisation of supply chains has been of more limited benefit to small open economies. Most are too small to play a significant role in the supply of components and inputs for manufacture in other countries; their strength is in the international supply of services. Small countries have had limited success in penetrating the global market for traded services. A handful of Caribbean countries have small niches in supplying cultural, telemarketing, data processing, educational and medical services, mainly to the North American market, but the services sector (other than tourism and related services) has made a very limited contribution to foreign earnings. Caribbean singers, songwriters and musicians have established a truly global reputation, establishing distinctive categories of world music, and the leading practitioners, past and present, have become household names. Caribbean street festivals, which have reached their fullest modern interpretation and inspiration from the Trinidad and Tobago Carnival, have defined style and content which has been imitated across the Caribbean, as well as in New York (the Labor Day Parade in Brooklyn), Toronto (the Caribana festival), London (the Notting Hill Carnival) and in cities throughout the US. The Dominican Republic and Jamaica have a significant business in telemarketing and data processing for the North American market, but Barbados had been driven out of that market by a combination of rising wages and small size. The only significant offshore educational services in the Caribbean are schools providing preparatory training to prepare medical students for the US market. The Dominican Republic has a sizeable business in cosmetic surgery for Americans but other countries have had little success in this field.

There is apparently limitless potential for the development of traded services in a future which is limited mainly by our ability to marshal new technologies to produce and trade goods and services that add value to human wealth and improve well-being. The tragedy of the COVID-19 pandemic has had the effect of accelerating some helpful innovation, for example by making flexible work practices commonplace in many countries, and enhancing the profitability and productivity of delivery, communications, ordering and marketing systems.

Many of the developments will not be reversed, and the enhanced delivery of services will be of benefit to all, including small communities in poorer nations. Where all this will lead cannot be known in advance. It does seem, however, that expectations that small open economies will be able to establish a foothold in the higher value added services such as banking, investment, accounting, legal, marketing and management services, will not be realised, not because of lack of competitive advantage, but because of the currents of international politics.

The reform of global governance is essential for reversing anti-globalisation sentiments

The current wave of anti-globalisation sentiment that is manifest across the planet will do nothing to arrest the ever-rising tide of international commerce, movement of people, ideas and finance. It will, however, make the interchange and interaction messier, more conflict-ridden, bloodier and altogether more unproductive, with consequences for human well-being everywhere, worse than it needs to be. It will certainly put all the goals of sustainability and arresting the threats to climate change well beyond reach, and it increases the risks of occurrence of the worst nightmares of the human imagination. The stark reality is that, so long as policies are formulated, executed and monitored at national levels there is little prospect that solutions to global challenges can be found.

The response to the COVID-19 pandemic provides a graphic illustration of the problem. Contrary to the narrative that has gained currency in the West, the pandemic was reported from first suspicions based on the unusual incidence of pneumonia in Wuhan to the Chinese Centre for Disease Control with alacrity, and the virus was swiftly identified and immediately reported to the World Health Organisation (World Health Organisation, 2020a). The world body went into emergency mode, issuing daily advisories and holding daily international media conferences. Remarkably, the advisories of the world's leading health organisation were ignored by the leadership of the US and other Western nations, until the virus reached their shores. When it did, they found themselves defenceless, with deadly consequences which have traumatised populations in the world's richest nations. The leaders have been reluctant to admit that their slight of World Health Organisation advice has caused avoidable loss of life of their citizens.

To the contrary, Western countries reacted with a defensive stance which was the opposite of what was required. Their immediate priority was to arrest the dismaying levels of illness and death among the domestic populations, an effort which exhausted their human, production and financial resources, leaving nothing to contribute to the global fight against the pandemic. This was at a stage where the World Health Organisation and all leading experts warned that the virus should be suppressed in all countries, to reduce the risk of the emergence of new variants. Sadly, new variants did emerge, as feared, in South Africa, a country with limited resources and inadequate health services. The spread of new variants has led to new surges of infection worldwide, prolonging the COVID-19 crisis everywhere.

The lesson to be drawn from this experience is that global policy cannot be effectively designed and implemented by a collective of national entities. No rich country could contribute major resources to fight the pandemic elsewhere in the world while they were struggling to regain control of the health systems at home, even though they would have known that, by doing so, their domestic efforts could be undone by new variants from abroad. Similar conflicts of interest, between short-term expediency and long-term solutions, and between the needs at home and abroad, arise with respect to climate change, arresting the rate of species extinction, and all the sustainable development goals.

First steps in the reform of global governance

There is, as yet, little interest in the reform of the global institutions of governance. The most influential of them, the International Monetary Fund and the World Bank, have been demoted to a second tier of importance, symbolised by the fact that Christine Lagarde stepped *up* from the post of Managing Director of the Fund to that of the President of the European Central Bank. The current leadership of the Fund and the Bank are persons who are relatively unknown in international circles. The United Nations is dismissed as a talk shop, whose decisions have no impact on policy or strategy globally, even though several of its many agencies are very effective and influential in peacekeeping in countries such as Somalia, in the welfare and provision of services for refugees in countries around the world, in the publication of economic data and analysis for Latin America and the Caribbean, in services for children, and in the preservation of culture. No other institutions can boast universal membership, so the World Bank, the Fund and the United Nations must be the foundation for the reform of global governance.

The International Monetary Fund and World Bank both have a governance structure that reflects global power relationships. Countries are grouped into "constituencies" which have roughly equal proportions of the total capital of each institution; each constituency has a seat on the Executive Board of Directors that governs the institution. Small countries are grouped into constituencies by region, according to criteria that make sense in the circumstances of each country. Caribbean countries are grouped in one or other of the Canadian and Brazilian constituencies, Pacific island countries are members of the Australian-New Zealand constituencies, and small African and European countries are members of various constituencies grouped by language or other criteria.

A number of reforms are essential to restore the influence and effectiveness the Fund and the Bank once enjoyed. The first and most important must be to end the farce which perpetuates the European monopoly of the post of

Managing Director of the Fund and the US monopoly of the Presidency of the Bank. Every time either post has become vacant, for the past quarter century, we have seen a global media pantomime played out: speculation among knowledgeable journalists, financiers, think tanks and opinion makers quickly identifies the most qualified potential candidates, and the executive board of the institution issues a statement of its commitment to a transparent process of selection. In every case, this supposedly transparent process has produced a European managing director and an American president, and in no case was either of the candidates chosen from the list of world-recognised financial specialists that was the subject of initial speculation.

The second necessary reform is the revision of the capital contributions of the Bank and Fund to bring them in line with current realities of international economic relationships, and realignment of constituencies on the executive boards accordingly. If the decisions of the institutions are to reflect the interests of all members fairly, the Boards that make those decisions must be constituted in such a way as to be fully and fairly representative of those interests. As it stands, the decisions and initiatives of the Fund and Bank are too closely aligned with the policies and interests of the US and Europe, and it is therefore not surprising that they meet resistance in the rest of the world.

This is far from the minimum that is sufficient and necessary to restore the International Monetary Fund and World Bank to primacy in international economic finance and development, but it is the essential starting point. Without these reforms of the leadership and top decision structures, the necessary reforms of the staffing, analysis, policies and programmes face impenetrable barriers. Numerous attempts have been made over several decades to revise and re-orient financial support and advice offered by the institutions, but their record of success remains clouded, and for good reason. Apart from countries which were already in the highest category of human development, it is hard to find an instance where the intervention of the Fund or the Bank is associated with a public perception of improved well-being of any country.

The governance structures of the United Nations and its agencies must be reformed along the lines of the Executive Boards of the Fund and the Bank. The fantasy that the interests of Tuvalu or Trinidad and Tobago have equal weight with those of the US or China robs the UN General Assembly of meaning and relevance. A way forward would be to imitate the structures of the international financial institutions, where the executive committees overseeing all UN activities are composed of a limited number of representatives of countries grouped into constituencies of equal weight. The operations of the agencies would be structured to capture and distil the opinions of all, in proportion to each country's impact.

Far from reducing the influence of small open economies in the world's affairs or worsening the terms of their engagement of the world economy, the constituency system creates avenues for small economies to have an effective voice at the table when international decisions are made. Networks established within the Canadian and Brazilian constituencies in the Fund and

Bank afford Caribbean countries an avenue to have their views heard when decisions are being made that affect their interests. No comparable facility exists outside of these structures. Individual countries attend and make speeches at the annual meetings of the Fund and Bank, but like the speeches made at the General Assembly of the United Nations, these are rituals performed to provide photo ops for consumption back home. Unlike the Fund and Bank, the UN has no body that gives every country a say in decisions about actions and policies of the institution which affect their interests.

All international laws, frameworks, guidance, standards and regulations would ultimately need to be captured under the inclusive umbrella of the Fund, Bank and the United Nations. These functions are currently in the hands of ad hoc and legacy bodies such as the Financial Stability Board, the Bank for International Settlements, the Organisation for Economic Development and Cooperation, the International Association of Insurance Supervisors and others, where a handful of the world's richest countries set agendas which frustrate the aspirations of a majority of humanity.

These first steps are now urgent, in a journey to the destination of a global system of governance that gives humanity a fighting chance of reversing trends that, on our present course, threaten to wipe civilisation from this planet prematurely. Humanity can no longer resist these initiatives for reform, unless we are utterly fatalistic about our future. To continue as we are, on the basis of national commitments, means that the world moves further and further away from the goals for sustainability of the civilisation we now enjoy.

References

Dollar, David. 2021. China's Domestic and External Economic Challenges. Webinar by the International Relations Council, Kansas City, 29 January.

Economic Commission for Latin America and the Caribbean. 2020. "COVID-19 and the socioeconomic crisis in Latin America and the Caribbean," CEPAL Review no. 132. Special Issue.

Geithner, Timothy. 2014. *Stress Test: Reflections on Financial Crises.* New York: Crown Publishers.

Global Development Policy Center, Boston University. 2021. The Sources of China's Vision for Global Economic Governance. Webinar, September 7.

International Organization for Migration. 2020. "World Migration Report," *Grand-Saconnex*, Switzerland: The Organization.

Moyo, Dambisa. 2017. "Globalization's ongoing challenge." Interview, McKinsey and Company, 11 May.

Okonjo-Iweala, Nkozi, Tharman Shanmugaratnam and Lawrence Summers. 2021. "We don't have to fly blind into the next pandemic," *Washington Post*, 16 September.

Ortiz-Ospina, Esteban and Diana Beltekian. 2018. "Trade and globalization." *Our World in Data*, October.

Posen, Adam S. 2021. "The price of nostalgia: America's self-defeating economic retreat," *Foreign Affairs*, May/June.

Rodrik, Dani. 2020. "Will COVID-19 Remake the World?" *Project Syndicate*. 6 April.

Sachs, Jeffrey. 2022. The Future of Globalization. China Global Television Network, Youtube video.

Slaughter, Matthew. 2022. "Forward thinking on globalization and the evolving role of corporate leadership in the 21st century." *Global Interview*, McKinsey and Company.

Thunberg, Greta. 2018. "School Strike for Climate – Save the World by Changing the Rules," *TEDx Stockholm*. 24 November.

Mueller, Jan-Werner. 2021. "What's behind the 'Crisis of Democracy'?" *Project Syndicate*, August 6.

World Health Organisation. 2020a. "Archived: WHO Timeline – COVID-19, April 27." https://www.who.int/news/item/27-04-2020-who-timeline—covid-19.

World Health Organisation. 2020b. "UN Agencies Issue Urgent Call to Fund the Global Emergency Supply System to Fight COVID-19," April 20.https://www.who.int/news/item/20-04-2020-un-agencies-issue-urgent-call-to-fund-the-global-emergency-supply-system-to-fight-covid-19.

World Health Organisation. 2020c. "ICC-WHO Joint Statement: An Unprecedented Private Sector Call to Action to Tackle COVID-19," March 16. https://www.who.int/news/item/16-03-2020-icc-who-joint-statement-an-unprecedented-private-sector-call-to-action-to-tackle-covid-19.

World Health Organisation. 2020d. "Statement on Cases of COVID-19 Surpassing 100,000," March 7. https://www.who.int/news/item/07-03-2020-who-statement-on-cases-of-covid-19-surpassing-100-000.

Worrell, DeLisle. 2021. "Measuring China's economic impact in the Caribbean," *Global Discourse: An Interdisciplinary Journal of Current Affairs*, Vol. 11, no. 4. November.

19 Practical Guidance for Policy Makers in Small Open Economies

The IMF Staff Report on Barbados (International Monetary Fund, 2021) complements "the government led by Prime Minister Mottley [on] successfully implement[ing] a comprehensive economic reform agenda" which has

> restored confidence in the country's macroeconomic framework.... Macroeconomic stability was steadily restored with a combination of strong fiscal adjustment, a comprehensive sovereign debt restructuring with both domestic and external creditors, and structural reforms to increase macroeconomic stability. International reserves have gradually increased to US$1.4 billion by October 2021.
>
> (International Monetary Fund, 2021, p. 6)

Table 19.1 shows what Barbadians actually experienced between 2018, the year the economic adjustment programme was agreed with the IMF, and 2021. The level of economic activity was lower than it had been three years earlier: real GDP was 14 per cent lower. The job situation was worse: the unemployment rate had risen from 10.1 per cent per cent three years earlier to 14.1 per cent. Whereas in 2018 government had covered all its operating expenses and interest payments from tax revenues with a surplus on the current account equivalent to 1.6 per cent of GDP, in 2021 current expenditures exceeded tax receipts by the equivalent of 0.6 per cent of GDP, an amount which government was obliged to cover by drawing on loans borrowed from the IMF. Government's total expenditures had increased from the equivalent of 30 per cent of GDP in 2018 to 33 per cent, one third of all economic activity in the country. Foreign direct investment in the Barbadian economy had fallen further, from the already low $465 million recorded in 2018, less than half the total recorded ten years earlier, to $418 million. The only positive outcomes, apart from foreign reserves, were inflation, down by 0.7 of a percentage point and a one percentage point reduction in the tax burden, from 29 cents in every dollar of national income, to 28 cents. It should come as no surprise that the IMF's sentiment that the adjustment programme has been a success is not shared by the ordinary Barbadian.

DOI: 10.4324/9781003247609-23

Table 19.1 Barbados leading economic indicators

	2011	*2012*	*2013*	*2014*	*2015*	*2016*	*2017*	*2018*	*2019*	*2020*	*2021*
HDI				0.808	0.809	0.809	0.81	0.81	0.814	n.a	n.a
Real GDP, $b	9.0	9.0	8.8	8.8	9.0	9.3	9.3	9.3	9.2	7.9	8
Unemployment, %	11.2	11.5	11.6	12.3	11.3	9.7	10	10.1	10.1	13.6	14.1
Inflation, %	9.4	4.5	1.8	1.8	-1.1	1.5	4.5	3.7	4.2	3	3
Foreign reserve cover, weeks	18	20	16	15	11	8	5	13	19	41	41
Fiscal savings, % of GDP	-2.8	-6.7	-8.6	-5.6	-6.6	-3	-2.8	1.6	5.4	-1.7	-0.6
Revenue. % of GDP	27	27	25	26	26	28	29	29	28	28	28
Expenditure, % of GDP	31	35	36	34	35	33	33	30	24	33	33
FDI, $m	991	980	311	632	522	377	468	465	375	509	418

Source: Central Bank of Barbados (http://www.centralbank.org.bb/research-publications/statistics).

Note: As a result of a refinement of the HDI methodology in 2014, the published data for earlier years are not strictly comparable.

Economists and policy makers gain credibility by using the Human Development Index as the measure of economic success

This dissonance between the official story and what the woman and man in the street experiences would have been avoided by using the Human Development Index as the measure of success. The HDI score for Barbados is not yet available for 2021, a reflection of the reality that the effects of the new economic strategy would not have produced results within three years in terms of investment, productive capacity, foreign earnings, and national income, not to speak of the health and educational outcomes that have the largest impact on the quality of people's lives. In reality, we do not yet know whether the economic strategy implemented in 2018 has corrected for the policy deficiencies which occasioned the 2018 balance of payments crisis in the first place. The issues around which there is as yet no clarity are many: has the public sector been reorganised to reverse the declining productivity which negatively affects international competitiveness and the investment climate? Has the reorganisation reduced the overstaffing which drove the government's current account into dissaving? Has the capital budget been increased to cover depreciation and modernisation of the country's failing infrastructure? Have public services been reprioritised to optimise the use of available finance and skills? What has been the long-term impact of the restructuring of public sector debt on the management of government cash flows and the health of domestic financial markets?

The indicators we have to date are unpromising. There are no published reports for any government department, agency or state-owned corporation for any year since 2018, except for the Barbados Central Bank, whose most recent published report (in May 2022) is for 2020. As a result we have no early indicators on health, education, public sector productivity and the sustainability of public finances over the medium term. We also have no concrete information on important new initiatives such as renewable energy. Moreover, what indicators we do have are not encouraging: foreign direct investment has not increased, government's international credit remains far below investment grade, and there is no appetite for government debt, locally or internationally.

In contrast to what now obtains, an economic assessment based on the Human Development Index would have tempered expectations about what might have been expected from periodic economic updates in the early stages of the adjustment programme. In the policy framework advocated in this book, the overall economic strategy would be informed by published documents on the multi-year strategy and an annual budget setting out government's priorities and expectations for the current year, consistent with the medium-term targets. This framework would provide a benchmark against which quarterly and annual reports could be evaluated. This not only conditions immediate expectations, it also allows a basis for evaluating the impact of unanticipated challenges. In the case of Barbados, three such challenges are mentioned in the IMF Staff Report: the COVID-19 pandemic, an ashfall event from a volcanic eruption in a neighbouring island and a hurricane. The latter two events will have no lasting impact on the quality of life in Barbados, and they may therefore be ignored, but coping with the COVID-19 pandemic and the possibility of future global health crises require a major reshuffling of government priorities, of which there is as yet no sign.

The use of the HDI as the measure of economic success also puts focus on measures that may be taken by government to raise the average quality of life with the existing levels of national income. As we saw in Chapter 17, measures to reduce inequities in the distribution of income, and in access to health and education, would increase the well-being of the average Barbadian by as much as 17 per cent, at current levels of average purchasing power and with the existing levels of health and education provision. In addition, the HDI focusses attention on factors such as labour force participation – particularly of females – poverty alleviation, infant nutrition, school attendance, sanitation, youth unemployment and other qualitative factors. A fully articulated economic management framework would include the collection, analysis and timely publication of such data, so that the public could be kept abreast of improvements that might be expected as the economic strategy unfolds.

Small size does not limit the possibilities for economic prosperity

The achievements of Mauritius, Iceland and other countries we have discussed in this book are testament to the fact that size does not limit the possibilities of human development for small economies.[1] The populations of one quarter of the countries in our sample enjoy livelihoods which are of much the same quality, on average, as those of the world's richest countries. We have brought theory and evidence to bear to show that suitably-tailored macroeconomic policies play an essential role, along with many other factors and circumstances, in securing a superior quality of livelihood for the populations of small economies.

Economic management in the small economy requires a different mindset than for a large economy. The policy maker must understand that the nation is not the economy; the economy is the exchange of national output with the rest of the world, and the internal circulation which that exchange permits. The notion of local production for local consumption applies to Robinson Crusoe and primitive society, but it is not a useful way to think about the possibilities of a small modern economy. Instead the economic challenge is to build and constantly enhance the nation's capacity to produce goods and services that foreigners wish to buy at ruling US dollar prices, to put the foreign exchange earned to the most efficient domestic use, and to purchase the most affordable imports of every quality, from wherever in the world they may be had, to satisfy the needs of the resident population. Economies which rank lower in the quality of human development are those which don't produce enough internationally competitive goods, tourist services and other services, which use foreign exchange in ways that are wasteful, and which fail to secure value for money in the goods they import. As we demonstrated in Chapter 1, domestic circulation in the small economy is nothing more than an amplification of the foreign currency inflow, and domestic activity generates a need for an essential volume of imports which are paid for with foreign currency earnings and foreign borrowings. The foreign currency that comes in goes back out again, as the goods and services the country produces are sold in exchange for the goods and services the country needs.

This change of perspective makes for a clearer view of the economic potential and a more persuasive presentation of feasible economic strategies for small economies. Import substitution possibilities are limited to the production of electricity from renewable energy, and even in this case, the substitution is incomplete because the technology and equipment needed to build dams and solar and wind farms must be imported. The notion that a small economy can achieve a meaningful degree of food security by producing food for home consumption makes no sense from this perspective. Rather, providing subsidies, tax breaks, tariffs and quotas to promote domestic production of food which can be imported more cheaply is a wastage of foreign exchange, albeit one which we find in most small open economies.

Understanding that the small economy lives by its commerce with other economies clarifies the difference between foreign earnings, which enter domestic circulation, fuel activity and ultimately exit to pay for imports, and foreign reserves which bypass the domestic economy and are sequestered in central bank accounts at the Federal Reserve Bank of New York. If this were understood, the Barbados government would not want to squirrel away enough borrowed foreign currency to pay for over two years' worth of imports, as reported in the IMF Staff Report mentioned earlier, rather than invest those funds in projects of high priority, nor would the IMF staff consider that an indicator of the success of the adjustment programme.

Another misunderstanding that is cleared up by this view is the common belief that domestic ownership of hotels, banks and other businesses that earn foreign currency is preferable to foreign ownership because the foreign revenues remain in the domestic economy. In fact, all foreign currency that comes in is destined to exit in the end, so the relevant question is whether the transaction fuels domestic activity, as when the hotel pays workers and pays for laundry services, and whether the foreign currency provides the wherewithal to buy imports, as is the case when a hotel pays for supplies from abroad.

The formulation of macroeconomic policy begins with a model that captures the essential features of the small open economy

We have described the essential features of an economic model that captures the peculiarities of the small open economy in Chapter 6. We may deduce from the model the essential elements of a macroeconomic strategy that best secures the objective of sustainable improvement in the material well-being of the population over the medium term, in a manner that avoids fits, starts and crises in the balance of external receipts and payments. Highlights of such a strategy include the management of the finances of the public sector to ensure that current spending is always contained below the level of revenues, so that there are some savings to contribute to the financing of replacement for depreciated assets. All borrowing, domestic and foreign, should be for capital formation; the annual budget for capital formation should always include a provision for rehabilitation and upgrade of infrastructure, adequate to ensure the complete renewal of roads, transport infrastructure, equipment, buildings and facilities on a specified long-term cycle appropriate to each category, on a rolling basis. Apart from this, all borrowing should be for specific projects with deadlines for completion, and all projects should be presented with full documentation. All project implementation agencies should be required to issue progress reports at specific intervals, and a final report on completion.

The economic strategy should be anchored on a managed exchange rate, preferably one that is linked to the US dollar or other international currency. The anchor must be held firm by active management of total spending in the economy, using expected foreign currency inflows as a guide to the total value of imports that can be afforded. The tools to be used to manage spending in the economy are taxes, expenditures by the public sector and government borrowing, backed by interest rate policy and modest use, temporarily and if needed, of holdings of foreign currency held in reserve on deposit with the Federal Reserve Bank of New York. If, for whatever reason, the country is unable to establish a framework and track record of maintaining the exchange rate anchor, it is advisable to retire the domestic currency altogether, and adopt the US dollar or other foreign currency for domestic use. If this action is not taken in a timely fashion, the wealthier elements of society will increasingly protect the value of their savings by placing them in dollars instead of local currency, an action which widens income disparities in the society and thereby impairs average national well-being.

Priority has to be given to activities that earn and save foreign exchange, because they provide the essential fuel for the growth of the economy. These activities may not always attract adequate investor interest, however, because they may not yield returns comparable to alternatives such as real estate. This may be due to a variety of reasons, including ignorance of market opportunities, unfamiliarity with a new technology, the absence of needed legal, accounting or other specialised services and skills, or scarcity of finance on suitable terms. In these and other cases of market failure, government support is indicated for activities that increase foreign exchange availability. Such support, in whatever form, should be conditional on monitored performance within agreed targets.

Much more careful attention, with adequate data and analysis, needs to be paid to the allocation of government revenues and borrowed funds in the annual budget. The allocations to health and education should be large enough to produce improvements in life expectancy, years of schooling and other health and educational indicators. That tells the authorities that gains are being made in national well-being, because these are the most powerful contributors to overall human development. Budget allocations for all government departments and agencies should be tailored to the range and quality of services each institution produces, and should be adjusted in light of performance, based on suitable indicators. The results of this allocation, together with the results of the previous year's performance as evidenced by suitable indicators, should be made available in annual reports of each institution, published no later than three months after the end of each financial year. This detail has to be specified, after decades of official reports on improving efficiency of public services in many countries with no results to be seen in terms of improved efficiency and productivity.

Improved efficiency of health, educational and other public services not only improves well-being directly, it also contributes to international competitiveness and the country's attractiveness to foreign investors. Years of schooling, skills, life expectancy, the institutions for security of person and property, the burden of government regulation and other elements of public administration all enter into the competitiveness score of countries compiled by the World Economic Forum. The Global Competitive Index, which the Forum publishes annually, captures investor sentiment in 140-odd countries around the world.

Efficient electricity production and distribution, world-class telecommunications, universal availability of water and sanitation services are all critical elements in promoting development, contributing directly to well-being, and providing services that are essential for the productivity of all enterprise, and therefore critical factors influencing the decision of every potential investor. Whether the public sector provides these services directly, in partnership with the private sector, or sets the framework and price setting rules for private providers, government must put in place systems which feature the crucial elements of ensuring budget adequacy, performance monitoring and revision and adjustment on an agreed path to an announced target. This is an immensely complex issue, thanks to the long horizons involved for investments, the rapidly changing technologies, and many other factors, social, political and environmental. What may be said in general is that, in the final analysis, the provision of public services will be adequate only where the economic costs of providing the service are fully covered. If the full costs are borne by the consumer, those with low incomes will not be able to afford the service, even in the wealthiest of countries. Governments need to bear this in mind when making decisions about how public utility services are to be delivered, priced and subsidised.

The experiences of the countries we have analysed do not allow us to offer any suggestions for the public sector in the performance of its entrepreneurship role, even though Mazzucato's thesis (Chapter 8) that all governments perform this role in one way or another is a convincing one. It has long been recognised, particularly in small economies, that the government is the only institution with the resources to absorb the risks inherent in the early development of many new export activities, with the finances to support small enterprises that make a disproportionately large contribution to employment, and with the capacity to fund and support the upscaling of small export-oriented enterprises. Other than the observation that East Asian economies have been the outstanding performers in the area of state entrepreneurship, little insight has so far emerged from economic and business research to provide guidance on state entrepreneurship.

The framework for policy formulation and implementation

In Chapter 12 we described a structure of interlinked macroeconomic accounts, built to incorporate the relationships of the model in Chapter 6, which may be used to prepare forecasts, set benchmarks for expected outcomes, set targets to be achieved by official policy, and write scenarios to evaluate the magnitude of risks of various kinds that might affect economic performance. The accounts recommended are sufficiently detailed to capture all fiscal, monetary, financial or other policy tools. They should be continuously updated and the interrelationships between the variables refreshed through ongoing research activity. It is important that the public sector have a strong research capability, networked with universities, international financial institutions and think tanks worldwide that have an interest in open economy macroeconomics. As things now stand, there is no global institutional structure of this kind; the only dedicated research unit in the public sectors of small countries resides in the central bank, if there is one, and its main task is usually to prepare descriptive reports on the economy. Every policy maker is therefore obliged to build a unique network through personal contact, with the assistance of like-minded colleagues in universities and think tanks. In the absence of a model that suits their circumstances, most small economies use the IMF's framework of analysis for policy making, a framework which, as we demonstrated in Chapters 6 and 7, will lead to erroneous policies if applied to these economies.

Implementing the economic strategy

The process of implementation begins with the preparation of a set of accounts representing a forecast of year-end benchmark numbers for the next five years, prepared on the assumption that there is no change in policies. The benchmark forecast incorporates all developments that can be anticipated with respect to the factors that will affect exports, tourism and foreign investment, all expected investments and best expectations about import prices, interest rates and other variables over which domestic policy makers have no control. Clearly, most of these factors will have changed beyond expectations in five years' time. To take account of that the forecast is updated and rolled forward every year.

The five-year forecast is used to frame the public sector budget for the each year of the forecast, rolling the whole process forward year by year. In evaluating the outcomes for the fifth year of the forecast, the government's economic team will consider what policy changes would serve to improve the outlook, in terms of higher GDP, minimising unemployment, improving health and educational services, improving competitiveness and bettering the outcomes in all aspects of well-being. This evaluation would be informed by the declared objectives of government, the parliament and cabinet. Technical assessments and comparisons of different options and combinations should be distilled to a set of feasible options by the support team of the joint senior economic management committee, with the help of technical assistance and advice from experts in a variety of areas. There follows a process in which top decision makers arrive at decisions on the targets for the economy, and the changes in policy that they should undertake to move towards these targets.

Next comes the preparation of the public sector budget for the first year of the forecast, consistent with the revised benchmark five-year forecast, incorporating the newly agreed economic targets, and the policy changes required to improve on the original benchmark. The budget is subject to approval by the parliament; any changes made by the parliament must be incorporated in a new revision of the benchmarks.

Chapter 12 discusses in some detail how the process of implementing, monitoring, evaluating and adjustment might be conducted in order to keep on track to achieve government's development goals in an economy that remains stable and sustainable. The macroeconomic strategy for development and stability must be managed by a top level committee that is headed by the minister for finance, and that includes the governor of the central bank, the head of the treasury (the public sector's financial controller), the head of the tax revenue authority, the public debt manager and the principal economic counsellor in the public sector (usually the director of research at the central bank), together with their supporting staff. Experience suggests that the prime minister (the country's chief executive, whatever the title) assume the responsibility for the finance portfolio to minimise the risk that the economic strategy will run into difficulty or unravel at the level of cabinet or parliament.

There is merit in appointing the central bank Governor as co-chair of the committee. It is a public symbol of the fact that the committee's decisions are soundly based on data, analysis and informed opinion, and are feasible, internally consistent, and within the financial and human resources available for their implementation. These features must characterise the committee's decisions in any case if they are to have a chance of success. Having the governor, the public sector's principal financial officer, as co-chair removes any illusion that the committee's deliberations may be subject to political capture, or, even worse, that a new prime minister might conduct the committee's business on that assumption. The co-chairmanship does not in any way impair the final responsibility of the people's representatives to make all policy in the country, including all monetary and financial policy. The decisions of the economic management committee will have to be taken to the cabinet, which is where the decisions on tax, public spending and borrowing will be approved for implementation.

The macroeconomic management committee needs to meet monthly in normal circumstances, and weekly or more frequently in times of crisis, to review the macroeconomic accounts against the benchmarks. Their discussions should be informed by a report prepared by their support team which highlights matters for attention, worrying trends, and developments that deserve to be carefully watched. The committee makes course corrections as needed, maintains control over public sector spending, and takes the initiative when major changes are necessary to budgetary allocations, and when crises or natural or man-made catastrophe looms on the horizon.

The macroeconomic strategy

The macroeconomic strategy should be based on solid analytical foundations and it should be presented clearly and accounted for in timely publications. The macroeconomic strategy needs to be analytically sound, otherwise it is likely to fail. That means it has to be built on the basis of statistics, information and analysis presented in analytical reports. In the final analysis, however, the strategy must appeal to the general public, and to their representatives in the parliament. For this purpose it must be distilled into documents and presentations that are appealing and digestible, with targets and objectives that matter to the ordinary citizen.

No single document can fully represent the assumptions, interrelationships, judgemental factors and uncertainties that are embedded in the economic analysis, nor can any single document or media event or presentation convey fully the trade-offs that were made in arriving at the envelope of policies that comprise the strategy that is finally decided upon. The suggestion is therefore offered that the information and documentation process be managed separately. Reports prepared for and by the technical support team in the process of designing the strategy should be directed to the economic and policy community, and discussed in think tanks, universities, economic research agencies and in technical and academic seminars. They may be published through the normal channels through which such work is disseminated.

The content of the agreed-upon strategy, on the other hand, must be offered in short essays, opinion pieces, panel discussions and audio and visual sessions and events. Their content should be guided by the strategy, so that the feasibility and consistency of the whole is clear, and they should speak to the health, education and other factors that materially affect well-being. The use of the HDI, incorporating adjustments for inequity and the quality of services and infrastructure is helpful in this respect. If the improvements in the indices that go into the extended HDI are set as the targets of economic policy, not only does the strategy gain immediate relevance to everyone, it also becomes difficult to ignore the trade-offs that are necessary, given the burden of taxation, the government's credit-worthiness and the competing claims on the budget, all of which can be pointed out in the budget framework.

There is an urgent need for an international institutional network of research on the macroeconomics of the open economy

A renewed macroeconomic focus on the mechanisms of the open economy is now overdue. The closed economy thinking which informs most common approaches to policy, including the use of monetary policy to control inflation and the use of exchange rate policy to affect the propensity to trade, arguably are no longer particularly helpful even for the world's largest economies; they are certainly of no value for open economies, even economies much larger than those which are the subject of this book. Only very slowly, and very obliquely, are the essential issues of the open economy reappearing on the international policy agenda, in guises such as the "dominant currency paradigm" and the inflationary consequences of shortages in global supply chains.

Why is it that the everyday realities of economic interconnectedness across national borders are only slowly being reflected in policy analysis and opinion? Why is macroeconomics ruled by a closed economy mindset in a world of economies linked by commerce, finance, travel, technology, information and ideas? Could it be as a result of the fact that research in economics is networked around universities, research centres and think tanks in the English-speaking world, and in particular the storied schools of thought in the US and UK? It would surely be helpful to develop a counterpoint, a research programme networked among research institutions in Singapore, Hong Kong, South Africa, Ireland, Malta, Argentina, Chile and Mexico, which is motivated and informed by the experiences of countries in which inflation is imported, and the financial markets take their time from New York rather than from their own central banks and monetary authorities.

The use of an inappropriate conceptual framework is not an inconsequential matter. Once you understand that a small open economy like the Dominican Republic is essentially an import-export machine (understanding exports to include tourism and other services), the central bank's official commitment to maintaining the inflation rate at five per cent per cent maximum by raising interest rates, most recently (1 February 2022) by 50 basis points, can be dismissed as a futile gesture. Ordinary people on their way to the supermarket have no reason to pay attention to such announcements. That is precisely the point: policy only becomes effective when it motivates economic agents to take note and adjust their behaviour. The absence of a body of economic research and analysis which uses openness as the point of departure hampers policy makers in the design of policies that answer to the challenges of the open economy, in explaining their policies to the economic agents whose behaviour they hope to influence, and in defending those policies and strategies in discussion with international institutions on whose assistance they depend.

We may use the exchange rate of local currency to illustrate. It is generally believed that a scarcity of foreign currency for the imports needed for normal commerce is an indication that the local currency should be devalued, because when things are scarce their prices increase. If foreign currency is scarce its price has to rise. However, in an import-dependent economy, which all small economies are, devaluation raises prices, especially for the lowest income groups, and reduces the average well-being. The central theorem which informs the economic model described in this book shows that devaluation is the wrong policy for the small economy facing a foreign currency shortage, and that instead policies should be directed to reducing the demand for foreign currency. We are able to make a persuasive case for this approach because we use an alternative to the point of departure of the conventional way of addressing the problem.

Once you address the foreign currency problem as we do, with policies to reduce the amount of foreign currency people need to buy, the design of the economic policy focuses on the tax policies and expenditure reductions that would be needed. The advantage of using taxes is that the cuts may be targeted on things like motor cars and new government offices, where postponing spending will have the least impact on the average person. This alternative design makes the policy easier to sell to the population, and it is therefore more likely to be accepted and complied with, as compared with a devaluation. The fact that the policy is firmly grounded, in terms of its economic rationale, is the basis on which it can be sold to the IMF, credit rating agencies and others whose financial assistance may help to ease the burden of adjustment.

The economic programme and strategy must be sold to the public

Economic policy making is a complex process of design, implementation, monitoring, evaluation and adjustment, and it involves thousands and millions of economic agents, with scores of different interests and influence. Economic strategies cannot be fashioned in the public square, nor should they be subject to popular vote. The ordinary citizen, however well informed, cannot be expected to have the expertise to appreciate the full implications of economic policy decisions. As the exchange rate example illustrates, even the experts get it wrong when it comes to the actual responses to economic policies. The policy maker cannot assume that her or his task is done when the policy design, revision and approval is complete; the economic strategy needs to be sold to sceptical economists and policy specialists, to the public whom the policies are intended to benefit, and to all external interests whose activities bear on the domestic economy, including the IMF and other international institutions, credit rating agencies and potential investors. The governments of most economies under-invest in the research that underpins their economic strategy and in marketing that strategy to all interested parties. The economic strategy should be carefully designed by specialists who have a profound understanding of the economy, making use of the best expertise available domestically and internationally. The strategy needs to be sold to the local economy on its merits, with quantitative targets and deadlines with which everyone can mark its progress; and it has to be presented to the world in an informed, analytically sound and persuasive manner.

Domestically, the economic strategy should be put through a political process to establish its legitimacy and to build consensus around it. The process ought to make reasonable provision for revisions and amendments which need to be sent back to the technicians who designed the strategy, so that they can incorporate the changes and work through all the consequences in amending the strategy document. It is helpful to have a national convention with representatives of various interest groups to launch the strategy, once it is finalised and agreed. The convention should reassemble at three-year intervals, to review progress with the implementation of the economic strategy and the achievement of its targets. More frequent overall reviews are not helpful, because they set unrealistic expectations with respect to tangible results on well-being which may reasonably be expected to appear immediately. However, reports of all public sector entities should be published annually without fail, so that measures of public sector productivity and efficiency can be compiled and analysed by those with the requisite skills.

Vision and sensitivity to the needs of society are crucial to the successful implementation of policy

The reason that Mahatma Gandhi, Martin Luther King and Nelson Mandela are so revered is that they imagined a new world, one that had never previously existed, and set out on a quest to lead us into that world. Everyone has visions of a better world, but that world for many is a version of a fantasised past. It is rare to encounter a vision that is new, of something that has never before existed. Yet this is the reality of human existence. Every new day is a reality which has never before existed. Visionary leaders do not romanticise the past, nor try to recreate it; instead they imagine a future which they believe is realisable, and devote their lives to leading the way towards it.

As the economic strategy unfolds, leaders need to be sensitive to its impact on society, and to address concerns which emerge in the process of economic development and change. Unexpectedly, this has become more difficult, not less, in the era of global telecommunications networks. The indiscriminate dissemination of unfiltered "news" means that public opinion everywhere is less, not more, informed about the reality of the lives, circumstances, aspirations and possibilities of fellow humans all around the globe. Visionary leadership that defines a clear path forward for the small economy in the midst of the deafening noise of news and opinion from the media, traditional and social, is the secret sauce which makes the economic strategy come together.

Note

1 The small nation of Kiribati, three island archipelagos (only two of which, thousands of miles apart, are inhabited) isolated in the middle of the Pacific and threatened by imminent inundation as a result of sea level rise, is the only exception of which I am aware. However, the quality of life available in Kiribati, a country I

have visited, is so deprived that I doubt there are many i-Kiribati who would not opt for the superior lifestyles on offer in Australia or New Zealand, if offered the opportunity.

References

International Monetary Fund. 2021. "Barbados: 2021 Article IV Consultation." 17 December.https://www.imf.org/en/Publications/CR/Issues/2021/12/17/Barbados-2021-Article-IV-Consultation-Sixth-Review-Under-the-Extended-Arrangement-Under-the-511086.

International Monetary Fund. 2022. "International financial Statistics." International Financial Statistics – At a Glance.

Moore, Winston, Jamila Beckles and DeLisle Worrell. 2015. "Size, structure and devaluation." Working Paper. Central Bank of Barbados, March.

United Nations Conference on Trade and Development (UNCTAD). 2017. "World tariff profiles." Export Diversification Report. New York: United Nations.

United Nations Development Programme. 2020. "Human Development Report." New York: United Nations.

Index

Page numbers in italics refer to figures. Page numbers in bold refer to tables. Page numbers followed by 'n' refer to notes.